Praise for

*Shut Up and Keep Talking*

"I could tell right away when I met Bob Pisani as a guest on CNBC over 30 years ago that he was one of the sharpest observers of the markets. And that's still true today! *Shut Up and Keep Talking* gives a fascinating look into the history of trading, Bob's personal investing tips and great stories about the unique people he met on the NYSE floor. It's investing made fun!"
—**Barbara Corcoran, Founder of The Corcoran Group and Shark on** *Shark Tank*

"Bob Pisani has seen it all, said it all, and met them all. *Shut Up and Keep Talking* is his fun, breezy and irreverent look inside the famed New York Stock Exchange. Bob's book is a joy to read, and you walk away with insights on managing your own money from the titans of Wall Street. Whether you want a leisurely stroll through the Street's past three decades, or an in-depth meeting of the people behind the scenes and away from the camera, Bob is your best guide."
—**Ric Edelman, Ranked the #1 Financial Advisor in the nation three times by Barron's; bestselling author,** *The Truth About Your Future*

"Every investor will benefit from this engaging survey of what works on Wall Street, along with an irreverent and humorous rendering of the mistakes that can ruin any investment plan."
—**Burton G. Malkiel, #1 bestselling author of** *A Random Walk Down Wall Street*

"Bob Pisani has been embedded inside the NYSE for over 25 years. From his unique perch he has seen it all and does a masterful job of chronicling events in a way that makes you his partner on the journey. This is a must-read for anyone interested in the markets, money and what makes the world go round."
—**Kevin O'Leary,** *Shark Tank's* **Mr. Wonderful and Chairman of O'Leary Ventures**

"Bob Pisani has been covering the markets for more than 25 years. This well-researched book has perceptive insights into how markets operate, peppered with amusing anecdotes about the many celebrities who have rung the opening and closing bell at the NYSE. This book is at its best when Pisani gets personal, particularly when he examines his own investment failures and successes and the role that behavioral economics and bad thinking play in determining investing success."
—**Larry Swedroe, Chief Research Officer for Buckingham Strategic Wealth; author of** *Your Essential Guide to Sustainable Investing*

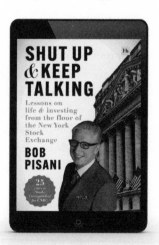

# SHUT UP & KEEP TALKING

## Lessons on life & investing from the floor of the New York Stock Exchange

# BOB PISANI

Harriman
House

HARRIMAN HOUSE LTD

3 Viceroy Court

Bedford Road

Petersfield

Hampshire

GU32 3LJ

GREAT BRITAIN

Tel: +44 (0)1730 233870

Email: enquiries@harriman-house.com

Website: harriman.house

First published in 2022.

Hardback ISBN: 978-0-85719-921-8

eBook ISBN: 978-0-85719-922-5

British Library Cataloguing in Publication Data

A CIP catalogue record for this book can be obtained from the British Library.

33614083141779

*For Suzanne*

*Wheresoever she was, there was Eden.*
*—Mark Twain*

# *Contents*

=====

# *About the author*

═══

B OB Pisani is the Senior Markets Correspondent for CNBC. A CNBC reporter since 1990, Bob Pisani has covered Wall Street and the stock market from the floor of the New York Stock Exchange for 25 years. In addition to covering the global stock market, he also covers initial public offerings (IPOs), exchange-traded funds (ETFs) and financial market structure for CNBC.

# *Foreword by*
# *Burton G. Malkiel*

$\equiv$

B OB Pisani has been a wise and perceptive observer of financial markets for over 30 years, most of it as CNBC's Stocks Correspondent at the New York Stock Exchange. He has enjoyed an inside view of what really matters on Wall Street. Distilled from that experience is a discerning set of lessons learned that provides insightful guidance for newbie as well as experienced investors. Every investor will benefit from this engaging survey of what works on Wall Street, along with an irreverent and humorous rendering of the mistakes that can ruin any investment plan.

The book is part memoir, part financial history, part inside look at CNBC and the perils of an interviewer, and part explanation of what we know about financial markets and what we can never know. We learn about the immense changes in how our stock markets operate and the new instruments available to ordinary investors enabling them to participate efficiently in the growth of our economy. Pisani accomplishes this not by writing a text or an historical essay, but by teasing insights and investment lessons from his years of interviewing Wall Street professionals and cultural celebrities.

The book presents a good summary of the financial history of the past 30 years as well as the monumental changes in how stocks are traded and packaged for investment. There is also easily accessible material on the academic theories of efficient markets and the evidence in favor of passive investing. Considerable attention is given to the emotional side of investing and the importance of understanding our behavioral biases.

We learn how the NYSE lost its dominant share of stock trading. The birth of electronic trading created a regime change that fundamentally altered how our financial institutions operate. Jack Bogle and several academic scribblers eventually convinced investors about the wisdom of indexing. ETFs and indexed mutual funds created a revolution in how investors bought and held stocks in their retirement accounts.

There are wonderful stories of vivid characters such as the legendary raconteur and grizzled trader Art Cashin, whose homey wisdom is both delightful to read and wise to remember. We are also introduced to mountebanks like Bernie Madoff and Black Jack Bouvier (Jackie Kennedy's father, described as "drunkard" and "s.o.b.") and the misguided professionals who mistakenly think they have found the keys to market success. Meeting Walter Cronkite, with his steady voice and refusal to editorialize, provided a template for Pisani's TV journalism career.

The stories of cultural celebrities that Pisani had the pleasure of interviewing are generally told with the lessons learned from their illustrious careers. Barry Manilow's career began with a string of big hits (26 Top 100 hits between 1974 and 1983). While he kept churning out albums and performing, the hits stopped coming. But Manilow refused to believe that the well had run dry, and he kept plugging along. He had to wait until 2002 when his album *Ultimate Manilow* went double platinum. In life there is a reward for sticking to something long term. There is no better rule for investing and building wealth. Save regularly, keep investing, take advantage of dollar cost averaging, and stay the course no matter how many people are assuring you that the world is falling apart.

A story about Mike Wallace illuminates the importance of decency. One about Norman Mailer reminds us that some people are devoid of civility. From Pisani's interview with the cultural icon Aretha Franklin we learn that if we want to get people to talk, find out what motivates them. All the interviews with famous people are described with humor and an appreciation of the broader lessons that can be learned from successful people. Sometimes interviews can go awry—while Pisani was interviewing Fidel Castro, he scratched an itch on his head and was immediately thrown against the wall with his cameraman as security guards mistook his gesture as an impending attack on the Cuban leader.

Much of the book centers on the (fruitless) search for the unique individuals and institutions who may be better able to select stocks that beat the market or make superior forecasts of economic conditions and market returns. Can we determine in advance whether stocks will go up or down? Can anyone predict the future? Can we find the perfect investor with the keenest market insights who can see what will happen before anyone else? The sad conclusion is that this is an impossible quest. There are no consistent superior stock pickers, and everyone (even the Federal Reserve, who controls monetary policy) is bad at predicting the future. When it appears that some person or institution has found the key to predicting the stock market, the market invariably changes the locks.

So what should a wise investor do? Pisani's answers are clear. Diversify broadly with low-cost index funds and ETFs. Buy and hold. Market timing does not work. Pay more attention to how your brain chemistry can lead you to stupid decisions than trying to outsmart the market. Avoiding mistakes—not brilliant insights—is the key to investment success.

In a charming section, written with abundant humor and humility, Pisani tells of his own investing mistakes. Two of the doozers involved underdiversification and overexuberance. Believing that Jack Welch was a true genius and that General Electric would continue to be the preeminent company in the United States, he put almost 50 percent of his 401(k) portfolio in GE stock and held it through most of the stock's precipitous decline. The overexuberant error came from being swept up in the excitement of an auction. As a collector of 1960s rock music posters, he paid almost 10 times the price of an equivalent poster for Black Sabbath (and he never even liked the group and its turgid style).

While certainly not a "how to" book, there are many important investment lessons in these pages that can help readers become better investors. While certainly not a history of the stock market over the past few decades, there are extremely lucid descriptions of how the market and the instruments available to investors changed for the better. While not a memoir of a successful financial reporter, the fascinating stories and vivid characters come to life with humanity and humor. Anyone interested in investing will find this love letter to the stock market a delightful read.

Burton G. Malkiel

Chemical Bank Chairman's Professor of Economics,

Princeton, and Author, *A Random Walk Down Wall Street*

# *Preface*

===

W HAT would you do if you could meet all your heroes—all the people you ever admired?

What would you say to them?

What if you could meet all the CEOs, politicians, kings and queens, movie stars and rock stars you ever wanted to meet?

Would you be amazed? Would you be impressed? Or would it be like that old saw, "Never meet your heroes, because you'll be disappointed."

I've met most of my heroes. For 32 years, I've been a financial correspondent for CNBC, and for 25 of those years I've covered the stock market on the floor of the New York Stock Exchange.

Every day, trading commences with an opening bell ceremony at both the NYSE and NASDAQ that is viewed by millions around the world. It's one of the grand traditions of the NYSE: a bell has been rung to start the day since continuous trading began in the 1860s. And every day, trading ends with the same ceremony.

A different person, or company, or charity, rings the bell each time.

In 25 years, that amounts to over 10,000 bell ringings.

Some of these bell ringers appeared on air in interviews with me or my colleagues. The majority did not, but they were available before and after the bell ringings, as they usually descended from the podium and came onto the floor.

That gave me an opportunity to meet a lot of exceptional people. CEOs. Rock stars. Government officials. Firefighters. Military heroes. Olympic athletes.

These people had one thing in common: they were all fabulously successful. That's how you get to ring the opening and closing bell at the NYSE.

This is a book about some of the people I have met in those 30 years, most of them on the floor of the NYSE, and what I have learned from them. Some of those encounters—like one with Robert Downey Jr., where we discussed the history of Iron Man—were brief, one-off affairs. Others—like meetings and discussions with Vanguard's Jack Bogle, or Yale University's Robert Shiller (winner of the 2013 Nobel Prize in Economics), or the Wharton School's Jeremy Siegel, author of *Stocks for the Long Run*, or Burton Malkiel, author of *A Random Walk Down Wall Street,* or UBS's Art Cashin, the doyen of floor traders—had an impact that has lasted decades.

Some of the discussions were with celebrities about what seems like frivolous matters: how to mount a comeback with Barry Manilow; how to ask for a favor from Mike Wallace when you're in a desperate situation; or talking with Aretha Franklin about her musical legacy.

Others were about profound questions on investing and decision-making in general.

Why is everyone so bad at predicting the future—not just about stock prices, but about everything?

Why do most stock pickers underperform the markets, and why does it appear to be getting worse?

What works in investing, and what doesn't? Does active investing outperform passive investing? Can you time the markets?

Why do investors make such bad decisions? If you're supposed to buy low and sell high, why do so many do exactly the opposite? Is there something in the structure of our brain that keeps telling us that certain actions seem right, but we know they are wrong?

All of these encounters, all of these discussions, had one thing in common: they profoundly influenced the way that I report, what I report on, what I believe matters, and even the way that I look at the world in general.

In writing this book, I had to make decisions every author confronts. In my case, I did not want to write a memoir. I also did not want to write a financial history of my times. Nor did I want to write a how-to investing book.

I did want to write what it was like to witness three of the most important developments in the financial world in the last 100 years: the birth of electronic trading, the growth of passive (index) investing versus active investing, and the development of behavioral finance, which went a long way toward explaining some of the crazy behavior of investors.

I'm going to describe what I've come to believe about these developments, but this isn't an academic book. I'm not going to bore us all to tears and act as a journalistic referee between competing schools of academic thought.

There are broader question as well: What have I learned covering financial markets for 32 years at CNBC? What do I know? How do I know what I know? Why do I believe I know these things?

These are difficult and unsettling questions. It's been a long journey. A difficult but rewarding journey. I learned a lot of things I didn't know when I started in 1990, but that's the least of it. I also learned to unlearn some things I thought I knew, particularly about the rationality of human beings.

Along the way, I met some brilliant people. I also met some lunatics, egomaniacs, mountebanks, jokers and fraudsters. It's all been part of the fun.

Let me take you on this journey. You're going to learn:

- How I decide what I want to say every day, who I think is important, and why I don't have a high opinion of stock analysts (Chapter 2).
- What it's like to go public on the floor of the New York Stock Exchange, and reveal my choice for the two biggest winners of all time in the IPO sweepstakes (Chapter 3).
- What Wall Street legend Art Cashin of UBS taught me about the interplay between the stock market and storytelling (Chapter 4).
- What news legend Walter Cronkite asked me during a brief meeting in 1999, the wildest year on Wall Street (Chapter 6).
- Why it was dangerous to your health to be a stock market reporter after tech stocks collapsed in 2000 (Chapter 7).
- Why my search for The Perfect Trader didn't pan out, but what the best traders taught me about the perils of groupthink (Chapter 8).
- How the birth of electronic trading destroyed the profits of the old brokerage community and gave us our modern trading system (Chapters 9 and 12).
- The lessons on investing I learned from Vanguard founder Jack Bogle (Chapter 10).
- The one thing I learned to do that saved me after witnessing the 9/11 disaster (Chapter 11).
- How the Great Financial Crisis of 2008–2009 finally forced everyone to acknowledge the role that irrational behavior played in investing (Chapter 13).
- Why I don't believe the stock market is predictable, why you shouldn't either, and why the future is so hard to figure out (Chapters 15–17).
- My dumbest investing blunder, and what I own today (Chapter 20).
- How an obsession with a Black Sabbath poster again taught me that I am not as rational as I think I am (Chapter 21).
- What I have come to believe about stock market investing, why market timing doesn't work, and why you shouldn't exhaust yourself looking for *outperformance* (Chapter 22).

- How to think about the future in a constantly changing world (Chapter 23).

I'll also share encounters with Barry Manilow, Mike Wallace, Aretha Franklin, Joey Ramone, and Fidel Castro.

Finally, for those who like pithy observations, at the end of the book I'll share my 58 Maxims on Television, Life, and the Stock Market.

## *Shut Up and Keep Talking*

When I'm on the air, I wear a wireless microphone attached to my lapel and an earpiece. It's called an IFB (short for "Interruptible foldback"—don't ask) and it enables the producer in the control room to talk with me and provide cues or directions on when my hit is coming up.

In practice, most communications between the producer and talent—particularly reporters in the field—consist of short commands. In my case, while I have many dear friends who are producers, 95 percent of the communication consists of two phrases: "Wrap"—meaning "Shut Up," and "Keep talking," or sometimes "Stretch," meaning "Don't shut up."

That's the life of an on-air journalist: shut up and keep talking.

The stuff you do in between—your reporting and how you interpret this endless cacophony of stock prices and economic data and screaming traders and panicky investors—determines whether anyone is going to give a damn about listening to you.

If you wanted to start listening about the stock market in 1997, there was no better place to be than the New York Stock Exchange. That's when I made my entrance.

# PART ONE

# *Working at the NYSE*

# CHAPTER 1

## *Welcome to the New York Stock Exchange*

═══

*S*EPTEMBER *1997. The floor of the New York Stock Exchange. My first day as On-Air Stocks Correspondent for CNBC. My first hit.*

*I'm waiting for the anchor, my friend Bill Griffeth, to toss to me. It's shortly after the open. The floor is buzzing with the sound of 4,000 brokers screaming orders at each other.*

*Bob Zito, the man in charge of communications and marketing for the NYSE and the one responsible for allowing reporters on the floor, is standing in front of me, just out of sight of the camera, which is mounted on the balcony and pointed toward me on the floor.*

*He is there to observe my first hit. About 10 seconds before I appear on camera, Zito walks up to me, smiles, and hands me a note.*

*It says, "YOUR FLY IS DOWN."*

*As I'm reading it, I hear in my ear, "Now let's go down to Bob Pisani on the floor of the New York Stock Exchange. Bob?"*

That was my welcome to the New York Stock Exchange. My fly was not down, but I spent several seconds staring at the camera, frozen, trying to figure out if I should check my fly, while Zito collapsed in hysteria just off-camera.

If that sounds like a fraternity party prank, it was appropriate. The floor of the New York Stock Exchange in 1997 was a giant fraternity (it was almost entirely male), and an elite fraternity at that.

Now I was trying to break into it, and I was having a tough time.

Here's a definition of loneliness for a journalist: some 4,000 guys in a room, they all know something you want to know, and not even one will talk to you.

That September was my first month as On-Air Stocks Editor. I had been the Real Estate Correspondent for CNBC from 1990 to 1996 and had spent the prior year doing CEO profiles (it was all the rage then: spend a few days with the CEO of Procter & Gamble to find out what kind of person they *really* were). Most importantly, I had spent part of 1996 and 1997 as a substitute reporter on the floor of the NYSE.

It was a wonderful time to be at CNBC. After several years with little or no ratings, we were not only getting ratings, but they were going up—and fast. The ratings weren't going up because I was the Real Estate Correspondent—they were going up because the investing world had discovered a shiny new toy: the internet.

Netscape, the first browser, had gone public in August 1995, and it was a sensation. We didn't know it then, but the next four years would form the tail end of the great stock market boom that had begun in 1982 when then-Federal Reserve Chairman Paul Volcker had broken the back of inflation.

From the beginning of 1982 to the end of 1999, the S&P 500 would rise an astonishing 1,200 percent. It would end in March 2000, with what is now known as the "dot-com bust."

But that was far in the future. Right now, it was intimidating, showing up on the floor of the NYSE. My predecessor, Maria Bartiromo, had been hired by CNBC in 1995. Other reporters had reported from the balcony of the NYSE, but Maria was the first to report on the floor, and she was a sensation from the very beginning. Many floor brokers resented the presence of a reporter on their turf, but Maria was having none of it. She was tenacious. She stood her ground and reported the news surrounded by a mob of men screaming at each other and occasionally at her. She was a huge success.

She became an anchor in 1997, and though she continued to do reports from the NYSE floor, I took over the job of doing most of the market hits.

Reporters need sources, and in theory, the floor of the NYSE was the ultimate source for a stock reporter. At that time, about 80 percent of all the volume that went through the NYSE was done on the floor. If you had access to the people doing that trading, your reporting would be far better than just watching the tape.

I set my sights on two groups: specialists and two-dollar brokers.

While the floor had brokers representing the most prominent firms—Goldman Sachs, Morgan Stanley, Merrill Lynch, JP Morgan—a significant part of the trading was done by small independent shops, known as two-dollar brokers. They executed orders for other brokers' clients, or for brokers who did not have a presence on the floor. They got their name because they were traditionally paid $2 to trade a round lot of 100 shares. Though most of the firms were small, they often had significant orders to buy and sell stocks.

The other group, the specialists, had an equally important role. They were market makers who helped facilitate trading in stocks. They had evolved in the late 19th century when many traders began specializing in trading individual stocks exclusively. Posts were set up where each specialist traded a particular stock or group of stocks. If you wanted to trade General Electric, for example, you went to the post where General Electric was traded, where you could meet other traders who wanted to buy or sell the same stock. The specialist conducted ongoing auctions that posted the best bid (the maximum price a buyer is willing to pay) and offer (the minimum price a seller is willing to take) and kept an inventory of the stock that they could also trade if there were insufficient buyers or sellers.

These were valuable groups of people to get to know if I wanted to have more depth to my reporting.

The problem was most of them did not want to talk to me.

I couldn't blame them. There was no apparent reason why they would want to talk to a reporter, even on background. They were part of a powerful, elite organization, and most felt they didn't need to have nosy reporters hanging around asking questions.

But the times were changing, and even at a conservative organization like the NYSE, there were many who saw the advantages that media coverage could provide.

Foremost was Bob Zito, Executive Vice President and a member of the Management Committee of the NYSE. Zito was essentially in charge of communications and marketing, but he was much more influential than that. It was Zito who thought the NYSE would benefit from allowing reporters on the floor as a branding effort to reach a wider, global audience. Richard Grasso, the head of the NYSE, signed off on the idea, but only if the floor broker community—the leadership of which was affectionately known as "the Animals"—signed off as well. The floor was controlled by dozens of companies independent of the NYSE; it amounted to a series of independent fiefdoms. Many of the Animals were outright hostile to the idea: "You want *those* media people to be down here with us while we're trading?" Zito recalled one of them saying to him.[1] He convinced the floor leadership to commit to a pilot program that became a huge success. He even began providing media training to some of the brave souls willing to speak on air.

But in 1997, many—perhaps most—of the floor leadership were not happy with reporters showing up on the floor. They viewed it as a distraction and an invasion. Most did not trust reporters. They had stories (many true) that they had spoken with reporters with the understanding that they would not be quoted and subsequently were, which got them into trouble.

I worked for months to win the trust of a small group of people. Unless I could convince them to trust me, I was going to be forever a stranger in a strange land, surrounded by a rich source of information with no way to access it.

The breakthrough came gradually, with two key people: Jimmy Maguire and Art Cashin. Maguire ran Henderson Brothers and was the specialist for Warren Buffett's firm, Berkshire Hathaway. By the time I got there in 1997, Maguire was already a legend on the floor. He had been there for more than 25 years and had been at the American Stock Exchange for decades before that. He was courtly, he was courteous, he was respected by all, including Warren Buffett, who regularly praised his ability to keep trading spreads tight. He was known as "the Chief."

One day Buffett came on the floor, and Maguire insisted I meet him. Buffett at that time did not give many interviews. We spoke for a few minutes, with Jimmy standing next to us. Buffett reiterated that he would keep holdings like Coca-Cola "forever." On a later trip to the floor, I got a photo of the three of us, with me engaged in a tug of war with Warren and his wallet. It's one of my favorite pictures.

Art Cashin was also a legend in his own right. By 1997, he had been at the NYSE for over 30 years, managing floor operations for PaineWebber. He wrote a morning newsletter that mixed history with commentary on the trading action that was widely read on the Street. He was a drinker and a raconteur. I would go on to spend decades sitting in saloons with Art after trading hours, learning how to describe markets and tell stories.

With those two on my side, the tide started turning. *He wasn't such a bad guy, Pisani. You could talk to him. Have a drink with him. He was trustworthy. If you told him something that was just on background, your name would stay out of it.*

The two of them controlled a very powerful tradition: every year, between Christmas and New Year's, traders assembled on the floor and sang "Wait 'Till the Sun Shines, Nellie," a 1905 ditty that had become a sentimental favorite ever since the Depression of the 1930s. Art and Jimmy took turns conducting.

I knew I was making progress when I stood by them during the singing in those first years, and no one objected.

Others, including several specialists, soon came forward and either spoke to me or let me stand by them and watch them work.

There were characters back then on the floor—bigger-than-life personalities, men who screamed profanities at each other, drank heavily, and took shit from no one. Many were impatient with my questions, but enough let me into their world that I was able to improve my reporting dramatically.

While orders to buy and sell stocks were fragmented among dozens of firms, if you were able to talk to a sufficiently large sample size, you could see, for example, that there were large orders coming in to buy oil stocks or large orders to sell pharmaceutical stocks.

At the same time, a steady stream of celebrities came and rang the opening and closing bells.

The bell was traditionally rung by an exchange official until 1956, when 10-year-old Leonard Ross became the first invited person to ring the bell after he won $100,000 on a television quiz show answering questions on the stock exchange and finance.

President Reagan gave the bell ringing a new cachet when he visited in 1985, his first of two visits.

Bob Zito ramped it all up. He was very conscious of the publicity value of having CEOs, rock stars, movie stars, and political figures come and ring a bell in front of cheering stockbrokers. Beginning in 1995, that's precisely what he engineered.

Spectacle had arrived at the NYSE.

I met a few of those celebrities (more on that later), but more importantly, over the next few years I met and became acquainted with the work of a small group of academics and financial advisors who had published important research on the history of investing and investor psychology:

- Jack Bogle, the founder of Vanguard, who had built an investing empire emphasizing low-cost index funds.
- Burton Malkiel, the author of *A Random Walk Down Wall Street*, who had popularized the idea that you can't beat the market, no matter how much technical or fundamental analysis you throw at it.
- Wharton Professor Jeremy Siegel, whose book, *Stocks for the Long Run* had recently (1994) been published, examining stock and bond returns going back to 1802, and arguing that stocks provided superior returns of 6.5 to 7.0 percent after inflation, but only over long periods of time.
- Yale Professor of Economics Robert Shiller, who had made groundbreaking contributions to behavioral economics and whose book, *Irrational Exuberance*, would be published in 2000, examining stock market bubbles and why they happen, and who would go on to win the Nobel Prize in Economics in 2013.

These men had been asking profound questions about investing and human behavior for several decades. They had firm opinions on what worked and what didn't, and in the case of Shiller, why people behaved in ways that seemed opposed to their own interest.

By 2000, when Shiller's book came out, at the very height of the stock market's dot-com boom (March), I had already spent several years on the NYSE floor, observing trading but also watching the trading behavior of the new group of retail investors. These investors were taking advantage of the new crop of electronic brokers that enabled them to trade from home.

It was the perfect storm for a bubble: new technology (hardware and software) that enabled investors to connect directly to their brokers without being on the phone and receive confirmation of the trade in a much shorter time, along with a stock market boom (fueled by intense interest in the internet) that moved the S&P 500 up nearly 90 percent in the three years from 1997 to the start of 2000.

It would not end well, but in between, it was a wild ride.

That was the environment when I arrived on the floor in 1997. I'll tell you what happened next in Chapter 5, but first I want to give you the answer to one of the most common questions I get asked by viewers: how do I decide what is news?

# CHAPTER 2

## *What's News?*

=====

AFTER "What's going on with the markets?" the most common question I get asked is, "How do you decide what to say?"

The short answer is, it's a distillation of everything I think is important in the trading world, filtered through the crucible of my own experience.

In this chapter, I'll show you how I review the thousands of pieces of information that comprise "the markets" to obtain a view on what is going on that day. Hopefully it will help you to do likewise!

It all starts with each day's morning meeting.

## *The morning meeting*

Want to feel like an idiot? Try calling into the morning meeting at CNBC.

Most newsrooms have a couple of daily meetings—in the morning and in the afternoon. It's a chance to discuss what should be covered that day. It's where reporters pitch story ideas to the Executive Producers and the Assignment Desk.

On busy days, there can be 100 people on the morning call, including producers, the Assignment Desk, editors for cnbc.com, the social media team, and reporters covering everything from aerospace to media, cybersecurity, real estate, biotech, retail, banking, technology, energy, bonds, personal finance, global markets, the Federal Reserve, Capitol Hill, and even Hollywood.

The call usually starts off with an overview of the news, and what we should be emphasizing today. We go over the story pitches, and often the reporters will comment on what is happening with their beats.

One thing's for sure: I'm usually the oldest guy on the call. Senior Stocks Correspondent. The Last of the Mohicans. Thirty-two years at CNBC, and most days, I feel like I'm not only the oldest on the call, I'm also the dumbest.

That's because these are the smartest people I've ever worked with. They're also what I call the glue people for the News Division: the muscle and bone of the company, the people that hold it together, make it cohesive.

This is a crowd that knows almost everything there is to know about the business world.

If you open your mouth in front of this crowd, you'd better be able to tell them something they don't know—and the shortest, most effective way it can be conveyed to the audience.

And you'd better not waste their time. Everyone is busy, everyone has a show to produce or appear on.

I have a broad portfolio. I'm not the biotech reporter, not the aerospace reporter. I'm the 30,000-foot guy. Big picture. My job is to describe what is going on with the markets. Is the trend up or down? What's winning, what's losing? What is everyone worried about? What will earnings look like? How will events in Washington or overseas affect the stock market? How's the IPO market looking? Where is the money going, and where is it leaving?

By the time of the morning call, I've already been up for a few hours, so I'm not flying blind. I usually get up a little after 5 AM. For the past 20 years, the first thing I have looked at is the S&P futures and the market in Tokyo. It's not perfect, but it gives a general sense of where things are.

By the time I get to my office at the New York Stock Exchange, a few hours before the markets open, I have a good idea of what will matter that day.

I'm partial to our outstanding website, CNBC.com, which is set up to give active investors a clear view of what will impact trading that day. I'll also check the major papers like *The New York Times*, *The Wall Street Journal*, *Barron's*, and *Financial Times*, along with Bloomberg and Axios, and a smattering of other online morning newsletters.

I will check on what, if any, IPOs have priced the night before and look at earnings releases of major companies.

The biggest chunk of time is spent going through my email; I get about 600 a day. Some of it is internal distribution of news stories, but most of it is from strategists and analysts at Wall Street firms, discussing everything from the big picture (the economy, earnings), to the very small picture (here's what our housing analyst had to say about the New Home Sales report).

Sounds like a gold mine of information, doesn't it? Everything Wall Street is thinking that morning.

Alas, much of the output from strategists and particularly analysts is garbage.

## Deciding what matters

The first rule is, not all sources are equal. Some sources matter more than others.

## ANALYSTS

Of the 600 emails I get a day, a good portion are analyst reports on every conceivable subject. Individual stocks like Apple or Caterpillar. Sectors like Technology or Industrials. Most of it—and I am talking 80 percent—is garbage.

At one time analysts were the lifeblood of Wall Street. Not anymore.

In 2003, then New York Attorney General Eliot Spitzer and other regulators reached an enforcement agreement between all the Wall Street brokerage firms, the SEC, the National Association of Securities Dealers (NASDA), and the NYSE. Spitzer had sued the big firms, alleging a conflict of interest between the investment banking firms and their analysis departments. The firms, it was alleged, were allowing their analysts to issue overhyped and, in some cases, fraudulent research reports in exchange for business from companies seeking to go public. As part of the settlement, known as the Global Analyst Research Settlement, the firms paid $875 million in penalties and disgorgement, and were required to erect a "Chinese Wall" to insulate their analyst departments from investment banking.[1]

With the lucrative payouts from investment banking no longer available, analyst pay dropped dramatically. The best and brightest analysts decamped, some to retirement, some to hedge funds.

Prior to 2003, I spent a lot of time with analysts, because they often had excellent insights. Since then, not so much. While there are still analysts worth reading, the majority do very little original research or thinking. They parrot companies' financial data and often only change their forecasts when a company announces a change.

You'd think that after the 2003 Settlement, analysts would have become more conservative and less willing to slap a "Buy" rating on a company.

Nope. In 2002, 45 percent of all the ratings were a "Buy" or "Strong Buy." Only nine percent were a "Sell" or "Strong Sell."

Today, 57 percent have a "Buy" or "Strong Buy" rating and six percent have a "Sell" or "Strong Sell" rating."[2]

The analysts are more bullish than they were 20 years ago!

There have been attempts to set up independent research organizations, but it is difficult to accomplish because most traders don't want to pay the real cost for research.

All this adds up to a crisis in covering companies. Many companies—particularly small caps—have no analyst coverage at all, and so they languish because there is no one to stir up interest. We've gone from overhyped to neglected, in less than 20 years.

## STRATEGISTS

Strategists are the intellectuals of Wall Street. Some are *macro* strategists whose views can range far and wide, covering the global economy and politics, though most cover more mundane topics like equities, fixed income, currency, commodities, and the futures markets. Some, like David Kostin from Goldman Sachs, Mike Wilson from Morgan Stanley, Mohamed El-Erian from Allianz, or Savita Subramanian from Bank of America/Merrill Lynch, have become superstar commentators and appear regularly on TV and in the newspapers.

I pay more attention to this group than analysts. I don't think they have better predictive power than analysts, but it's a more rarified group and the best will often have something original to say that makes it worthwhile to stop and read.

## CORPORATIONS

In theory, public relations (PR), which are set up to talk to the media, and investor relations (IR), which are set up to talk to investors, are great sources of information.

PR is important when trying to confirm information from sources other than the company. IR can be very important for beat reporters that need to drill down into a company's earnings or other company development.

Most reporting on corporations relies on the company's quarterly earnings report. In recent years, the quarterly earnings call—a telephone conference with analysts—has become more important. Twenty-five years ago, this was an exclusive event—analysts were usually the only participants present, and the media was generally excluded. That has changed in recent years because the earnings calls now provide far more color than a bland earnings press release, and there are now readily available transcripts of the calls that can be poured over.

## TRADING DESKS

Trading desks represent the sell-side of Wall Street. They're the brokerage firms that act as intermediaries, buying and selling stocks on behalf of clients, and sometimes for their own account. Because they see a lot of orders to buy and sell, the best ones have a good sense for the flow of the market. Often, traders at mid-size firms are less constrained by their PR and legal departments, and have better observations than their brethren at the largest firms.

## THE NYSE FLOOR

The traders on the floor—independent brokerage firms, large brokerage houses, and the Designated Market Makers (DMMs)—are also part of the sell-side. Twenty years ago, about 80 percent of all the trading done in NYSE stocks was done on the floor. Today, it's less than 20 percent, but it's a mistake to think there is no information. Many of the DMMs are still among the largest traders in their stocks, so if a stock is showing unusual activity, there's a good chance the DMM knows what's going on.

I walk the floor several times a day to chat with the traders and see what is on their minds.

## MUTUAL FUNDS

This is the buy-side—the people who buy, sell and manage stocks for clients, many of whom are CNBC viewers. The largest, like those run by Blackrock, Vanguard, and Fidelity, publish regular reports on trading activity, fund flows, and even 401(k) activity that can be very useful in understanding where people are putting their money. Still, most of their observations are only useful for intermediate and long-term viewpoints. Their observations also tend to be conservative because they need to appeal to the largest possible audience.

## EXCHANGE-TRADED FUNDS (ETFS)

ETFs are like mutual funds in that they can hold assets like stocks, bonds, currencies, and commodities—but unlike mutual funds, they can be bought and sold during the day, have lower costs, and are more tax efficient. Most use indexes and are passively managed. While many of the big fund families also run ETFs, this universe is more dynamic than the mutual fund universe. Companies like Invesco, ProShares, WisdomTree, ARK, VanEck, Amplify, and O'Shares run innovative investment strategies. Many set up funds that invest in technology themes like clean energy, cybersecurity, 3-D printing, or blockchain. Others avoid market capitalization-weighted indices and instead invest on the basis of dividend growth or earnings growth. ETFs can be quickly created around themes that have suddenly become popular, like cannabis or work-from-home. The people who run these ETFs have strong opinions on the themes behind their funds. I run a show focusing on this area, *ETF Edge*, and I often consult with this group.

## HEDGE FUNDS

In the 1990s and 2000s, I spent considerable time talking to hedge fund traders of a very particular type: long/short equity funds. These funds were typically siloed by sector. A manager might be responsible for trading retail stocks. He or she might be long a basket of retail stocks, and short others. Good managers, if they were willing to talk to you, were great sources of information. Many were very innovative in gathering information outside normal channels. Traders covering retail, for example, were counting cars in parking lots at large malls around the country decades ago, as a way of gathering information about retail store flows. They were also paid to have strong opinions: a trader could give you five reasons why Home Depot might outperform Lowe's in the next year.

They may be great sources of information, but there's big problems with them. First, most hedge funds will not talk to the media, and those that do will usually not disclose their current positions. Large hedge funds are required to file a quarterly report, but these reports have little value because by the time the report is filed the positions may have changed significantly.

Another problem for long/short funds is that the relentless rise of the markets in the last decade has caused the short book to dramatically underperform, so even if someone managing a long/short book has some success picking winners, their picks for losers often do not pan out.

Finally, hedge funds suffer from the same issue that afflicts all active managers: as a group they underperform their benchmarks. While there are indeed some outstanding hedge funds, most are poor stock pickers because market timing (deciding when to get in and out of investments) tends to underperform simple benchmarks like buying and holding the S&P 500. Most do not come anywhere near justifying their typical fee of two percent for administration and 20 percent of profits.

## COMMENTATORS AND BLOGGERS

There's a lot of nonsense and garbage in this group, but there is also some real gold. Two of my favorites are DataTrek, a terrific quant-driven report run by Nicholas Colas, and the Morning Bullets from Greg Valliere, Chief US Policy Strategist at AGF Investments. Greg writes a succinct newsletter each morning on the intersection between Washington and Wall Street.

Ben Carlson at Ritholtz Wealth Management writes a great blog, *A Wealth of Common Sense*, that focuses on wealth management and investor psychology. His colleague, Josh Brown, also runs a great blog and podcast, *The Reformed Broker*. Morgan Housel tweets wise and witty observations on personal finance and wrote one of my favorite books on investing, *The Psychology of Money*.

Jeffrey Sonnenfeld is the Lester Crown Professor in the Practice of Management at Yale School of Management, and Senior Associate Dean for Leadership Studies. He writes insightfully on corporate governance matters and is a regular on CNBC. Much of his writing can be found on the Yale Insights page.

Other people who cover the broad markets and investing that I follow closely include Jeff Cox and Patti Domm at CNBC.com, Christine Benz, John Rekenthaler, and Ben Johnson at Morningstar, Eric Balchunas at Bloomberg, Kathleen Smith and Matt Kennedy at Renaissance Capital, Jason Zweig and Greg Ip at *The Wall Street Journal*, Mark Hulbert at MarketWatch, Dave Nadig at ETF Trends, Sam Stovall and Todd Rosenbluth at CFRA Research, and Larry Swedroe, Director of Research at Buckingham Strategic Wealth.

Matt Hougan, Chief Investment Officer at Bitwise Investments, has been a friend for many years and one of the sharpest minds in the ETF and crypto space.

While there are many good websites for investors who want information on mutual funds and ETFs, my go-to source has always been Morningstar. ETF.com is also an outstanding resource for data and articles on ETFs.

The American Association of Individual Investors (AAII) is an excellent resource for small investors. Their website contains a wealth of information on investing, retirement, and financial planning.

Renaissance Capital does terrific research for investors in upcoming IPOs and maintains a calendar of events.

## SOCIAL MEDIA

Social media is a blessing and a curse. A blessing, because it's a fast and convenient way to stay in touch with other professionals who cover the markets. I can see what topics are dominating the conversation that day. It's also a great way to stay in touch with thoughtful viewers who have constructive observations and suggest topics they believe are worth covering.

It's a curse because it has become a magnet for angry people. The loudest, most vociferous people are usually associated with a brand I call "aggrievement." They're mad. Sometimes they're mad at me, but usually they're mad at something else. The Federal Reserve. The stock market. The president. Their boss. Their life. Social media has given everyone a platform to air their grievances, and while it may feel good, it doesn't necessarily advance the conversation.

It was a wise person who said, "In the future everyone will be anonymous for 15 minutes."

## THE VIEWER

There's another player in this game: the viewer. Most don't work on Wall Street. Some are active traders, but most just have money in the markets and want to know what is going on.

Thirty-two years ago, when I started at CNBC, I had a major problem: I wasn't sure who I was talking to. I was the Real Estate Correspondent, but I had no idea what the sophistication level of the viewer was. Did they know what a mortgage was? If they did know, did they know what a mortgage-backed security was?

It bothered me, staring into a camera not knowing who I was talking to.

So I invented a viewer.

She was 48 years old, lived in Minneapolis, and worked part-time as an accountant for MMM. She was married, with two boys, one of whom was 25 years old, had just gotten engaged, and was interested in buying a house.

She had a basic knowledge of real estate—she knew what a mortgage was and a little about the process of buying and selling a home, but not much.

She was interested in learning more.

She was, for me, the perfect viewer. She knew a few things, but not too much. I knew at what level I could speak to her. I knew she would understand a mortgage, but I would have to explain a mortgage-backed security.

When I developed stories I considered what interested her, and I knew what level of sophistication I needed to use.

I still use that idea. I try talking to a viewer who may or may not be an active trader, but who is interested in broad trends in the market. I try to keep the financial terms at a consistent level. You do need to make assumptions about what the viewer knows, but I always consider what the viewer *wants to know* as the main question to answer.

Different viewers want to know different things, but I've found that the typical viewer wants a Senior Stocks Correspondent like me to describe: 1) the main buying and selling trends at that moment, with an emphasis on sector momentum; 2) the main earnings trend in the market—is it up or down; and 3) the main risks in the intermediate term (next three to six months).

Why intermediate term? Because I found that is the timeline most people tend to think about. Sure, there are day traders who only care what is happening that day, and there are long-term buy-and-hold investors who aren't likely to change their portfolios no matter what happens. But I've found that most people who ask me, "What's happening with the markets?" are asking about what could happen in the next several months. It's a time horizon everyone, from day traders to long-term buy-and-hold investors, can relate to.

## *What's it all mean?*

Put it all together, and what I have is a mosaic of several hundred different facts and opinions.

*How do I make sense of it?*

I visualize this as a blank white wall. On the wall are hundreds of small, yellow Post-it notes, each with one fact or idea.

My job is to show how they are connected; to put all the facts together and make a coherent narrative out of it.

I don't have to use everything. Not everything is important or worth mentioning. That's where experience comes in.

After the morning meeting, I'll email and call my producer, Kirsten Chang, to chat about what I will say in my first hit, which is usually right after the market opens, about 9:40 AM.

Kirsten has been with me for several years and she's become a great market observer on her own. She will email her own observations and those of other sources as well.

I'll also usually call a few traders before the open. I've known most of them for many years.

The most valuable source is a person who: 1) knows what they are talking about; and 2) can provide an honest opinion.

They are not necessarily the same things.

The first thing I learned covering the stock market is that Everyone Talks Their Book. Everyone has something they are selling. If it's not stocks, it's ideas, or it's just the prestige of talking to a reporter.

I have learned to filter this out. It doesn't mean there is no value.

Over time, I have developed sources that I can trust, that will tell me what's going on, and whether it's good or bad—even if it is detrimental to their stocks, or to their firm, or even to their career.

One source like that is far more valuable than calling 10 other sources and trying to figure out whose narrative you should be following.

## Squawk on the Street: the smartest guys in the room

By the time 9 AM comes around, we've already had three hours of *Squawk Box*, with Becky Quick, Joe Kernen, and Andrew Ross Sorkin interviewing many of the major newsmakers.

*Squawk on the Street*, kicking off at 9 AM, is a different animal. The first hour revolves around three very strong personalities: Jim Cramer, David Faber, and Carl Quintanilla.

Jim Cramer has one of the toughest jobs at CNBC. He doesn't just comment on the markets; he gives opinions on stocks he likes and doesn't like. I still marvel at the level of granularity on hundreds of stocks that he keeps in his head. He also gets all the important CEOs on *Squawk on the Street* and his evening show, *Mad Money*.

Cramer's granularity is matched only by David Faber. I have known David for more than 30 years and have watched him for just as long. He covers mergers and acquisitions, but he can, and does, talk about anything that he finds interesting: IPOs, SPACs, earnings. His real specialty—which he often covers in a brief segment called "The Faber

Report"—is making observations about the news of the day from a single company. He'll connect the dots on dozens of facts, ask questions, and draw conclusions.

It's masterful journalism—bringing disparate facts into a coherent narrative, adding to the story without editorializing. It's difficult to do, even with a deep knowledge of the subject matter.

The true star of the show is Carl Quintanilla. He is the perfect anchor.

Cramer and Faber are two mighty planets, and Carl is the sun that the show revolves around.

He rarely shows his hand. You would be hard-pressed to know his opinions, even on subjects that come up on a daily basis.

Instead, he makes observations about stocks, the economy, earnings. He throws out facts from the weekly jobless claims, or an earnings report, or a comment from a hedge fund manager, and asks Jim and David what they think.

This sounds simple, but, as the ancients used to say, the art is in the artlessness. The trick is to inform and entertain, to move from one complex subject to another, but make it seem like a conversation between friends.

## The opening bell

The first few minutes after the open is often the busiest part of the day. *Squawk on the Street* is on the air with Carl, David and Jim, live from Post 9 in front of the bell podium. Gillian Austin, our Segment Producer, is planning segments, booking floor traders, executing production requests, running scripts to the set and making sure the guests are checked in and have makeup. Brad Rubin, our floor manager, is making sure the technical operations are running smoothly.

I will usually come on shortly after the open.

The mission is simple: in three or four minutes, explain the most important things the average viewer needs to know that day.

Go.

## MOMENTUM: SECTORS

I usually start with a look at momentum—what're the main buying and selling trends? Absent specific company news, stocks tend to move in groups—bank stocks tend to move together, Industrials tend to move together. There are 11 sectors in the S&P 500: Financials, Industrials, Technology, Materials, Consumer Discretionary, Consumer Staples, Health Care, Energy, Communication Services, and Real Estate Investment Trusts (REITs).

What's the trend? What sectors have been outperforming, what sectors have been underperforming? Is there an obvious reason?

## THE BIG THEME

What're the main themes driving stocks? Have these themes changed in the last week, or even overnight?

## INDIVIDUAL MOVERS

Jim, David and Carl will likely have covered the major stock stories of the day. Is there something I can add? Are there other stories they didn't mention that were significant, that could shed light on the broader market? If one company reported they were having supply chain problems, or suddenly had higher raw material costs, could I extrapolate that to other companies?

## IPOS

Watching IPOs is my favorite part of the job. It's a chance to witness the American dream: building a company, watching it grow, going public, and, yes, getting rich.

In some cases, very rich.

If the IPO is generating a lot of investor interest and it's trading on the NYSE, I'll often stand in front of the post, talking about where it priced and what the expectations might be.

I'll usually stick around after my first hit and chat with the people whose firm is going public. I could be talking to an oil company, insurance salespeople, scientists looking for a cure for cancer, or a waste hauling company. It's a wonderful front-seat view of corporate America.

For more than a decade the bulk of IPO activity has gone into two sectors: technology, particularly software, and biotechnology, a subsector of health care. Why? Because that's where the growth is. Software to make the world run more efficiently, and cures for diseases. Every imaginable disease. I've had discussions about neuron excitability disorders, infectious diseases, oncology drug development, everything.

I'll talk more about what it is like to go public on the NYSE in the next chapter.

——————

After chatting with a few of the floor traders, I go back to my office. The rest of the day is spent prepping for afternoon hits. In between, I am reading reports from analysts and strategists that I care about, making phone calls, and, most importantly, coming up with story ideas.

The rest of the time, like everyone else, I am watching the tape.

# *Reading the tape*

Tape reading is a high art on Wall Street. Of the roughly 3,000 stocks that trade on the Street, I watch about one third of that—about 1,000.

Tape watchers can be arranged into two basic groups—the *technicians* and the *fundamentalists*.

To a fundamentalist, the stock market is a discounting mechanism to figure out a future stream of earnings and dividends.

It's based on the idea that it is possible to figure out the true, intrinsic value of a stock by estimating a future flow of dividends and earnings, and then determining if the present price is trading at a premium or a discount.

How does an analyst know how much earnings and dividends a company is going to make in the future? They don't. They make educated guesses.

If the stock of a company the analyst is interested in—let's say it's Caterpillar—might make X amount of earnings in five years and throw off Y amount of dividends, what would be the correct price to pay for Caterpillar today?

Technicians, instead, use technical analysis. At its basic level, this is the study of crowd behavior. It's watching price and volume trends, which reflects what the crowd is doing, and it's also about trying to figure out how long the trend will continue.

I have a fondness for technical analysis, because the assumptions behind it seem to make sense.

Technicians, for example, do not worry about why a stock price is up 25 percent in a month or how overvalued or undervalued a stock is. They're not concerned with trying to figure out what a company's earnings are going to look like two years in the future.

They're just concerned with trying to figure out crowd behavior.

I often talk about trading patterns on the air, so much so that in 2014 I received a Recognition Award from the Market Technicians Association, the main organization of technical analysts, for "steadfast efforts to integrate technical analysis into financial decision making, journalism, and reporting."

That doesn't mean I don't have problems with technical analysis. I'll discuss some of the problems I have with day trading and market timing in Chapters 15–17.

Regardless: technical analysis is widely used, particularly by short-term traders.

My stock screen is arranged by sectors and subsectors. A couple of times a day, I run screens, looking for technical trends:

- Biggest percentage movers up or down.
- How many stocks are at new highs, how many are at new lows.
- Relative Strength Indicators, which measures how much a stock has been moving up or down over a short period of time, often just a few weeks.
- How many stocks are advancing versus declining.
- Overall trading volume, and unusually heavy trading in individual names.
- Moving averages of stocks and indexes for different periods, such as 50- or 200-day moving averages.

Many traders also incorporate sentiment indicators, such as how many mentions stocks are receiving in chat rooms, as an additional factor to watch.

I spend a good part of my day looking at technical trading patterns, but I am far more interested in fundamental analysis like earnings growth (increasing earnings growth is good) and profit margins (increasing margins are also good). In the long term I believe there is a relationship between expectations of future earnings and future dividend growth, and stock prices, even though the value investors put on that future stream of earnings and dividends (the P/E ratio) can vary over time (I discuss this in greater detail in Chapter 10).

In practice, there are very few pure technicians and fundamental investors. Even fundamental investors who might consider technical analysis to be "voodoo" watch technical indicators, if only because the focus of many traders is much more short-term than it used to be. These are what I call "closet technicians." They will give you all sorts of reasons why they like the fundamental story of the company under discussion, and then they'll say, "Oh and by the way, the chart looks great."

This process—of reading endless research reports, talking to traders, staring at stock charts until your eyes bleed (mine have)—is all for one purpose: to construct a narrative that explains what's going on for the viewers.

The viewers, of course, are not a homogenous group; they have many different beliefs on what works and what doesn't.

Something that every viewer likes to see is an IPO. In many cases, it's a chance to watch their favorite brands go public.

There's another reason viewers like to watch IPOs. There's a voyeuristic quality to it.

While it takes years to build a company to the point where it can go public, the founders and early investors can—and do—get rich quickly. Very quickly.

# CHAPTER 3

## *My Favorite Part of My Job*

===

MEETING movie stars or rock stars is fun, but Initial Public Offerings (IPOs) are my favorite event. It's a chance to watch people realize the American dream, up close and personal.

For most, it's the biggest day of their professional lives. It's the day their company is going public. It's the day they get to tell the whole world, *I have succeeded.*

For many, it's also a day when they become wealthy, in some cases fabulously wealthy.

When your company is going public at the NYSE, your day begins early. Senior management will arrive at the NYSE about 7 AM, often with their families and other hand-picked employees, anywhere from a few to a few hundred.

There's usually a banner out front of the NYSE trumpeting the company's name. There's a display of the company's products, anything from sports cars (Ferrari) to exercise equipment (F45 Training) and everything in between. If there's no apparent product that can be displayed (software), there's often a band and free food.

# The NYSE Board Room: welcome to the club

There's a reception, usually in the Board Room on the sixth floor.

It's breathtaking: an open room, 40 by 100 feet, crowned with a glass ceiling made by people who had worked for Louis Tiffany himself.

In the corner is a seven-foot-tall stone and silver urn carved from red malachite, mounted on a green malachite pedestal and bearing the crest of the Russian Tsar, Nicholas II. It was created in 1903 by Carl Fabergé and given to the NYSE from the Tsar as thanks for its help floating a $1 billion loan to the Russian government, a considerable amount of money for that time. After the Tsar was deposed in 1918, the Russian government defaulted on the bond.

On the far wall, opposite the urn, is the only object that was formerly in the old New York Stock Exchange building, which was next door until the NYSE opened this building in 1903.

It's the Trading Floor Clock, and it's a very peculiar clock. The face does not have hour numbers, just five-minute markers. At that time, the NYSE traded only one stock at a time in an auction setting, for just five minutes at a time. The NYSE went to trading all stocks at once in the early 1870s, but the clock remained.

The festivities begin with a short welcome video, reminding everyone of the long and illustrious history of the NYSE.

An NYSE official, often the President of the NYSE, will welcome the guests and congratulate them on their accomplishments.

It's a carefully choreographed message: You are a public company. You have arrived.

The company's CEO will usually speak, reminding everyone how far the company has come and the long road it has traveled to get here.

# Bell ringings and gavel pounding

After the reception, everyone takes the elevator down to the trading floor.

The principals ringing the bell will sign the NYSE book under the podium, with the adoring gaze of staff, friends and family. More pictures.

The bell ringers will climb a short flight of steps to the bell podium. The rest of the staff and families remain on the floor, directly below the podium, cheering them on.

The bell ringing has its own elaborate ritual. When the NYSE went to continuous, simultaneous trading of all stocks in the 1870s, a Chinese gong was the bell of choice. When the NYSE moved into its new building in 1903, the gong was replaced by a large brass bell rung via an electric push-button.[1]

While the bell is rung electronically, the button must be held down by the bell ringer. It's supposed to ring for 10 seconds.

There's a digital clock above the post in front of the podium. The bell ringer is told by an exchange official standing with them that they are supposed to press the button at 9:29:50 and then release it at 9:30:00.

That doesn't always happen. Some get nervous and their fingers slip off the button. Some get so excited with all the cheering that they will ring it for 10 seconds and then push the button so it starts ringing again.

That's considered bad form. It invites booing from the traders.

There's one other piece of tradition: banging the gavel. After ringing the bell, the person ringing the bell strikes a wooden sounding block. This tradition goes back to the time before continuous trading started, when stocks were traded one at a time, and the banging of a gavel would signal the start and end of trading in a particular stock.

If bell ringers get overly enthusiastic at times, they get positively giddy pounding the gavel. I've seen bell ringers beat the gavel so furiously you'd think the podium was going to collapse.

Not surprisingly, the gavel breaks several times a year.

One thing that hasn't broken: the sounding block that the gavel hits. It's an original block of wood, used by the NYSE since the 1870s.

There's one other odd bit of history: the bell rings for 10 seconds in the morning, but 15 seconds in the afternoon. This tradition likely goes back to the opening of the new building in 1903, which had pneumatic tubes installed that whisked orders all over the building. The extra five seconds bought more time: if you dropped your order into the tube, as long as you got it in for the first strike of the bell, it would get to the post within that 15 seconds.[2]

After the bell is rung and the gavel is pounded, pictures are taken, and everyone exits out the back door.

Still more ritual: bell ringers sign the wall outside the podium. Bell ringer graffiti!

There are several ways you can go after you leave the podium: up a short flight of stairs to the elevator that will take you back to the sixth floor, or you can go down the stairs. Make a left, and you go on to the floor. Make a right, and you go down a short flight of stairs that take you onto Broad Street.

That is the way taken by people who don't want to come on the floor.

It's happened. In May 2005, Edgar Bronfman Jr. came to the NYSE to ring the opening bell for the IPO of his new company, Warner Music Group. He brought along Led Zeppelin guitarist Jimmy Page, who performed a thunderous short version of "Whole Lotta Love" while the opening bell rang, drowning out the bell and the traders who were screaming at the top of their lungs for Jimmy to keep playing.

After the open, Bronfman came down on the floor and I was set to interview him and Page. There were hundreds of floor traders clutching worn vinyl copies of *Led Zeppelin II* and *Physical Graffiti* they were hoping to get signed by Page.

Bronfman appeared without Page. "He's not coming down," he told me, explaining Page had taken the right turn and left the building, though he knew everyone was waiting to say hello.

It is well known that Page suffers from stage fright and performance anxiety, but the traders were bitterly disappointed their guitar hero had appeared and then just slipped away.

Fortunately, most people who ring the bell don't pull a Jimmy Page. They make a left, and they're on the floor.

They will walk to the post where their stock will be trading.

And they will wait. There are two principals involved in the IPO opening process: the Designated Market Maker (DMM), in charge of making a market in that stock; and the bookrunner, the firm that is the lead underwriter for the offering (usually Goldman Sachs, Morgan Stanley, or JP Morgan). Together, they will "build the book," where they are putting together those who want to sell stock they have received from the offering the night before with buyers who wish to purchase at the open. This can take anywhere from 15 minutes to several hours. The game is to find the correct opening price that matches the most buyers with the most sellers.

While they are waiting for their stock to start trading, everyone is taking pictures, hugging each other, looking around, but mostly they are staring at the panel above the post, which has the name of their company and the IPO price.

Floor traders who have orders to buy and sell at the open are standing in front of the post, waiting for early indications from the DMM on where it might open.

At some point, a public "indication" is posted on the panel. For example, if the stock was priced at $18, it might say "$19–$20," indicating that at the current level of interest, it would open between $19 and $20.

That's when the cheering begins in earnest. Everyone is staring at the panel, and they're all doing the same thing.

They're calculating their net worth.

Because that's when it gets real—that's when they realize that the minute the stock starts trading, they're going to be worth a lot more than the minute before.

How much more? It depends.

A typical IPO might seek to raise anywhere from $100 million to $500 million, but it can go much higher. For example, the biggest IPO of all time, Alibaba Group, raised a staggering $25 billion when it went public on September 19, 2014.[3]

The amount of shares floated varies, but it is typically anywhere from 10 million to 40 million shares. The trend in the last decade has been to float a smaller number of shares—often as low as 10 percent of the shares outstanding—because limiting supply will help support the price. A typical IPO might price in the $20 range.

All of the senior management have been granted substantial shares, usually for free, as part of their compensation. Others, such as venture capital investors, may own shares at a fraction of the price of the IPO.

It would not be unusual for senior management to own 100,000 shares in the company. If the stock opens at $20, that's $2 million.

In seconds.

No wonder they're staring at the panel.

In some cases, those insiders may be able to sell a portion of their shares at the open, but in most cases all or a substantial part of their shares are locked up for some time, often six months or more.

No matter. The minute the company goes public, their net worth is substantially higher, even if it's only on paper.

The NYSE will have a "floor bell" next to the post. It's a smaller replica of the bell on the podium. When the stock begins trading, the CEO or founder will "ring" the bell.

"Ring" does not quite describe what many end up doing. They beat the hell out of that bell, they're so happy. Other senior members of the team grab the hammer and chime in. More pictures are taken. Jokes are told. A lot of "Remember when…" stories are told. A lot of backs are slapped.

And then, slowly, the party winds down. NYSE officials escort the crowd back up to the sixth floor. More refreshments, and then the crowd is again escorted down the elevators and out onto Wall Street.

Literally, out onto Wall Street. To the corner of Broad and Wall, the site of Federal Hall, where more pictures are often taken. The original building was New York's first City Hall, then after the establishment of the United States in 1789 it was the site of the first Congress and the location of George Washington's first inaugural address that same year. The current building on the site, completed in 1842, was the U.S. Custom House for the Port of New York and is now a national memorial. A statue of the first President, his right hand extending outward, stands on the site.

## Who's rich, and who's really rich: Jack Ma and Mark Zuckerberg

Earlier, I used an example of an executive who might have 100,000 shares in a company that went public at $20, so on paper, that executive has $2 million in stock.

That's likely the low end. It can go way, way higher, and many also include stock options. Co-founders can own 20 percent or more of the company.

In those cases, their net worth can go into the billions.

Billions? Yes.

I'm often asked, "Of all the people you've met, who made the most money on their IPO?"

I don't know who the record holder is, but Jack Ma certainly is up there.

On September 19, 2014, Alibaba co-founder and executive chairman Jack Ma came on the NYSE floor after an elaborate welcome at the

NYSE. He had brought an entourage of Alibaba executives and employees, along with a smattering of celebrities like actor and martial artist Jet Li.

It was a Big Event, the largest IPO in history. A staggering $25 billion had been raised, with a market capitalization north of $230 billion.

Ma owned about six percent of that.

Even before the stock opened, Ma had already spoken with David, Carl, and Jim. The interview would be memorable because he was asked who inspired him.

Everyone expected him to cite someone like Warren Buffett, but Ma said his hero was the movie character, Forrest Gump. Ma said he had seen the movie many times and had taken inspiration from the main character, who faced tumultuous change in the 1960s and 1970s, but always remained true to himself. "No matter what changed, you are you," Ma said.

Ma was going to need some of that Forrest Gump patience to get through the day. The sheer size and complexity of the deal would make it one of the most extended IPO processes in NYSE history.

At that time, a typical IPO might start "building the book" right after the open, and usually open between 9:45 and 10:15 AM.

Not this one.

After pricing overnight at $68, the first indications came at 9:45 AM: $80–$83. From there, it stepped up in $3 increments, then $2 increments, then $1 increments.

Ma had come over to Post 8 and was standing with Glenn Carell and Patrick Murphy from GTS, the market maker who had won the right to trade the stock on the floor. Carell and Murphy were veterans of many IPOs and were explaining the process to Ma.

I was inside the post, looking out at Ma, providing a running commentary of what was going on to the viewers.

About 11 AM, Ma came into the post to say hello.

This is what makes my job so unique: not only am I on the floor of the NYSE covering the biggest IPO of all time, but I am also now standing next to Jack Ma, making small talk.

I joked that the process was taking so long we were all ordering lunch and did he want anything. How about the pastrami?

I asked him how he felt about the IPO process.

"It's a good process I am very happy by that. Yeah I learned a lot, I'm learning how can we do better next year for our Single's Day. It's exciting. It's very transparent."

He had good reason to be excited. He had just steered the largest IPO in history. The stock, which had priced at $68, was indicating it would open around $90 by the time I spoke to him.

When it finally opened at $92.70 at 11:53 AM, it had a market cap north of $300 billion, making it larger than Facebook or Amazon.

Ma instantly became one of the richest men in the world.

He owned 206 million shares. He sold 12.75 million on the offering at $68, which got him $870 million in cash. When Alibaba opened at $92.70, the remaining roughly 193 million shares were worth $17.8 billion.

The value of his stake at the open, including the value of the stock he sold, was almost $18.7 billion.

Significant as that haul was, it wasn't a record.

Mark Zuckerberg took Facebook public on May 17, 2012. The stock priced at $38, raising $16 billion in what was then the third-biggest IPO in U.S. history and the largest ever by a tech company. Facebook was valued at $104 billion, at that time the largest ever valuation for a newly public company.[4]

Zuckerberg owned 533 million shares. He sold 30.2 million at the open at $38. When it opened at $42.05 (after a delay due to technical problems at Nasdaq), the value of his holdings, including the value of the stock he sold, was $22.3 billion.[5]

He had beaten Jack Ma by more than $4 billion.

Ma stepped down as executive chairman in 2019, claiming he wanted to focus on his philanthropy efforts.

He very nearly pulled off the IPO Feat of the Century: he almost had a hand in steering the biggest IPO of all time, a second time.

Ant Financial, an affiliate of Alibaba, owned China's largest digital payment platform, Alipay. It was set to go public in November 2020 on both the Shanghai and Hong Kong exchanges. It attempted to raise an estimated $34.5 billion, 40 percent higher than the record-breaking $25 billion Alibaba had raised six years before. Its valuation would have been north of $300 billion, making it larger than some of the biggest banks in the United States, including Goldman Sachs and Wells Fargo.[6]

It didn't happen.

Ma stepped down from the board of Alibaba in early October 2020. On October 24, Ma gave a speech in which he heavily criticized China's regulatory system. Shortly after, the IPO was canceled, and Alibaba became the target of an antitrust investigation by Chinese authorities.[7]

Ma resurfaced in January 2021. Even after selling a good part of his Alibaba shares the prior year, he was still one of the wealthiest men in the world, worth north of $50 billion.[8]

## *What to see at the NYSE on the day of your IPO*

If you're ever lucky enough to attend an IPO or any other event at the New York Stock Exchange, make sure you get to the Board Room to see the Russian urn.

In 1992, for the 200th anniversary of the NYSE, President Ronald Reagan visited the NYSE for the second time and brought along a special guest: former Soviet leader Mikhail Gorbachev. More than a decade earlier, the Russians had expressed interest in having the urn returned to Russia. Then-NYSE chief executive John Phelan told the USSR Ambassador in the 1980s that the urn was a gift for a bond that was never repaid, and if the Russians wanted it back they could buy it with the principal and interest due on the $1 billion loan. Gorbachev also expressed interest in having the urn returned, and NYSE officials reiterated that he would have to pay back the bond with interest.[9]

Gorbachev didn't take them up on the offer.

There's one other item you shouldn't miss.

On the seventh floor, near the old members' luncheon club, there's a small stand that displays the most important document in the building, and one of the most important documents in American history: the Buttonwood Agreement, the founding document of the NYSE, signed on May 17, 1792. It's called the Buttonwood Agreement because the early traders met under a sycamore tree near what is today 68 Wall Street, a block away. Sycamore trees were called "buttonwoods" because they were used to make buttons.

It's remarkably short. There are only 24 signatories. It says two things: the signatories are only going to buy and sell with each other and no one else, and the commissions will be 0.25 percent.

Look for the signature of Leonard Bleecker. It's the first one, on the left side.

Anthony Lispenard Bleecker was a prominent banker, merchant and auctioneer. Around the time the Buttonwood Agreement was signed, Bleecker bought 160 acres "out in the country," several miles north from where he lived on lower Broadway. His friends laughed at him for wasting his money, but that land became summer vacation homes for wealthy New Yorkers.[10]

Today, that land Bleecker bought is called Greenwich Village, and one of its main thoroughfares is Bleecker Street.

That story about the founding of Greenwich Village is one of many I heard from one of Wall Street's master storytellers. In a friendship that has spanned 25 years, Art Cashin would teach me that storytelling and a compelling narrative was far more effective in conveying the lessons of the market than academic treatises on fundamental or technical analysis.

# CHAPTER 4

# *Art Cashin and the*
# *Art of Storytelling*

———

No one ever made a decision because of a number. They need a story.
—*Daniel Kahneman, in Michael Lewis,* The Undoing Project[1]

I F you encounter Art Cashin on the street outside the New York Stock
Exchange you might think you were meeting a man one step removed
from homelessness.

His suit is usually rumpled. His ties are 20 years old, knotted carelessly,
and skewed to one side. He is typically wearing a dilapidated trench coat
straight out of *Casablanca*.

He looked like he might have slept outside on the pavement.

But for 60 years, Art Cashin has been one of the most influential men
on Wall Street. Head of floor trading for PaineWebber, and later UBS, he
is old-school Wall Street to the core—a market historian, a great drinker,
but above all a raconteur: a teller of stories.

There's a lot of great market historians—men and women who
can tell you what moved when, where, and why. Those types know
what they're talking about, but most don't *sound* like they know what

they're talking about—they can't explain what they know for a general audience. Then there's the opposite problem: the vast hordes of Wall Street bullshitters that don't know much, but *sound* like they know what they're talking about.

Cashin is that rare exception: a man who knows what he is talking about *and* sounds like he knows.

He never went to college and had little use for academic theories. His "education" consisted of attendance in the only "universities" he had ever known: the floor of the NYSE and the many bars surrounding it.

Holding forth at the bar on the seventh floor of the New York Stock Exchange with a glass of Dewar's on the rocks in his hand, or at Bobby Van's steakhouse across the street, or any one of dozens of Wall Street watering holes he frequented with a coterie of friends and hangers-on he dubbed the "Friends of Fermentation," Cashin would engage anyone in an analysis of what was going on in the markets and the economy, but disdained academic and scholarly digressions on why the market was behaving in a certain way, or whether one trading style or another was more successful than others.

It wasn't that he didn't care: he cared very much. He just preferred a different style than academics.

He preferred to tell stories.

The stories always had a point. The purpose was to educate, but also to amuse.

Often, in an attempt to explain why people should think deeper about what they are doing, he told stories that illustrated a favorite theme: why the obvious answer is not always the correct answer.

For example, you would think a nuclear attack would be a horrible event, and it certainly would be. Cashin had to live through the constant specter of such an attack in the early 1960s, and one such incident taught him that sometimes investment decisions are not entirely logical.

He was spending a considerable amount of time then with one of his earliest mentors, an over-the-counter trader in silver stocks whom he called Professor Jack. As Art tells it:

We were not quite to the Cuban Missile Crisis. We were getting there and I was still not a member yet. It was the early 60s, and word spread that something had happened and that the Russians had actually pressed the button and that the missiles were flying.

The option market wasn't on an exchange in those days, it was over-the-counter and you had to call around. I had virtually no money and I was looking to see if I could make a $100 bet by buying a put or some such things. And everywhere I called I couldn't get anything done.

So I cleaned up and rushed down to the bar. And Professor Jack was already in the bar, and I came bursting through the doors as only a 19- or 20-year-old could. And I said, 'Jack, Jack. The rumors are that the missles are flying.'

And he said, 'Kid, sit down and buy me a drink.'

And I sat down and he said, 'Listen carefully. When you hear the missiles are flying, you buy them, you don't sell them.'

And I looked at him, and I said, 'You buy them, you don't sell them?'

He said 'Of course, because if you're wrong the trade will never clear, we'll all be dead.'

Usually, Art's stories illustrated some aspect of investing, such as what price discovery is about.

Volumes have been written explaining the concept of "price discovery"—how anyone determines what the right price to pay for a stock should be. Scholarly papers have been written about supply and demand, and the information available to buyers and sellers at the time of the transaction.

To explain price discovery, Cashin liked to tell the story of the time the jeweler Charles Lewis Tiffany tried to sell an expensive diamond stickpin to JP Morgan.

Tiffany, Cashin said, knew that JP Morgan loved diamond stickpins, which he used to put in his tie. One day he sent a man around to Morgan's office with an envelope and a box wrapped in gift paper. Morgan opened the envelope, and in it was a message from Tiffany: "My dear Mr. Morgan, I know of your great fascination with diamond stickpins. Enclosed in this box is an absolutely exquisite example. Since it is so exquisite and unusual, its price is $5,000." In those days, Cashin noted, $5,000 was north of $150,000 in present dollars.

The note continued: "My man will leave the stickpin with you and will return to my office. He will come back tomorrow. If you choose to accept it, you may give him a check for $5,000. If you choose not to accept it, you may give him the box back with the diamond stickpin."

He left, and the next day, Tiffany's man came back to see Morgan. Morgan presented him with the box rewrapped in new paper, along with a note, which said, "My dear Mr. Tiffany, as you've said, the stickpin was magnificent. However, the price seems a bit excessive. Instead of $5,000, enclosed you will find a check for $4,000. If you choose to accept that, you may send the pin back to me, and if not, you may keep the pin and tear up the check."

The man returned to Tiffany, who read the note and saw the offer for $4,000. He knew he could still make money on the offer, but felt the pin was still worth the $5,000 he was asking.

He said to the man, "You may return the check to Mr. Morgan, and tell him I hope to do business with him in the future." Tiffany then took the wrapping off the box, opened it up and found not the stickpin, but a check for $5,000 and a note that said, "Just checking the price."

That is price discovery, told in a way people can understand it!

# *The master storyteller who couldn't type*

In a lot of ways, Art Cashin was the least likely person to be a great storyteller.

One obvious problem: he can't type. He can't use a computer, either. His notes are handwritten and then sent to his assistant, who types them up for distribution.

A filing system? Forget it. His desk at the NYSE was piled high with papers he had accumulated over the decades. At times it resembled a recycling facility.

And if you needed to get hold of him after hours? Good luck. He refused to buy a smartphone—for years he used an obsolete flip phone that he rarely answered.

Dinner is straight out of *Mad Men*. In 25 years of hanging out in saloons with Art, the night invariably begins with several scotches or bourbons, on the rocks. It progresses to "Irish caviar" (pigs in a blanket), then fries, burgers, or an occasional steak.

On many nights, we never got past the scotch or bourbon.

When it comes time to pay the tab, wads of $20 bills emerge from his pockets. He refuses to use credit cards: everything, including his voluminous bar bills, is paid in cash. "You pay by credit card, people know where you went to drink, how much you drank, and what you were drinking. If you want to keep the anonymity in there, you pay cash," he once said to me.[2]

Though he has the appearance of a person on the verge of homelessness, there is nothing haphazard about his inner self. Art Cashin is a study in irony: everything about his persona was carefully constructed.

It is partly molded around a fierce desire to protect his privacy and guard against the intrusiveness of the digital age.

"You can protect your personality," he told me. "You don't allow people to invade who you are. I don't mean to be overly protective, but this way,

I know who I am, and you may think you know who I am. But you don't know all about me that you would, if I were in the digital world."[3]

His brief foray into the use of email many years ago ended in disaster: "I got inundated. I had hundreds of thousands of people who, for some bizarre reason, wanted to talk to Arthur Cashin. And I didn't think I could fully handle that, so I kind of backed up into the forest, and remained not quite so evident."

Why had so many people tried to contact him? "It could be low standards," he quipped.[4]

It was a lot more than that. In the intensely competitive and often vicious world of stock market commentary, Cashin was that rarest of all creatures: a man respected by all—bulls and bears, liberals and conservatives—alike. He seemed to have no enemies.

## *"I was destitute"*

Cashin's upbringing gave no indication he would become a Wall Street guru, either.

He was born in Jersey City, New Jersey in 1941. His parents were superintendents of an apartment building.

"My dad died when I was a senior in high school," he told me one night while we were sitting in Bobby Van's. "And I had to go to work to support the family. I tried to go to work for the Port Authority of New York, hoping to go to college at night."

That didn't work out.

"I was destitute. My uncle, who was a bartender, looked a little down in the dumps. And one of his customers said, 'What's wrong?' He said, 'My nephew is a bright kid. He was hopin' to get a job to take care of the family. It didn't work.' The customer wrote down the name of Thomson McKinnon—a large-scale brokerage firm at the time. He said, 'Tell him, go there. See this guy. And tell the guy he doesn't wanna work in the back office. He wants to be where the action is. 'Cause if he's got any brains, people will notice that. And he'll get promoted.' And that's the story of my life."

On December 30, 1964, at the age 23, Cashin became a Member of the New York Stock Exchange, proudly signing his name in the members' book that included the signatures of JP Morgan and John D. Rockefeller.

When Cashin became a member, the vast majority of all trading took place on the floor of the NYSE. The sensory experience was overwhelming.

"You could hear the floor itself. And when I used to have guests who came down, they'd say to me, 'Noise, so much noise. How can you put up with it?'

"And I would say, 'The noise is my friend.' Then they said, 'What do you mean?' When I hear the noise pick up, I know the activity's picking up. And after several years of doing it, you could tell, by the pitch of the noise, whether there were buyers or sellers. There is something, apparently, macho about accumulating stock. And the buyers would shout, 'Take 'em, take 'em,' and sound like a Russian chorus. And the sellers, somewhat panicky, would be higher pitched. And you'd hear, 'Sell, sell!' And so if the pitch of the noise was high, I would know the sellers were headed my way. Or if it was a rumble, I would know that it was probably buyers coming."

It was so crowded on the trading floor that the NYSE had passed a regulation decades before banning men from wearing stiff-brimmed hats, out of concern the sharp edges would injure traders who were jostling for positions.

"They were very serious about enforcing that regulation," Cashin told me. "There was a guy who used to work on the floor who really liked fancy clothes. He used to wear seersucker suits from Brooks Brothers and a skimmer [a straw hat with a stiff brim], but he had to hang up the skimmer in his booth as he went to work on the floor."

Cashin claimed to have never given a thought about another career, with the exception of one lone foray into politics. In the mid-1970s, disgusted by the corruption in his hometown of Jersey City, Cashin ran for mayor: "I think I ran 12th in a field of five. But once they discovered I was honest, there wasn't much chance I was gonna get elected."

He returned to Wall Street. In 1980, he joined PaineWebber and managed their floor operation, continuing to do so even after PaineWebber was bought by UBS in 2000.

At the NYSE, he served as a Governor, Member of the Market Performance Committee, and on virtually every other committee. He chaired the NYSE "Fallen Heroes Fund" which assists the families of NYC police and firemen killed in the line of duty. After 9/11, the Fallen Heroes Fund provided over $6 million in assistance.

## How do you tell a story about the stock market?

By the time I met Cashin in 1997, he had been writing a daily column, Cashin's Comments, for nearly 20 years. It was estimated to reach as many as two million people a day. It invariably began with an analysis of an important event:

> On this date in 1918, the worldwide flu epidemic went into high gear in the U.S.

And after a brief history lesson, tied that event to the day's market events:

> Pre-opening Wednesday morning, U.S. stock futures looked like they might be coming down with the flu. Several earnings reports were less than glowing and some of the outlooks were cloudy.

Cashin never took a course in literary theory, but he understood that some stories were far more persuasive than others, and that condensed narratives that had a clear storytelling arc were the most memorable and therefore the most effective way to convey information.

For Cashin, storytelling is only partly about facts: a series of Post-it notes on the wall, each with a separate fact about something going on in the market that day, is not a story. It's how you connect the facts and weave it into a narrative that makes it a story.

"I have been fortunate enough over the years to be able to look at very complicated situations or problems and be able to reduce them to understandable items by using a story or a parable," he once said to me.[5]

He not only uses stories, but he also anthropomorphizes the entire market: he routinely described the market as "in a tizzy," or that traders were "circling the wagons" to defend a particularly important level of the Dow Jones Industrial Average.

Let's get back to the story about JP Morgan, Tiffany, and price discovery. For Cashin, understanding what a stock was worth was not about a mathematical formula—it was about trying to understand what the other guy was willing to pay:

How can I, in a real estate transaction, in a stock transaction, whatever, delve into your mind and find out what will you really accept? You offer your house at three quarters of a million dollars. Is that really your price? How do I find out what the difference was? And Morgan, in his natural genius, figured out that he would offer the guy somewhat less, and if the guy took it, that was to Morgan's advantage. And if the guy refused, then that was the price and he had to pay.[6]

Cashin's secret sauce was a natural gift for telling stories with a "dramatic arc," that is, stories with rising action, a climax, falling action, and a resolution. Even the short Tiffany story contains all these elements: the action rises when Tiffany's man presents the stickpin to Morgan with a $5,000 asking price, and Morgan counters with a $4,000 offer. The climax occurs when Tiffany declines the counteroffer. The falling action occurs when he sends the courier back with the note. The resolution occurs when Tiffany opens the box and found not the stickpin but a check for $5,000 and a note that said, "Just checking the price."

Cashin grasped that these kinds of stories pack more emotional resonance than stories that don't have the dramatic arc, and that's why people remember them.

Why? Neuroeconomist Paul Zak studies how economic decisions affect our brain chemistry. In a now-famous 2015 paper, Zak showed that narratives that possess this dramatic arc release hormones into the bloodstream.[7] One of these hormones—oxytocin, often referred to as the "love hormone"—helps to facilitate relationships. In other words, it makes people more empathetic.

Zak noted there were other hormones that get released when this narrative arc is presented effectively, including cortisol, which plays a part in regulating stress and in helping memory function.

What's the effect of all these hormones getting released? It causes us to pay more attention and get more emotionally involved with the characters. Zak says: "This structure sustains attention by building suspense while at the same time providing a vehicle for character development. The climax of the story keeps us on the edge of our neural seats until the tension is relieved at the finish."[8]

Cashin had never read Zak's study, or other studies by neuroeconomists or psycholinguists. He would likely laugh at the thought of even using a word like "neuroeconomist." But he understood what they had discovered: that an effective story "transports" you into the narrative and makes the story—and its lesson—easier to remember.

Unfortunately, compelling narratives also make it easier to confuse people and drag them into investments that make no sense.

# *How do smart people read the tape?*

Cashin passionately believed that the market did indeed reflect all available information—even if some were able to come to different conclusions than others. And often when the market moved for reasons that were not obvious, Cashin would come up with some plausible but not obvious reason why.

"The truth is on that tape," he told me. "Don't just go for the obvious. If you're good at this business, you gotta be Sherlock Holmes. The improbable, as long as it's not the impossible, may turn out to be the true fact. And you will learn far more than you ever thought."[9]

As far as I knew, Cashin never said that to anyone but me. To everyone else, he told a story about a man who looked at the markets during a national disaster and read the tape in a very different way than everyone else.

It was November 22, 1963—the day Kennedy was assassinated.

"I was upstairs," Cashin told me, "And the market was selling off. And a broker on the floor, Tommy McKinnon, called up. I was in the order room. And he said, 'Is there anything on the tape about the president?' And I said, 'No. Why do you ask?' And he said, 'Merrill Lynch is all over the floor, selling.' And I asked him why, and he said, 'Something about the president.'"

"So I went back. The news ticker had a bell that would ring once for ordinary news, twice for something that was special, and three for really dynamic news. And the bell rang three times. And I ran back about 15 feet to where the news ticker was. And the headline was, 'Shots Reported Fired at President's Motorcade in Dallas.' And I ran back to call the floor of the Exchange to tell Tommy. And before he could pick up, the bell rang three times again. And it said, 'President Rumored to Have Been Hit.' And I went back to call him again. And again, the bell rang three times. And it said, 'President's Motorcade

Diverted to Parkland Hospital in Dallas.' And that's when they shut the Exchange down."

"The amazing thing, to me, was how did Merrill Lynch know before anything was on the news ticker? And it was a lesson to me in Wall Street. Presidents didn't travel much in 1963 and so the manager of the Merrill Lynch Dallas branch said, 'You guys go out and watch the parade. I'll keep a skeleton crew here.' They went out to watch the parade. A little while later, they all came in down in the dumps. And he said, 'What's the matter? You were supposed to watch the parade.' And they said to him, 'The parade got cancelled.' And he said, 'What do you mean?' And they were here. And the parade was way up there. And they heard the sirens go loud. And the parade turned right."

"And this guy was a good manager. And he called the salesmen together. And he said, 'Give me a good bullish reason to pull the president out of a parade.' And nobody could think of one. And he said, 'Give me a bearish reason.' Nobody thinks, assassination. They were nowhere near there. They were 10 blocks away. But they start thinking, nuclear catastrophe, natural disaster, blah, blah, blah. They find 100 reasons to sell. He said, 'Begin to sell for the discretionary accounts. Start calling our clients. And tell them, 'We think something bad happened at the parade.'"

For Art, that Merrill Lynch manager was the perfect stock market Sherlock Holmes: Don't just consider what you hear. Think beyond what happened.

# The great curmudgeon

I like Art for many reasons, but I particularly like him because beneath the warm and fuzzy exterior there beats the heat of a true curmudgeon.

People misunderstand curmudgeons. They're often mistaken for misanthropes, or people who hate mankind. Curmudgeons don't hate mankind; they just hate the stupidity of mankind.

They look around at mankind, and they are not terribly impressed. They realize, as Tallulah Bankhead once said, that there's less here than meets the eye.

They are acutely perceptive, aware that much of life is full of absurdities. They're pissed off because they feel things differently than others, deeper than others, and they believe there's a lot to be pissed off about.

Curmudgeons have standards, a way of measuring themselves against the world. And aside from stupidity, curmudgeons are most at war with mediocrity. They dislike the middle ground because it breeds groupthink. They believe, as Mark Twain did, that whenever you find that you are on the side of the majority, it is time to reform.

Because they hate groupthink, curmudgeons are very discerning. They have opinions. Strong opinions.

They are often great drinkers. Art certainly is.

Because they are at war with mediocrity and absurdity, curmudgeons do not play defense. They are perfectly willing—in fact eager—to go on the offensive.

Curmudgeons have a style they have developed over many years, a way of looking at the world. They won't put on a phony display of cheerfulness because they see so much horseshit around them, and so they are often mistaken for being bitter. Some are. Most are a little bit neurotic and a little bit weird as well. Some might be tempted to attribute this state of mind to an unhappy childhood, but most curmudgeons will say it's dealing with the stupidity of the world that has driven them to the state they are in.

So it is with Art. As he has gotten older, he has gotten a bit surlier. His medical problems have multiplied.

When I asked what he was going to do about his physical decline, he shrugged. "Keep seeing the doctors."

That's Art. There is a type of man from that generation that will tell you everything that is wrong with them, will discuss in detail their medical conditions, but when you suggest they do something about it, that they change their diet, their drinking, their lifestyle, their exercise habits, they look at you like you have crossed a line, like you are invading their privacy.

Art possesses a quality the Germans call *Weltschmerz*, "world-weariness." Like Mark Twain, one of his literary idols, he has seen enormous change in his lifetime, has been a participant in those changes, and like Twain, Art Cashin exudes a sense of weariness that suggests he understands he is a dying breed.

Still, his health—however precarious it is—does not dominate his thinking. It is not the source of his attitude toward the world. Art's *Weltschmerz* is understandable when you consider he had only two loves in his life: his family and the New York Stock Exchange.

His wife Joan passed away in 1998 and his daughter Jennifer died in 2007. His son Art Jr. remained in New York, but his other son Peter eventually moved to North Carolina.

His beloved trading floor had gone from 4,000 strong in 1997, controlling 80 percent of the trading volume, to less than 400 people who controlled less than 20 percent of the volume 25 years later. He had entered the stock world in *Mad Men* times, when trading was transacted on pieces of paper between men (they were almost all men) whose word was considered their bond. The world changed, and stock trading changed, becoming more electronic with each year.

He was never resentful or bitter, but he wasn't accepting either.

He longed for the world he had helped create: "I miss those magnificent days when your spirit hung on the fact that you were good for your word, or you're outta here," he told me.

Even as his scotch glass went from half full to half empty, his most endearing traits did not change: his humor, his eagerness to tell stories, and his modesty. When *The Washington Post* ran a long profile of his career in September 2019, calling him "Wall Street's version of Walter Cronkite,"[10] we proceeded to celebrate at the bar at Bobby Van's. After his second or third Dewar's, he said, "I think I owe an apology to Walter Cronkite."[11]

Years ago, Cashin gave me a copy of a menu from Eberlin's, a restaurant founded in 1872 and a fabled Wall Street hangout, long since departed. It was from the mid-1960s: a Martini or Manhattan was $1.20.

On the list of entrées, there is this:

SPAGHETTI (a l'Arthur Cashin) .................................................... $2.75

Why was a spaghetti dish named after him? "It was a hangover cure," he told me. "Eberlin's opened at 6:00 AM, and all the guys who had been out drinking the night before came in for something to eat. My preferred breakfast was spaghetti in a red sauce, so they named the dish after me."[12]

In February 2020, just weeks before the NYSE shut down due to the Covid-19 outbreak, Art was across the street at Bobby Van's having his usual pre-prandial Dewar's. His car, with his driver, was waiting outside, as usual. Art got into the car in the back seat, but before he could get the seat belt on, the driver accidently hit the gas pedal and the car hit the wall by Bobby Van's. Art was thrown against the back seat, fracturing his hip.

He spent the rest of 2020 in rehab. We did get him back on the air numerous times from his home. There he was, in the same rumpled suit and tie, still lucid, still watching the markets every day, still writing his newsletter late into the night.

He returned to the floor on September 11, 2021, the 20th anniversary of 9/11, to reminisce with me about that terrible day and how Wall Street had coped with the loss of so many friends and family. It was the first time he had been back in 18 months.

As with everyone who has outlived most of his competition, Art's world has gotten smaller. The fabled Friends of Fermentation, which used to encompass dozens at the bar, is down to a few old friends. But when Art can come into the city, we still gather and hoist a few glasses, debate the current state of the markets and remember the long, wild, uneven party that Wall Street was.

What did Art Cashin do for me? I told you in Chapter 2 how I decide what I'm going to say each day. I said the way I look at the news is like having hundreds of Stick-em notes on the wall each day, each with a separate fact.

Cashin helped show me that the Stick-em notes weren't nearly enough. It was how they were arranged that mattered. It was the narrative. Even with the stock market, you could show rising action, a climax, falling action, and a resolution.

Art Cashin may indeed have been the Walter Cronkite of Wall Street, but meeting the real Walter Cronkite at the very end of the 1990s threw me for a loop. I'll describe that meeting in Chapter 6.

I barely knew Art when I encountered my first great crisis on the floor in 1997. There was trouble brewing in Asia, and it was about to hit the U.S. shores. I desperately needed Art's storytelling skills, because my ability to tell this particular story was going to be sorely tested.

# PART TWO

## *Looking Back*

≡

# CHAPTER 5

# *How Do You Stop People from Panicking?*

═══

Y OU can learn a lot about people by watching how they react when they wet the bed.

On October 29, 1997, I saw a lot of people wet the bed.

People ask me if I ever get nervous when I'm on the air. I never get nervous, but I'm constantly in a state of mild agitation. I've always been that way. Most TV people are, and if you ask them about it, they'll say that nervous energy is part of their success—that it helps keep them sharp and edgy.

This makes being around TV people both wonderful (they're full of ideas) and exasperating (they always act like they are in a crisis and don't have time to talk to you).

But there are times when something suddenly comes out of left field, and I get frazzled. It happens because I'm struggling to get my head around something that I don't fully understand.

When that happens, my voice tends to pitch up, and I talk faster.

Much faster.

At the close of trading on October 27, 1997, I was on the air talking to my colleague, Ron Insana, at 100 miles an hour.

I was frazzled. So was everyone around me. My head was ready to explode as I struggled to understand a very complicated global event that was blowing up the U.S. stock market.

It was about six weeks after my first appearance as On-Air Stocks Editor on the floor of the NYSE, and I had just watched a lot of traders wet the bed.

The Dow Jones Industrial Average had just recorded its largest single point drop in history (554 points), the 10th largest percentage decline in the index since 1915 (7.2 percent), and the stock market had seen its heaviest trading day ever.

On any normal trading day, the market closes at 4 PM, but this was anything but normal.

The market had already closed, a half hour before.

"If you are just joining us and are preparing for the closing bell on Wall Street, you should know that it already rang," Ron said on-air, and tossed to me for an explanation.

"The mood started turning ugly right after we reopened about 3:05 and that's when traders started getting very, very nervous," I said to Ron.

I was standing on the trading floor, which normally would have been buzzing at this moment (just after 4 PM ET). Some traders were wandering about, looking like they had spent the night in a washing machine on the spin cycle.

Traders had good reason to be in an ugly mood.

*What the hell had happened?*

## The Asian Financial Crisis: a study in herd mentality

You could blame much of it on the desire to kick Asian economies into high gear, along with the greed of foreign investors. In the 1990s, countries in Southeast Asia like the Philippines, Thailand, Indonesia and Malaysia were trying to grow, and grow fast.

The narrative they sold was simple: along with China, millions of people were being lifted out of poverty. Millions would become middle class citizens, make money, and trade with the rest of the world.

Global investors rushed in. To make sure those investors were happy, those governments tried to maintain very high interest rates.

It worked for a while: the economies and the stock markets of those countries went on a tear. Thailand's economy grew over nine percent a year from 1985 to 1996. GDP growth was in the 8 to 12 percent range for many other countries.

Then, it started going bad. In early 1997, interest rates began rising in the U.S. and so did the dollar.

This resulted in a double whammy for these *Asian tigers*:

1.  Foreign investors began pulling money out to reinvest in the U.S.
2.  These countries had their currencies pegged to the dollar, so their currencies also rose as the dollar rose. The Asian countries were trying to grow by exporting, but a stronger currency made their exports more expensive and less competitive.

The Thai government was the first that was forced to abandon its fixed peg to the dollar and devalue its currency, on July 2. The Thai stock market, which had been on a tear, lost about half its value in 1997.

Other governments too were then forced to abandon their fixed pegs to the dollar and allow the currencies to float. The IMF had to step in with a series of bailouts.

For U.S investors, it all came to a head on October 27.

# Can you stop the market from falling?

It's traumatic enough when the market has a big drop in a few hours, but it's really traumatic when trading is halted before the market closes.

This was the first time that circuit breakers that had been adopted in the wake of the October 1987 crash were used. These circuit breakers were designed to prevent the kind of crazy panic that occurred on October 19, 1987, when the Dow dropped 508 points (22.6 percent), still the largest percentage decline in history.

After that debacle, circuit breakers were implemented that allowed exchanges to temporarily halt trading when large declines occurred.

The problem was defining "large." The goal was to slow things down and stop people from panicking without shutting down markets for a long period of time, which would also cause people to panic.

This proved a lot trickier than anyone imagined. Initially, trading was to be halted for one hour when the Dow dropped 250 points from its previous day's closing level and for a subsequent two-hour trading halt if the Dow dropped 400 points from its previous day's close. That was modified in 1996 and 1997: the market would halt trading for a half hour when the Dow dropped 350 points, and for an hour when it dropped 550 points. If trading hit that second level in the final half hour, the market would stop trading for the day.

At 2:36 PM on October 27, 1997, the Dow dropped 350 points, which triggered a 30-minute halt in the market. After trading reopened at 3:06 PM, the market quickly resumed the downward trend until it dropped 550 points, which triggered a second circuit breaker. Under those circuit breaker rules, the market closed at 3:30 PM, ending the trading session 30 minutes prior to the close.

This first ever use of the circuit breakers shocked the hell out of everyone.

Turns out, halting trading before the close doesn't necessarily make everyone more thoughtful, it just makes them more uncertain about when the market is going to stop going down.

"Several traders said they were looking to buy but they wanted to see blood in the streets," I said to Ron. "Another said they are looking for wide spreads between the bid and the ask, another sign of a classic market bottom, and are also looking to see individual stocks halted because of trading problems."

For me, this was an early lesson in what came to be called "behavioral finance"—the study of herd behavior. During a panic, traders will look for all sorts of signs of a bottom. In this case, the trading halt—and the problem of future halts—had itself become a sign: more individual stock trading halts (specialists on the floor were permitted to halt individual stocks that were excessively volatile) was a sign of intense panic, and in the trader world, when everyone wet their pants at once, that was usually a sign of a bottom.

"Most of the traders I am polling are anticipating a down open tomorrow," I told Ron.

Sure enough, the next day, the market opened down but rallied midday. The Dow closed up 337 points (4.7 percent), on then-record share volumes of over a billion shares each on the NYSE and Nasdaq.

## *Fixing the circuit breakers*

The shock of the trading halt reverberated on Wall Street. SEC Chair Arthur Levitt asked his own people in the Division of Trading and Markets to "reconstruct" the market events and make recommendations. They sensibly concluded that the circuit breakers were set at the wrong levels: the Dow halt of 350 points was only a 4.5 percent drop—not enough to justify halting trading. The rule was subsequently changed to respond to a *percentage* drop, not a *point* drop.[1]

Second, closing the market a half hour early was a bad idea— the second drop of 550 points was only a seven percent decline, not enough to justify shutting the market down. Concern that the market may close early was cited as one of the reasons for the selloff when the market reopened at 3:05 PM. A normal close should have been permitted.

But even after the event, getting the circuit breaker level *right* proved very difficult.

In 1998, new circuit breaker rules went into effect that halted trading when the Dow dropped 10, 20, and 30 percent.[2] That sounded fine, until it was needed.

Oddly, there were no trading halts during the worst crisis since the Great Depression: the 2008–2009 Great Financial Crisis. In October 2008, at the height of the crisis, there were eight sessions when the S&P 500 slid by seven percent, but the closest it got to down 10 percent was on October 15 of that year, when it was down 9.4 percent at one point.

On May 6, 2010, in what became known as the Flash Crash, the S&P 500 fell as much as 8.6 percent in the middle of the day, then recovered and closed down 3.2 percent. Because it never dropped 10 percent, no trading halt was triggered.

Turns out, 10 percent was a bit too much for everyone to handle. This time, the level was too high.

"Setting it at 10 percent, that's like setting the speed limit at 100 miles per hour," Rob Hegarty, then global head of market structure at Thomson Reuters, told *The Wall Street Journal*.[3]

The market-wide circuit breaker levels were subsequently adjusted several times. The index used was changed from the Dow to the S&P 500, and in the last adjustment in 2013, three circuit breaker levels were instituted:

- Level 1: S&P 500 decline of seven percent or more before 3:25 PM halts trading for 15 minutes. A similar decline after 3:25 PM will not halt trading.

- Level 2: S&P 500 decline of 13 percent or more before 3:25 PM halts trading for 15 minutes. A similar decline after 3:25 PM. will not halt trading.
- Level 3: S&P 500 decline of 20 percent at any time during the trading day will halt market-wide trading for the remainder of the trading day.

These levels appeared to have the virtue of being sufficiently high that they were almost never needed. Almost.

It took a pandemic. Following the initial shock of the coronavirus epidemic in March 2020, there were Level 1 (15 minute) trading halts on March 9, 12, 16 and 18.

## *Do trading halts work?*

What's the verdict? Do these market-wide trading halts work?

The SEC, in its report on the October 27, 2009 drop, said trading halts:

> were designed to operate only during significant market declines and to substitute orderly, pre-planned halts for the ad hoc trading halts which can occur when market liquidity is exhausted. Circuit breakers also provide opportunities for markets and market participants to assess market conditions and potential systemic stress during a historic market decline.[4]

If that's the definition, trading halts work. They do substitute orderly, pre-planned trading halts for ad hoc trading halts. They do provide an opportunity to assess market conditions.

But that dry definition ignores the very real psychological issues that arise when you force trading to stop. The circuit breakers have an impossible task: they must be set high enough so they are almost never needed, but if they are needed, everyone must agree that it was certainly a good thing that they kicked in, and also that they were necessary.

One thing's for sure: they do not prevent a debacle. March 2020 saw two of the five largest drops in the history of the Dow Industrials. On March 12, after the World Health Organization declared coronavirus a pandemic, the Dow dropped 10 percent despite a trading halt, it's fifth largest percentage loss in history. On March 16, in what was the third trading halt in a week, the Dow Industrials dropped 12.9 percent, its second largest percentage loss in history.[5]

But that's not what trading halts were designed to do: they were not designed to stop the markets from dropping when they had a legitimate reason to drop, and coronavirus was certainly a legitimate reason for the markets to drop.

They were designed to make people stop and think during a panic, and perhaps more importantly, to look for liquidity—that is, to look for other people who want to buy and sell.

That's why I think trading halts are useful. They may not stop traders from wetting the bed, but maybe it will make the bed a little less wet.

## More bed-wetting to come

As for the Asian Financial Crisis, as it came to be known, what was a wrenching emotional experience short term turned out to be a momentary blip for U.S. investors: the S&P 500 was up 31 percent in 1997. Asian markets, on the other hand, would take several years to recover.

Standing on the NYSE floor on that day in October 1997, watching panicky selling and two trading halts, I had my first lesson in herd behavior on a personal level.

I also learned a painful lesson about what the term "crowded trade" meant. Many hedge funds in the mid-1990s touted the advantage of investing in emerging markets, particularly in Southeast Asia. But it was a new strategy, the global base of investors was not large enough, and global investors did not have enough staying power. Most attempted to get out all at once. It was yet another study in herd behavior.

I didn't know it, but that day was the first of many bed-wetting days I would have at the NYSE. The next one would come the following year, when I learned another lesson: *these events have unforeseeable knock-on effects that are almost impossible to calculate.*

Because of the Asian crisis, global oil demand dropped. This was a factor in several large oil company mergers in 1998 and 1999, culminating in the merger of Exxon and Mobil in 1999.

It also was the cause of a second crisis—the Russian financial crisis of 1998. The Russians defaulted on their debt that summer due to a reduction in oil revenue largely caused by the Asian crisis. This caused the hedge fund Long-Term Capital to collapse and forced the Federal Reserve Chairman, Alan Greenspan, to intervene, saving the markets from yet another crisis.

More bed-wetting experiences were ahead of me, but not before 1999. That was a one-year celebration of internet madness, and the greatest party Wall Street ever threw.

# CHAPTER 6

# *1999: Walter Cronkite, Muhammad Ali, and the End of the Party*

———

O N December 31, 1999, Muhammad Ali came on the floor to ring the final opening bell of the year.

As he wound his way through the floor, traders lined up to say hello. He wasn't doing interviews, but I didn't care. I introduced myself and walked with him for a few moments. He was a good three inches taller than me. His shoulders were wide. When we shook hands, his right hand completely enveloped my own. He was practiced at the art of serenity: he smiled and nodded at the crowd but didn't stop to banter.

It was the last day of one of the greatest years of my life. Everyone should have a year like 1999 at least once in their career—a year when the wind is at your back and everything is going right, when you're proud of what you have accomplished, but you know some of it was just good luck.

But what luck: the right company, the right time, the right job, the right location.

I was working for one of the hottest networks on television. The country had become obsessed with the stock market, and with good reason: the internet. Between 1990 and 1997, the proportion of households owning computers increased from 15 percent to 35 percent, the Bureau of Labor Statistics reported. The amount spent by the average household on computers and hardware more than tripled.[1]

Like the railroad, the telegraph, the telephone, and the computer before it, the internet was having a profound impact on the way people communicated. The first viable web browser, Mosaic, was released in 1993, followed in 1995 by Netscape Navigator and then Microsoft's Internet Explorer.

It's hard to say when the speculative craziness that became known as the "dot-com bubble" began, but it's reasonable to date it from the Netscape IPO, an event of such improbable success that it became known as the "Netscape moment."

It happened on August 9, 1995, a little more than a year after the company was founded. Originally set to price at $14, it was doubled to $28. It hit $74.75 at its peak on the first day of trading and closed at $58.25.[2] Netscape had a value close to $3 billion.

All this, without making a dime in profits.[3]

The public responded with a buying frenzy. Between 1995 and that last day of December 1999, the Nasdaq Composite, the main index for young tech stocks, rose 440 percent.

Volumes on both exchanges, but particularly the Nasdaq, soared between 1995 and 1999. The number of U.S. households with investments in the market doubled from 1990 to 1999.[4]

CNBC was having its own bull market. Our ratings had been going up, almost in parallel to the Nasdaq. "Viewership in 2000 is triple that of 1995, according to Nielsen Media Research," Fast Company wrote in a 2000 story on CNBC.[5] "And that's just the viewers CNBC knows about." Indeed: everyone knew there was a vast audience watching in bars, restaurants, and on trading desks that was difficult to calculate. No matter: the numbers were good. CNBC beat CNN in daytime ratings for the last three months of 1999.

I was not only working at the hottest network on television, I had the hottest job: On-Air Stocks Correspondent. I was up at 5 AM every day. I spent my days trying to figure out the stock market and was out late into the night with an assortment of brokers, hedge fund traders, strategists, analysts, and soothsayers—anyone who could give me a handle on what was going on.

We had morphed from a rather ragtag operation since our founding in 1989, where we went through several years unsure of what we wanted to be, into a battle-hardened group that knew exactly what we wanted.

We wanted to cover the horse race: the daily ups and downs of the market.

Along the way, we had gone from a bunch of nobodies that were looked down upon by our broadcast brethren as amateurs with inferior equipment, to mini-celebrities. David Faber, Joe Kernen, and Mark Haines were killing it as hosts of *Squawk Box* in the morning. Maria Bartiromo was on fire anchoring both *Business Center* and *Market Wrap*. Ron Insana was anchoring *Street Signs* at 3 PM. Bill Griffeth was hosting two hours of *Power Lunch* in the middle of the day, all by himself.

The old-school broadcast guys may have laughed at us in 1990, but they weren't laughing in 1999. We were leaner, meaner, smarter, and—most important of all—we were making money.

It wasn't just the broadcast guys that stopped laughing. The print media, long dismissive of the "talking heads" on television, started paying attention. Andy Serwer, writing in *Fortune* in 1999, called CNBC "the TV network of our time."[6] "Every week more than seven million of us flip it on, many even more obsessed than I am," he wrote.

Serwer was smart enough to realize that there was more than just a stock market rally fueling CNBC's rise. By 1999, the typical baby boomer born in the 1950s was well into his or her forties, the age when people typically start worrying about retirement and savings. Thanks to the decline of pensions and the rise of the 401(k), much of the responsibility for that retirement sat squarely on the shoulders of individual investors, most of whom knew little or nothing about investing.

Throw in the growth of online brokers like E*Trade, Ameritrade, and Charles Schwab, and you had millions of investors who didn't know what to do, who suddenly had a medium to help them and the technology to act on it.

It was the perfect storm—a combination of economic necessity (retirement fear), with a frenzy for a new technology (the internet), enabled by the development of new hardware (the personal computer) and trading software (used by the online brokers), all fueled by a *hot* medium (CNBC) that presented financial news in a different way, with a bit more *attitude*.

It helped that the rich and famous watched, wanted to be on air, and wanted to be part of the story. Stories floated around that His Royal Highness Saudi Prince Al-Waleed Bin Talal Al Saud, a member of the Saudi royal family, was a regular viewer. He had written to our President, Bill Bolster, about his "addiction" to CNBC.[7]

In August 1999, it all came together. We moved *Business Center*, an hour-long broadcast at 6:30 PM, from the studio in Fort Lee, New Jersey to the NYSE floor. We had been broadcasting reports from the floor since 1995, but this was the first time a full show was done. Ron Insana and Sue Herera were the anchors, and I was the floor reporter.

One of the first pieces I did was a three-part series explaining how trading was done on the floor of the NYSE. It was a primer on how the specialists and the floor traders interacted with the public's orders.

# The NYSE leverages its trading floor

While Nasdaq listed most of the tech start-ups and was the focus of attention, the NYSE was also going through its own red-hot moment. It too was benefitting from the broader rally being driven by tech.

On March 29, the Dow Jones Industrial Average crossed 10,000 for the first time, a feat celebrated with cheering on the floor. "Dow 10,000" hats were passed out. The S&P 500, the broader index of the largest 500 stocks, had risen 34 percent in 1995, 20 percent in 1996, 31 percent in 1997, 26 percent in 1998, and would end 1999 up nearly 20 percent, not including dividends. Altogether the S&P had risen over 200 percent in five years, one of the greatest bull markets in history.

The NYSE also had something the Nasdaq did not: a trading floor, and an opening and closing bell ceremony that was getting more elaborate by the day.

Bob Zito, the man in charge of communications and marketing for the NYSE, was determined to modernize and promote the NYSE to a new generation of investors, and his tool was television. In 1995, he convinced a skeptical crowd of old-school floor brokers to allow reporters on the floor, and it was a success. At the same time, he changed the dynamics of the bell ringing, from a staid internal affair to an international media event.

# The open bell goes global

A bell had been rung to start the trading day at the NYSE since the 1870s.[8] When the NYSE moved to its new building in 1903, a brass bell was rung on the newly built podium. But up until the mid-1990s, most bell ringings were quiet affairs done by NYSE staff.

Zito changed that. Beginning in the mid-1990s, he began inviting CEOs, political figures, and even celebrities to ring the opening and closing bells.

The market rally, along with the public's obsession with the internet, turned these ringings into media events. Eventually, the NYSE would claim that the bell ringing was the most widely viewed daily news event on Earth, watched by as many as 110 million people all over the world.[9]

And it all came to a head in that final month of 1999.

Zito had masterminded an event he called the Millenium Bell Series to recognize distinguished leaders of the 20th century whose influence would be felt into the next millennium. In the space of a few weeks, Zito brought in a who's who of global celebrities to ring the opening or closing bell:

- 12/15: GE CEO Jack Welch
- 12/15: Art Buchwald
- 12/17: Hank Aaron
- 12/20: Joe Namath
- 12/22: Walter Cronkite
- 12/24: Archbishop Desmond Tutu
- 12/27: Neil Simon
- 12/30: Abby Joseph Cohen (Goldman Sachs)
- 12/31: Muhammad Ali

It was a lollapalooza of celebrities, all fueled by end-of-the-century frenzy and a five-year stock market rally.

Most of my encounters with these bell-ringing celebrities were brief affairs, a couple of minutes to say hello, welcome to the NYSE, maybe get a quick comment, something that could be relayed on air. These were designed to be fast-moving media events.

My encounter with broadcasting legend Walter Cronkite was different.

# Meeting Walter Cronkite

By the time Cronkite came onto the floor on December 22, 1999, he was already 83 years old. It's hard to overestimate how important he was to my generation, the baby boomers who had grown up with television in the late 1950s and into the 1970s.

He covered World War II, then went with Edward R. Murrow to CBS News in its infancy, in 1950. He covered the Democratic and Republican National Conventions and, most famously, the John F. Kennedy assassination on November 22, 1963, when he came on air sitting at a desk with no jacket and teared up announcing that the president had died of his wounds. He was so famous that when he announced he was opposed to continuing the Vietnam War in 1968, President Lyndon Johnson reportedly said, "If I've lost Cronkite, I've lost middle America." His sign-off, "And that's the way it is," was a cliché often used after someone said something that was deemed particularly important. He anchored the *CBS Evening News* for 19 years, from 1962 until his retirement in 1981.

When he came on the NYSE floor that December, he had been retired for 18 years. He had still kept active: he was a special correspondent for CBS News and was particularly involved with covering the space program, which he called "our last great adventure."[10]

The people I met or interviewed who came to ring the bell were all accomplished and famous to one degree or another, but most of the time they didn't mean too much to me *personally*. I didn't grow up admiring them or wanting to be them.

Walter Cronkite was different.

I wasn't doing an on-camera interview with him, but I didn't care. I went up to him, introduced myself, thanked him for his work and told him, "You're one of the reasons I wanted to be a journalist."

I sounded like a gushing teenager in front of his pop star idol, but I didn't give a damn. This was Walter Cronkite.

Cronkite meant something to me. He had taught me the value of straight reporting, without editorial content. And he also taught me something even more important that I used every day as a journalist: the value of being a steady voice.

That's why Cronkite captivated the country. He was always there, always a steady voice. The few times he ever broke that façade—as when he teared up at Kennedy's assassination or shouted "Go, baby, go!" at the Apollo 11 moon launch in 1969—made headlines.

By 1999, the airwaves were full of "opinion journalism." The whole Cronkite ethic—be a steady voice, don't editorialize—was out of fashion.

Not for me. The ups and downs of the stock market were now national news. I tried to keep the Cronkite ethos. If the market was down big, viewers didn't want to hear a screaming, hysterical person come on the air and imply, "The end of the world is here." In a time of great stress, the viewer is stressed. My job was to inform the viewer and not leave them in an even more hysterical state.

That's what Cronkite had taught me. And now he was standing in front of me.

Then something wonderful happened. Cronkite said he was amazed by the sudden importance of financial journalism, and did I think it would continue?

*Oh man*, I thought, *Walter Cronkite is interviewing me. How cool is this?*

Rather than me asking him about all of the famous events and interviews I always wanted to ask him about, he had turned around and asked me a question. He was still curious about what was going on.

It was a surprise because I was half expecting him to lecture me about the evils of allowing reporters to express opinions. Cronkite had been a vociferous opponent of the rise of "opinion journalism," and I had been worried he might include CNBC in that group. His memoir, *A Reporter's Life*, had been published just three years before, and he made clear his distaste for the trend: "Among this new generation of better-educated journalists, there is an urge to break out of the reportorial straight-jacket by slipping a point of view into a supposedly impartial item. I think the new press cynicism is a fad that will fast fade. I see self-correction coming across the horizon."[11]

He was wrong about that, but there was none of that in our brief discussion.

As he was leaving, I said, "Can I ask something? You're still so vital. Why did you leave in 1981?"

For the first time, the smile that had been on his face during our entire discussion changed. He patted me on the shoulder and said, "I left too soon."

I wasn't surprised. Cronkite had stepped down from the anchor job at CBS at the then-mandatory retirement age of 65, which he reached in 1981, and he insisted it was his own choice. It was well known that there had been some tension with those who went on to run CBS after his retirement, including his successor, Dan Rather.[12] Cronkite had said he was "disappointed" that CBS hadn't used him more: "It turned out to be more retirement than I thought it would," he told *The Washington Post* in 1986, five years after he stepped down.[13]

No matter: I got my chance to pay my respects to Walter Cronkite.

And I took his comment to heart. I wasn't going to leave too soon. After 10 years at CNBC, my contract was up for renewal. Many of my friends who had helped build CNBC in the early days were now jumping ship to CNN, Bloomberg, ABC, or CBS, eager to cash in on the shine that working at the hottest network on television gave to their careers.

Briefly, I thought of leaving myself. I got offers to "come in and talk" from other networks. I met with a well-known agent who was eager to shop me around.

I decided to stay, because nothing I could think of came close to the exhilaration of covering the stock market. No other network had the prestige of CNBC, and no other job I could think of was more important than the job of On-Air Stocks Editor. And no other place afforded the opportunity, every single day, of meeting famous and important people ringing the opening and closing bell.

Those bell ringings had become a central part of my life. I didn't have to do anything except be there and every day, some CEO or rock star or head of government came by. I walked up to them, introduced myself, and chatted. Much of the time there was no formal interview, but even a few minutes alone with the CEO of Chevron will do wonders to inform your reporting.

The NYSE was well aware of this. It was soon promoting the opening bell as the most watched news event in the world and the NYSE itself as "the most recognized brand in the world."[14]

None of us knew it in those final, heady days of 1999, but the financial world was about to change.

Stocks had been going up steadily since 1995 and the rally reached a crescendo toward the end of 1999, particularly in the IPO market. That year, 457 companies went public, most of them internet stocks. Of those, 117 doubled in price on the first day of trading—25 percent of the total.[15]

It wasn't just the stock prices going up. Everything was going up. Everything was getting bigger. The frenzy of stock trading had reached such a crescendo that Wall Street firms were paying exorbitant prices to buy each other.

In June 1999, Merrill Lynch bought Herzog Heine Geduld for the incredible price of $914 million. Herzog Heine Geduld was a respected Nasdaq market maker, the third largest with eight percent of the Nasdaq market, but $914 million for a market maker?[16]

In September, Goldman Sachs paid $6.5 billion to buy Spear Leeds & Kellogg. Spear was one of the largest specialist firms on the New York Stock Exchange. It seemed like an odd bet at the time. A bet on Spear was a bet that the traditional auction method used on the NYSE floor would continue to dominate over the electronic trading that prevailed at the Nasdaq. Many—including Henry Paulsen, Goldman's chairman and chief executive—believed that electronic trading was the future and clearly said so. No matter: "Goldman's most senior executives are saying that Spear, Leeds will put Goldman Sachs at the forefront of a global boom in stock trading, no matter which direction the markets take," *The New York Times* said in announcing the deal.[17]

Even the NYSE's floor traders were caught up in a speculative frenzy.

In 1999, LaBranche & Co. was the first NYSE specialist to become a public company. Among the 30 or so specialist firms on the floor at that time, LaBranche was one of the oldest and largest. It ranked third in the number of stocks listed but was first in dollar volume traded on the exchange. The NYSE floor was akin to a private club, and LaBranche's IPO—which showed the public exactly how lucrative the stock trading business could be at that time—was not well received by many of LaBranche's fellow specialists.[18]

It wasn't just the deals that were getting bigger. Even the drinks got bigger.

In the bars that the traders frequented, the martinis and Manhattans had gone from staid affairs served in 4- or 5-ounce coupes to V-shaped monstrosities twice that size—so big you could float a goldfish in them. The prices increased too: martinis were routinely $12, but many bars were now charging $15 and up. There was a joke going around that Wall Street needed to replace the Big Mac Index—which had been created by *The Economist* a decade before as a way of measuring the relative purchasing power of different currencies—with a Martini Index.

Even the bars where people drank were changing. Many traders still flocked to old-school places like Harry's downtown, run by Harry Poulakakos, or the standing bar at the 21 Club. But a whole new generation of bars and bartenders were descending on the city, and traders were eager to belly up.

At Blackbird in Midtown, Dale DeGroff, who had formerly been head bartender at the Rainbow Room, was transforming American cocktail culture with fresh ingredients and new takes on old classics. And I mean old classics. The Cosmopolitan may have been the national drink of the moment (thanks to the success of *Sex in the City*, which had debuted the year before), but traders for the most part stuck to Manhattans, martinis, and beer.

Dale was one of the first celebrity bartenders, a man who garnered a passionate following. He would later go on to become one of the first cocktail "consultants," making custom cocktails for restaurants and beverage companies.

Big as everything was getting, nothing was bigger than the NYSE. In December 1999, Richard Grasso, the NYSE Chairman, threw a party on the floor of the NYSE. It was a party for the times. The band was loud. The lights were bright.

The shrimp were almost as big as my fist.

It would all soon change. A new sobriety was about to descend on Wall Street. The change would be fueled not just by the bursting of the speculative excess known as the "dot-com bubble," but also by technological change. The same hardware and software companies that made investors rich (at least on paper) was now being turned on Wall Street.

The trading business would not be the same again.

## CHAPTER 7

# *The Dot-Com Bust and the End of the Rainbow*

===

I knew things were getting bad when I started to receive death threats.

The dot-com bubble ended with a breathtaking two-month drop. On Friday, March 10, 2000, the Nasdaq Composite peaked at an intraday high of 5,132.52. From that high point, it dropped almost 40 percent to its (temporary) low at the end of May 2000.

That wasn't the end of it. The bottom wouldn't come until mid-2002. By then, the Nasdaq Composite was down about 75 percent from that March high.

The broader market declined significantly too. From its peak in March 2000 to the bottom in September 2002, the S&P 500 declined 50 percent.

I had an old-fashioned phone message machine, with a cassette tape recorder. I turned it on when I left for the day.

By mid-2000, the messages started getting nasty.

Here was one: "You'd better find some way to stop the markets from dropping or we are going to come down there and take care of you."

There were others. They all had some variant of the same message: *I lost a lot of money trading tech stocks. How come you didn't warn us the market was going to drop? How come there weren't more bears to tell us to sell?*

When I casually mentioned to the head of security at the NYSE that I was getting nasty messages, he advised me not to erase them, and to keep the cassettes in storage.

I didn't have to ask why. He wanted a record, in case something happened.

I didn't take his advice.

I didn't need angry phone messages to remind me that life was very different toward the end of 2000 than it was at the end of 1999. I could see it everywhere I went.

There was a bar in midtown Manhattan that was a favorite of traders and those who followed the markets. It had a row of maybe eight TV sets above the bar, and in 1999 all of them would be set to CNBC.

When I walked into the bar one day in late 2000, the TV sets were still there, but they were all set to ESPN.

In retrospect, there were plenty of warning signs of what the traders jokingly called "Peak Martini."

## *Assigning blame*

Why did the market peak on March 10? No one knows, but concerns over lack of profits had long been debated.

Morgan Stanley's Mary Meeker estimated that the market cap of the 199 internet stocks she tracked was $450 billion in October 1999. The total sales, however, were a measly $21 billion. And profits? There were none. They collectively had lost $6.2 billion.[1]

On March 13, the Nasdaq dropped nearly three percent. Traders cited the 1.4 percent contraction in Japan's GDP; the country was now in a recession. Suddenly, there was concern that a slowdown in demand might slow earnings growth—not a crazy concern with prices at these levels. "The Nasdaq (was) certainly overdue for a reality check," Howard Ward from Gabelli Funds told CNN.[2]

From there, one worry after another pounded stocks for the next two months.

On March 20, Jack Willoughby of *Barron's* warned that internet startups were burning through cash at an alarming rate.[3]

That same day, software maker MicroStrategy dropped 62 percent because the SEC forced them to restate results for the past two years. The SEC was cracking down on aggressive accounting practices, promulgating new accounting guidelines on reporting revenue.[4]

The next day, the Federal Reserve raised rates—the fifth increase in less than eight months.

On April 3, Microsoft dropped 15 percent when a federal judge ruled the company had violated the Sherman Antitrust Act, leading to concern the company could be broken up. The Nasdaq dropped another eight percent. "A lot of people assume that what's bad for Microsoft is bad for technology, and that's what's hurting the Nasdaq," Art Hogan, chief market strategist at Jefferies, told CNN.[5]

By the middle of April, the dam had fully burst. As tax week loomed, the Nasdaq collapsed again, falling nine percent on April 14, capping a decline of 25 percent that week.

For the Nasdaq, it was the worst weekly loss in history.

*What caused that particular whoosh?*

Some cited surprising strength in consumer prices, triggering fears the Fed would again hike rates (they would). Others noted that taxes on big gains in 2000 were now due. Some cited margin account requirements. Most simply threw up their hands: "Still, analysts say little fresh fundamental news was behind the week's losses," one report said. "Instead, months of greed that fueled one of the greatest bull markets in history turned to fear on changing sentiment that the highest-flying technology stocks rose too far, too fast."[6]

## Who was responsible for the dot-com bust?

As always, there was plenty of blame to spread around. Some claimed that changes in the tax code, particularly the Taxpayer Relief Act of 1997 that lowered the maximum tax rate on capital gains for individual investors from 28 percent to 20 percent for assets held more than 18 months, made speculative investing more attractive.[7]

Another source of blame: the Federal Reserve. The Fed had historically been a killer of economic expansions and bull markets when it raised interest rates, and it certainly bears some blame for killing this bull. The Fed had begun raising interest rates in the second half of 1999 because the economy was doing so well. Between June 20 and February 2 of 2000, the Federal Funds Rate—the target rate the Fed sets for commercial banks to borrow and lend their excess reserves to each other overnight—went from 5.00 percent to 5.75 percent. Even after the market began moving down in March 2000, the Fed continued to hike, this time to 6.00 percent on March 21 and then to 6.50 percent on May 16.[8]

Another easy target: the companies themselves. The standard narrative—created mostly after the bubble had burst—was that they were greedy and profligate, "invented" metrics that made no sense, and worst of all, had business plans that made no sense.

That was certainly true. In those heady days, it seemed like you could sell anything online. Why not pet food and supplies?

The poster child for all the frothiness, Pets.com, went public on the Nasdaq in February 2000 and raised $82.5 million. It had considerable competition in the form of Petopia.com, PetsMart, and even Petstore.com, which was backed by Animal Planet. To get ahead of the competition, it spent a fortune on advertising, hiring a big-name advertising firm that created the famous sock puppet. The strategy was relatively simple: massive advertising combined with heavily discounted pet food.

But problems emerged immediately. It lost money because it was selling merchandise below what it cost to buy it. It also offered free shipping.

Do you know how much it costs to ship a 10-pound bag of cat litter?

The biggest problem: most people in 2000 were not interested in ordering dog food online. There was no perceived value added for this service at that time.[9]

It made no sense, but could you blame Pets.com?

How about blaming the company's backers? Before going public, private investors and venture capitalists were throwing money at Pets.com. Amazon.com purchased 54 percent of the company in its very first round of venture capital funding, in March 2009. Hummer Winblad Venture Partners and Bowman Capital Management both invested $10.5 million at the same time.[10]

Given this ocean of financing, could you blame companies for being fiscally irresponsible?

On November 9, 2000, 10 months after going public, Pets.com announced it could no longer continue as a business. It announced final liquidation plans in January 2001. Its stock price had fallen from $11 when it went public to $0.19. It had been public less than a year.

Tough competition and no profits were a problem for most startups at this time. What about Netscape, which arguably started the whole mania? Its IPO on August 9, 1995 was so spectacular, investors had coined the phrase "Netscape moment" to describe the point at which the potential of the internet was realized.

Netscape's star quickly faded. The market share for its main product—the web browser—peaked near 80 percent a year after its IPO, in 1996. After that, Microsoft's Internet Explorer steadily gained market share.

AOL bought Netscape in 1999 in a deal that valued the company near $10 billion. Most of that $10 billion came from the deal structure: AOL agreed to give Netscape shareholders 0.9 AOL shares for every Netscape share. When the deal was initially announced, the price was $4 billion. But as AOL's share's skyrocketed after the announcement, so did Netscape's, so the final price at the time of acquisition was $10 billion.

From $4 billion, to $10 billion. In four months.

Was it a good deal for AOL? No one seemed to care. By then, Netscape's browser share was down to about 50 percent.

By 2002, its share was down to 10 percent.[11]

Bankruptcies became commonplace by this time. There were online retailers boo.com (filed for bankruptcy in May 2000), eToys.com (filed for bankruptcy in February 2001), and many others, most notably theGlobe.com.

Founded as a social networking service by two Cornell students in 1995, theGlobe.com went public on the Nasdaq on November 13, 1998. Pricing at $9, it went as high as $97 on its first day before closing at $63.50, up 606 percent.

It was the largest first-day gain of any IPO in history.[12] It was all done without making a dime in profits—theGlobe.com would never make a profit. By the start of October 2000, it was trading for $0.75. The flagship site closed in August 2001, the company laid off 50 percent of its staff,[13] and it was delisted from Nasdaq.

## Let's blame the media

There's a final piece of the "who-to-blame-for-the-dot-com-bust" puzzle: the media.

That would be me—and my colleagues.

Remember those death threats and nasty messages I got on my message machine after the bubble burst? Were my colleagues and I also responsible, or at least a contributing factor?

I had a hard time feeling personally responsible because I had gone to great lengths to avoid appearing as a cheerleader. That meeting with Walter Cronkite in December 1999 was a big moment for me. I was dedicated to the Cronkite ethos of being a reporter, and I certainly did not feel that reporting on the fact that the markets were going up made me complicit as a cheerleader.

Regardless: did the financial media bear any collective responsibility?

I think we did—but not in an obvious way.

Robert Shiller taught me the right way to think about it.

In one of the most fortuitous timing events in book publishing history, Robert Shiller, then Stanley B. Resor Professor of Economics at Yale University, published *Irrational Exuberance* in March 2000, the exact height of the stock market boom.*

Shiller devoted an entire chapter to the influence of the news media on speculative bubbles. The very first sentence of the chapter on the news media declares: "The history of speculative bubbles begins roughly with the advent of newspapers."[14]

That was an important insight: bubbles need access to mass media in order to form. They also needed some investment vehicle, which included stocks and futures.

Both of these—mass media and stock markets—began appearing in the 1600s, and that is when we find the first large-scale bubbles, including the fabled tulip mania bubble (which collapsed in 1637). For the most part, the bubbles centered around new technology, including turnpike construction in England (1600s), and in the U.S. in canals (1820s),

---

* Shiller acknowledged that the title came from Alan Greenspan's now-famous comment four years before.

railroads (1830s), the telegraph (1830s), undersea cables (1860s), the telephone (1870s), and radio (1920s). The radio, in particular, was truly the internet of its time.[15]

After reviewing media coverage of the stock market crashes of 1929 and 1987, Shiller gets to the heart of the issue: "The examples given in this chapter illustrate that the news media are fundamental propagators of speculative price movements through their efforts to make news interesting to their audience."[16]

That certainly sounds damning. But Shiller points out something about the financial media that is far more important.

He asks a simple question: how do we know that there is a relationship between stock prices and what the media claims is moving those prices?

What the media doesn't do a good job of, Shiller claims, is explaining *why* the markets are moving. He noted that in many cases reports of why the stock market moved were not plausible, and that the media often failed to explain why very large movements in stock prices often occurred on days when there was little or no news.

The reason this happens, Shiller says, is because the markets move almost instantaneously to adjust for any new information, and market reporters are simply striving to explain such movements after the fact.

What market reporters are good at is getting the public to focus: "They sometimes strive to enhance such interest by attaching news stories to stock price movements that the public has already observed, thereby enhancing the salience of these movements and focusing greater attention on them."[17]

Shiller uses the phrase *attention cascade* as a way to describe how the media can focus on past price changes and influence future price changes.

*What's all this got to do with whether the media shares part of the blame for the dot-com bust?*

Shiller's criticism of the media was far more subtle and intellectually significant than merely placing blame on the media. The financial media,

Shiller says, explains market behavior after the market has reacted. The focus on certain narratives to explain the movement of stock prices can itself further influence prices.

In other words, the media can definitely influence the markets.

But did the media fail to warn the public about the danger of an overpriced market going into 2000? Shiller recognized this was nonsense. Here's what Shiller concluded after examining prior speculative bubbles in 1901 and 1929, and comparing them to the 1990s:

> I could not find 1990s accounts that were as expansively and breathlessly optimistic as some in 1901 or 1929, and although there is much optimism in the media in the 1990s, it is usually a matter of background presumption rather than bold assertion. There appears to have been a media attitude change, and optimistic hyperbole was out in the 1990s. Many writers seemed, if anything, rather more influenced by concerns about market overpricing and speculative mania.[18]

In the third (2015) edition of *Irrational Exuberance*, Shiller further amplified this by adding, "There appears to have been a media attitude change, and optimistic hyperbole was out in the 1990s, *just as it is still out of fashion today in the second decade of the twenty-first century.*" (emphasis my own).[19]

Shiller's conclusion: "The possibility that the stock market boom was a speculative bubble was certainly thrust before the minds of readers in the 1990s."[*20]

In other words, don't blame the dot-com bust on the media.

---

* In the second edition, published in 2005, Shiller added: "But the evidence in the markets is that the public in the 1990s found these possibilities at best mildly amusing; they were far more swept up in the new era thinking symbolized for them by the coming of the new millennium."

But that didn't make me feel any better. Shiller made me realize that much of what I assumed I knew for sure, like why the markets move up or down on any given day, may not be so certain.

How did I really know the market dropped two percent because the GDP of Japan was down? How did I know for sure that there was a causal relationship between those two events?

I didn't—I used my experience to infer what I believed traders and investors cared about, and thus what would matter to the markets. I also engaged in what would come to be called "confirmation bias," by speaking with traders and strategists who would enforce what I already believed. I was willing to report on a contrarian opinion, of course, but even then only within certain norms. I was *not* going to report that the markets were up due to favorable astrological signs, for example.

What the media does—all media, not just the financial media—is construct narratives. The statement, "The Dow rose 100 points" can have many narratives associated with it. We can explain it by associating it with corporate profits, economic news, global events, or any other occurrence that we can plausibly argue might be linked.

Some narratives can become far more powerful than others. Narratives around making money quick—which is what happened to a small group of people in the 1990s—can have particular resonance.

The media is adept at picking up narratives with strong resonance and running with it.

The media ran with the "get rich" narrative, but it also ran with plenty of narratives warning that it was getting out of control.

## The aftermath

Regardless of what caused the dot-com bust, there was an otherworldly quality to it. It seemed as if some kind of collective mania had descended on the investing public. But it was a mania around a very real and viable concept: the internet. Like the railroad boom of the 1800s, which also led to a bust, the internet (and the railroad) survived and did indeed change the world.

But not before a lot of damage was done. D. Quinn Mills, a Harvard Business School professor, expressed the majority opinion a few months after the collapse in an article in the *Harvard Business Review*: "The share prices collapsed simply because they had been bid up to irrational and unsustainable levels. The bubble burst because it was a bubble."[21]

Really? It was all due to the "irrational exuberance" that Alan Greenspan had famously warned of in a speech about three years before the dot-com collapse?[22]

I found it hard to believe. I shouldn't have, but I did. "It was all just a bubble" is not intellectually satisfying. Sure, manias and bubbles had been part of the stock market—indeed, part of all markets—throughout human history. Why would this be different?

But I still clung to the silly notion that humans were rational creatures, that they would act in their own self-interest. In the case of the stock market, that interest was expressed in "buy low, sell high." No rational actor would do the opposite.

But there it was—clear evidence that they do indeed do the opposite.

And that's when I started to take people like Robert Shiller a lot more seriously.

By 2000, Shiller and a small group of colleagues had been publishing evidence for more than 20 years that humans did not act rationally at all. Applying this knowledge to markets yielded a new field, behavioral finance, which purported to show how people really act, not how they are supposed to act, particularly when they are investing. These studies all noted the same thing: humans don't act rationally. They exhibit biases that influence the way they make decisions. The biases often result in wrong decisions.

Ignoring the growing evidence of behavioral economics had been a costly mistake for many of us.

The experience affected my reporting. I began spending more time looking at the growing mass of evidence about behavioral finance.

But I also continued a quest I had begun several years before. I thought I could find The Perfect Trader. The one trader who knew all.

I thought I could find the Wizard of Oz.

## CHAPTER 8

# *The Wizards of Oz*

===

In addition to trying to determine how to make money one must also try to keep from losing money. It is almost as important to know what not to do as to know what should be done.

—*Jesse Livermore*, Reminiscences of a Stock Operator, *1922*[1]

TALK about chasing dragons.

Shortly after I got to the NYSE in 1997, I became obsessed with a quest that consumed me for several years.

Somewhere, I was convinced, there was someone who knew everything. Someone who had figured out the markets, who had conquered irrationality and either had stunning natural instincts that never failed or had turned human instincts into a computer program.

This Wizard of Oz, I believed, was the one person who had perfect knowledge of the markets. He or she saw trends before anyone else. He or she could see turns in the market. He or she insisted on anonymity and remaining as a background source. He or she was wealthy, but in a quiet, inconspicuous way, because this was The Investor Behind the Curtain.

This person was the perfect source—the perfect trader.

With this man or woman as my confidant, I would be admitted into the Illuminati of Secret Traders Who Know All. I would learn The Things No One Knows About the Markets Except Us and ultimately would be shown The Secret Sauce, the perfect recipe for making money year after year.

Armed with this information, I would pepper my market observations with pithy words of wisdom and come off as fabulously well-informed.

I read books. Jack Schwager's *Market Wizards*, a book of interviews with well-known traders, was very popular at the time, helping to burnish the reputation of the traders who were included: William O'Neil, Jim Rogers Jr., Larry Hite, and Paul Tudor Jones.

I was struck by how the principal focus of most traders was on avoiding repeating mistakes and avoiding losing money as much as making it. It was the same mantra as that of Jesse Livermore, perhaps the most famous of all traders in the early 20th century. Livermore was the subject of Edwin Lefevre's investment classic, *Reminiscences of a Stock Operator*, which had been published 67 years before Schwager's book.

Hedge fund manager Michael Steinhardt was typical of Schwager's Market Wizards, when he opined, "There is a very good investor I speak to frequently who said, 'All I bring to the party is twenty-eight years of mistakes.'"[2]

I was looking for someone who made very few mistakes. I took a lot of people out. I bought a lot of drinks and asked a lot of what I thought were probing questions about the market.

By 1999, I had a contact list that exceeded 500 people.

I wasn't necessarily looking for stock pickers. I had boatloads of them. I wasn't even looking for *successful* stock pickers. I knew by then there weren't many of them, either. I wasn't even looking for people who had successful investment systems, though I was always interested in hearing about them.

What I was really looking for was *attitude*. I was looking for people who had a way of looking at the world in general, but also specifically people who had the attitude that was necessary to succeed in the trading world.

This idea—that there were indeed market wizards who had figured out everything—was the exact opposite of the idea the indexers were talking about. The indexers questioned the very wisdom of trying to outperform the markets, or that anyone could be expected to outperform the markets on a consistent basis.

Why would I believe this? It seemed like a Don Quixote quest; a folly doomed to fail.

But I convinced myself otherwise. Surely, I thought, there were people who had figured this out. There were people who had removed all human emotion from trading, who had studied all the trading patterns of the past and who had devised The Perfect Trading Algorithm and would show me The Secret Sauce.

It was a ridiculous quest, that would cost me several years of my life and a small fortune in bar bills.

## *John Mulheren: how to play against the crowd*

There's a lot of crazed, bizarre people on Wall Street, but finding crazed, bizarre people who are consistently brilliant is tough, even on Wall Street.

John Mulheren Jr, the man who went after Ivan Boesky with a shotgun, was one of the smartest, funniest, most eccentric, and most generous men I ever knew. He was also nuts. He could go from calm and coherent to bat-shit crazy over the course of two sentences. I first met him in a dingy wine bar in 1999, at the very height of the stock market and all the craziness around the internet boom.

By the late 1990s, I had been On-Air Stocks Correspondent for several years, and the market had done nothing but go up, despite all sorts of crazy things happening overseas, including the Thai Bhat crisis in 1997, and the Russian debt default in 1998. No matter: Wall Street—and the country—was gripped by the first wave of Internet Fever. It had started with the IPO of Netscape in August 1995 and it had gotten progressively crazier.

By then Mulheren was one of the great trading legends of Wall Street. He had made his early reputation trading stock options and was so successful he was recruited to Merrill Lynch in the 1970s by Merrill's chairman, Donald Regan, who went on to become Secretary of the Treasury under Ronald Reagan,[3] then moved to Spear, Leeds & Kellogg, at that time the largest specialist firm at the NYSE, and after 1985 set up his own firm, Jamie Securities.

In the late 1970s and early 1980s, Mulheren entered into a very profitable relationship with Ivan Boesky, who owned his own brokerage firm that specialized in corporate takeovers.

By the mid-1980s Mulheren had made a ton of money and wasn't afraid to spend it. He bought a beautiful home in Rumson, New Jersey that had been formerly occupied by Francis Cardinal Spellman, the Archbishop of New York. He was known to commute to work from there in a speedboat he docked at the South Street Seaport.

His trading prowess was legendary. During the October 1987 crash, his firm lost $80 million, but he plunged back into trading and still finished the year up 18 percent.[4]

It all went to hell after 1987 when Boesky was indicted on insider trading charges. He cooperated with the government and implicated others, including Michael Milken and Mulheren.

One night in February 1988, a deeply distressed Mulheren got into his car with a gym bag that held a shotgun, an assault rifle, a semi-automatic pistol, and a .357 Magnum. His wife, alarmed about his emotional state and his ravings that Boesky had betrayed him, had alerted the local police. They stopped him as he was leaving the house, saw the pistols, and seized them without arresting Mulheren, since he had a permit and hadn't yet left the property.[5] Later that afternoon Mulheren left the property and was stopped by the police again. He still had the assault rifle in his car. He was arrested and spent several days in jail before being released.

Mulheren was convicted of conspiracy and stock fraud in 1990 and sentenced to a year and a day in prison, but the conviction was overturned on appeal the following year. As James Stewart noted in *Den of Thieves*, "It seems obvious that Boesky manipulated Mulheren, not that Mulheren manipulated the market."[6]

Boesky, however, was convicted and received a sentence of three and a half years and a $100 million fine. He never worked on Wall Street again, but the story of Mulheren getting into his car, reportedly with a clear intent to kill Boesky, became the stuff of Wall Street legend.

By the time I met Mulheren he was head of Bear Wagner Specialists, a stock trading firm and market-maker.

We had arranged to have drinks and dinner at Lea Wine Bar in Midtown, next to Bobby Van's Steakhouse.

Mulheren arrived 20 minutes late and wasted no time.

"You've probably heard a lot of stories about me," he said.

"I sure have."

"They're all true."

"They're all true?"

"All of them."

"Even the ones about you and Boesky, and the shotgun…"

"Especially about Boesky and the shotgun."

He stopped and stared at me. He wasn't overtly hostile, but there was a coldness in his eyes. I felt like I was in one of the *Godfather* movies.

"I hear you're a nice guy, so I agreed to meet with you," he said. "I'm going to tell you how this is going to work. We're going to chat for a few minutes. At the end, I'm going to decide if I want to keep talking to you. But I'm going to tell you something right now: if I ever hear my name on your TV station, I'm going to kill you."

He spat out the phrase "TV station" like it was a curse word and put extra emphasis on the words "kill you."

I thought about him and Boesky.

There's two lines of attack you can adopt with this kind of guy: you can swing back and gain a grudging respect by convincing them that, even though you work in a business they disdain, you're a lot like them. You can be a nice guy, but you're not going to be intimidated.

I calculated that this route of attack would likely get me a whisky glass slammed against my forehead.

I opted for the second line of attack.

"I understand," I said, making circles with my arms. "No problem, everything is on background. My job is to try to figure out the markets and explain it to the public. I talk to a lot of people. Some of them are great, some of them are bullshit. A lot of them just talk their book. I've got to figure out what to cover, and what to ignore. I'm looking for the right way to look at the markets, and you're one of the best out there. I'm looking for guidance."

Soft around the edges. Respectful. I squinted slightly, trying to look like Sollozzo talking to Luca Brasi in the first *Godfather* movie. Except I felt like Luca Brasi.

He stared at me, and instead of busting a glass over my head he began to talk. He talked about how most traders were sheep that didn't know how to think independently. Most were lazy and didn't fully understand how their markets worked. Most didn't know how to really practice their craft.

He warned against following herds, and how the bigger money was always made playing against the expectations of the majority.

He was right. Wall Street is one of the great sources of groupthink in the world. We tell ourselves stories to order the universe, to make sense of the world. Wall Street does the same thing: the endless stream of stock quotes is not how anyone understands the stock market. It's understood by taking the stock prices and the economic numbers, and the deals and promotions, and creating a narrative. The economy is expanding and so are earnings. The internet is on fire, and here's the next hot stocks and why. The Thai baht is overvalued and profits in Asia are evaporating.

Stories. Not numbers. But the stories everyone told themselves were usually the same as everyone else's story, so investors often made—and lost—large sums of money, all at the same time. There were only a few great ideas at any one time, so most moves were "crowded trades."

How to work against that "crowded trade?" I asked him how he got ideas. He left the impression that it was more an attitude, more a way of questioning assumptions, and more trusting instincts honed by years of experience that whispered an opportunity might be available.

He told me to look for information in places that were not obvious. He said, for example, that he monitored message boards for clues on what retail traders were thinking.

That was a surprise. At that time, most professional traders viewed computer bulletin boards on stocks as cesspools of misinformation and stupidity, and strictly for amateurs. But Mulheren saw it as a great opportunity because the speculation in the message boards often was followed by temporary swings in prices—what Wall Street called "volatility."

Volatility was a trader's dream: big price moves presented great opportunities. It didn't matter if the stock was up or down: it only mattered that you were on the right side of the trade.

It went like this for about an hour. He talked, and I asked questions. At the end of the hour, he said: "OK, this is what's going to happen. I'm going to give you my phone number. You can call, but not very often. I mean it. Not more than once a month."

"Understood."

So began an odd relationship. I honored his terms, I never called more than once a month—and he honored my terms, his take was almost always warped through the unique prism of his brain.

A typical conversation went something like this: "John, I hear that XYZ stock is getting ready to take off…"

"That's bullshit. Those people telling you that are full of shit." And he would give me a completely different take on the story. A different way to look at it. A different group of stocks to buy or sell.

That's the way all the conversations went. It didn't matter what the topic was. Tech stocks. Consumer stocks. Individual stocks. The economy.

Each time, I called to ask about an issue, and each time my take on the topic was usually "bullshit." He hated investment bankers. He hated analysts.

And he *really* hated journalists.

I finally got it. Mulheren had made his reputation staking out new and different ways to profit from trading. Every time I called him I began by representing the consensus. Because he made his career playing against that consensus, everything was "bullshit."

## THE CONTRARIAN AS AN ARTIST

Mulheren was a genius trader, but much of it came from his willingness to be a contrarian.

What does it mean to be a contrarian in the stock market?

Edward C. Johnson II was one of the early titans of the mutual fund industry. He founded Fidelity Investments in 1946. In a famous 1963 lecture entitled "Contrary Opinion in Stock Market Techniques," Johnson, who had spent a lot of time with traders and prognosticators, reviewed the various approaches to picking stocks and the traders who supported each approach and asked, "There's no one god in the investment world, so how are you going to decide which one of these indicators you're going to pick?"[7]

Surprisingly, Johnson expressed considerable sympathy for the contrarian thinkers like John Mulheren. While he described himself as a "pragmatist" (this was the founder of Fidelity Investments, after all) he said it took real "artists" to get outperformance in the markets, just like it took a great artist to play a violin well:

> Now this means that we don't want an orthodox investment approach. [A]n orthodox investment approach, handling as it does stupendous amounts of investment funds, more or less has to obtain average investment results. There isn't any other way of doing it. Unusual results in securities, as I say, have to be looked for in the basically artistic camp, which is relatively small in number as are all artistic groups.[8]

## Buzzy Geduld: still looking for the Wizard of Oz

I'd learned a lot about contrarian thinking from Mulheren, but it wasn't an all-encompassing way of looking at the markets.

I spent a lot of time with other traders, looking for the secret. I asked to sit on trading desks to watch how famous traders moved stock around.

I sat with Kenneth Pasternak, the co-founder of Knight Securities, then one of the biggest market makers in the United States. I watched him move large blocks of stock around prior to the open. I asked a lot of questions.

About 1998, I did the same with Buzzy Geduld, one of Pasternak's biggest competitors. His firm, Herzog Heine Geduld, specialized in trading Nasdaq stocks. He was president and chief executive, but Buzzy was known as a trader's trader, a man who lived and breathed the markets. I was introduced to him by one of his traders.

Buzzy was not fond of having outsiders sit on his trading desk, but he graciously allowed me to shadow him for a couple days.

I turned into a source of annoyance for him.

The trading desk was shaped in the form of a large rectangle. It was very noisy. The traders were yelling orders at each other. It was about two minutes prior to the open, and I was still pestering Buzzy with questions. It looked like a very large amount of stocks were about to be moved around, but I wasn't sure what he was doing.

He stood up, spread his arms wide, and screamed, "Will somebody please take this guy off my hands?"

What Buzzy was doing was making a market in stocks, which he insisted was a very particular art form.

"You have to distinguish between day trading/investing and market making, because they are two different things," he later told me.[9] "We weren't investing for Herzog. We were making markets and had positions."

Herzog Heine Geduld became one of the most successful Nasdaq market makers, which Buzzy attributed to his insistence on hiring the right people and making his customers happy.

We hired people who were A, street smart, and B, hungry. I wanted a kid who would say to me in an interview, 'I'll mop the floors, I'll get here at 5 in the morning. Don't pay me, see how well I'll do.' Hungry and smart, that's how you got a job. The most important thing was street smarts. That was more important than an MBA, it was more important than a Harvard degree.

Once the right people were in place, making the customer happy was the priority, regardless of the size of the order.

Whether an institution calls for 100 shares or a million shares, I don't care. Same thing. I want that guy to come back 10 years from now. So what we concentrated on more than anything else was client satisfaction. On Intel, they had 40 people to go to, why would they go to Herzog? It had to be because we would do a better job than Goldman Sachs.

What made customers happy—and what kept them coming back—was superior execution. Getting the best prices for his customers.

To get that, Buzzy had simple rules for his trading desk:

- *Market makers are not investors:* "Traders don't have opinions on how a company will do, that's not what a trader gets paid for. A trader gets paid to make a market for buyers and sellers and to be on the right side. It's very simple. Supply and demand. Smart buyers go long the stock. Smart sellers go short the stock. I only cared about who was buying and who was selling. If you have more buyers than sellers, you should be long the stock. I could be long at 10 o'clock, and I could be short at 10:05. The world changed."
- *Manage the downside:* "You always want to limit your risk. You always want to limit the downside. Making money took care of itself. Losing money was your concern."
- *Don't hang on to losing positions:* "You cut losses as quickly as you could. Praying is for Saturday and Sunday, not Monday through Friday. So you never trade around a position hoping it is going to go back up or if it's short that it's going to go back down. People have a tendency because they bought something, to hold on to it and hope it's going to go back up. There was no room for that in my trading desk."
- *Don't fall in love with stocks:* "I never talked to the CEO. I never wanted to be influenced or fall in love with them. To us they were just numbers. We were traders, not investors. They were all just numbers to us. It didn't matter if it was XYZ, the greatest company in the world.

We didn't analyze it, we didn't look at it that way. If the market told us that the stock was going up because there was more buyers than sellers, we'd want to own the stock."

Don't lose money, limit your losses, take care of your clients. It all led to one thing: more orders. And order flow was the mother milk of trading success for a market maker like Buzzy Geduld.

"Order flow created more order flow. Order flow is what made you money. The firms that did the most volume made the most money."

Buzzy's precepts for success—don't lose money, limit your losses, take care of your clients—were principles I heard over and over again in the next few years.

## *Ace Greenberg: memos from the Chairman*

I kept asking stupid questions of famous traders and got similar annoyed responses.

I later spent a day with Bear Stearns' Alan "Ace" Greenberg. Greenberg was a trading legend and one of Wall Street's bigger-than-life characters. He had started at Bear Stearns at the very bottom, as a clerk making $32.50 a week, shortly after graduating from the University of Missouri in 1949.[10]

He rose through the ranks to become CEO of Bear Stearns from 1978 to 1993, and Chairman of the Board from 1985 to 2001. Aside from managing Bear Stearns, he had two other passions: bridge and magic. He could often be found after the markets closed at the Regency Whist Club playing bridge. He was also a member of the Society of American Magicians.

He emphasized a small number of basic principles which he conveyed to his staff in a series of memos, some of which were later published in a short book, *Memos from the Chairman*.[11] He was obsessed with cost savings (his memos on reducing the use of paper clips, rubber bands, and scotch tape, and only licking one side of an envelope so it can be reused by licking the other side, are comedy classics and still read today).[12] But many of the memos were addressed to a smaller audience—the trading desk and the salespeople.

To get the points across, Greenberg frequently quoted Haimchinkel Malintz Anaynikal, whom Greenberg called "the dean of business philosophers."

Except Haimchinkel didn't exist. He was a fictional character, Greenberg's doppelgänger.

Over and over, the memos emphasized principles very similar to Buzzy Geduld's:

- *Paying very close attention to what you own:* "I want all partners in the trading area to pay particular attention that our positions do not increase dramatically in size."[13]
- *Limiting losses:* "When the going gets tough, the tough start selling."[14]
- *Avoiding the herd mentality:* "Big money is usually made by contrarians… our best moves were made against the thinking of the masses… it is incumbent upon us to stress that the contrarian point of view is the intelligent course."[15]
- *Favoring internal hires and instead of looking for MBAs, looking for people who are PSDs (Poor, Smart and with a deep Desire to become rich):* "They built this firm and there are plenty around because our competition seems to be restricting themselves to MBAs."[16]
- *Not getting caught up in investing euphoria or gloom:* "Bear Stearns will *not* get caught up in the hysterical optimism and the people at Bear Stearns will *not* get careless or conceited… Humans tend to get sloppy when making money is easy."[17]
- *Staying humble:* "A man will do well in commerce as long as he does not believe that his own body odor is perfume."[18]

In late 1992, Bear Stearns suffered significant trading losses: "I may have had a more difficult 14 days, but I cannot remember when," Greenberg wrote to the staff.[19]

He told his traders to forget about it and move on, quoting his favorite source, the sage Haimchinkel Malintz Anaynikal: "You cannot fly with the eagles and poop like a canary."

"Our losses have been taken, our minds are clearer and our job now is to get rolling in the right direction," he wrote.

When I spent the day with him, I asked why so many of his principles seemed to be directed at traders, like avoiding herd mentality, use of common sense, insistence on taking losses quickly: the same principles Mulheren had emphasized to me.

Why was trading so important to Bear Stearns' operation?

Ace had the same annoyed look on his face that Buzzy Geduld and Kenny Pasternak had when I kept peppering them with what must have seemed like obvious questions.

"Because this *is* the operation, kid," he sneered, referring to the trading desk.

Mulheren, Geduld, Pasternak, and Greenberg were all great traders, but they weren't the Wizard of Oz.

But they did have similar character traits (none of them were born wealthy, they loved their craft, and they were workaholics), and they had all come to very similar conclusions about trading, particularly risk management.

What kind of thinking do these people use that causes them to look at the same activity everyone else is looking at but come up with completely novel solutions for tackling the problem?

That thinking pattern got clearer when I met Joe Zicherman.

# *Joe Zicherman: what is a successful trader?*

During the 1980s and 1990s, Joe Zicherman was Morgan Stanley's Broker to the Stars. He was the epitome of Ace Greenberg's most desirable trait for a successful trader—he had no MBA, but he was a genuine PSD: Poor, Smart and with a deep Desire to become rich.

Like many great traders, he had traits associated with attention deficit disorder (ADD): inability to pay attention, the ability to hyper-focus on tasks that interested him, and bouts of excessive energy. He didn't read books (they required too much sustained concentration), but he could concentrate for short bursts and was a wizard at spotting trading trends. He could also be impulsive, was not afraid to take risks, and was comfortable with rapidly generating and receiving new ideas.

He had another critical skill: he was adept at making friends and gaining trust.

He was born into a poor Bronx family in 1942 in the shadow of Yankee Stadium, playing stickball on the street, a game related to baseball played with a broom handle and a rubber ball, typically a Spaldeen. For many of his generation, stickball was a metaphor for life: "You learned to make something out of nothing," he told me.[20] The game usually "appeared out of thin air... There was a parking lot on Girard Avenue, right near the stadium. And we couldn't hit the ball far because it was a parking lot that was in between two buildings. So a single was a ground ball past the pitcher, a double was a line drive past the pitcher, a triple was above the third window, and a home run was above the sixth window."

After a nondescript college career at the University of Vermont, Zicherman eventually landed a job in the Purchase and Sales (P&S) department at Merrill Lynch in 1968, where he processed trades.

"They had these pneumatic tubes," he recalled. "These brokers used to write out these orders, and these tubes came out of the sky... they came right at me and I take them and I take the ticket out of the tube and I turn it over to a fellow… and he would take the order and timestamp it, type it and it would go to a post on the floor, and the report came back in 12 or 13 minutes, and then I take the report and I wrap it up in that thing and stick it in the ceiling. I'd slip it in and it would go right back to the broker, he had a thing coming out of his ceiling, these pneumatic tubes, and that's how we communicated."

After two years in P&S, Zicherman went to Merrill's training school, emerging in 1970. He survived the brutal bear market years of the early 1970s by constantly hustling for clients.

"I never did cold calling because I thought it was a mortifying way to do business. I did referrals… I was in restaurants, I was at openings I was at parties, and I was just meeting and greeting. People would say what do you do and I started to meet people and started to do business."

As the market began to rise after the bear market in the early 1970s, the hustling slowly began to pay off, with small accounts from people who talked to other people about the markets.

"I used to give out [business] cards, anywhere, everywhere. And I wound up having the account of the maître d' at the Hotel Pierre."

His big break came in 1978, when he moved to Morgan Stanley after it opened a division to cater to high-net-worth clients. He was the third person hired in the division.

The cultural shift from the Queens office of Merrill Lynch to the Wall Street office of Morgan Stanley was jarring. It was, he said, "Like you're selling suits at John's Bargain Stores in Queens and all of a sudden you just got hired at Brioni."

At that time, going after high-net-worth clients was a novel idea, and not a popular one.

"When you have an institutional client, like say an AT&T, the zeros don't end. When you have the CEO of AT&T, nobody cares about an $8 million account or a $12 million account, they care about an $8 billion account."

But the division was a hit. High-net-worth people flocked to the company, and Zicherman got his first taste of what real influence felt like, because for the first time in his life he held the most powerful cards.

"I'm sitting there with ten cannons, and they're sitting there with a pistol. I have all the ammo. I have the Morgan Stanley research, I've got the power of trading, I have the power of order flow, I've got the power of information, I have the power of flexibility."

The new, high-profile job also helped him acquire the trappings of a new, bigger personality. He bought a full-length beaver coat, bought the right suits, hung out with the traders and analysts.

"I learned how to work the room," he told me.

His second big break came in 1982, when he was introduced to Lloyd Zeiderman, who ran Zeiderman Oberman & Associates, which handled high-profile Hollywood accounts.

In Hollywood, "You have to have somebody do your real estate, your insurance, your taxes, your cars, your investing." Joe told me, explaining the role of people like Zeiderman. "They do every single thing for you, for a fee."

In 1985, Zeiderman invited Joe onto the set of a new TV show.

"I was invited by Lloyd to meet Bruce Willis and Cybill Shepherd. They were starting a show on the Fox lot on Pico Boulevard called *Moonlighting*. And that began a wonderful friendship."

Zeiderman introduced him to legendary entertainment lawyer Jake Bloom and influential business manager Page Jenkins. Eventually, he had a roster of clients that included, at various times, Sly Stallone, Jon Peters, Peter Guber, Sam Waterston, Michael Crichton, Arnold Schwarzenegger, and others.

"I developed this reputation for handling all these folks in Hollywood, and I was going out to LA once a month. Morgan Stanley was very generous in funding me to go out there and stay, stay there for five, six days once a month, and visit the studios."

In 1991, he met Barbra Streisand and began managing money for her as well. He accompanied her to the Fire and Ice Ball in Los Angeles in 1993, and for a series of shows at the MGM Grand over New Year's in 1993, her first paid public performances in 27 years.

In 1996, he was, by his own account, managing $600 million and doing roughly $17 million in commission business, making him one of the top brokers on the street.

But the street was changing. Up until then, while he did not control how much money went into or out of the accounts, he did have much of the say in what was in those accounts. After 1995, Morgan Stanley began to push to have the accounts go into Morgan Stanley Asset Management (MSAM), which would have paid him an annuity but left him with no control over his accounts.

Wall Street was moving away from generating profits from commissions on trading, and toward asset gathering, where a flat fee was charged for the money that was under management. Trading, and especially human trading, was on the way out. Computer models that picked stocks were in.

It was, Zicherman said, part of a larger plan to reduce risk.

"The pressure began in 1995 to turn my entire book into the asset-backed model, and I refused to do it," he told me.

It wasn't just that he would have no control over the accounts: he would also lose control over the clients. "It's not my account anymore," he said. Friendships developed in Hollywood with people like Streisand would no longer matter: "I would have no more relationship with her. And she didn't want that, she wanted me to run her money."

Zicherman left Morgan Stanley in 1998. He had come a long way from the P&S department at Merrill Lynch 30 years before. He took some of his Hollywood clients and had a two-year stint running a hedge fund. He closed that in 2001 and has been trading his own money for the past 20 years, often keeping concentrated positions in a dozen or so names, often using options to hedge his positions.

It is, he admits, a practice that is getting tougher and tougher as he competes against machines and increasingly sophisticated traders.

The market often baffles him, and not just when he's having a bad day and losing money. He will often call and rail against investors who he says have "no respect for the markets," traders who care nothing for fundamentals. He'll point out trades that make no sense to him.

It infuriates him, but he does not leave the markets, even as he approaches 80.

He doesn't leave for three reasons. First, he still makes money, though the odds are increasingly stacked against him.

Second, he believes his mental abilities have not significantly deteriorated. "I think my brain is about as good as it's always been, maybe 95% of where I was. But it's all because I exercise it daily. The great thing about what I do that nobody ever talks about is it's a different job every day."

Third, he can't stop trading, because it is what he is. He is a trader. For most, trading is just a means to an end, a way of making money, of parlaying their perceived defects (in this case, ADD) or strengths (the ability to hyper-focus) into a business that is perfectly suited to their temperament.

But for a small minority, including Joe, it is much more than just the money. It is what you are; it is a part of the very fiber of your being. It is what you live and breathe and think about, even when you're not doing it.

"I could retire tomorrow, and deal with my beautiful family here and deal with all the incredible things that I've been so fortunate to have, but I don't want to retire," he told me.

## JOE'S RULES

Like all the great traders, Joe has "rules" that he swears by, and they are remarkably similar to those espoused by Geduld and Greenberg.

- *Risk management is your principal job:* "I'm never worried about making money. My biggest issue is losing money, because I have to manage my risk very carefully."
- *Take losses fast:* "People say, 'Oh, if I make 50% one year and I lose 50% the next year, I'm even. You're not. You cannot let losses get away from you. When you buy something at $30, and you sell it for $13, oh my God, you have to have a lot of winners to make up for that. I always assume that there are much smarter people out there than I am... The first thing I do is sell first and then I bother to figure it out."
- *Never average down:* Don't buy more of a losing stock. "Why would I buy more of a food I didn't like?"
- *Never meet a margin call with money:* "You sell stock, and you get small. That's the way."
- *Respect the market:* "You need to understand that you're in a world where anything can happen, and bad things happen."

# *What I learned from all of them*

After a few years talking to successful traders, it became obvious that there were "rules" that everyone lived by, that everyone believed in, because violating them usually led to ruin. In most cases, they were the same rules.

- *Success in trading is not necessarily predicated on technical or even fundamental skills:* You cannot succeed without an understanding of trading patterns, but it was surprising how few ever boasted that this was the critical skill that made them successful. Experts in technicals rarely make fortunes. Same with fundamentals: most traders had a good grip on the outlook for the stocks they were trading but rarely cited that knowledge as critical to their trading.

- *Managing the downside is more important than managing the upside:* Everyone made a lot of money, and they also lost a lot of money. When you have a lot of money, figuring out how to avoid losing money by managing positions is the primary goal for most.

- *Personality traits perceived to be negative can be positive in the right circumstances:* What seems like a defect (ADD, bipolar disorder) in certain situations provides an evolutionary advantage, and what seems on the surface like a con game (the ability to get important people to trust you) can be parlayed to an advantage. Joe Zicherman believes his ADD has been, on balance, a major advantage: "The plus side is that you can do many things at one time. Another plus is that you have this enormous memory where you just don't forget a lot of things… I'm a great tape reader and instant analyzer of news. There's times when I actually feel like I'm inside my machine. That's how close I get to it."

- *Idea generation and going against the herd were more important than going with the crowd:* In one sense, everyone is a momentum trader. Everyone told me that it was important to "let your winners ride," but the best were able to find winners in nooks and crannies that were not obvious to others. A disdain bordering on contempt for investment ideas that were wildly popular with the average investor was a common theme. The study of groupthink and crowd behavior has been around a long time. Gustave Le Bon, a French polymath, wrote one of the earliest accounts of group psychology in an 1895 book, *The Crowd: A Study of the Popular Mind*, in which he noted that several things happen to people who succumb to crowd behavior: they develop overconfidence ("a sentiment of invincible power that allows him to yield to instincts that, had he been alone, he would perforce have kept under restraint"), they are consumed by a contagion ("an individual readily sacrifices his personal interest to the collective interest"), and they become lost in the sentiment of the crowd ("All feelings and thoughts are bent in the direction determined by the crowd itself."). His conclusion: "in crowds it is stupidity and not mother wit that is accumulated."[21]

John Mulheren would have readily agreed.

## *Where are they now?*

Kenneth Pasternak retired from Knight Securities in 2001 and now runs a hedge fund.

Buzzy Geduld and his partners sold Herzog Heine Geduld at the top of the market (June 2000) to Merrill Lynch, for about $900 million.[22] You'd think someone with that much money would stop and smell the roses, but not Buzzy. He formed a new shop, a family office called Cougar Trading, and is still at his desk. Prior to Covid, he hosted an informal salon with chosen friends at the Friars Club in New York.

John Mulheren died of a heart attack on December 15, 2003. He was 53 years old. My friendship with Mulheren lasted only four years, but he made a profound impact. He was not only a great trader: he was a great philanthropist. He gave away large amounts of money to his alma mater, Roanoke College, and to many other charities. I attended his funeral at Holy Cross Church in Rumson, New Jersey, along with 1,500 other mourners, including Bruce Springsteen, Jon Bon Jovi, NYSE Chairman Richard Grasso, Home Depot co-founder Ken Langone, and, yes, Ace Greenberg. Springsteen ended the ceremony singing, "Santa Claus Is Coming to Town," a request from Mulheren's wife.[23]

Ace Greenberg died at the age of 86 on July 25, 2014. After nearly 60 years at Bear Stearns, he had presided over the sale of his beloved company to JP Morgan after the firm collapsed in March 2008. He placed much of the blame for the company's problems on his successor, Jimmy Cayne.

Like Mulheren, Greenberg was involved in many charities, and more than a few oddball ventures, including donating $1 million to New York City's Hospital for Special Surgery to fund Viagra prescriptions for impotent men.

"You do some nutty things," Greenberg said, telling *People* magazine that his wife told him, "you've made your money, and you can spend it any way you want."[24]

Joe Zicherman left Morgan Stanley in 1998, but still trades his own money.

He is, by his own admittance, a dying breed. He still calls me with observations on trading activity, and still rails against trades that he insists make no sense and against traders who have "no respect for the markets," which usually means he is losing money.

And he still tells some very funny stories.

In 2015, I went to the premiere of a movie, *Rock the Kasbah*, starring Bill Murray and Bruce Willis. It was a terrible movie, but there was a party after, and Murray and Willis were there.

At one point, the stars aligned and my wife Suzanne and I found ourselves standing next to both of them.

Suzanne was a huge Bill Murray fan, so she was in heaven chatting him up. He was charming.

Which left me standing next to Bruce Willis. I dislike being around movie stars, because I don't have anything to say to them. I'm more comfortable with CEOs.

I remembered Joe talking about Willis from the 1980s, and the times he had been with him while he was doing *Moonlight* and the early *Die Hard* films.

Lacking anything else to say, I asked Willis if he remembered Joe Zicherman. He paused for a couple of seconds, then looked at me funny and said, "You know Joe Zicherman?"

I said, "He's a good friend of mine. I talk to him almost every day. Did you know him?"

He said, "I knew Joe Zicherman a long time ago. We had a hell of a lot of fun together, and I don't remember any of it. If you see Joe, you tell him I said hello."

And that was it. The party rotated, and they went on to talk to other people.

I called Joe the next day, amused and a bit bewildered.

"Bruce Willis said to say hello, but he says he doesn't remember anything. What happened?"

Joe laughed and said, "We behaved very badly."

## *Goodbye to all that*

In time I gave up the quest to find the Wizard of Oz. I had learned a lot about human behavior and what makes a great trader by hanging out with great traders, but I wasn't any closer to uncovering The Secret of the Markets.

I began hanging around with a new group of traders—upstarts who were challenging all the old rules and causing panic at the Nasdaq and a great deal of worry at the NYSE.

It started when I got an unsolicited phone call from a fellow who said he wanted to show me something. He had been part of a group that had set up an electronic trading system to compete with the stock exchanges.

And he claimed to have a plan to take down the New York Stock Exchange.

## CHAPTER 9

# *"We're Going to Take Down the NYSE"*

═══

I was sitting in my office at the NYSE in late 1999 or early 2000 when the phone rang.

"Mr. Pisani, my name is Matt Andresen, I work at Island. We're an electronic trading network, and we're right next door to you, at 50 Broad. I really think you should come and see our operation."

"Why would I want to see your operation?" I asked.

"Because we're going to take down the NYSE. And we don't think much of Nasdaq either."

My instinct was to hang up immediately. On the surface, Andresen sounded like a nutjob.

Take down the NYSE and Nasdaq? Both were at the height of their influence at the end of the 1990s. The Dow Jones Industrial Average topped 10,000 on March 29, 1999. The NYSE was unveiling a third trading floor. The Nasdaq was home to the hottest tech stocks and the Nasdaq 100, the 100 largest non-financial stocks listed on the Nasdaq, was challenging the Dow Jones Industrial Average as the index everyone watched. The idea that something could challenge the NYSE and Nasdaq seemed ludicrous.

Except there were whispers. More than 80 percent of the volume traded at the NYSE was still conducted on the floor, but there were signs that business was starting to slip.

The NYSE already had its hands full competing with the Nasdaq, which had captured much of the younger tech listings that were the talk of investors. Unlike the NYSE, the Nasdaq operated an all-electronic trading system that was starting to make the traditional, floor-based trading championed by the NYSE seem antiquated.

Both exchanges were worried about a new crop of competitors known as Alternative Trading Systems (ATS). The electronic version of ATSs, known as Electronic Communication Networks (ECNs), were a major source of anxiety.

Island was one of them. I knew very little about how they operated, but I knew the floor guys were worried.

And that's what piqued my interest. I knew they were becoming more influential, I knew the floor was worried, but I still had a hard time believing they were going to bring down *anything*.

Andresen kept talking. "Just come over and take a look," he said.

A few days later I walked into Island's office at 50 Broad Street.

## *Meet the revolution*

At first glance, there didn't seem to be much to be impressed with. Calling it an "office" would be a stretch. Andresen greeted me and I immediately asked to see the trading desk.

"The trading desk?" Andresen said, looking at me askance. Several years of hanging out on the NYSE floor had not quite prepared me for what I was about to see.

"Just show me the operations," I said.

Andresen took me into a small room. It was a little bit larger than a walk-in clothes closet, but not much. It was full of racks of off-the-shelf Dell computers, all strung together.

It looked like a high-school computer experiment gone wrong.

"This?" I said, staring at him. "This is what you're going to use to take down the NYSE?"

He looked at me like he was trying to explain something very complicated to an imbecile.

"Bob, it's not so much about the hardware, it's about the software, and about the software our clients are using." The Dell computers, he said, were designed to be modular. There was no single mainframe computer that could seize up during heavy trading. Each computer had a particular function that could be quickly backed up.

"What software?"

"They're writing algorithms to trade stocks."

"What are these algorithms doing?"

He described, patiently, how much of the trading was a form of arbitrage—rapidly buying and selling stocks or indexes on one platform and buying or selling on another.

"Who are your clients?"

"I can tell you, but you won't know any of them. They're not big institutions."

"Just tell me who your biggest client is."

"Automated Trading Desk."

"Where are they?"

"Charleston, South Carolina."

That piqued my interest. I had vacationed with friends in Folly Beach, outside of Charleston, for many years. I knew the area well.

"Who runs this Automated Trading Desk?"

"His name is Steve Swanson."

"Can you provide me an introduction?"

"Sure."

On the way out, Andresen introduced me to Island's general counsel, Chris Concannon. He looked very young to be general counsel.

———————

That summer, I was in Automated Trading Desk's office in Mount Pleasant, South Carolina, a bedroom community of Charleston, on the other side of the Cooper River.

Steve Swanson greeted me, and I immediately made the same mistake I had made with Andresen: I asked to see his trading desk.

"Trading desk?"

"Yes. Trading desk."

"OK, I can show you our trading desk, but you're not going to be impressed."

He walked me into a wood-paneled room. There was a large table in the middle, with two men seated across from each other. Each had a computer monitor. One was staring at the monitor, looking very bored. The other had his feet on the table and was reading *USA Today*. There were no other papers of any kind on the table. There was no paper anywhere.

"This is the trading desk?" I asked.

He looked at me sympathetically, like Andresen had done.

"Bob, these guys are not trading, they're just here to monitor the trading. The trading is being done by algorithms."

"What are the algorithms trading?"

"A lot of things."

I asked for an example, and he said one trade was to arbitrage the difference between S&P futures trading on the floor of the Chicago Mercantile Exchange, and the same instrument that was simultaneously trading electronically.

"Can you make money doing that?"

"Yes."

"How much?"

"That's proprietary information."

He gave some simple examples, though—enough for me to see that there was a persistent enough gap between prices to offer what seemed like a consistently profitable business of buying one instrument low and selling the (same) instrument slightly higher a few moments later.

There was more to it than just arbitrage. ATD had developed a pricing engine that estimated the fair value of any given name they might be trading in the very near future, literally seconds ahead of time. So if the pricing engine estimated that the stock might rise in the very near term, the engine would cancel any offer to sell, and depending on how aggressive the buy signal was, it could improve the bid.[1]

That was the aha moment for me. By then I was a believer in the Efficient Market Hypothesis, the widely held belief that asset prices reflected all available information. But here was an example where a firm was exploiting what clearly seemed like micro-inefficiencies in the market.

The limitations of this approach were obvious: the more algorithms written to exploit the micro-inefficiencies, the more trading occurred, and the less profitable the trades would become.

But that was far in the future. For the moment, ATD and Island seemed to be prospering.

## The computer era and the birth of Nasdaq

What I was witnessing was the birth of a new world of trading, and the death of an old world.

Island was part of a much larger movement toward electronic trading that began in the 1960s with the very first attempts at computerized trading. It was largely brought about by institutional traders who were demanding change and by then were eager to exploit the new electronic frontier that computerized trading had opened up.

It was about time. The 1960s were a boom time for the markets, but the largely paper-based NYSE was woefully unprepared for the explosion in stock trading that occurred. For several months in 1968, the NYSE was forced to close on Wednesdays just to try to catch up with all the orders.[2]

The biggest changes were occurring away from the NYSE. By the late 1960s, there was a vast market in over-the-counter (OTC) securities, which were not listed on a stock exchange because they did not meet the listing requirements. There was also considerable trading in listed stocks in the OTC markets. Bid-ask spreads—the difference between the highest price a buyer was willing to pay and the lowest price a seller was willing to accept—were often very wide. A study by the SEC concluded that automation might enable improved trading in OTC securities.[3]

The National Association of Securities Dealers (NASD) was founded in the late 1930s and had primary oversight of brokerage firms. The NASD founded Nasdaq (National Association of Securities Dealers Automated Quotations) in 1971 with the express purpose of helping to automate the market in OTC securities.

In some ways, Nasdaq was the anti-NYSE: there was no physical trading floor. It would link only market makers—there was no way for the retail public to interact with it. Most importantly, there was no trading in NYSE-listed stocks.[4]

Nasdaq was the world's first electronic stock market, though initially it simply displayed prices on a computer screen. The actual trading was still done on the telephone.[5]

Regardless: simply displaying quotes on a computer screen was revolutionary. Bid-ask spreads did indeed begin narrowing, and the profits of brokers began declining.

Among those OTC-listed stocks were many tiny technology companies that could not meet the listing standards of the NYSE. Nasdaq's support for those early technology companies, eventually including Microsoft and Apple, was instrumental in its success. The NYSE had assumed that companies would eventually "grow up" and move over to the Big Board (as the NYSE was called). That was a huge miscalculation: by the time those companies grew up, they didn't need the NYSE.

Even then, Nasdaq had competition in the electronic sphere. There were attempts to develop private networks to trade stocks, which came to be known as Alternative Trading Systems. These were non-exchanges that simply matched buyers and sellers for execution of trades. The electronic version of ATSs came to be known as Electronic Communication Networks (ECNs).

The first ECN—Instinet—started in 1969. It was a slow start for all-electronic trading, but better technology pushed it forward.

## SOES bandits and the birth of day trading

The dramatic growth of electronic trading was creating plenty of opportunities: for the exchanges, for market makers, and, in an interesting twist, for the little guy as well.

The 1987 stock market crash highlighted a major problem for a system, like Nasdaq, that was based on orders taken over the phone: many traders simply stopped answering their phones. Small traders got ignored, and the dealers only picked up the phone for their biggest clients. In response, the NASD set up one of the earliest automated trading platforms, the Small Order Execution System (SOES), to automatically execute orders of up to 1,000 shares at the best bid or offer. The intention was that SOES would execute trades for small retail order flow. The big guys—the market makers and institutional traders—would come after the small orders.

That was the way it was supposed to be, but traders quickly found a flaw in the system. Since the SOES orders were automated and executed immediately, traders could use SOES to trade stocks far faster than large investors, who were not able to use SOES. A smart trader could buy 1,000 shares in SOES and then sell the same 1,000 shares a few seconds later on another network to market makers who weren't paying too much attention. It came to be known as "scalping" and it was so successful that it led to the birth of an entire industry, known as "SOES bandits."

At this time, orders were being executed at the NYSE mostly on the floor, and orders on Nasdaq were executed mostly on the phone. SOES bandits were able to trade stocks electronically, where buy and sell orders were executed almost immediately. The SOES bandits did not have an informational advantage, they were just faster.[6] And they were often able to provide improved pricing. It proved to be a huge advantage.

A small group of these SOES bandits were very vocal about what they were doing and soon became media darlings. Harvey Houtkin, a founder of All-Tech Direct, was the most famous of the group, even penning a book, *Secrets of the SOES Bandit*, in 1998 and claiming he was "democratizing" the market by taking advantage of the big guys.[7]

Big traders complained vociferously that the SOES bandits were circumventing the rules—and indeed they were. Houtkin and his crowd turned SOES, which was meant to help small traders execute orders quickly, into a big business. Houtkin and others were routinely investigated and fined by regulators for rules violations, but the cat was out of the bag. There was big money to be made in electronic trading, if only because the rest of the world was still trading at a much slower pace.

# ECNs conquer the trading world

The growth of electronic trading had many advantages (including improved bid-ask spreads and faster executions), but it also came with problems. One was the ease with which informed market makers could trade ahead of a customer's order.

By the early 1990s, there was evidence that some Nasdaq traders were colluding on prices.[8]

A 1996 report by the SEC alleged that the Nasdaq market "has not always operated in an open and freely competitive manner. Nasdaq market makers have engaged in a variety of abusive practices to suppress competition and mislead customers."[9]

The other problem was that a two-tiered trading system had developed: one with the ECNs which usually had better pricing, and the other with Nasdaq. Because ECNs were private networks and Nasdaq was public, a perception developed that the public was not getting as good a deal as those who traded in the private ECNs.

To address the problem of brokers trading ahead of their clients, the SEC adopted the Manning Rule in 1994, which prohibited dealers from trading ahead of a customer's order. They were now required to give any better prices they had to the customer, rather than trade it in their own account.

To address the two-tiered trading system that had developed, the SEC adopted Order Handling Rules in 1996 that required market makers to display ECN quotes on their terminals right next to the Nasdaq quotes. Market makers were no longer allowed to publish quotes in private ECNs that were better than the public was getting.

The Order Handling Rules proved to be a game-changer that "broke the pricing conventions used in the NASDAQ market," as Schwartz and his colleagues wrote.[10] Spreads collapsed, but even more importantly

ECNs were suddenly able to provide direct matching and execution of stock trades.

Who wanted to be a SOES bandit when you could become an ECN?

## The SOES bandits turn into ECNs

The SOES system proved to be the death knell for executing most orders by phone. Who wanted to pick up a phone when you could execute an order by computer, even if—in the beginning—humans still had to manually make the trades?

Online trading began to explode as internet traffic dramatically increased. Small traders were beginning to have access to the same real-time pricing as professional brokers.

An entire industry developed around the SOES bandits, and when regulators tried to rein in the abuses with new regulations like the Order Handling Rules, a lot of the old SOES bandits decided it could also be profitable to become an ECN, especially after the SEC gave a formal blessing to the ECN format in a series of rules called Regulation Automated Trading System (Reg ATS) in 1998.[11]

One of them was Datek, which had been founded in 1970 and which by the mid-1990s had successfully morphed into a SOES bandit operation that had been repeatedly fined and censured by the NASD.[12]

Datek hired smart people. They included Sheldon Maschler, who opened Datek's trading operation in downtown New York in 1987, 17-year-old Jeff Citron, and a young programming genius named Joshua Levine.[13]

Citron and Levine developed a software program called Watcher that allowed day traders to exploit the weakness in SOES: because SOES orders were executed immediately, those who executed those trades had a significant time advantage over those whose orders did not execute immediately. Datek traders could buy stocks at a lower price than the competition and sell them seconds later at a higher price.

For example, suppose the public market for Disney was a bid (offer to buy) at $24.25, and a $24.38 ask (offer to sell). Someone trading on an ECN might see a lower offer to sell—say, at $24.25—which might enable the trader to buy that stock at $24.25 on the ECN and sell it seconds later—at, say, $24.31—on a public exchange. The key is that the order would get executed almost immediately on the ECN, whereas simply posting an order to buy at $24.25 through a market maker would have taken much longer to execute. It's likely the prices would have changed in the seconds it took to execute and the order may not have been executed at all.

It was a perfect one-two punch: the SOES automatic execution advantage combined with Watcher's superior technology. It was a matter of pennies on each trade, but executed on a sufficiently large scale, there was a lot of money to be made.

And scale is what Datek created, by recruiting legions of young traders to use their system.[14] It was against the spirit of the SOES system, which was meant to be used only to execute small orders and specifically banned firms from trading for their own accounts, but it was an enormous success.

Levine's next project was also a success. All Nasdaq trades had to go through a middleman, known as a market maker. Levine observed that many trades on Nasdaq were never executed because buyers and sellers could not find a match. Levine built an ECN that enabled traders to connect directly to each other without going through a market maker.

Levine had circumvented both the Nasdaq market makers and, potentially, the traders on the NYSE floor.

The Island ECN, as it was called, was launched in 1996. It was a hit right from the start, because it had a brilliant matching engine and it had Datek sending huge amounts of orders to it. By the end of 1999, the firm had 40 employees and was trading 6.6 billion shares in a single quarter.[15]

By the late 1990s, these ECNs were cannibalizing Nasdaq's business because they were faster and able to provide better pricing.

ECN share volume in Nasdaq-listed stocks grew rapidly. Other competitors to Island launched in 1997, including Archipelago and RediBook. By the end of 1999, ECNs were handling more than 20 percent of the securities listed on Nasdaq, and almost four percent on the NYSE.[16] By 2000, there were nine ECNs competing for the Nasdaq share volume.[17]

Matt Andresen was named president of Island in 1998. I met him shortly after that.

## *The NYSE vs. the world*

I went back to New York and talked with some of the guys on the floor about my experience with Island and Automated Trading Desk. Take down the NYSE? You're joking, right Bob?

But electronic trading was going to be very serious competition to the "open outcry" floor model that the NYSE had helped pioneer.

It was only the latest in a long series of challenges the NYSE had faced since its founding in 1792. The 1800s were a golden age for stock exchanges: there were about 250 exchanges in the U.S., one in every major city. Over 100 stock exchanges were still functioning in the United States as late as 1900.[18]

In the Midwest, there were the Chicago, St. Louis, Cincinnati, Cleveland, and Minneapolis/St. Paul Exchanges. In the Northeast, there was the Boston Stock Exchange, the Washington Stock Exchange, the Baltimore Stock Exchange, and the Pittsburgh Stock Exchange.

By the mid-1970s, many had merged or gone out of business, because technology made it more efficient to send orders to larger markets (like the NYSE) where it was easier to find other traders to interact with.

By then, there was just a small group left to pick at the crumbs of the NYSE, including the Philadelphia Stock Exchange, the nation's first stock exchange, founded in 1790, and the American Stock Exchange, long considered the poor cousin of the NYSE, the place where companies that couldn't meet the NYSE standards would list. Both Philadelphia and American survived by moving into the hot new trading field of the early 1970s—options—which took off after the establishment of the Chicago Board Options Exchange (CBOE) in 1972.[19]

Still, there were enough trading venues to make life difficult for the average trader: trading was fragmented, and there was plenty of evidence that investors were getting bad executions on their trades. In 1975 Congress directed the SEC to clean up the mess by developing a National Market System (NMS) for securities. A cornerstone of this NMS was to make prices in all markets available to all investors. This sounded perfectly reasonable, but it was a revolutionary idea: Congress wanted all the markets to be linked together. They also wanted to oblige broker-dealers to seek the best prices for their customers' orders.[20]

Hooking everyone together in this way proved to be very difficult, mainly because the exchanges saw no advantage to linking up. Neither did the trading community: what were the advantages to them if the system got smoother, more efficient, and (gads!) cheaper to use? Baruch College professor Robert A. Schwartz put it this way: "Market intermediaries are not interested in getting out of the way of orders—that is, allowing orders to simply interact with each other. It is hard to make much money if you just let orders interact with each other."[21]

In 1978, the Chicago Stock Exchange launched an Intermarket Trading System (ITS) that allowed orders to be sent from one exchange to another, but it would be decades before the exchanges would be effectively linked.

# The NYSE and slow markets

By the late 1970s, even the NYSE had taken notice of the electronic trading revolution. The NYSE had made some concessions to electronic trading. They started a Designated Order Turnaround (DOT) system in 1976 to electronically route smaller orders directly to specialists on the floor.

These were not true electronic orders because the specialist still matched the orders, but it did bypass the floor brokers. It was expanded again in 1984, when the SuperDOT system allowed up to 100,000 share orders to be directly routed to the floor.

Still, the NYSE was not prepared to give up floor-based trading. There was still a lot of information on the floor of the NYSE that could enable traders to get a leg up on trading. And floor trading was still a very profitable business.

Unlike Nasdaq, the NYSE had several potent weapons to keep the upstart ECNs at bay. One was Rule 390, which prevented member firms from trading NYSE-listed stocks away from the floor of a traditional exchange.

"Rule 390 was like the monopoly rule for the NYSE," Baruch College Professor Robert Schwartz told me.[22]

A second potent tool was the "best execution" standard. By their very nature, ECNs were fast, and the NYSE, because it was floor-based, was slow. Very slow. ECNs could execute orders in sub-second intervals, but it was not unusual for the NYSE to take 15 seconds or longer to confirm execution. Being slow doesn't sound like a competitive advantage, but it was for the NYSE.

Brokers were required to adhere to a "best execution" standard that prevented them from accepting trades at prices inferior to those quoted in the National Market System. Those prices were quoted on the NYSE floor. Any ECN trying to compete with NYSE floor prices would have to halt their trading and wait for the NYSE floor to respond to their orders.[23]

That—for a time—partially insulated the NYSE from the ECN onslaught. But the trading world was changing.

In late 1999, the NYSE Board eliminated Rule 390. The SEC, which had been critical of the NYSE's attempts to fend off competition, signalled its approval: "Off-board trading restrictions such as Rule 390 have long been questioned as attempts by exchanges with dominant market shares to prohibit competition from other market centers," the SEC said in a statement approving the rule change.[24]

That opened the door for even more electronic trading from competitors like ECNs.

Serious as that was, the NYSE had even bigger problems: the traditional blue-chip stocks the NYSE was famous for were out of favor. The trading public was obsessed with all things internet-related, and most of those names traded on the Nasdaq.

By 1994, the Nasdaq's annual share trading volume was larger than the NYSE's for the first time.[*25] In 1998, Nasdaq moved to all-electronic trading. By then it was calling itself "the stock market for the next hundred years."[26]

## Maker-taker: let's pay people to trade with us!

Andresen and the folks at Island had yet another novel idea to get more people to trade on their platform: pay them.

This was the start of what is now known as the "maker-taker" model, otherwise called "payment for order flow." Island offered a rebate for

---

* As Brian Nelson noted, "Technically, the NASDAQ was not a national stock exchange from its founding. It was actually a securities marketplace overseen and regulated by the NASD." It became an exchange in 2006.

anyone "making" liquidity—that is, anyone who put an order in their book that added volume, whether to buy or sell. They charged traders for "taking" liquidity—that is they charged anyone who placed a market order that would trade immediately, whether it was to buy or sell. It was, as Sang Lee and Paul Zubulake put it, "an ideal transaction model to attract aggressive participation of high-frequency trading firms."[27]

Island was not the originator of the concept. Bernie Madoff, who ran the Cincinnati Exchange in the 1970s and 1980s, was one of the early pioneers of payment for order flow.*

But Island was particularly effective in utilizing the model.

Paying to have someone come onto your trading platform was controversial then, and still is. But as multiple exchanges and trading venues proliferated, the "maker-taker" model won out over the traditional commission model.

It was not surprising. When you have many different venues to trade in, someone is going to try to get a competitive advantage. Why not offer a rebate? But could you offer a rebate and still fulfill your requirement to offer best execution to your clients? This was not clear—and it still isn't clear today.

## Trading in pennies

The final blow to the profitability of the brokerage industry was the move to trading in pennies.

It had been a long time coming. For 200 years, the minimum price variation for a stock quote was an eighth of a dollar (12.5 cents).

---

* Madoff, who ran Bernie L. Madoff Investment Securities, was later convicted of running one of the largest Ponzi schemes in history.

It was a great business: buy at, say, $25.125, and sell at $25.25. A minimum 12.5 cent spread.

But quoting in fractions was a problem. It was awkward. The world used decimals, not fractions. In mid-1997, the SEC began urging the exchanges to study pricing in decimals. That year, trading switched from quoting in eighths of a dollar increments to sixteenths (6.25 cents), largely at the instigation of Bernie Madoff, who was then a minority owner in the Cincinnati Stock Exchange and helped turn it into the first electronic stock exchange in 1980.[28] After a transition period, trading finally went to penny increments in early 2001.[29]

Once again, it was great news for buyers and sellers of stocks: it dramatically reduced bid-ask spreads, resulting in improved pricing.

Stiff competition from ECNs, lower commissions, pressure from regulators, and now the move to pennies were all beginning to seriously erode the profits of brokerage firms.

It was a boon for their clients, the so-called buy-side. Trading became cheaper and more efficient for institutional firms like Fidelity and Vanguard. It enabled institutions with large orders to divide up their orders to reduce the impact of their trades.

If an institution wanted to buy 100,000 shares of Pfizer, they previously had limited choices: they could bring in a block trader to execute the entire trade at once (risky since it might significantly move Pfizer's price), or they could have their broker on the floor of the NYSE try to execute it throughout the day in smaller pieces (also risky since other brokers were likely to quickly notice that a fellow broker was buying an awful lot of Pfizer throughout the day).

The growth of ECNs made it a lot easier to take that 100,000 share order and slice it up into 1,000 orders of 100 shares each, which could be placed in an ECN and executed throughout the day in a manner that was relatively cheap, relatively less risky (spreads were only 1 cent), and had much less impact on the price of the stock.

By 1999, the term VWAP (Volume Weighted Average Price) had become a standard metric among traders. It was the average price of the stock throughout the day, based on volume and price, and the goal of all institutional traders was to trade at the VWAP. It was a sign, essentially, that the institutional trader was not getting ripped off. [30]

## Electronic trading changed everything

By the end of the 1990s, the Nasdaq and to a lesser extent the NYSE were losing order flow to Island and a raft of other upstarts, and there was panic in the air.

The world of 1999 was completely different from the world of 1989.

It was brought about by a combination of:

- *An exciting new technology (the internet)*, that spawned dozens of new companies, as well as online trading and chat rooms;
- *The explosion of online trading and the proliferation of online brokerage firms* like ETrade, Ameritrade, and others;
- *Improved hardware and software*, that allowed trades to occur in sub-second intervals;
- *New competition for the NYSE and Nasdaq* in the form of Electronic Communication Networks (ECNs), which offered faster trading, improved prices, and new pricing models;
- *U.S. regulators*, who began pushing for more transparency, and eventually, more electronic trading; and
- *A move from trading in eighths of a dollar* in 1996, to sixteenths of a dollar in 1997, and finally, in early 2001, to pennies.

# The victors get bought out

Matt Andresen's prediction that Island would take down the NYSE and they would successfully challenge Nasdaq proved to be only partly true, but it was the part that mattered.

Island's dream of taking down the big boys was cut short by the usual route: the big boys bought them. The dot-com bust in 2000 was devastating to the trading community. Island was spun off from its parent, Datek Online Holdings, in December 2000. In June 2002, Island was bought by its chief competitor, Instinet, for $508 million in stock.[31] The Island operating platform was renamed INET. In December 2005, Nasdaq acquired Instinet for $1.9 billion.[32]

Nasdaq now controlled the company that was, six years earlier, the greatest threat to its existence. It was no coincidence: just seven months before the NYSE had bought Island's rival, Archipelago.

Electronic trading had won. The victors were acquired.

In the end, no one took down the NYSE or Nasdaq. But the world was changing very fast and going into the new millennium these were two still very magnificent, but very wounded, creatures.

As for Datek, arguably the most important player in the electronic trading revolution, an effort to go public in 1998 fizzled due to a sea of regulatory issues. Its day trading unit, Datek Securities, was sold to Heartland Securities in March 1998. It paid a $6.3 million fine in 2002 to settle a raft of securities fraud charges. Sheldon Maschler, Jeff Citron and others separately paid over $70 million in 2003 for allegedly fraudulent use of SOES from 1993 to 2001.[33]

Datek Online, the brokerage firm that evolved out of the day trading unit, was sold to Bain and a consortium of private investors in 2000, and was subsequently sold to Ameritrade in 2002. Ameritrade paid a hefty price of $1.29 billion—about $600 million more than analysts' initial valuation.[34]

Ameritrade realized what the trading community had long known: online traders traded a lot more than everyone else. Joe Moglia, Ameritrade's CEO, said that Datek's clients did 20 to 25 trades per account a year, compared with just ten or so at Ameritrade.

Overnight, the Datek deal turned Ameritrade into the largest online brokerage firm in the U.S., as measured by equity trades per day.[35]

## The founders move on

The founders of this revolution all went on to other careers. Matt Andresen was named chief operating officer when Instinet acquired Island, then became co-CEO of Citadel Derivatives Group, and is now CEO of Headlands Technologies, a global quantitative proprietary trading firm.

Chris Concannon, the kid I met standing in the hallway at 50 Broad Street, went on to a long and illustrious career at Instinet, Nasdaq, Virtu Financial, BATS Global Markets, and CBOE Global Markets. In 2019 he became President and Chief Operating Officer of MarketAxess.

In July 2007, Automated Trading Desk (ATD) was sold to Citigroup for $680 million.[36] Steve Swanson, whom I had met in Charleston, became global co-head of electronic trading for equities. It was part of a major move by Citigroup to expand its stock trading activities and it seemed like a triumphant transaction, because by then ATD was executing six percent of the volume on both the NYSE and Nasdaq. But the deal could not have come at a worse time for all parties involved.

Of the $680 million, $102.6 million was in cash. To pay for the rest, Citi issued about 11.17 million shares, the value of which plummeted several months later as the Great Financial Crisis took hold.

Swanson left Citi/ATD in 2010 and has been involved with several startups in New York and South Carolina.[37]

Harvey Houtkin, the original SOES bandit, did not survive the dot-com bust in 2000, when so many of the day trading army he helped create went under. In 2001 he was fined and suspended from trading, and All-Tech was closed.

Regardless, when he died in 2008, *The Wall Street Journal* called Houtkin the "Father of Day-Trading."[38]

He would have been honored.

## *The start of a different quest*

What did it all mean? Looking back, my obsession with traders—and the quest for the Wizard of Oz—was misplaced; a product of the fact that I was spending most of my time on the floor of the NYSE with, well, traders.

I thought understanding active trading was the way to understand wealth accumulation. I thought traders could give me insight into how to trade and make money by doing it actively—by moving in and out of stocks. I thought this was the way to wealth.

But it wasn't. What I learned hanging out with traders was the mental attributes that make for a successful trader. That was valuable insight into how Wall Street works, but it didn't have anything to do with helping CNBC viewers get wealthy in the long term.

And that's what interested me. Fortunately, by then I had met a small group of people who, between 1994 and 2000, had produced a half-dozen books that profoundly influenced me and helped erase my quest to find the Wizard of Oz, and end my obsession with people who traded the markets all day.

It began with a brief phone call with Jack Bogle, the founder of Vanguard.

## CHAPTER 10

# *Lessons from Jack Bogle,*
# *and Other Masters*

═══

I N 1997, just as I was becoming On-Air Stocks Editor, I had a telephone conversation with Jack Bogle, the founder of Vanguard.

That conversation would end up changing my life.

## *How I became a Bogle convert*

Jack was by then already an investing legend. He had founded Vanguard more than 20 years before and had created the first indexed mutual fund in 1976. Due to health issues, he had relinquished his role as CEO of Vanguard in 1996.

CNBC had been in the regular habit of having investing "superstars" like Bill Miller from Legg Mason, Bill Gross from Pimco, or Jim Rogers on the air. It made sense: let the people who had been successful share their tips with the rest of us.

Bogle, in our brief conversation, reminded me that these "superstar" investors were very rare creatures, and that most people never outperformed their benchmarks. He left the distinct impression that CNBC was spending too much time building up these "superstars" and not enough time emphasizing sound investment principles, like long-term buy-and-hold, and the power of owning index funds. He reiterated that most actively managed funds' fees were too high and that any outperformance they might generate was usually destroyed by the high fees. His tone was cordial, but not overly warm.

Still, the impact of the conversation was such that I did two things. First, I opened a Vanguard account for my wife, who was a real estate agent. She put that first money into the Vanguard Real Estate Index Fund, a passively managed fund of the biggest real estate companies. She also put money into Vanguard Explorer, a highly regarded actively managed fund. My personal foray into index investing—and low-cost active management—had begun.

I also started paying much more attention to Bogle's investment precepts. Bogle may have been famous among a small group of low-cost converts in 1997, but most of the investing public ignored him. Even he admitted that much of the investing community viewed him as a "fringe fanatic."[1]

The truth was, many investors wanted excitement and action, and active managers were happy to oblige. Who wanted boring old "buy and hold?"

People wanted to buy high-priced, speculative tech stocks. Everyone had an online trading account. People swapped news on the latest hot chat room for stock tips.

Who wanted to bother figuring out whether they were being overcharged a few percentage points by greedy mutual funds, or if commissions were stupidly high?

Invest in an index fund? What kind of loser does that? We're all going to get rich owning Netscape!

The irony is that Bogle's buy and hold approach would have delivered superb returns in the 1990s. The market in the mid-1990s was on a tear:

the S&P 500 was up 34 percent in 1995, 20 percent in 1996, 31 percent in 1997, and 26 percent in 1998.

Bogle stuck to his guns. By then, he had been sticking to them for a very long time.

## The birth of Vanguard

From the day it began operation on May 1, 1975, Vanguard Group was modeled differently from other fund families. It was organized as a mutual company owned by the funds it managed; in other words, the company was and is owned by its customers.[2]

One of Vanguard's earliest products proved to be the most historic: the first index mutual fund, the First Index Investment Trust, which began operation on August 31, 1976.[3] Modeled on the S&P 500, Bogle piggybacked on earlier work done by William Fouse and John McQuown of Wells Fargo Bank, who had attempted to develop an index account for the pension fund of Samsonite Corporation based initially on an equal-weighted index of all the equities on the New York Stock Exchange.[4]

Bogle estimated that the cost of the fund would be about 0.5 percent per year: 0.3 percent in operating expenses and 0.2 percent in transaction costs. Given that the total cost for the average mutual fund was then about 2.0 percent, Bogle believed investors would be enthusiastic about investing in a fund that right from the outset would provide returns 1.5 percentage points above the average mutual fund.

He was mistaken. The mutual fund industry correctly saw that Bogle was attacking its core business. They were not enthusiastic about buying into the concept.

Bogle was hopeful he would raise $150 million for his index fund, but the initial offering raised only $11.4 million.[5]

# *Indexing is championed by the academic community, but few others*

By then, the academic community was aware that index funds outperformed actively traded mutual funds of all stripes. In 1973, Princeton professor Burton Malkiel published *A Random Walk Down Wall Street*, drawing on earlier academic research that showed that stocks tend to follow a random path, that prior price movements were not indicative of future trends, and that it was not possible to outperform the market unless more risk was assumed.

In the conclusion to his book, Malkiel suggested that what the public really needed was an investible index fund: "What we need is a no-load, minimum-management fee mutual fund that simply buys the hundreds of stocks making up the broad stock-market averages and does no trading from security to security in an attempt to catch the winners."[6]

In 1975, Charles Ellis, a managing partner at Greenwich Associates, wrote an article, "The Loser's Game," in the *Financial Analysts Journal* in which he noted that 85 percent of professionally managed funds had underperformed the S&P 500 during the past ten years.

His conclusion: "money management has become a Loser's Game."[7]

Other academics also weighed in. Paul Samuelson, a revered figure in financial circles and the first American to win the Nobel Memorial Prize in Economic Sciences in 1970, had published a paper in 1974 critical of the investment community, entitled "Challenge to Judgment." It argued "that some large foundation set up an in-house portfolio that tracks the S&P 500 Index—if only for the purpose of setting up a naïve model against which their in-house gunslingers can measure their prowess."[8]

Bogle later acknowledged that Samuelson's paper "caught me at the perfect moment."[9]

Not many other people paid much attention to the academics, or to Bogle. "For a long time, my preaching fell on deaf ears," he lamented.[10]

But Vanguard, under Bogle's leadership, kept pushing forward. In 1986, they did for bonds what they had done for equities and introduced an indexed bond fund, the Vanguard Bond Market Fund. That year, Vanguard's stock index fund approached $500 million in assets under management.[11]

In 1987, Vanguard introduced its second index fund, the Extended Market Portfolio, which attempted to replicate the entire U.S. stock market, not just the 75 percent of the market represented by the S&P 500 fund.

In 1994, Bogle published *Bogle on Mutual Funds: New Perspectives for the Intelligent Investor*, in which he argued the case for index funds over high-fee active management and showed that those high costs had an adverse impact on long-term returns.

In 1995, Bogle felt he had enough data to clearly demonstrate the outperformance of an index strategy. He published a pamphlet, "The Triumph of Indexing," in which he declared, "Index funds have come of age."[12]

In 1997, the year I had that conversation with him, Bogle published a paper that described the history of his efforts to develop an investible index fund, wherein he outlined what he called his "simple theory that underlies index investing:"

Investors as a group cannot outperform the market, because they are the market. And from that theory flows the reality: Investors as a group must underperform the market, because the costs of participation—largely operating expenses, advisory fees, and portfolio transaction costs—constitute a direct deduction from the market's return. Unlike actively managed funds, an index fund pays no advisory fees and limits portfolio turnover, thus holding these costs to minimal levels. And therein lies its advantage. That, essentially, is all you need to know to understand why index funds must provide superior long-term returns.[13]

Between 1997 and 2000, several books were published that reinforced Bogle's worldview, and indexing and the corrosive effects of high costs in the mutual fund industry began to get wider coverage. Charles Ellis had expanded his original essay into a book-length treatise, *Winning the Loser's Game*, that printed its third edition in 1998. Two years before, Burton Malkiel's *A Random Walk Down Wall Street* had come out in its sixth edition, and Wharton Professor Jeremy Siegel had explained the superiority of long-term stock investing over all other investments in *Stocks for the Long Run* in 1994.

Bogle's second book, *Common Sense on Mutual Funds: New Imperatives for the Intelligent Investor*, came out in 1999 and immediately became an investment classic. Bogle made an extended case for low-cost investing and took on all the objections to it, in 445 pages of mind-numbing detail.

On the very first page, he laid down his investment thesis, almost exactly as he had done with me a couple of years before: "Investing for the long term is central to the achievement of optimal returns by investors. Unfortunately, the principle of investing for the long term... is honored more in the breach than in the observance by most mutual fund managers and shareholders."[14]

In a 1999 interview on CNBC with my colleague Tyler Mathisen that was done as the book was coming out, Bogle ridiculed the idea of trying to pick baskets of stocks that would consistently outperform the market:

I don't think there is such a thing as a stock pickers market. All investors are picking all stocks. To the extent an index fund owns all stocks, it's a sort of contradiction in terms, because if a good stock picker takes all the good stocks, the other half of the market will be owned by the bad stock pickers who pick the bad stocks. It all comes down to a sum of one.[15]

More than 20 years later, the basic precepts that Bogle laid down in *Common Sense on Mutual Funds* are still accurate.

# *Bogle's precepts*

## THERE ARE FOUR COMPONENTS TO INVESTING: RETURN, RISK, COST, AND TIME

Return is how much you expect to earn. Risk is how much you can afford to lose "without excessive damage to your pocketbook or your psyche."[16] Cost is the expenses you are incurring that eat into your return, including fees, commissions and taxes. Time is the length of your investment horizon; with a longer time horizon, you can afford to take more risk.[17]

## STOCKS PROVIDE HIGHER RETURNS THAN BONDS OVER THE LONG TERM

While there are some periods where bonds have done better, over the long term stocks provide superior returns, which makes sense because the risk of owning stocks is higher.

Bogle drew heavily on the research of Wharton professor Jeremy Siegel, whose book *Stocks for the Long Run* had demonstrated that stocks provided real annual returns (corrected for inflation) of 6.7 percent a year since 1802. Long-term government bonds, by contrast, returned only 3.4 percent a year, and considerably less than that in the modern era after 1926.[18]

In the fifth (2014) edition of his book, Siegel updated the results, but the overall trend was still the same, even through the dot-com bust, 9/11, and the Great Financial Crisis of 2008–2009.

**Stocks vs. bonds, 1802–2012 (average yearly return, inflation-adjusted)[19]**

| Stocks | 6.6% |
|---|---|
| Government bonds | 3.6% |
| Government bills | 2.7% |
| Gold | 0.7% |

Even in the modern period, from 1926 through 2012, stocks grew at a 6.4 percent rate per year.[20]

The longer the time period, the better chance stocks would outperform. For 10-year horizons, stocks beat bonds 80 percent of the time, for 20-year horizons, about 90 percent of the time, and over 30-year horizons, nearly 100 percent of the time.[21]

The advantage of bonds is that they moderate the short-term volatility of stocks. As a starting point, Bogle recommended an allocation of two-thirds stocks, one-third bonds, but admitted that could easily be changed depending on the investor's risk profile.[22]

## FOCUS ON THE LONG TERM, BECAUSE THE SHORT TERM IS TOO VOLATILE

Bogle noted that the S&P 500 had produced real (inflation-adjusted) returns of seven percent annually since 1926 (when the S&P 500 was created), but two-thirds of the time (one standard deviation) the market will average returns of plus or minus 20 percentage points of that. In other words, about two-thirds of the time the market will range between up 27 percent (seven percent plus 20) or down 13 percent (seven percent minus 20) from the prior year. The other one-third of the time it can go outside those ranges.[23] That is a very wide variation from year to year!

## FOCUS ON REAL (INFLATION-ADJUSTED) RETURNS, NOT NOMINAL (NON-INFLATION ADJUSTED) RETURNS

While inflation-adjusted returns for stocks (the S&P 500) have averaged about seven percent annually since 1926, there were periods of high inflation that were very damaging. From 1961 to 1981, inflation hit an annual rate of seven percent. Nominal (not inflation-adjusted) returns were 6.6 percent annually during this period, but inflation-adjusted returns were –0.4 percent.[24] Yikes!*[25]

## THE RATE OF RETURN ON STOCKS IS DETERMINED BY THREE VARIABLES

These three variables are the dividend yield at the time of investment, the expected rate of growth in earnings, and the change in the price-earnings ratio during the period of investment.[26]

The first two are based on fundamentals, the third (the P/E ratio) has a "speculative" component. Bogle described that speculative component as "a barometer of investor sentiment. Investors pay more for earnings when their expectations are high, and less when they lose faith in the future."†[27]

This offers an explanation for why stocks go up or down based on a rational, fundamental basis (dividends and earnings growth) as well as an irrational basis: the P/E ratio reflects the extent of investor enthusiasm for stocks in the form of how much investors are willing to pay for a dollar of

---

* Still, over very long periods of time, stocks do well even against inflation. Jeremy Siegel noted: "Stocks turn out to be great *long-term* hedge against inflation even though they are often poor *short-term* hedges." And in the 2014 edition of *Stocks for the Long Run*, Siegel noted: "Stocks represent real assets, which in the long run appreciate at the same rate as inflation, so that real stock returns are not adversely affected by changes in the price level." And "Over time stocks, in contrast to bonds, compensate investors for higher inflation." The key is the ability to raise prices in line with costs, which enables companies to maintain profit margins. Stocks go south during periods of high inflation when companies don't have pricing power or sudden spikes in inflation leave companies unable to raise prices fast enough.

† Bogle was able to demonstrate that this fairly simple method of valuation produced very accurate results, at least over 10-year intervals. For example, the period from 1990 to 1999 produced an initial yield of 3.1 percent, an average annual earnings growth of 7.7 percent, and a 6.7 percentage point increase in the price/earnings ratio, for a calculated return of 17.5 percent. The actual (nominal) return was 18.2 percent. The return for the period 2000-mid 2009 was -2.5 percent, the actual return was -2.0 percent. Close enough on both counts!

earnings. At extremes it implies investors are likely acting irrationally (but we already knew they are capable of doing that).

## WHEN PROPERLY ADJUSTED FOR RISK, INVESTMENT STYLES TEND TO PRODUCE CONSISTENT AVERAGE RETURNS

Large-cap growth stocks are more volatile than large-cap value stocks, so by definition they are riskier to own and should offer higher returns. However, over long periods of time, the risk-adjusted returns are similar, whether you are talking about small, mid-, or large market cap funds, or value, growth or blended funds.[28]

## HIGH COSTS DESTROY RETURNS

Whether it is high fees, high trading costs, or high sales loads, those costs eat into returns. This holds for broad funds that own the whole market, but it also holds regardless of what size (small, medium, or large market cap), style (value or growth), or sector (technology, industrials, health care) of the market you invest in. Always choose low cost.[29] If you need investment advice, pay close attention to the cost of that advice.

## KEEP COSTS LOW BY OWNING INDEX FUNDS, OR AT LEAST LOW-COST ACTIVELY MANAGED FUNDS

Actively managed funds charge higher fees (including front-end charges) that erode outperformance, so index investors earn a higher rate of return. As for the hopes of any consistent outperformance from active management, Bogle concluded, as Burton Malkiel had, that the skill of portfolio managers was largely a matter of luck, that gross returns (before costs) did indeed exhibit elements of a "random walk:" "For managers in the aggregate, the heavy handicap of cost is simply too heavy to overcome."[30] Bogle was never against active management, but believed it was rare to find one that outpaced the market without taking on too much risk.[*][31]

## VERY SMALL DIFFERENCES IN RETURNS MAKE A BIG DIFFERENCE WHEN COMPOUNDED OVER DECADES

Take a fund that charged a 1.7 percent expense ratio versus a low-cost fund that charged 0.6 percent. Assuming an 11.1 percent (nominal) rate of return, Bogle showed how a $10,000 investment in 10 years grew to $25,900 in the high-cost fund, but $30,800 in the low-cost fund. After 25 years, the high-cost fund grew to $108,300 but the low-cost fund grew to $166,200.[†][32] The low-cost fund had nearly 60 percent more than the high-cost fund!

Bogle said this illustrated both the magic and the tyranny of compounding: "Small differences in compound interest lead to increasing, and finally staggering, differences in capital accumulation… A higher-cost investment loses ever more ground to a lower-cost investment as years roll on, leading to sharply lower capital accumulation."[33]

---

* Bogle wrote, "I believe that it is possible for some managers to apply judgment born of wisdom and experience in the selection of a stock portfolio that will outpace the market over time, without assuming undue risk. Those managers will be extraordinarily difficult to identify in advance, but investors have a fighting chance to win if they seek experienced professionals with individuality, training, experience, savvy, determination, contrarianism (or sheer iconoclasm), and a capacity for hard work."

† Bogle went to great lengths to explain that most investors never get that roughly seven percent real rate of return. He estimated that the average operating expenses for a professional advisor was 1.5 percent of assets, and additional transaction costs were an additional 0.5 percent, which means instead of a seven percent real rate of return, the average investor has a five percent real rate of return. Put differently, costs consume about 28 percent of the real return (two percent for costs divided by seven percent real return – 28 percent). That is a lot to pay for advice! Bogle was writing in 1999, when costs were somewhat higher, but the thrust of his argument is still valid.

## DON'T TRY TO TIME THE MARKETS

Investors who try to move money into and out of the stock market have to be right twice: once when they put money in, and again when they remove it. Bogle said: "After nearly 50 years in this business, I do not know of anybody who has done it successfully and consistently. I don't even *know* anybody who knows anybody who has done it successfully and consistently."[34]

## DON'T CHURN YOUR PORTFOLIO

Bogle bemoaned the fact that investors of all types traded too much, insisting that "Impulse is your enemy."[35]

In a later edition of *Common Sense on Mutual Funds*, he noted that during the stock market crash of 2007 to 2009, the turnover rate for the average fund was 36 percent, meaning the average shareholder held a fund for just about three years.[36]

Bogle noted about professional fund managers: "The evidence that I have seen shows that the overwhelming majority of funds would earn higher returns each year if they simply held their portfolios static at the beginning of the year and took no action whatsoever during the ensuing 12 months."[37]

## DON'T OVERRATE PAST FUND PERFORMANCE

Bogle said: "There is no way under the sun to forecast a fund's future absolute returns based on its past records."[38]

Funds that outperform eventually revert to the mean.[*39] This was true

---

* Bogle wrote, "Reversion toward the market mean is the dominant factor in long-term mutual fund returns."

regardless of investing by size (small, medium, or large market cap), style (value or growth), sectors (technology, industrials, health care), or geographic area (U.S. vs. international). Over long periods of time, all tend to revert to a mean.[40]

## BEWARE OF FOLLOWING INVESTING STARS

Bogle said: "These superstars are more like comets: they brighten the firmament for a moment in time, only to burn out and vanish into the dark universe."[41]

## OWNING FEWER FUNDS IS BETTER THAN OWNING A LOT OF FUNDS

Even in 1999, Bogle bemoaned the nearly infinite variety of mutual fund investments. He made a case for owning a single balanced fund (65/35 stocks/bonds) and said it could capture 97 percent of total market returns.*[42] Having too many funds (Bogle believed no more than four or five were necessary) would result in over-diversification: the total portfolio would come to resemble an index fund, but would likely incur higher costs.

## STAY THE COURSE

Once you understand your risk tolerance and have selected a small number of indexed or low-cost actively managed funds, don't do anything else. "I am absolutely persuaded that investors' emotions, such as greed

---

* The competition—actively managed balanced funds—did not even come close, mostly because of the higher costs: they captured only 76 percent of the total return. It was the same with owning a single broad equity fund (like the Wilshire 5000): it outperformed a broad actively managed fund in the same period.

and fear, exuberance and hope—if translated into rash actions—can be every bit as destructive to investment performance as inferior returns."[43]

## STAY INVESTED

Short term, the biggest risk in the market is price volatility, but long term the biggest risk is not being invested at all.[44]

# Bogle's Legacy

These investment precepts are well-known to most in the investment community, but few investors adhere to them. It's not surprising: Bogle often blasted the investment community for having interests that are not in line with their clients. There's simply too much money in high-priced active management.

Because of that, he never tired of reiterating what he stood for. He was, in a sense, in a constant state of war with the investment community.

Any telephone conversation I ever had with him was like a conversation with one of my college professors about a point I had made in an essay for his or her class. It was a friendly conversation, but he never passed up the opportunity to reiterate what he stood for and correct me if he thought I was deviating from the core teachings.

I will describe the impact Bogle had on my own investment portfolio in Chapter 20, "Trading Hits and Misses."

After Bogle relinquished his role as CEO of Vanguard in 1996, he spent much of his time after that as president of the Bogle Financial Markets Research Center.

He wrote many more books, notably *The Little Book of Common Sense Investing* in 2007 and his final book, *Stay the Course: The Story of Vanguard and the Index Revolution*, in 2019.

But *Common Sense on Mutual Funds* was his masterpiece. Syndicated columnist Scott Burns called it "the definitive book on index-fund investing."[45] Jane Bryant Quinn called it "the finest book on mutual funds ever written."[46] ConsumerAffairs.com listed it #2 on their list of "15 Business Books that could actually Help Make You Rich."[47]

Bogle never deviated from his central theme of indexing and low-cost investing, and there was no reason to do so. Time had proven him correct.

Surprisingly, he was skeptical of Exchange-Traded Funds (ETFs) because he felt it encouraged too much trading and discouraged long-term investing.[48] Fortunately, John Brennan, who served as Bogle's successor as CEO from 1996 to 2008, ignored those concerns and Vanguard subsequently became a powerhouse in ETFs as well.

Jack Bogle passed away in 2019. From those humble beginnings in 1975, Vanguard now has 30 million investors in about 170 countries and manages over $7 trillion in assets. True to its original purpose, it is still the low-cost leader in the investment industry, with an average expense ratio of 0.09 percent.[49]

And that first Vanguard index fund? Now known as the Vanguard 500 Index Fund, it had $658 billion in assets under management as of March 2021.[50]

As for the battle over indexing, a battle Bogle spent his life fighting, today there is over $12 trillion indexed to the S&P 500, and much more if closet indexers are included (those who try to replicate the index but do not pay Standard & Poor's for a license to be an official tracker fund) representing about 30 percent of the entire S&P 500.

Now, *that* is the triumph of indexing.

Unfortunately, Bogle would not be of any help to me in my next ordeal, an event which would bring the downtown financial community to its knees.

## CHAPTER 11

# 9/11 and the Search for Calm

═══

A T 8:48 AM on September 11, 2001, I was in a car on the West Side Highway, just north of the World Trade Center, heading to work at the NYSE. I was reading *The Wall Street Journal*.

Suddenly, in the middle of the road, my driver skidded to a halt.

"Look, look!" the driver yelled, pointing at the North Tower.

The top of the building was on fire. All the traffic on the highway had stopped.

I got out of the car. A man was standing outside his own car, staring at the building.

"What happened?" I said to him.

"A plane just flew into the building." He didn't look at me. He just kept staring at the building. His mouth was open.

I called the Assignment Desk at CNBC. Nick Dunn answered, and we agreed I should go right to the building.

I ran toward the building, and got to Church and Dey Street, near the Century 21 department store, around 9 AM. Fire engines were everywhere.

People were out in the street, staring at the North Tower. No one was sure what was going on.

CNBC was reporting that S&P futures had dropped a very modest 5 points, about a half percent, and within minutes had started rising as some speculated it was an accident.

At 9:03 AM, the second plane hit the South Tower.

The top of the South Tower exploded in a fireball. After the initial explosion, the next sound was almost as loud: the tens of thousands of people who had by that time gathered at the scene all gasped at once.

That was followed by a few seconds of silence, as everyone stared at the fireball, trying to take in what was happening. But there wasn't much time to think. A few seconds later, metal from the explosion began dropping in the street around us, making very loud "clang" sounds.

That is when all hell broke loose. Thousands of people turned and ran as fast as they could.

I ran too. The crowd around me broke and ran east toward Broadway. There was such a panic some tripped and fell to the ground. Others ran over them, right onto their backs, slamming them back down. One man who had been slammed down had gravel embedded in the side of his face from the impact and was bleeding. Another woman grabbed a man by his shirt collar, trying to lift him off the ground, only for him to get slammed back down again.

With metal landing with loud "clangs" around us, this was not a crowd you were going to stop and ask to calm down.

We got to Broadway, and many collapsed onto the sidewalk, panting and crying. I ran to the NYSE and entered the building.

In the minutes following the second plane hitting the South Tower, S&P futures had dropped another 25 points, nearly three percent. Then, just as it had done right after the first plane hit, it rallied again. The futures session ended at 9:15 AM down about 15 points, a loss of a little more than one percent.

We were not sure if the markets were going to reopen.

"People here are a bit shell-shocked," I told my colleague Mark Haines when I got on the air, "But Dick Grasso, the head of the New York Stock Exchange, just got off the loudspeaker system, saying the opening would be delayed. We don't know exactly when, but there will be a delayed open. They will give a 10-minute notice prior to the open."

Mark Haines, in one of his finest hours, perfectly defined the problem Grasso and other market leaders were grappling with.

"It's a conundrum of sorts," Mark said to me. "On the one hand, great damage has been done to buildings in which many people who work on Wall Street work, and we have no idea how many of them have been hurt or perhaps even lost their lives. On that score, one would think that the New York Stock Exchange would decide not to trade today. On the other hand, the other part of that equation is, the New York Stock Exchange officials may well feel that to not trade today would be to admit that the terrorists, if terrorists they be, have won a round and perhaps they do not want to do that. So it would not be an easy decision either way, so I suppose the suspension or postponement would be the best thing to do at the moment."

He was right. We didn't know it then, but the markets would not open that day, or for the rest of the week.

At 9:37 AM, a third plane crashed into the Pentagon.

At 9:39 AM, the South Tower collapsed. The North Tower collapsed at 10:28 AM.

The NYSE, which was several blocks away, shook both times as the buildings fell.

At 10 AM, as I was coming down the stairs from my office onto the floor, I saw my colleague Maria Bartiromo coming into the NYSE moments after the towers fell. She was covered in white soot. I hugged her and almost cried.

At 11:30 AM, Maria, my producer Bianna Golodryga, and I emerged from the NYSE onto a deserted Broad Street. White ash was floating in the air, along with still-burning paper.

At 2 PM, I walked alone onto the Trade Center site, deserted, the collapsed buildings still burning. It was disorienting: it took me a few minutes to figure out where I was, because everything was destroyed.

I stood on a steel girder and phoned in a report to my colleague Bill Griffeth:

Bill, I'm standing on the corner of what was Liberty and Trinity Place, I am on the site of what is left of the South Tower. As I left you about an hour ago I came down the street and came onto the site along with the first wave of EMS people that were allowed in. There is an enormous pile, a 30-foot pile of wreckage, that is now being scaled by emergency EMS people looking for any signs of life. Firemen are trying to scale this small mountain of rubble here. It is rather difficult to breathe, there is still enormous amounts of smoke and debris in the air, and there is also an unstable building to the left of me, and the firemen are not getting near it, and they are a bit concerned about it, I see them not even getting near it, just sort of staring at it. The sky is dark, although the sun has come out as I have been walking around outside the Exchange, which is about a quarter mile away. On the site itself, which is where I am standing, it is black all around us. You cannot even see the sun right now. So Bill, you can imagine, they are just climbing, like ants climbing the side of a mountain, looking for any signs of life, obviously a rather grim business. Within the last 20 to 25 minutes was the first time they were letting people on top of the mountain. There are big, 30-foot-tall twisted curtains of the side of the Trade Center that is standing here like some surreal scene in front of us and I think they are a little concerned about the stability of that as well, they won't let us anywhere near it. I am 75 feet away right now, watching a large number of firemen just starting to scale the side of this mountain of rubble looking for people.

At 7 PM, Maria and I were sitting in NYSE chief Dick Grasso's office on the sixth floor. Grasso was grim but calm. When would the exchange reopen? He wasn't sure but was in touch with everyone in Washington and the goal was to open as quickly as was safely possible.

At 8 PM, I walked with Maria to the subway stop at Canal Street. The streets were almost empty. Many had walked over the East River bridges to get home.

Just getting the markets open would take a heroic effort. Many of the brokerage firms had offices in the World Trade Center and would not be able to easily reopen.

## Getting the NYSE reopened

With the NYSE closed, I spent the next several days mostly on the West Side Highway, where an army of reporters had camped just outside of the Trade Center site.

I spent the weekend at the Soho Grand Hotel, just north of Canal Street. The NYPD had indicated that they would be restricting access to anything below Canal Street, and I wanted to make sure I could get to the NYSE.

The NYSE reopened on Monday, September 17. I was there early, standing outside with NYSE Chairman Richard Grasso as Treasury Secretary Paul O'Neill drove up to help ring the opening bell with firefighters and policemen, led by NYC Police Commissioner Bernie Kerik and Fire Department Commissioner Thomas Von Essen, along with U.S. Senators Hillary Rodham Clinton and Charles Schumer, Mayor Rudy Giuliani, New York Governor George Pataki, and SEC chairman Harvey Pitt.

"I'm very proud to be included in this group, to send the message to the American people that all will be well," O'Neill said.

"The market is ready, the country is ready, we're back to business, don't bet against America because you'll be wrong," Grasso said.

On the floor, the mood was tense but patriotic, and why shouldn't it be?

Warren Buffett had gone on *60 Minutes* saying he would not sell any of his holdings when the market reopened. There had been numerous calls in the week before from investors insisting it was the patriotic duty to buy.

The floor is always especially noisy a few minutes before 9:30 AM, when orders to buy and sell at the open go back and forth among traders, but this day was different. It was going to be one of the heaviest trading days in a long time, likely years, and while the decibel level was high the mood was subdued.

Then, suddenly, everything went quiet. The room went from the collective sound of 4,000 traders talking to each other to complete quiet as two minutes of silence were observed. Members of the New York City police and fire departments, representing the heroes of 9/11, had come on the floor. The entire room sang "God Bless America," and then the police and firefighters, led by all the dignitaries, rang the opening bell.

With that kind of opening, the trading that ensued was anticlimactic. An hour before the markets opened, the Federal Reserve had cut interest rates by a half-point, but it didn't seem to make a difference. The S&P 500 dropped nearly five percent, the Dow seven percent, to the lowest levels in nearly three years. Airlines and aerospace stocks, not surprisingly, got hammered. Defense stocks rose, as did a smattering of consumer names like Merck and Johnson & Johnson.

By the end of the week, the S&P 500 had dropped nearly 12 percent from its pre-9/11 level.

No one cared. The market had been closed almost a week, the longest closure since the Great Depression.

What mattered was that it was open again.

# The aftermath

The next month, on Sunday, October 7, my wife Suzanne and I were in a cotton field outside of Clarksdale, Mississippi. We had just spent three days in Helena, Arkansas, at the King Biscuit Blues Festival. We were driving to New Orleans down a dusty side road, surrounded by cotton fields.

My cell phone rang. It was my boss, Bruno Cohen, the Executive Vice President of News at CNBC.

"Where are you?" he asked.

"I'm in a cotton field in Mississippi."

Long pause. "What are you doing in a cotton field in Mississippi?"

I started to explain, but he cut me off.

"Never mind. The United States has invaded Afghanistan. I need you to get back immediately. How far are you from an airport?"

"Well, we are driving to New Orleans. It's probably six hours."

"Six *hours?* Isn't there anything closer?"

"I guess we could drive to Memphis. It's less than two hours."

"Do that. Go immediately and get the first plane back to New York. I want everyone in place on Monday morning."

We drove to Memphis, where we were the subject of intense scrutiny at the airport because we had made a last-minute reservation and asked to be seated up front so we could make a connecting flight.

The security people eyed us suspiciously. Security had been dramatically beefed up at every airport in the United States in the month since 9/11.

You made a last-minute reservation, and you want to sit up front?

I explained who I was and where I was going, but it didn't matter. They went through every inch of our luggage, and we barely made it on the plane.

The next day, Monday, October 8, proved to be anticlimactic. The S&P dropped less than one percent.

On the surface, it looked like the market was recovering. Within a month, the S&P was back to its level prior to 9/11. The government had announced billions of dollars in stimulus. The Federal Reserve had cut interest rates dramatically.

But all was not right.

## The preacher disappears

For many years, every Friday afternoon near the close of trading, a preacher appeared in front of the New York Stock Exchange and delivered a sermon. The traders, eager to get to their Friday night fun, scurried past him, and while a few curious tourists stopped to listen and take pictures, most of them ignored him as well.

The preacher didn't seem to mind. He preached with the same fervor, regardless of whether there was a crowd of tourists gawking at him, or there was no one but the statue of Washington in front of Congress Hall listening.

One Friday, he failed to appear. He didn't show up the next Friday, either.

Or the next. Finally, after a month, he reappeared. I don't know why, but I was relieved to see him.

I had never spoken to him, but I walked up to him and said it was good to see him again, and where had he been?

He smiled, looked down at his shoes, and said, "I needed to get away."

## The worst winter ever

That winter after 9/11, we all needed to get away, but most of us couldn't.

By the spring of 2002, the markets were fried, and so were a lot of us at the NYSE.

The winter of 2001/2002 was spent mostly trying to handicap the effects of 9/11. Unfortunately, the market was dealing with more than just that disaster. There was the lingering effect of the dot-com collapse, with many companies like Pets.com filing for bankruptcy. There was the collapse of Enron, which filed for bankruptcy in December 2001, and other accounting scandals, including the bankruptcy of WorldCom in July 2002.

The summer of 2002 was a disaster: the S&P 500 dropped more than 20 percent in June and July.

The psychological scars were much worse, particularly among those of us who lived and worked downtown, which was only just surfacing. Everyone who worked in the Financial District had friends who had died in the disaster. I had several, including Bill Meehan, the chief market analyst at Cantor Fitzgerald, a raconteur with a fondness for Hawaiian shirts and with whom I spent many wonderful after-hours in restaurants, talking about life and markets.

There was also the grim reality of working downtown. The Financial District had morphed into a partly-closed armed camp. It was almost impossible to cross Canal Street, the dividing line between Soho/Chinatown and the Financial District, unless you were a resident or worked at the NYSE or on Wall Street. Police were everywhere, on every corner. No one knew if another attack was coming.

There was, above all, the smoldering pit of the World Trade Center. The smoke would not disappear for many months, and could be seen for miles around. Worst was the smell: the acrid odor of still-burning paper, office furniture, and building materials.

And yet, everyone at the NYSE came to work. They were, like me, anxious and many were depressed. But we all came to work.

But work had changed. The lingering effect of the dot-com bust, combined with the 9/11 disaster and the ensuing recession, had caused the wild enthusiasm for technology and internet stocks to evaporate.

CNBC responded by increasing coverage of real estate (my old beat), as well as what was then considered to be an unorthodox asset class: collectibles of any kind.

We covered car collecting. Wine collecting. Comic book collecting. Baseball card collecting. It was a lot of fun, since collectibles usually involved individuals with particular obsessions that make for great human interest stories (I should know: I collect 1960s rock posters).

What was not in favor, in that long winter of 2001/2002, was the stock market. That was a disaster for me, since I was On-Air Stocks Editor.

The stock market, of course, did not go away. But the atmosphere changed. Wild speculation was out. What replaced it was a calm, sober atmosphere that was focused on fundamentals, not speculation.

I changed too. That winter, I went into a tailspin.

## *Burning out*

It wasn't the first time I had burnt out.

Nine years earlier, in the summer of 1993, I found myself in a cardiologist's office at Pennsylvania Hospital in Philadelphia with chest pains. I had been at CNBC for three years, working very hard.

While the cardiologist was examining me, we chatted about what I was doing. We were a startup, essentially, and it was fun but very demanding. I told him I loved the job and I thought I had a good shot at making a career out of being a broadcast journalist.

"You're not going to make it," the cardiologist said, in a flat voice.

I was stunned. How did he come up with this conclusion? Was I dying? Was I in imminent danger of a heart attack?

"You're not having a heart attack, but if you keep this up you're going to have serious problems," he said.

He showed me how my chest muscles had contracted over my chest. They were rock hard. He said this was a sign of continuous stress.

I was still young, he explained, but the ongoing stress was going to start causing much more serious problems than just chest pains in the future.

"You need to change what you've been doing," he said. Take more time off, get more exercise. And, most importantly, *calm down.*

I took his advice, mostly. I did join a gym and take more time off.

The calming down part was not so easy. Edgy people like me have a love/hate relationship with our edginess: we love the adrenaline that it forces through us because it aids the creative process. We hate the resulting anxiety because it creates mental distractions and physical manifestations that we know are bad in the long run.

This time, in the dark days after 9/11, was very different than 1993. I had made a decision years before to stay on as the stocks reporter because I loved the job: I loved being with the traders on the floor, I loved talking to the CEOs and celebrities who were ringing the opening and closing bells, I loved CNBC, and I loved going out with the traders at night.

I loved the whole damn job, and when my friends at CNBC started taking lucrative jobs at other firms as we became more popular in the 1990s, I decided to stay put.

Now, I wasn't so sure.

Had I screwed up? Had I stayed too long at the party? Should I have been more realistic and concluded, "It's been 12 great years, but it's time to move on"?

I wasn't the only one asking these questions. The NYSE floor was changing too. Off-exchange trading was increasing dramatically as electronic trading was increasing. New competitors in the form of Electronic Communication Networks (ECNs) were springing up. Technology stocks may have gone into a decline, but technology was rapidly changing the way trading had traditionally been conducted.

With profits eroding, many decided to leave the business.

I watched many friends go into a tailspin—much worse than a midlife crisis—when they quit or lost their prestigious job on the NYSE floor, or as an analyst or strategist at some Wall Street firm. They had trouble leaving because being a trader on the floor or a Wall Street analyst or strategist is what they were—if they weren't that, they ceased to exist.

Of course, that is ridiculous. We are more than our jobs. We are husbands, wives, sons, daughters, friends, lovers, and just plain human beings.

That's true, but for many of us what we do defines what we are.

I needed more clarity on what I should be doing. I needed to find a way to get clarity.

One night, in early 2002, I was sitting in a small room on the second floor of a nondescript building in midtown Manhattan.

I was going to learn to meditate.

## Hearing Seventh Avenue

I had had an interest in Buddhism for nearly 20 years, after I had monitored a course in college on Buddhism and physics taught by Fritjof Capra, a Berkeley physics professor who had written a book, *The Tao of Physics: An Exploration of the Parallels Between Modern Physics and Eastern Mysticism*, in 1974. I had seen people meditating, knew of the benefits, but had never bothered to try it myself.

The room contained about 15 people: a dozen women, myself, and two or three other men. We were sitting cross-legged on the floor on yoga mats. I noticed most of the women had that nearly perfect spinal curvature associated with people who meditated and did yoga. It annoyed me. The other two or three men, like me, slouched and appeared uncomfortable.

This is typical of my behavior: even in a benign setting, I am scanning the room, checking out the competition.

The instructor, a man, looked at me looking at everyone, and began talking.

"This is a guided meditation," he began. "The purpose is to introduce you to the basic precepts of meditation. This is *not* a competition," he said, looking at me. "Don't worry about whether you are sitting properly or not, or what anyone else is doing. Just try to be comfortable. Now, listen to the sound of my voice."

He started by telling us to concentrate on our breathing. This was, he said, a trick to keep us focused on the present. He spoke about becoming aware of how we think. We are always thinking about where we are going next, what we are going to do this evening, this weekend, next year. We are perpetual day planners. But learning to be in the moment will make us more aware of ourselves and our surroundings. This will make us calmer, more peaceful, less frantic.

This continued for an hour. His voice was low, drone-like and just loud enough to be heard.

At the end of the hour, I was intensely aware of the hissing in the steam pipes. I left the class, and for the first time I saw Seventh Avenue.

I don't mean it was the first time I was on Seventh Avenue. I mean I experienced it in a completely different way than I had in the past.

Most of the time, New Yorkers walk down the street oblivious to everything around them. The goal is to get where you are going as quickly as possible. People who walk too slowly or block your way are annoying.

It was an unusually warm late-winter night, and the windows in the bars and restaurants were open. I could hear the conversations through the windows.

More than that: I was *aware* of the conversations.

I was aware of everything: the temperature, the colors, the other people around me.

*This is what they're always talking about,* I thought. *This is what all that "be here now" stuff I heard about in the 1970s is all about.*

It was all true. I was hyper-aware I was walking down Seventh Avenue. I wasn't trying to get everyone out of my way, I wasn't thinking of what I was going to do tomorrow, or on the weekend.

I was just there. The flood of awareness. This is what they are talking about. Now I understand.

I was so moved that I stayed with the classes for many months. It was a Tibetan center, but with no religious or ideological overlay.

They gently insisted that I also do yoga classes, largely to help make it easier to meditate. I moved briefly into a single-room occupancy hotel down the street so I didn't have to go back to my apartment in Fort Lee, New Jersey every night.

I got better at meditating. The hard part was resisting the urge to let my mind wander, which they called "monkey mind."

Pull yourself back into the present, don't fight yourself. Be gentle. When thoughts arose, take note of the thoughts, but let them drift off. I became adept at recognizing thoughts I had—a problem at work, or what I was doing that weekend—but then flicking the thoughts away, like flies. I was getting better at controlling the flood of thoughts in my head.

## What meditation did for me

About six months after I started meditating, I felt much better. I felt calmer, more in control. I stopped agonizing about the stock market and my job. What had changed, I realized, was not me but the circumstances around me. The world had changed, but I had not. I was still working under an old paradigm. There was nothing wrong with me—the markets didn't fall apart through my neglect.

I needed to change too. I needed to be more accepting of the changed circumstances and adjust my life accordingly.

What I didn't need to do was quit my job, because all the things I liked about it were still there.

As for the stock market, it didn't bottom until October 9 of 2002, but by then I had stopped wringing my hands about it.

Meditation helped me get through a lot of other crises, including the Great Financial Crisis that would descend on us six years later. I find I get into trouble whenever I stop mediating for long periods, and do better when I get back into it.

I haven't attained a Buddha-like state and never will, but at least I am aware of the source of my weirdness.

It doesn't mean I stopped caring or obsessing about the stock market. One of my oldest friends at CNBC, Ellen Egeth, once called me up to ask me how I was doing. I started off by describing what had happened in the S&P 500 that day.

"I didn't ask how the S&P was doing, I asked how you were doing," she said.

I thought about it, and sheepishly said, "Some days, I can't tell the difference."

I need to keep meditating.

No amount of meditating was going to help the NYSE trading floor. It was going through one of the greatest transformations it had ever seen, and it would re-emerge at the end of the 2000s a very different animal.

# CHAPTER 12

# *"They Killed It": the NYSE 2000–2008*

═══

I knew it was bad when the NYSE fired its barber.

Gerardo Gentilella, known to all as Jerry the Barber, had been cutting hair at the NYSE for 43 years. He was a no-nonsense guy.

You did not tell Jerry how to ply his craft. He cut your hair the way he wanted to.

The one time he cut my hair, in 2000, I suggested the way I wanted it cut.

He stood in front of me and stared at me sternly.

"Bob, you don't tell me how to cut hair, OK?"

Even though he cut everyone's hair the same way, he was a beloved figure, and I often stopped in to say hello.

In August, 2006, shortly after the NYSE went public, Jerry was fired.

The day he was fired, he called me in tears. He didn't understand why he was being fired, and so abruptly. Was it that bad? Could I do anything?

This was emblematic of everything that was happening at the NYSE. It was all going to hell.

I did something I had rarely done before: I stuck my nose into the NYSE's business.

I called upstairs.

*For cryin' out loud, this does not look good for the NYSE. You're firing the old barber who's going to retire in a couple of years anyhow? All the guys on the floor are talking about it. Why don't you keep him on for a few months, past Christmas, and then let him go in January?*

The answer was no.

# Happy Birthday, NYSE

On May 17, 2006, a cake was wheeled onto the trading floor. It was the NYSE's 214th birthday.

Instead of cheering, traders booed.

It wasn't surprising. For the traders on the floor, there wasn't much to cheer about. The last few years had been ugly.

Two months earlier, on March 8, 2006, the NYSE had gone public, ending 214 years of independence. No longer was the NYSE a private club, owned by its members. Now, it had sold shares to the public: the vast, unwashed public, who had no interest in the cherished open outcry trading business that had made the NYSE floor so famous.

No wonder the floor was booing.

The year before, my boss—Mark Hoffman, the president of CNBC— had made a sizeable investment in our floor reporting by installing a wireless camera on the NYSE floor. Dubbed the "Eye on the Floor," it was a dream come true for me. For the prior eight years, I had been mostly confined to a fixed camera that was mounted on a platform above one of the stairwells.

Now I could stick my microphone into anyone's face. Traders. Bell ringers. Celebrities.

I could go anywhere on the floor.

Except the floor was falling apart.

"They killed it, Bob," one trader said to me at the time. "They killed a beautiful business."

## Ghosts on the floor

By 2006, the floor was starting to thin out. Old-timers, angry at the slow descent of the floor business, would tell stories about the outrageous characters that had eaten, drank, and traded with them in the decades before.

There were a lot of ghosts on that floor.

One of them was Jackie Kennedy's father.

I was standing in the middle of the floor in October 2005 when Jerry Daly walked up to say hello.

Jerry was a retired floor member who had come in for the annual meeting of the Buttonwood Club, which was founded in 1962 as a society of senior members of the NYSE.

"You know where you're standing, Bob? That's where Black Jack Bouvier stood. He was a drinker, and a son-of-a-bitch."

By all accounts, John Vernou Bouvier III, known as "Black Jack Bouvier," was indeed a drinker, and a son-of-a-bitch.

His great-grandfather, Michel Charles Bouvier, had migrated from France to Philadelphia in 1815, became a cabinetmaker, made a fortune in real estate, and had several sons who became successful financiers on Wall Street. Jack's father bought an estate in the trendy hamlet of East Hampton, Long Island, where Jack was born in 1891.

Jack went to all the right schools, including Yale, where his classmates included Cole Porter, Dean Acheson (later Secretary of State), and Averell Harriman (later Governor of New York and political mentor to John

F. Kennedy), but he showed little interest in anything but clothes and women, acquiring the title "Black Jack" from his perpetually tanned skin and extravagant lifestyle.

After being discharged from the Army in 1919, Jack used his family money to buy a seat on the New York Stock Exchange for about $115,000, a small fortune back then.[1]

His first child, Jacqueline (Jackie) Lee Bouvier, was born on July 28, 1929, mere weeks before the stock market crash that began the Great Depression. The crash almost ruined Bouvier, who responded by increasing his alcohol consumption.[2]

By all accounts, his stockbroking career on and off the floor was unassuming. He had squandered most of the Bouvier fortune by the time his daughter Jackie married John F. Kennedy in 1953.

Bouvier was present at the wedding but did not walk his beloved daughter down the aisle. By one account, Bouvier was drunk, and Jackie had her stepfather, Hugh Dudley Auchincloss, Jr., walk her down the aisle. By other accounts, Bouvier was prevented from walking Jackie down the aisle by his ex-wife Janet, who had divorced him in 1940 and who now reportedly had schemed to keep him drinking and delay him from attending the wedding.[3]

Regardless, Bouvier spent the last several years of his life in a four-bedroom apartment on the Upper East Side of Manhattan, drinking alone.[4]

Two years later, in January 1955, he gave up the NYSE seat he had held for more than 30 years. Even that had declined in value. In 1929, seats on the exchange had sold for over $600,000—Bouvier sold his for $90,000.[5]

He died two years after that, of liver cancer.

———————

A lot of cherished traditions were dying in those years, including the many pranks traders pulled on themselves—and their guests.

One of the oldest was "dusting" a visitor's shoes, where a trader would sneak up to someone with a bottle of baby powder and secretly sprinkle it on the visitor's shoes. When they noticed their shoes were white, they would try to shake off the powder by shaking their feet, which caused a cloud of white powder to rise up, an excuse for the traders to begin shouting "heya heya!"

It was a silly ritual performed on hundreds of guests through the years, including Edward G. Robinson and Kirk Douglas.

Not even that silly ritual survived. "We dusted some shoes today," Daly told me on that day in 2005, "but we did it quietly so the floor officials wouldn't see us."

## An ocean of troubles: scandals, competition, going public

What a difference a few years had made.

At the start of 2000, the NYSE floor was revered as the temple of capitalism. By 2006 a series of disasters—some of them self-inflicted—had wounded the NYSE to the point where the floor had become a dark and fearful place. Disagreements broke into shouting matches. Friendships came under stress, and many ended in acrimony.

When I came to the NYSE floor on a full-time basis in 1997, 4,000 traders (almost all men) were on the floor. Eighty percent of all the volume traded occurred on the trading floor.

By 2006, more than half of the traders were gone and the NYSE's floor share of total trading volume was dropping fast.

The decay had begun even as I arrived in 1997. As we saw in Chapter 9, upstart alternative trading systems, known as Electronic Communication

Networks (ECNs) with funny names like Island, Instinet and Archipelago had sprung up, bypassing Nasdaq and even the NYSE. That year, the SEC had passed Order Handling Rules that required that bids and offers from ECNs be included in the national market quotes. In 1998, the SEC formally recognized the role of ECNs in Regulation Automated Trading System (Reg ATS).

The upstarts had invaded the country club. That was the beginning of the end for the Nasdaq, and eventually the NYSE, monopoly.

As pressure mounted to move more rapidly toward electronic trading, the very idea of who should run the NYSE began to change.

From the outset, the NYSE was owned by its members—specifically the roughly 1,300 people who held seats that entitled them to trade on the floor.

It also entitled them to make their own rules and to self-govern.

These members were more than a little reluctant to embrace electronic trading. They were downright hostile to the idea.

And with good reason. The profitability of the business had plummeted as trading had gone from increments of an eighth of a dollar in 1996 to a sixteenth of a dollar in 1997 and then finally to a penny spread in 2000. Now there were proposals to allow trading to be conducted easily off the floor.

The math was very simple:

lower profitability + loss of trading volume = death of the trading business

But the pressure to change was unrelenting, and finally the very model under which the NYSE was governed came under attack.

Instead of a mutual society owned by its members, the NYSE would have to go public and become a shareholder-owned entity.

In the heady days of 2000, that was still a bridge too far. The NYSE and Nasdaq did their best to control information and order flow. NYSE

Chairman Richard Grasso was an early supporter of the concept of going public and was revered by traders for his defense of floor-based trading, but the big brokerage firms, along with the SEC, were demanding more change. By 2000, the NYSE was allowing bigger blocks to trade electronically, without floor trader involvement.[6] Even specialist firms began merging at a breakneck pace.

The years from 2000 through 2007 brought one blow after another. The dot-com bust had led to the evaporation of day traders and a loss of confidence in Wall Street. The 9/11 disaster had caused the death of many friends, and turned downtown into a smoking pit for over a year.

That wasn't the end of it. Market share continued to erode as competition kept springing up. In 2000, the Pacific Stock Exchange and Archipelago Holdings created a new all-electronic national securities exchange, Archipelago Exchange.[7] Archipelago itself went public in 2004.

In September 2003, the floor lost its biggest supporter.

Grasso was forced to resign over controversy on a deferred compensation package said to be worth almost $140 million.

It was an ugly time to be on the NYSE floor. Grasso had been the floor's biggest defender, it's "guardian angel."[8] Bitter disputes erupted between those who supported Grasso and those who felt he had become a liability and an embarrassment.

The floor had little to feel superior about. The reputation of the specialists also suffered under investigations for securities fraud. The NYSE settled those allegations for $241 million in 2004. The SEC found that some specialist firms had been trading ahead of customer orders.[9]

Reputational decline. Market share decline. Profit decline.

By 2005, prices for NYSE seats had dropped by half since 2000.[10]

In 2004, Grasso was replaced by John Thain, who had been president and co-chief operating officer of Goldman Sachs from 1999 to 2004, and who was far less interested in protecting the floor trading business.

Thain didn't waste any time. On April 21, 2005, he announced plans to merge with Archipelago and become a public, for-profit company.

The NYSE Group began trading on March 8, 2006. The 1,366 seat owners received 80,177 shares of the newly public company, plus $300,000 in cash and $70,571 in dividends. The stock ended the day up 25 percent.*[11]

At least the seatholders made some money. It was one of the only pieces of good news in many years.

One month later, the NYSE Luncheon Club on the seventh floor, an exclusive enclave where Andrew Carnegie and the entire elite of Wall Street had dined for decades, was closed. UBS's Art Cashin, whom I described in Chapter 4 and who was a beloved fixture at the bar for many years, decamped with his many friends to Bobby Van's steakhouse across the street.

Four months later, Jerry the Barber was fired.

## *New rules: Reg NMS*

Going public was the least of the problems for the dwindling population left on the floor.

In 2005 the SEC codified years of debate over electronic trading into Regulation National Market System (Reg NMS), the biggest overhaul of market trading in decades.

The final Rule filing ran for a mind-numbing 523 pages, but the essence could be summed up in three rules.[12]

---

* The NYSE's rival, Nasdaq, had embarked on the road to going public far earlier. The National Association of Securities Dealers (NASD), which controlled Nasdaq, had begun selling restricted shares of Nasdaq in a private placement in 2000. Shares began trading on the OTC Bulletin Board (over the counter) in 2002. On February 9, 2005, NASDAQ listed its shares on NASDAQ following an offering of secondary shares.

First, the "Order Protection Rule" required trading centers to execute trades at the best possible prices. Trades could not be executed at inferior prices on other trading centers.

Second, the "Access Rule" required that quotations must be displayed uniformly across all trading platforms, with no discrimination against other trading centers.

Third, the "Sub-Penny Rule" prohibited traders from posting bids or offers in increments smaller than a penny in stocks priced above $1.00 a share.

It doesn't sound like much, but these rules gave formal sanction to trends that had been going on for several years.

With the Order Protection Rule, the SEC had decreed that price was the priority—it required that an order be executed at the best possible price. This sounded perfectly reasonable. Who wants to have their order executed at an inferior price? Speed of execution would also be a priority, but only after the best price.

Unfortunately, this created a perverse incentive for the trading community. To succeed in this new world, market makers needed to 1) have a lot of liquidity (money to quote and execute bids and offers), and 2) be fast, really fast, because whoever offered those best prices first got their trades executed ahead of everyone else.

That new emphasis on speed proved to be a disaster for the NYSE floor model, which was, due to the human interaction, a "slow" market. Reg NMS allowed market participants to bypass any market that was not executing orders in an automated fashion. The NYSE attempted to maintain a "hybrid" model whereby they could shift into "slow" mode to do a floor-based auction when they need to, and then resume electronic trading.

In practice, because markets and exchanges were now linked, the fast (electronic) trading created an automated cross-market execution system, and the NYSE floor was often left out when it decided to "go slow."[13]

# What Reg NMS created

It wasn't intentional, but Reg NMS led to the spectacular growth of what came to be known as "high-frequency trading," or trading stocks at very high speeds.

The practice of trading stocks at high speeds, or more specifically the practice of attempting to trade at speeds faster than everyone else is doing, has been around since the birth of trading. Any time new technological advancements have occurred (turnpikes, telegraph, telephone, pneumatic tubes, the computer), traders have exploited these technologies to trade faster.[14]

Computerized trading has existed since the 1980s, but rapid advances in hardware and particularly software (algorithms to execute trades) led to execution times going from several seconds to milliseconds.

Reg NMS came along at the perfect time for these high-frequency traders. They now had hardware and software to engage in a massive arms race.

One effect: since speed was of the essence, there was a mad dash to put the high-speed servers of these traders as close as physically possible to the Nasdaq and NYSE servers (a process known as colocation).

A second effect: the rapid growth of multiple trading platforms, whether they were Alternative Trading Systems (dark pools, which were private trading venues, or Electronic Communication Networks) or exchanges.

An enormous food fight erupted in the trading community, which was trying to figure out who the winners and losers would be.

In theory, this was a positive for the average retail trader. Many argued that it made trading more efficient, since the liquidity these new market makers provided narrowed the bid-ask spread.[15]

Others argued that the SEC had made a big mistake trying to micro-manage the trading markets. In the old days, market makers (like the specialists on the NYSE floor) had informational advantages, but they also had duties and responsibilities to the public and could be fined or even banned if they failed in those responsibilities. In this new scheme, the market makers on the floor had given way to new market makers, who had far fewer obligations.[16]

The debate reached a crescendo in 2014 when Michael Lewis published *Flash Boys: A Wall Street Revolt*, where he argued that high-frequency trading had evolved into a method to front-run orders. This involved placing trades ahead of other investors by, for example, buying before other investors when the market makers believed a stock or the market was about to rise and then selling at the higher price.

In the most widely quoted accusation, Lewis claimed that the market had become "rigged."[17]

It created a huge brouhaha, even forcing then-SEC Chair Mary Jo White to tell a House of Representatives hearing that the market "was not rigged" and that there was no evidence yet that high-frequency traders were doing anything illegal.[18]

She was right. Even if some bad actors did emerge that tried to bend the rules by front running or other abuses of the system, the SEC had approved the practice of trading fast, in and out of multiple venues.

It was a new world, sanctioned by the SEC.

The markets of the future would be fast, competitive, and fragmented.

## *Trying to keep up*

The NYSE tried hard to keep up. First it attempted to modernize the trading floor to recognize the new reality of electronic trading.

The NYSE Hybrid Market initiative was designed to combine auction-based trading with electronic trading. Customers had a choice of electronic trading or using the floor. The idea was the floor would offer "the opportunity for price improvement over the published best bid and offer," the NYSE explained.[19]

Switching to a "slow" floor mode to enable price improvement was a noble attempt to preserve the floor auction process. Unfortunately, switching to that "slow" mode during periods of high volatility only caused traders to bypass the floor and go straight to electronic trading.

Next, it continued a furious pace of mergers. If there was less money to be made in the stock trading business per transaction, the only solution was to scale up and get bigger.

In April 2007, the NYSE merged with Euronext, the largest stock exchange in Europe. The European exchanges were facing very similar pressures to merge because their monopolies were being lifted as well.

In October 2008, at the height of the Great Financial Crisis, NYSE Euronext (as the new company was called) bought the AMEX, the third largest options market.

An attempt to merge Deutsche Börse with NYSE Euronext was blocked by the European Union in 2012, which said the merger would have created a "near monopoly" in European trading.[20] The following year, Intercontinental Exchange bought NYSE Euronext and spun off Euronext.

*What did it all amount to?*

By 2010, a crazy-quilt pattern of stock markets (more than a dozen) were operating in the United States, along with nearly 40 dark pools.

Institutional traders quickly realized that in the new world of high-frequency trading, the mere act of expressing interest in buying and selling stock on an exchange could move the price even before the institution executed a trade.

Dark pools were not, for the most part, accessible to the public. It enabled large blocks of stock to trade privately without requiring the institution to publicly display its intent. The size of the trade is not revealed until after the trade is filled.

This furthered the main goal of institutional traders: to get the best prices at the lowest cost with the least impact on the markets.

What wasn't clear was whether the average retail trader was getting a better deal. While dark pools are required to execute at the best bid and offer, the fact that so much trading occurs off the exchanges means retail investors usually cannot interact with that institutional order flow. We don't know if better prices would have been available had everyone been trading on exchanges that were "lit," that is, where everyone could clearly see what was available to buy or sell.

Regardless: Reg NMS had fully opened the door to electronic trading, along with all the consequences.

One of those consequences was the slow death spiral of the floor.

## Electronic trading wins out

Surveying the changes in 2010, the SEC Historical Society noted that as late as 2005, the NYSE handled 79.1 percent of its own listed shares.

By 2009, it was down to 25.1 percent.

By 2010, high-frequency traders accounted for an estimated 50 percent of the market.[21]

They not only were the biggest traders, but they also became the specialists.

In October 2008, the NYSE replaced specialists with a new term, Designated Market Makers (DMMs). On the surface, there wasn't much of a difference. The new DMMs were still required to maintain fair and orderly markets. They could run fully electronic trading platforms but also intervene manually to trade, which the NYSE called a "high touch" model.[22]

But there was one big change that was not obvious: the NYSE made sure the DMMs would not be able to see incoming orders as they had in the past, which had given them an information advantage. The DMM's algorithm would no longer receive a "look" at those orders. "This ensures that an intermediary will not see orders first, and that DMMs compete as a market participant," the NYSE said in a press release.[23]

Regardless, in the new world, the DMMs had become one of many market makers, even if they were still preeminent.

The old financial firms, which had dominated trading and the floor for decades, were losing interest fast. The cost of maintaining and updating the technology to trade as fast and efficiently as possible was so high, it drove the old financial firms out of the business.

It was the price that had to be paid to improve market efficiency. The NYSE had completed an enormous transformation in seven years, from a privately owned to a for-profit publicly owned company. The NYSE floor was in decline and far less influential than it had been seven years earlier, but its parent, NYSE Euronext, was now in many more businesses, including European equities.

The brokerage firms who worked on the floor with the specialists also saw their business shrink. Why bother using a floor broker when a trader could push a button and have his order executed electronically in a sub-second interval? Even if the floor broker had a chance to explain they could (often) provide price improvement, the ease of use and rapid confirmation proved to be irresistible, particularly to a younger cohort who had had no experience dealing with the old floor-based model.

Today the DMMs left on the floor are all market makers that came to prominence during the growth of high-speed trading: Citadel, GTS, and Virtu.

## *Down for traders, but up for investors*

The slow descent of the floor was occurring at an up-moment for investors.

By mid-2007, the markets, along with real estate, had made a dramatic recovery: the S&P 500 was up almost 90 percent from the bottom in September 2002.

Regardless, the NYSE was still the emotional heart of Wall Street. When the markets had big down days, news trucks still lined up outside the NYSE.

There hadn't been a lot of big down days in the last five years: the trend was almost straight up.

That was about to change. In the next year, the news trucks would be outside the NYSE a lot more.

## CHAPTER 13

# *The Financial Crisis and the Death of the Baby Boomers*

$$\equiv\equiv\equiv$$

I was standing outside the New York Stock Exchange in April 2009 when I realized that a good portion of my entire generation was screwed.

I mean the baby boomers: that giant rat in the belly of the boa constrictor of 20th-century America, 40 million strong.

Homo Economicus—the perfectly rational investor who always bought low and sold high—had already proven to be a fiction, but 2009 was the year I finally became a true believer in behavioral economics. This branch of economics purported to show how people really behaved, particularly in a crisis, and not how they were supposed to behave.

And the way they behaved was the opposite of rational behavior: many wet the bed and sold at or near the bottom.

# Assigning blame for the Great Financial Crisis

The S&P 500 declined roughly 50 percent from its peak in October 2007 to its bottom in March 2009, and the value of a typical existing home declined roughly 30 percent from mid-2006 to mid-2009.[1]

My generation had never seen anything like it. Hell, *no one* had seen anything like it since the Great Depression.

There were many causes of the Financial Crisis: excess consumer borrowing (particularly in real estate), easy credit conditions caused by the Federal Reserve, predatory lending practices, an explosion in subprime lending, deregulation, the development of complex financial instruments which were poorly understood, and—perhaps most importantly—the inability of market participants to correctly price risk.

The primary conceit, that somehow the development of increasingly complex financial instruments could spread out risk in a way that was perfectly measurable and containable, proved to be a disastrous assumption. In the aftermath it was clear that increasing complexity did not decrease risk, it *increased* risk.

Regardless of the cause, the effect was qualitatively different than the prior market meltdown I had also witnessed. The dot-com meltdown of 2000 was caused primarily by speculation in internet-related stocks. It had contributed to a mild recession and a fair amount of howling from a small group that was heavily invested in technology stocks.

The 2008 meltdown involved the entire stock market as well as real estate, an asset class with a far larger ownership base than technology stocks. By 2002, the average baby boomer was in his or her mid-forties, approaching peak income and prime real estate buying years. Some put money into stocks, but as the Federal Reserve lowered rates in 2003 to deal with the recession (partly caused by the 9/11 disaster), the baby boomers rushed to buy property. From 2002 to 2007, boomers bought first homes, second homes, and empty lots.

And who could blame them? The Fed was lowering rates, and mortgage rates followed. Second, and most importantly, there was a proliferation of new mortgage instruments that allowed almost anyone to get a loan. Lending standards were dramatically loosened, first by reducing the 80 percent loan-to-market ratio that had characterized most mortgage lending until then, and then by granting mortgages to a large group of people that would not have otherwise qualified for a loan.

By January 2006, the National Association of Realtors reported that 43 percent of first-time buyers purchased their homes with no money down; the median down payment was a mere two percent.[2]

Not surprisingly, real estate prices began accelerating at the end of the 1990s: real (inflation-adjusted) home prices increased 130 percent from 1997 to 2006, well beyond inflation and well in excess of growth in median family income.[3]

And then, it all reversed, starting in 2007.

## *Mispricing risk*

Wharton professor Jeremy Siegel, who has chronicled the ups and downs of long-term stock market trends in successive editions of *Stocks for the Long Run*, noted that "the primary cause of the 2008 financial crisis was the rapid growth of subprime mortgages and other real estate securities that found their way into the balance sheets of very large and highly leveraged financial institutions."[4]

The crucial mistake, Siegel notes, was a dramatic mispricing of risk: the belief that default risk could be reduced or eliminated by packaging mortgages from many different localities into a single security. Home prices, after all, had almost never declined in the many decades since World War II and had been on a gradually increasing upward ascent in nominal terms since then. The primary risk was not that prices would drop substantially, but that the borrower would default. But if there was even modest collateral behind the loan, and prices almost never dropped, then it might be possible to reduce default risk by creating a security that incorporated many different mortgage loans from different localities.

This mortgage-backed securities industry grew rapidly in the 1980s and 1990s. What made it more deadly in the 2000s was the explosion in the subprime lending business.

As Siegel explains, this was based on the faulty notion that real estate prices would never go down:

> as long as the real estate behind the mortgage was virtually always going to be worth more than the mortgage, the creditworthiness of the borrower should not be important to the lender. If the borrower defaults, the lender can take over the property and sell it for more than the value of the loan... This assumption provided the impetus for the sale of hundreds of billions of dollars of subprime and other 'nonconventional' mortgages backed by little or no credit documentation as long as the loan was collateralized by a pool of geographically diversified mortgages.[5]

What would have been a perhaps modest real estate drop turned into a much greater systemic issue for the entire economy because Wall Street banks had loaded up on subprime mortgages and sold them to investors. When prices began dropping far more than the models had suggested, outraged investors complained they were not fully warned of the risks, and firms like Bear Stearns had to buy back many of those subprime funds at huge losses.[6]

Lehman Brothers was one of many firms that had borrowed a lot of money to buy subprime mortgages. When lenders stopped lending to the firm, Lehman appealed to the lender of last resort: the Federal Reserve. The Fed had already agreed to guarantee the loans of Bear Stearns as part of its deal to sell the firm to JP Morgan in March 2008, but considerable political pressure against government bailouts meant there was not going to be a rescue of Lehman.

The government's refusal to bail out Lehman Brothers forced Lehman to file for bankruptcy on September 15, 2008. The Dow dropped 508 points that day, its worst decline in seven years. In quick succession, Merrill Lynch was acquired by Bank of America. The next day, the Federal Reserve took over American International Group with $85 billion in debt and equity funding.

## The Federal Reserve steps in

Surveying the wreckage on the floor after the close on September 15, I tried to put a positive spin on the grim news: "There's some optimism down here that there's a little bit less moral hazard because the Fed did finally say no, and there is additional liquidity coming into the system from a number of different sources," I said in my closing bell report.

That proved to be heroically optimistic. The S&P closed at 1,192 that day, down 4.7 percent, and would not bottom until March 6 of the following year, at 683, another 42 percent drop.

In theory, the Fed had unlimited power to lend to any financial institution in a crisis. But the Fed wanted political cover, and so Congress attempted to pass the Troubled Asset Recovery Program (TARP) to provide billions in support to financial institutions.

On September 29, 2008, the House failed to pass the legislation. The Dow Industrials dropped 777 points, a nearly seven percent loss.

Standing on the floor as the market closed that day, it was obvious what the market was saying: there were no alternatives.

"Now you're left with the other do-nothing proposal which is not acceptable to anybody at this point," I said as the markets were closing that day. "And the problem is that the one-bankruptcy-a-day plan is not working, and the one-shotgun-wedding-a-day plan like Citigroup and Wachovia, how many of those are you going to arrange at this point? That's why traders down here are somewhat in a state of despair."*[7]

The House reversed itself and passed the legislation four days later.

Ultimately, the Fed managed to stabilize the economy by pumping massive amounts of money into the system. Fed Chairman Ben Bernanke was a student of the Great Depression, and in his book, *Essays on the Great Depression*, made it clear that he sided with the group who felt that the Depression was caused by 1) adherence to the gold standard, and 2) a dramatic contraction in the money supply that reduced demand for goods.[8]

The Federal Reserve shared a good deal of the blame for prolonging the Great Depression, since it failed to adequately expand the money supply, even after the United States went off a strict gold standard in 1932, and failed to act as a lender of last resort during the banking panics that started in 1930 and extended into 1933.[9]

Ben Bernanke was not going to make that mistake. Long before the crisis, Bernanke, in a 2002 speech honoring Milton Friedman on his 90th birthday, apologized for the Fed's role in prolonging the Depression: "Regarding the Great Depression ... we did it. We're very sorry. ... We won't do it again."[10]

---

* Citigroup had agreed to buy Wachovia's retail banking operations in an FDIC-brokered deal that day. On October 3, Wells Fargo agreed to merge with Wachovia in an all-stock transaction that did not require government involvement.

# Lessons from the Crisis

Here are two important things I learned from this disaster:

1. *Don't put too much faith in expert opinion:* My faith in "experts" was already low after witnessing the Asian Financial Crisis in 1997 and the dot-com blowup in 2000. It got lower still after 2008. In the run-up to the Great Financial Crisis, it was amazing how long everyone was in denial. On July 27, 2007, I was quoting bulls who were arguing that "housing and credit issues do not represent systemic risk to the global markets." They were wrong.

2. *Bold, swift action works better than slow, indecisive action, or no action at all:* The Federal Reserve stepped in to make sure banks would not fail, and that finally stopped the free fall, though the economic fallout continued for many years.

Jeremy Siegel had noted that the end of the Depression came when both the United Kingdom and the United States ended the gold standard and began pumping money into their economies: "The lessons from history: liquidity and easy credit feed the stock market, and the ability of the central banks to provide liquidity at will is a critical plus for stock values."[11]

In a sense, John Maynard Keynes' interventionist ideas won out. Keynes had argued decades before that in a true crisis (like the Great Depression), just regulating the money supply—the Federal Reserve's main tool—is not enough. Government needs to step in, prop up critical institutions and spend a lot of money. That is precisely what Congress, the president and the Federal Reserve under Ben Bernanke did.

Global central banks in Europe and Japan also began buying up assets, and governments ran big deficits. Dire warnings that all this stimulus would ignite massive inflation were ignored.

Just how long this extraordinary stimulus should be continued is not clear. It is still being debated. This remains one of the risks for financial markets in the future.

Many questions from the Great Financial Crisis remain unanswered: Is the financial sector too big to fail? (The answer so far is yes.) How much regulation should banks be subject to? What limitations should be placed on financial innovations that may pose a systemic risk to the markets? How active should the Fed be in deflating asset bubbles? How much scrutiny and regulation should *nonbanks* or *shadow banks* that have become important players in the financial markets receive?

Stick around a few more years and we will have better answers to these questions. And, most likely, we will kill a few other Wall Street chestnuts along the way.

That brings me to a third lesson I learned living through this crisis: that I should have paid much closer attention to the work of the behavioral economists. It wasn't that I didn't know about them: I was familiar with their work by the late 1990s.

But knowing about an idea is different than understanding and accepting it.

My failure to truly understand and accept the findings of the behavioral economists earlier cost me dearly.


## *Forget buy low, sell high*

You can talk until you're blue in the face about subprime mortgages, the shadow banking system, excessive leverage in financial markets, and Federal Reserve policy, but it all comes down to how people react to losses, particularly after they have what they believe are significant gains.

They panic. They sell. They sell at any price.

In the Great Financial Crisis, they sold stocks *and* real estate. By the end of 2009, the average household was 20 percent poorer than just a couple of years before. The net worth of U.S. households and nonprofit organizations went from $69 trillion in 2007 to a trough of $55 trillion in 2009.[12]

I was reporting all this from the floor of the New York Stock Exchange, in real time. The market bottomed on March 6, 2009, but neither I nor anyone else knew that was the bottom.

February 2009 was a fearful time. An attempt to bottom had been made in October 2008 (October is a traditional month for market bottoms), but it had failed. Then, in November we hit new lows.

Here's what I wrote in my Trader Talk blog on February 17, 2009: "We are at the November lows, the hope now is that a final capitulation in second half earnings will create a new low that may be the bottom we need."

But it got worse. You could smell the despair in my March 5 blog, the day before the market bottomed: "We go down for three weeks and cannot even sustain a two-day rally."

The next day—March 6, 2009—was the bottom, but my blog sounded even more desperate: "Traders believe a rally is coming, but few are positioned to take advantage of it. Why? Because no one can afford to be wrong ... 'no one can afford another 10 percent down month,' as one analyst said."

A week later, the main index for bank stocks—which had dropped 80 percent from its 2007 highs—was up 45 percent from the previous week on positive comments from bank executives.

But investors did not believe a bottom was in. I noted several weeks later that the data firm Trimtabs was reporting there were continuing outflows from equity funds in February and March.

By the last day of July that year, I was still lamenting that investors were continuing to put money into bond mutual funds but not stock funds:

Despite a notable stock market rally in the first six months of the year (the S&P was up 1.8 percent, but up 36 percent from the March lows), there were OUTFLOWS from stock mutual funds in the first half of the year of $396 million (there's about $4 trillion in stock funds). What's up? Retail investors have been so badly burned by stocks last year that they still do not trust the market; they are showing classic signs of risk aversion by continuing to put money into bonds.

And that's what troubled me most. I had seen my share of modest panics, but I still believed that investors were fundamentally rational in their economic decision-making. Not here: "Buy low, sell high" went out the window. Waves of investors sold stocks at their lows, and many, particularly those of my generation, never returned.

That was when I started paying a lot more attention to behavioral economics.*

## Behavioral economics and the Great Financial Crisis

Even during the Financial Crisis, most investors realized the U.S. economy was not going to zero.

They knew this intellectually, but they didn't act like it emotionally.

---

* The terms "behavioral economics" and "behavioral finance" are often used interchangeably. However, according to Investopedia, behavioral economics is "the study of psychology as it relates to the economic decision-making processes of individuals and institutions." It studies how people maximize utility (satisfaction) and profit. Behavioral finance, on the other hand, is a subfield of behavioral economics, and "proposes that psychological influences and biases affect the financial behaviors of investors and financial practitioners." It is "an area of study focused on how psychological influences can affect market outcomes." To avoid confusion, I am sticking with the term "behavioral economics" when describing aspects of both fields.

It was one thing to have been an early seller in late 2007 or early 2008, but if you had held on until early 2009, selling with the S&P 500 down 50 percent from its historic high made no sense.

But that isn't what happened. Selling of mutual funds *increased* going into the end of 2008, near the market bottom.[13] Panicked investors, seeing the market decline of 50 percent approaching, couldn't stand the pain anymore.

Never mind that this 50 percent *loss* was largely illusory because investors had bought at various times over the years at much lower levels than the legendary market *top*. Most investors had a hard time calculating gains and losses.

Why do people act like this? Much of the *ex post facto* analysis centered around behavioral economics, which emphasized how people really behaved under economic stress, not how they were supposed to behave.

Way back in 1979, Daniel Kahneman and Amos Tversky noted that human beings did not act the way classical economics said they would act. They were not necessarily rational actors. They did not buy low and sell high, for example. They often did the opposite.[14]

Kahneman and Tversky proposed an alternative model, which they called *prospect theory*. Their key insight was that individuals don't experience gains and losses in the same way. Under classical theories, if someone gained $1,000, the pleasure they feel should be equal to the pain they would feel if they lost $1,000.

That's not what Kahneman and Tversky found. They found that the pain of a loss is greater than the pleasure from a gain.

This effect, which came to be known as *loss aversion*, became one of the cornerstones of behavioral economics.

In later years, Kahneman and Tversky even attempted to quantify how much stronger the loss was. They found that the fear of an emotional loss was more than twice as powerful as an emotional gain.[15]

That went a long way toward explaining why so many people who may have been inclined to sell early in the Great Financial Crisis did not do so: the pain of taking the loss was too great, at least until it became unbearable. People will hold their losers for a long time. The opposite is also true: people will tend to sell their winners to lock in gains.

## *You have more biases than you think*

Over the years, Kahneman and many others went on to describe numerous biases and mental shortcuts (heuristics) that humans have developed for making decisions.

Many of those biases and aversions are now a common part of our understanding of how humans interact with the stock market.

These biases can be broken down into two groups: cognitive errors due to faulty reasoning, and emotional biases that come from feelings.[16]

Loss aversion is an example of an emotional bias. They can be very tough to overcome because they are based on feelings that are deeply ingrained in the brain.

See if you recognize yourself in any of these emotional biases.

Investors will:

- Come to believe they are infallible when they hit a winning streak (*overconfidence*).
- Blindly follow what others are doing (*herd behavior*).
- Value something they already own above its true market value (*endowment effect*).
- Fail to plan for long-term goals, like retirement, because it's easier to plan for short-term goals, like taking a vacation (*self-control bias*).
- Avoid making decisions out of fear the decision will be wrong (*regret-aversion bias*).

Cognitive errors are different. They don't come from emotional reactions, but from faulty reasoning. They happen because most people have a poor understanding of probabilities and how to put a numerical value on those probabilities.

The most important of these biases is the tendency of humans to jump to conclusions.

Daniel Kahneman, in his seminal 2011 book *Thinking, Fast and Slow*, said that "Jumping to conclusions on the basis of limited evidence is so important to an understanding of intuitive thinking, and comes up so often in this book, that I will use a cumbersome abbreviation for it: WYSIATI, which stands for what you see is all there is."[17]

When applied to markets, Kahneman means that investors fail to examine the quality of information they are presented with and fail to question what other information might be missing.

Philip Tetlock, in his book *Superforecasting: The Art and Science of Prediction*, called this bias "the mother of all cognitive illusions."[18]

But there's plenty of other cognitive biases.

Investors will:

- Select information that supports their own point of view, while ignoring information that contradicts it (*confirmation bias*).
- Believe that because a stock has done well in the past it will continue to do well in the future (*the gambler's fallacy*).
- Overreact to certain pieces of news and fail to place the information in a proper context, making that piece of news seem more valid or important than it really is (*availability bias*).
- Rely too much on a single (often the first) piece of information as a basis for an investment (such as a stock price), which becomes the reference point for future decisions without considering other pieces of information (*anchoring bias*).

- Give more weight to recent information than older information (*recency bias*).
- Convince themselves that they understood or predicted an event after it happened, which leads to overconfidence in the ability to predict future events (*hindsight bias*).
- React to financial news differently, depending on how it is presented. They may react to the same investment opportunities in different ways or react to a financial headline differently depending on whether it is perceived to be positive or negative (*framing bias*).

## *Behavioral economists get their due*

I wasn't the only who paid more attention to the behavioral economists following the Financial Crisis. By 2008, everyone was reading their books, or trying to explain what they were saying. *The Wall Street Journal's* Jason Zweig, one of my favorite financial reporters, even came out with a book himself: *Your Money and Your Brain: How the New Science of Neuroeconomics Can Help Make You Rich.*[19]

By then, Daniel Kahneman had already won the Nobel Memorial Prize for Economic Sciences in 2002 for his work on prospect theory, specifically for "having integrated insights from psychological research into economic science, especially concerning human judgment and decision-making under uncertainty."[20]

Another key figure was Yale professor Robert Shiller, who had been publishing research since the 1980s that concluded that the volatility in the stock market could not plausibly be explained by rational expectations of future returns. Shiller concluded that investors often make decisions on emotions rather than rational calculations.

He was awarded the 2013 Nobel Memorial Prize in Economic Sciences (with Eugene Fama and Lars Peter Hansen) for his contribution to our understanding of how human behavior influences stock prices.

Richard Thaler, who teaches at the University of Chicago Booth School of Business, won the Nobel Memorial Prize in Economic Sciences in 2017.[21]

Thaler, too, had demonstrated that humans acted irrationally, but they did so in predictable ways, giving hope that some form of model could still be developed to understand human behavior.

## What does behavioral economics teach us?

Robert Shiller surveyed the history of behavioral economics in his Nobel Prize lecture and concluded that humans are a lot more suggestible and irrational than we care to think, and that the sum of all those biases influences the way we act: "insignificant changes in context or suggestion can produce profound differences in human behavior," he said.[22]

*What's all this psychological insight mean for investors?*

Life was a lot simpler in the old days, when we assumed we were all rational actors who bought low and sold high, and stocks were efficiently priced on a future stream of dividends and earnings.

But we're not going back to that. My understanding of the stock market and human behavior is far messier and less precise than it was when I started in 1990, but it is a lot more satisfying.

Here are my key takeaways:

### THE GROWTH OF BEHAVIORAL FINANCE GAVE A BIG BOOST TO THE PASSIVE INDEXING CROWD

Read even a short summary of the many biases and heuristics that have been developed by behavioral economists and your head will be spinning.

The one sure thing you will take away is that humans have so many mental pitfalls to clear, unbiased thinking that it's just about impossible to sort it all out.

Billions of dollars flowed into passive (index-based) investing strategies after the Great Financial Crisis, and with good reason: unless you want to endlessly analyze yourself and everyone around you, passive investing made sense because it reduced or eliminated many of those biases. Some of these passive investments can have their own biases, of course.

Some people concluded the opposite: that if there are so many investors making irrational decisions, maybe we can find a way to eliminate the irrational decisions. Does that mean that *smart* people can take advantage of *dumb* investors, which is the basis for active management? Under some circumstances, yes, but even Richard Thaler thinks it's just about impossible.

"The active management industry as a whole doesn't really provide much in the way of value," Thaler said in a 2016 interview. "I say that as a principal in an active money management firm where we do think we provide value."[23]

## STOCKS CAN BE MISPRICED: IT'S NOT ALWAYS TRUE THAT A STOCK PRICE IS EXACTLY EQUAL TO THE INTRINSIC VALUE

If there is anything we have learned from behavioral economics, it's that psychology plays a large part in setting at least short-term stock prices. It is now a given that markets may not be perfectly efficient and that irrational decisions made by investors can have at least a short-term impact on stock prices. Stock market bubbles and panics, in particular, are now largely viewed through the lens of behavioral finance.

# IT'S POSSIBLE TO TRAIN PEOPLE TO THINK MORE RATIONALLY ABOUT INVESTING, BUT DON'T EXPECT TOO MUCH

With all this brilliant insight into how people really think (or don't), you'd think that as investors we wouldn't be repeating the same dumb mistakes we have been making for thousands of years.

Alas, investing wisdom and insight remains in short supply because 1) financial illiteracy is widespread—most people (and sadly most investors) have no idea who Daniel Kahneman or Richard Thaler or Robert Shiller are, or what they have taught us, and 2) even people who know better continue to make dumb mistakes because overriding the brain's "act first, think later" system that Daniel Kahneman chronicled in *Thinking, Fast and Slow* is really, really hard.

I should know. I'm one of many investors who have made some really dumb investment decisions. I'll tell you more about that in Chapter 20.

---

In Part One, I described what it was like to work on the floor of the NYSE, covering the markets and IPOs. I described how I decide what is news, and my relationship with Art Cashin and what he taught me.

In Part Two, I took a look back at important moments in recent financial history, including the 1999 Asian Financial Crisis, the wild year of 1999, the dot-com bust, the 9/11 disaster, the birth of electronic trading, and the Great Financial Crisis.

In Part Three, I'm going to go deeper into the most important question for any investor: does anything work?

# PART THREE

## *Does Anything Work?*

=

## CHAPTER 14

# *What Makes Stocks Go Up and Down?*

═══

E VERY day, I go to work at the New York Stock Exchange, and I try to describe what the markets are doing.

I do a lot of work. I talk to a lot of people, I read a lot of research.

And I try to make sense of it all.

But if you think I'm going to say that I know precisely why the market moves up or down every single day, you are mistaken.

Some days the markets are up or down for obvious reasons. Economic reports. Wars. Elections. Recession fears.

But not all the time, and maybe not even most of the time.

That's what I want to explore in this short chapter. This is important because a lot of the time, it's hard to figure out what the market is doing.

In Chapter 10, I described Jack Bogle's insight into what makes stocks go up or down. He emphasized three determinants: the rate of return is based on the dividend yield at the time of investment, the expected rate of growth in earnings, and the change in the price-earnings ratio during the period of investment. The first two are based on fundamentals, the third (the P/E ratio) is a "speculative" component.

That's fine for understanding a stock's long-term rate of return, but it doesn't fully explain why the market behaves the way it does.

After staring at the stock market for a few years, I came to the same conclusion that a lot of market observers come to: most of the time, the market looks like it just wanders around.

## Are markets efficient?

Eugene Fama, in a famous 1965 paper, concluded that stocks tend to exhibit a "random walk" and prices were not forecastable based on prior movements.[1]

Even though future prices were not forecastable based on prior movements, academics concluded that the market was "efficient," in that it incorporated all known currently available information.

This became known as the Efficient Market Hypothesis (EMH).[2]

The main tenets of the EMH are:

- Asset prices reflect all available information.
- Price changes follow a "random walk," that is, they are random and their future trends cannot be predicted from past trading patterns.
- Prices change when new information becomes available.
- Because prices reflect all available information about the future payout of dividends and earnings, there is no good or bad time to enter the market.

## EMH is troubling for market analysts

EMH was a direct challenge to many in the investment community.

For active managers, who made their living buying and selling stocks, the idea that there was no good or bad time to enter the market meant that market timing—deciding when to enter or leave the market, which is one of the main functions of active management—was a waste of time.

For those engaged in technical analysis, which sought to forecast future prices by studying prior price and volume trends, EMH implied they too were wasting their time.

As Professor Jeremy Siegel has pointed out:

> Proponents claim that technical analysis can identify the major trends of the market and determine when those trends might reverse. Yet there is considerable debate about whether such trends exist or whether they are just runs of good and bad returns that are the result of random price movements.[3]

There were also troubling implications for fundamental analysis, which tries to determine the intrinsic value of a stock by forecasting a future stream of dividends and earnings and then "discounting" that future stream to a present value.

However, if it is true that the market also incorporates all publicly available information, then attempting to divine how much a future stream of dividends or earnings a company can generate would seem like a waste of time as well. Investors have already figured that out and it is reflected in the price.

## *Weakness in the EMH*

EMH seems to make sense, particularly the idea that the market incorporates all known information. Yet it has been attacked for decades because it seems to fail to explain some facts about the stock market and the behavior of investors.

For example, how do you explain bubbles? How do you explain collective manias, where investors suddenly drive up the price of stocks, or real estate, or Bitcoin, and then just as suddenly decide that they don't want them or they aren't worth the price? How is the market efficient in those cases?

Yale economist Robert Shiller was one of the first to note problems with EMH, in a 1981 paper.[4] If investors were perfectly rational, stock prices would be based on fundamentals, that is, expectations of future dividends, discounted to a present value.

But that isn't what Shiller found. After examining stock prices going back to the 1920s, Shiller concluded that the volatility of the stock market was far greater than would be justified by those future dividend expectations: "We have seen that measures of stock price volatility over the past century appear to be far too high—five to 13 times too high—to be attributed to new information about future real dividends."[5]

The implication was that the markets were not perfectly efficient and investors were not perfectly rational.

Shiller, who won the Nobel Prize in Economics in 2013, expanded on this idea over the years, including in his book, *Irrational Exuberance*, published in 2000.

In his Nobel Prize lecture in 2013, as he had done in *Irrational Exuberance* 13 years before, Shiller described the fault line between the "EMH crowd" and the "behavioral finance crowd:"

There is a troublesome split between efficient markets enthusiasts (who believe that market prices incorporate accurately all public information and so doubt that bubbles even exist) and those who believe in behavioral finance (who tend to believe that bubbles and other such contradictions to efficient markets can be understood only with reference to other social sciences such as psychology).[6]

Shiller noted that there was then and is now very little consensus on why the stock market moves up and down every day:

> The history of thought in financial markets has shown a surprising lack of consensus about a very fundamental question: what ultimately causes all those fluctuations in the price of speculative assets like corporate stocks, commodities, or real estate? One might think that so basic a question would have long ago been confidently answered. But the answer to this question is not so easily found.[7]

Shiller then gets to the meat of his argument: the role of psychology in the setting of prices.

> At the same time, there has been an equally widespread acceptance in other quarters of the idea that markets are substantially driven by psychology. Indeed, since 1991 Richard Thaler and I have been directors of the National Bureau of Economic Research program in behavioral economics, which has featured hundreds of papers that seem mostly at odds with a general sense of rationality in the markets.[8]

So which is it? What really drives the stock market? Is it fundamentals like expectations of future dividends and earnings, which are immediately incorporated into all available stock prices, or is it all just a shouting match between hysterical participants who alternate between moments of head-snapping buying climaxes and teeth-rattling selling frenzies?

It is, Shiller concluded, a little bit of both:

> The financial institutions that we have today are the product of centuries of experience with the volatility of speculative asset prices, with the important information discovery that these market prices can

reveal, as well as the potential for erratic behavior in these markets. The reliability of these markets in revealing genuine information about fundamentals is not terrific, but it is certainly not negligible either, and the reliability might be improved through time with better financial institutions. Efficient markets should be considered a goal, not an established fact.[9]

## *Making sense of the debate*

Are markets efficient? Or should we believe that everyone is so irrational that we should all just give up trying to make sense of it all?

I don't worry much about this debate anymore.

Markets sure don't seem to be perfectly efficient, though in most situations they seem to be efficient enough. But there are also bouts of irrationality that do help explain bubbles and manias. I'll speak more about what causes bubbles in the Appendix.

Investors may act irrationally at times, buying high and selling low and driving prices into the stratosphere, but in the long run they are rational enough.

One of the lessons of behavioral finance is that investors are trend followers. That means that technical analysis—efforts to look for trends in prices and volume—is unlikely to go away. As Siegel has noted: "The very fact that many traders believe in the importance of trends can induce behavior that makes trend following so popular."[10]

The fact that prices are often driven into the stratosphere makes fundamental analysis useful as a means of pinpointing when a stock may be overvalued or also undervalued.

Of course, you have to believe that there is a relationship between a company's stock price and a future stream of dividends and earnings.

If you doubt that, you should consult the Oracle of Omaha.

Warren Buffett, in a famous essay titled "Beating Costs With Indexing," said "the most that owners in aggregate can earn between now and Judgment Day is what their business in aggregate can earn."[11]

In other words, that future stream of dividend and earnings is what matters. It may be really hard to forecast what that future stream will be, but it is still what matters.

Finally, don't let this discussion about market efficiency and irrational behavior plunge you into despair or inaction.

In the next chapter, I will take you into the heart of the debate: the studies indicate the majority of active traders, whether they are rational or not, do not outperform the markets over any length of time when costs are factored in.

Philip Tetlock, in *Superforecasting*, summed it up best: "[E]ven if markets are far less efficient than ardent proponents of the EMH suppose, it is still very hard to consistently beat markets, which is why so few can plausibly claim to have done it."[12]

Which begs the question: can anyone beat the market?

# CHAPTER 15

# *Can Anyone Predict the Market?*

---

Everyone has a plan until they get punched in the mouth.

—*Mike Tyson*

Mike Tyson came on the NYSE floor on November 13, 2013 to talk about his life and his new book, *Undisputed Truth*. This was one of those times when the person you met was not at all like the person you thought you were going to meet.

There's a small balcony overlooking the trading floor where a good part of the CNBC staff works, and where guests come to get makeup. It's a great place to chat with the guests before they go on. I was expecting to talk with the brash and quotable Mike Tyson, the Tyson who once said, "When I fight someone, I want to break his will. I want to take his manhood. I want to rip out his heart and show it to him."[1]

That's not the man who showed up. He was quiet, spoke in a low voice with a measured tone, didn't make much eye contact, and seemed like a man very much interested in healing, rather than intimidation.

I shouldn't have been surprised. It was seven years since he had retired from the ring, and a lot had happened since then, including bankruptcy 10 years earlier.

While the boxing part of his life was the stuff of legend, much of the rest of it was not a pretty story, particularly when he got to the part where he had made—and lost—$400 million in boxing winnings.

"I had bad associates and I had made bad decisions, and those decisions led to me getting into a lot of trouble, and being in a lot of places at the wrong time, real bad places," he said in the CNBC interview that day.[2] "I trusted the wrong people."

It was something to watch. He had a plan—to be the greatest boxer of all time—and then he got punched in the mouth.

## Is the stock market predictable?

At least Tyson recognized that his plan wasn't working, and when he figured that out, he changed the plan.

Everyone on Wall Street has a plan, too: a plan to make money. A lot of them sell these plans to the public and charge money for their advice. Others are employed as economic forecasters by Wall Street investment houses. Even the Federal Reserve and other government agencies are involved in forecasting future economic activity.

Whether it's stock prices or the GDP, there's an army of people that are trying to predict the future.

What's surprising is how poorly most do. You'd think that, when they look at the evidence, most would do what Tyson did and change the plan, or at least change the methodology.

It would make sense to do that because a lot of people get (figuratively) punched in the mouth when they suddenly discover their investments haven't been outperforming or their forecasts are either 1) wrong, or 2) not any better than anyone else's.

I've met all sorts of investors at the NYSE with all sorts of systems. The more sophisticated are based on fundamental and technical analysis, or even on quantitative analysis, which uses statistical models to search through large databases looking for patterns. Others are based on systems that are a bit more unorthodox, including combining technical analysis with astrology, I kid you not.

The central question in all of investing is this: does the stock market—or any investible market—follow a pattern? If it does, is it predictable?

Oceans of research, entire careers, have been spent trying to get the answer to this one question right: is the stock market predictable?

And the answer seems to be: probably not.

The thing about systems is, they all can work for a little while, but most break down after longer periods. There is a lot more randomness in events—in sports, in investing, in life in general—than most people care to admit.

In investing, this means that you can make money for a few days using almost any system, but if you're doing it for a longer period—if you use the same system every day for, say, five years—you will not likely outperform the market.

God help you if you are rude enough to point this out to the investment community. Oh sure, there are plenty of below-average professional investors out there, but not me. Hell, I've been an investment advisor for 20 years, haven't I? Do you think I've stayed in business all these years because I didn't make money? Do I look like a phony to you, Bob? Just what are you implying?

Hrumpf!

But just because an advisor makes a living charging people for investment advice, does not make him or her a genius. The issue is this:

after accounting for taxes, fees and trading costs, do investment advisors make money above and beyond simply holding a low-cost basket of stocks that represent the overall stock market?

The overwhelming majority of advisors do not.

If you are a self-directed investor that decides on your own what and where to invest, is there any evidence that day trading or market timing outperforms the overall market for extended periods of time once taxes and trading costs are considered?

The overwhelming evidence is no.

## *Predicting the future: no one gets it right*

No one is more obsessed with predicting the future than Wall Street, and with good reason: if you get it right, you make a lot of money.

Except almost no one gets it right. Almost no one has a consistent track record of outperforming the market over many years.

How could this be? A massive prediction industry exists on Wall Street, employing tens of thousands of people studying every conceivable aspect of the U.S. and world economy. The purpose: to predict the future. To tell clients where the economy will be in one month, one year, one decade, and where the stock market will be as well.

The dirty secret: it's mostly baloney. From the highest to the lowest levels—from street corner pundits to famous hedge fund managers to the economists at the Federal Reserve—the track records of the best and worst minds are the same: from mediocre to outright terrible.

## Picking stocks as a beauty contest

Way back in 1936, John Maynard Keynes, the most famous economist of his day, recognized that forecasting the stock market was a fool's errand:

> If we speak frankly, we have to admit that our basis of knowledge for estimating the yield ten years hence of a railway, a copper mine, a textile factory, the goodwill of a patent medicine, an Atlantic liner, a building in the City of London amounts to little and sometimes to nothing; or even five years hence.[3]

But don't investment professionals have more knowledge than the "dumb money," the average investor who knows little about what they are investing in? In a now-famous passage in his magnum opus, *The General Theory of Employment, Interest and Money*, Keynes said the average professional investor was not trying to estimate the future value of stocks years into the future; he or she was merely trying to guess what the general public thought the valuation of a stock might be in the near future (three months to a year).

Keynes described stock picking by professionals as akin to a beauty contest. Imagine, he said, a newspaper competition where the competitors had to pick out the six prettiest faces from a hundred photographs.

Keynes recognized that the winner of this contest could not win by picking the faces that most appealed to him or her; the goal was to pick what the average participants thought was the prettiest. Keynes said that this model could be continually refined:

> It is not a case of choosing those which, to the best of one's judgment, are really the prettiest, nor even those which average opinion genuinely thinks the prettiest. We have reached the third degree where we devote

our intelligences to anticipating what average opinion expects the average opinion to be.[4]

Since each investor would have his own opinion on what other investors' opinions would be, this thinking could be extended almost indefinitely, making efforts to guess the ultimate intent of the entire market unknowable.

It's worse than that: Keynes described the whole stock-picking process as essentially a parlor game, like Old Maid or Musical Chairs, with the investor passing the Old Maid to the next investor before the game was over, or who secured a chair for himself when the music stopped.

Isn't it possible to pick stocks for the long run and ignore all these efforts to second-guess other investors? Keynes said it was, but those who were able to do it successfully were rare animals: "Investment based on genuine long-term expectation is so difficult today as to be scarcely practicable… life is not long enough—human nature desires quick results, there is a peculiar zest in making money quickly, and remoter gains are discounted by the average man at a very high rate."[5]

Keynes came to the conclusion that most professional investing ends in disappointment: "[I]t is probable that the actual average results of investments, even during periods of progress and prosperity, have disappointed the hopes which prompted them."[6]

## Fund managers have a terrible track record

It's been over 85 years since Keynes made those observations, and the evidence we have since then has proven him right. In Appendix 1, I go into a little more depth about the empirical evidence that was accumulating even in the 1930s that Wall Street was terrible at forecasting the stock market. That mounting evidence eventually led to the birth of indexing and the creation of Exchange Traded Funds (ETFs), which have revolutionized investing.

But first let's just look at the terrible track record that fund managers have.

S&P Dow Jones Indices—the company that determines the stocks that go into the Dow Jones Industrial Average and the S&P 500—has been studying the performance of fund managers for nearly 20 years. Each year they issue a report on how active fund managers (professional stock pickers) perform against their benchmarks.

Their conclusion: active managers have a dismal track record. In mid-2021, for example, the majority (58 percent) of funds that invested in large companies lagged the S&P 500, the benchmark for investors in large companies, over the previous 12-month period.[7]

This is not a one-year phenomenon. The longer you look out, the worse it gets. After 10 years, 82 percent of funds that invest in large companies underperformed the S&P 500; after 20 years, nearly 94 percent were trailing the index.

Here's a critical point S&P Dow Jones discovered: fund returns look better than they really are. Many funds are liquidated because of poor performance, so the survivors give the appearance the overall group is doing better than it really is. S&P adjusts their study for this "survivorship bias." For the 2018 study, S&P found that over 15 years, 57 percent of domestic equity funds and 52 percent of all fixed income funds were merged or liquidated.[8]

Still, some managers do outperform, particularly on a one-year basis. But it doesn't last, and even the small percentage that outperform over more than a few years aren't even doing better than sheer dumb luck: "[T]he persistence of fund performance was worse than would be expected from luck," S&P concluded in a 2019 study.[9]

Worse than would be expected from luck!

# *Retail traders aren't any better*

Retail investors are often derided as "dumb money" because its widely believed that professionals have information and technology advantages over them, but with the trading records of the professionals so bad, you'd think the retail investors would at least have a shot at outperforming.

Nope.

In 2019 and 2020, Robinhood became a trading sensation, with its easy-to-use interface, and the fact that millions of young investors were sitting at home due to Covid-19 restrictions, had stimulus money to burn, and often had no sporting events to otherwise occupy their attention.

It didn't take long for results to come in. One study examined Robinhood traders from May 2, 2018, to August 13, 2020.[10] The authors focused on "extreme herding events," where traders had crowded into certain stocks.

They concluded that during these events, "the top 0.5 percent of stocks bought by Robinhood each day experience return reversals on average of approximately five percent over the next month whereas the more extreme herding events have reversals of approximately nine percent."

The conclusion: "[I]ntense buying by Robinhood users forecast negative returns."

When these day traders bought en masse, it was a signal that the stocks would do badly!

Why did that happen? The authors noted that most Robinhood investors are inexperienced, so they tend to chase performance. The layout of the app, which draws attention to the most active stocks, also causes traders to buy stocks "more aggressively than other retail investors."

Finally, the ease of use of the site, and the fact that it is commission-free, may also encourage trading. "As evidenced by turnover rates many times higher than at other brokerage firms, Robinhood users are more likely to be trading speculatively and less likely to be trading for reasons such as investing their retirement savings, liquidity demands, tax-loss selling, and rebalancing."

Why do stocks that spike when Robinhood traders pile in so quickly drop off? In addition to reversion to the mean, the authors suggest that short sellers are perfectly aware of Robinhood trading patterns. "These reversals seem to be well known as stocks Robinhood users herded into attracted significant short interest," they wrote.

A Robinhood spokesperson declined to comment on the study, but in a statement emailed to CNBC said: "[W]e see evidence most of our customers are buy and hold, and 98 percent of our customers are not pattern day traders."

Other studies of day traders have come to similar conclusions.

Another study of almost 1,600 Brazilian day traders that tracked their activity for one year concluded that only three percent made money.[11] The authors avoided claims that day traders can make money over short periods of time (a day or a week) and concentrated on day trading activity over longer periods.

Their conclusion:

We show that it is virtually impossible for individuals to day trade for a living, contrary to what course providers claim. We observe all individuals who began to day trade between 2013 and 2015 in the Brazilian equity futures market, the third in terms of volume in the world. We find that 97 percent of all individuals who persisted for more than 300 days lost money. Only 1.1 percent earned more than the Brazilian minimum wage and only 0.5 percent earned more than the initial salary of a bank teller—all with great risk.

Yikes.

A 2011 study of Taiwanese day traders over a 15-year period, from 1992 to 2006, showed only slightly better results.[12] Day trading is popular in

Taiwan. In an average year, about 360,000 Taiwanese individuals engage in day trading, according to the authors.

Their conclusion: "Consistent with prior work on the performance of individual investors, the vast majority of day traders lose money." They do note that a small group (about 15 percent) do earn higher returns net of fees, but that "some outperformance would be expected by sheer luck."

A later version of the paper published in 2013 concluded: "Less than one percent of the day trader population is able to predictably and reliably earn positive abnormal returns net of fees."[13]

What about the tiny group that might do better than sheer luck? The authors speculate that "one way in which day traders could be earning profits is by supplying liquidity through passive limit orders to uninformed investors who are too eager to pay for quick execution."

In other words, the tiny fraction of day traders who do make money in Taiwan do so by trading with "dumb money"—other day traders and general investors.

In an older study, going back to 2000, day traders fared no better.[14] The authors analyzed 66,000 trading accounts at Charles Schwab from 1991 to 1996. They found that those who traded the most earned an annual return of 11.4 percent, while the market overall returned 17.9 percent. Their conclusion: "Our central message is that trading is hazardous to your wealth."

## *Why do so many keep trying to beat the markets?*

With such overwhelming evidence, it might be puzzling why so many smart investors continue to believe they can beat the markets.

It's not puzzling at all.

My friend Larry Swedroe, who has spent decades analyzing the stock market at Buckingham Strategic Wealth, outlined four reasons:

1. *Financial illiteracy.* Investors are not sufficiently educated about the facts.
2. *The triumph of hope over experience.* Hope springs eternal: people continue to play the game because they believe they may be part of the tiny minority that succeeds in beating the markets.
3. *Active management is exciting, passive management is boring.* Who wants to invest in an index fund for the rest of your life?
4. *Overconfidence.* Many believe they have either discovered a manager that has unlocked the secret to beating the markets, or they believe they have themselves acquired some secret insight that no one else has obtained.[15]

Fortunately, there have been significant inroads into investor education in the past decade, as the investing public has become aware of the value of indexing and the use of Exchange Traded Funds (ETFs) as investment vehicles, which I discuss in Appendix 1, and which has forced many investment advisors to change course.

# *Analysts*

Retail traders don't seem to have much long-term success trading, but what about professional stock analysts? Can they make accurate predictions?

Analysts have a mixed picture. Since the market tends to rise over time, being eternally bullish is probably a good strategy. One study concluded that analysts who are more bullish were more accurate. The study found that buy and strong buy recommendations have greater returns than do holds, sell, and strong sells.[16]

Other studies have concluded that even being eternally optimistic didn't necessarily help analysts. One study examined 45 research papers and concluded that "Analysts were generally inaccurate and optimistic."[17] The authors, Andrew Stotz and Dr. Wei Lu, separately studied global analyst reports over a 12-year period from 2003 to 2014 and concluded that analysts were 25 percent optimistically wrong in their 12-month earnings forecasts during this period. That is a big number to be off. Even in the best years, when they were most accurate, they were still optimistically wrong by 10 percent. In 2008, the worst year, when earnings collapsed, they were wrong by 55 percent. Notice that the analysts were always wrong on the optimistic side: "Analysts were never pessimistically wrong," Stotz concluded.

Why aren't analysts pessimistic? Probably because it's bad for their careers. That was the conclusion of one study that found that brokerage houses rewarded optimism over accuracy.

Specifically, the authors found that analysts who were more optimistic than consensus got better jobs: "Brokerage houses apparently reward optimistic analysts who promote stocks."[18]

Other studies have found that the inaccuracy of analyst forecasts increases when the economic environment is more uncertain, which makes sense.[19]

## Hedge funds have a hard time, too

Hedge funds, which charge a hefty premium for their services, certainly imply they can do better, but it's been tough for them as well.

One study that looked at hedge fund performance from 1997 to 2016 found that while hedge funds with equally weighted stock and bond portfolios outperformed in the first 10 years, they significantly underperformed between 2008 and 2016: the hedge fund portfolio returned 25 percent between 2008 and 2016, but the stock and bond portfolio was up 70 percent. The authors said that this was likely because the Fed's accommodative monetary policy had increased the correlation between individual stocks.[20]

## Economists aren't any better

OK, so neither professional nor retail stock pickers are very good at figuring out the future. Surely economists must be better.

They aren't.

The Survey of Professional Forecasters is the oldest quarterly survey of macroeconomic forecasts in the United States. The survey began in 1968; the Federal Reserve Bank of Philadelphia took over the survey in 1990. It surveys the top macroeconomists on short-term (one quarter to one year) economic trends: GDP, unemployment, job growth.

Surely these people could get a short-term forecast right, no? After all, they only had to guess what GDP might be a few months to a year out. But they didn't. A 2013 survey by two economists found while there was some ability to predict GDP one to two quarters out, there was no "significant skill" in the ability to predict a one quarter decline in the GDP just one year into the future.[21]

## Ah, but the Federal Reserve knows what they're doing, right?

If anyone should be able to get economic forecasting right, it should be the Federal Reserve, but the evidence that the Fed is better than anyone else is remarkably scarce.

Jimmy Maguire (right) was a legend on the NYSE floor and was Warren Buffett's friend and the specialist for Berkshire Hathaway for many years.

Muhammad Ali, 1999. The NYSE orchestrated a series of bell ringings in December 1999 to ring out the old millennium and ring in the new. Ali rang the opening bell on the final day of 1999.

Walter Cronkite, 1999. Cronkite was a legendary TV anchor and was at one time considered "the most trusted man in television." He was retired as an anchor by the time I met him in 1999, but he was fascinated by the rise of financial television.

General Electric CEO Jack Welch (right) (with Richard Grasso, NYSE chairman (left)), 1999, was an enormous influence on CEOs in the 1990s, and a personal influence on me, and my investment in GE stock.

Christmas Eve on the NYSE floor, c. 2000. Barbershop quartet singing during the holidays had been a staple on the NYSE floor since the 1860s, but the singing of one particular song—"Wait 'til the Sun Shines Nellie"—became a favorite during the 1930s and has been sung every year since then. Many retired members came to the floor each Christmas or New Year's Eve to participate.

Outside the World Trade Center site, after 9/11. The disaster struck the Wall Street community particularly hard: everyone at the NYSE knew friends or colleagues who had died, and for more than a year the smoke from the site was a constant reminder of the tragedy.

The World Trade Center site, about 2:30 PM on September 11, 2001. Within a few hours of the collapse of the Twin Towers, members of the New York Fire Department and the New York Police Department were on site, combing through the wreckage and looking for survivors.

Fidel Castro, 2006. My brief meeting with him did not end well.

Aretha Franklin came to the NYSE on December 4, 2008, for the annual Christmas party and to debut her first Christmas album. She was already thinking about making a biopic of her life.

Princeton Professor Burton Malkiel (right) authored *A Random Walk Down Wall Street* in 1973, which helped spread the gospel of indexing.

Jack Bogle, 2009. Bogle's philosophy of sticking mostly to low-cost index funds had a profound impact on the way I look at the markets.

With Stan Lee, 2010. One of my childhood heroes. Lee helped revive Marvel and the comic book business in the early 1960s by co-creating a series of flawed but still heroic superheroes, starting with the Fantastic Four and then X-Men, Iron Man, Thor, the Hulk, Daredevil, and many others. Disney paid $4 billion to acquire Marvel in 2009.

In April 2013 Robert Downey Jr. came to the New York Stock Exchange to ring the opening bell as part of a promotion for *Iron Man 3*. My copy of the first *Iron Man* comic book got him to stop and chat with me.

With Alibaba chairman Jack Ma (left) and the NYSE's Scott Cutler on September 19, 2014. Alibaba raised $25 billion in the largest IPO in U.S. history.

With Mötley Crüe, 2015. It wasn't all CEOs and finance. Plenty of rock stars came down to ring the bell, often in conjunction with a new album to promote, or, in Mötley Crüe's case, for their Final Tour concerts.

I was not a big fan prior to meeting him, but when Barry Manilow came to the floor in 2017 I was very impressed with his view on success and the arc of his career.

UBS's Art Cashin was a master storyteller, market historian and legendary Wall Street barfly. We spent many nights analyzing markets at the NYSE bar and across the street at Bobby Van's.

The Fed's own research staff studied the Federal Reserve's economic forecasts from 1997 to 2008 and found that the Fed's predictions for economic activity one year out were no better than average benchmark predictions.[22]

This doesn't seem to make sense. There are some obvious reasons why the Fed should do better at forecasting than the private sector. First, they should have an informational advantage—they get access to data before the public, even if only by a few days. Second, the Fed's predictions are predicated on the fact that their policies will directly impact the forecasts. To the extent the Fed knows what its monetary policy will be, but the private sector does not, the Fed again has an information advantage. Finally, given the size of the Fed's research team, you would think that no one devotes more time and effort than the Fed to getting the predictions right.

One paper by an economist at the Federal Reserve Bank of San Francisco concluded that the Fed's forecasts about the future path of GDP can be more accurate than private sector forecasts, not because the Fed are forecasting geniuses, but because of the persistent belief the Fed does indeed know more than everyone else, whether it is true or not: "If people change their views based on a belief that the Fed's announcements contain inside information, then this is another way monetary policy can influence the economy."[23]

The Fed thus causes private sector forecasts to change just because everyone believes they have information no one else has.

In another survey, researchers at the Federal Reserve Bank of Saint Louis did find that the Fed was better at predicting inflation trends than surveys done by the private sector in the period from 1968 to 1991, though the Fed's predictions often deviated substantially from actual inflation.[24] Yet the same survey acknowledged research indicating that any forecasting advantage the Fed may have had over private forecasts has been eroding in the last 20 years.

Why? One reason may be that the Fed's increasing communication and transparency that began in 1994 has eroded any information advantage the Fed may have had.

But that's small potatoes—the real insight the authors have is noting that the nature of forecasting itself may have changed over time: "Since 1984, the volatility of many U.S. macroeconomic variables, including GDP and inflation, has declined. During the same period, economists have found that it has become harder to beat even the simplest forecasting models." If volatility for these variables has indeed declined, the conclusion makes sense: it wouldn't matter how many resources the Fed threw at forecasting, getting more sophisticated or throwing more resources at the problem would not necessarily improve the accuracy of the forecasts.

The inability to get the future right goes far beyond the stock market: nobody seems to be able to get it right. Not stock pickers. Not movie producers. Not weather forecasters. No one.

Why not? We'll talk more about why the future is so hard to figure out in Chapter 16.

Wall Street, of course, for the most part refuses to acknowledge that stock forecasting doesn't work. Why refuse? Because there's too much money in forecasting.

## At least Tyson changed his plan

Tyson, at least, figured out long ago that his plan did not work out as he had anticipated, and he changed course.

His original goal—to be the greatest fighter in the world—evolved into a new plan. He remarried, for the third time, in 2009, and launched a whole new plan.

"My goal now is to be healthy people, and to be sober, and to be responsible for our children, and to be present for the day," he said in that 2013 interview on CNBC.

"We decided to embark on a different lifestyle, clean up our life, clean up our debt, and go into the entertainment business."

And the new plan was successful. He played a fictionalized version of himself in the film *The Hangover* in 2009, which garnered a whole new generation of fans. It was one of the biggest movies of the year. He debuted a one-man Broadway show directed by Spike Lee in 2012. He briefly had an Animal Planet reality TV series, *Taking on Tyson*, about competitive pigeon racing.

He came on CNBC several times since that 2013 appearance. "I've got more fans than I ever did in my boxing career and you know how come I know?" he said in a 2015 interview.[25] "Because I have the internet," he said.

And indeed he did. He had nearly five million Twitter followers by then and was paying off his debts.

He kept moving. In 2016 he launched a digital wallet for Bitcoin. He started a podcast and wrote another book in 2017, *Iron Ambition*, about his time with trainer and mentor Cus D'Amato.

In 2020 he attracted even more attention when he fought Roy Jones Jr. in an exhibition fight that ended in a draw. "I'm happy I'm not knocked out," Tyson said. "I'll look better in the next one."[26]

A few months before Tyson came to the NYSE in 2013, Robert Downey Jr. had come on the floor to promote his new movie, *Iron Man 3*. I wanted to ask him what made the Iron Man movies so successful, but I was eager to ask him a broader question: can anyone predict what will make a successful movie? Predicting what would make a movie successful seems a lot simpler than predicting the stock market or the economy.

The problem was getting him to talk to me.

## CHAPTER 16

# *Can Anyone Get the Future Right?*

≡

NOBODY KNOWS ANYTHING. Not one person in the entire motion picture field knows for a certainty what's going to work. Every time out it's a guess and, if you're lucky, an educated one.

—*William Goldman,* Adventures in the Screen Trade:
A Personal View of Hollywood and Screen Writing

M Y *Iron Man* comic book got Robert Downey Jr. to talk to me.
In April 2013, Robert Downey Jr. came to the New York Stock Exchange to ring the opening bell as part of a promotion for *Iron Man 3*. I'm a lot more comfortable talking to CEOs than to movie stars: I just don't have much to say to actors.

But I did have something to say to Robert Downey Jr. I wanted to talk about *Iron Man* and ask him about the secret sauce that had made these movies so incredibly successful.

The problem was getting to him. It was just about impossible.

Movie stars had been ringing the opening bell since the mid-1990s. For most of the time, they were relatively accessible. Even if an interview wasn't scheduled beforehand, you could walk up to them on the floor, introduce yourself to them and their PR person, and they would usually grant you a few minutes.

That all started to change in the 2010s with the rise of superhero movies.

Suddenly it became more difficult to get a simple, quick, off-the-cuff interview with a movie star visiting the floor.

It wasn't surprising. These films had been massively successful. The first *Iron Man* film in 2008 had grossed $585 million worldwide.[1] Walt Disney bought Marvel Entertainment in August 2009 for $4.24 billion, and the franchise only got bigger. *Iron Man 2* (2010) grossed $624 million worldwide. And from there it went straight up: *The Avengers* (2012) had grossed $1.5 *billion*.

These were now big properties. *Iron Man* was a big property. Because these were huge investments, the studios and the PR people became very careful in passing out information and who they made available to whom. They didn't want anything out of the ordinary. They didn't want anybody—particularly the stars—saying anything weird or off-putting, because they're an investment. They're a part of the property. Access became very tightly controlled.

The morning Downey Jr. was ringing the bell, his PR people came up to me. They didn't look happy. They said, "We know who you are. We know you want an interview, but he's not doing an interview, with you or anyone else."

I love it when PR people try to act like they're muscle for the mafia.

I said, "He'll be on the floor. Maybe he'll come by."

More dirty looks. "He's not going to come by. He's not going to say anything to anybody, okay?"

Okay.

This really pissed me off. I was used to being able to walk up to anyone and ask for an interview. I had been doing it on the floor for more than 15 years. Almost nobody ever stopped me in the past because there weren't people trying to stop me, and how could you? You were on my turf. I've got a microphone and a cameraman. I walk up to you, say "Hi, how are you? Welcome to the stock exchange. I'm Bob Pisani with CNBC. What brings you here?"

And now these gatekeepers were telling me not to go near him, *or else*. Damn.

I had spoken with the executive producer of *Squawk on the Street*, Todd Bonin, the day before. Todd is one of the best producers at CNBC, a consummate professional. And he said, "Downey is ringing the opening bell. You'll be with a cameraman on the floor. Do whatever you can do."

Now I am set up for a perfect conflict. Getting to chat with Robert Downey Jr. on the floor would be fun and a great way to start the trading day. But his people had told me to stay away from him.

## *What do you say to Robert Downey Jr.?*

We came up with a simple plan.

The bell is on a podium overlooking the main trading floor. After he had rung the bell, if he descended from the podium to the left, onto the trading floor, that's where I would be standing, at the entrance to the floor, with microphone in hand and cameraman behind me.

The problem was, how to get him to stop and talk. I knew from experience that he would be walking briskly and that the PR people would have a wall of guards between him and me. I would have about three seconds to get his attention.

The key was the comic books.

I was an avid comic book reader and collector in the 1960s—what came to be called the Silver Age (the Golden Age was in the 1940s). It was mostly about the rise of Marvel—*X-Men, Fantastic Four, Avengers*—but DC was still going strong with *Batman* and *Superman*. I amassed a substantial collection, including the very first *Iron Man* (*Tales of Suspense #39*), and *Avengers #1*, which also featured Iron Man.

Beginning in the 1980s, the value of these comic books had been rising, but with the stunning success of the superhero movie—*Superman* in 1978, then *Batman* in 1989, and culminating in the *Iron Man, Avenger* and *X-Men* movies—the prices, particularly for first appearances—had reached stratospheric heights. Even poor copies were going for north of $10,000—and much of that rise was because of Robert Downey Jr. and these movies.

He was part of a phenomenon. And I was curious if he had any idea about what went had made this franchise so successful.

The night before Downey Jr. was due to be at the exchange, I took the train home and found my copies of *Tales of Suspense #39* and *Avengers #1*. Iron Man looked a lot different in those first appearances: he had a gray, clunky suit on that first cover, which proclaimed: "He lives! He walks! He conquers!"

The next day, Downey Jr. and his entourage rang the bell and came down the stairs. The wall of guards was there. But I had the comic books, and as he passed in front of me, I held *Tales of Suspense #39* above my head and waved it at him: "Robert, first *Iron Man*! Say hello!"

He saw it, and he stopped walking. He came over, and said, "Hey, man. How are you doing? Is that real…?"

And I said, "Hell, yeah. Come on, say hello to the viewers."

He said, "Yeah. How's it going?" And I told him these were from my childhood, and Iron Man looked a lot different in the very early days, and then we were on the air, and he was talking about what it was like to be Iron Man.

"It's been a great gift gig and I'm just really pleased to be here opening the stock exchange, hanging out with my fellow New Yorkers, it's really been a blast."[2]

The movie had already grossed $195 million worldwide, and it hadn't even opened in the U.S. yet. I looked at him, searching for an explanation. I was wondering *why* these movies were so successful, and had Disney finally found the magic formula everyone had always looked for?

Much of it, he implied, was star power and a massive PR effort on his part.

"I think having traveled around the world and done a pretty effective press tour, you realize no matter how you slice it, in the information age people still want to see people," he told me. "This is more interesting than Facetime."

I didn't get a chance to follow up, but I was happy to get some time with him. Todd was happy. Everyone was happy except the PR people.

They came up to me as he was leaving, one of them waved their finger at me. "We told you—no interviews!"

"Excuse me," I said. "I am the reporter here. He chose to come over and talk to me, okay?"

The PR waved me off, the universal sign for "whatever."

## *No one knows what will make a successful movie*

*Iron Man 3* was an even bigger success than its two predecessors, grossing $1.2 billion worldwide. And from there it got even bigger: *Avengers: Age of Ultron* (2015) grossed $1.4 billion. *Avengers: Infinity War* (2018) $2.0 billion. *Avengers: Endgame* (2019) $2.8 billion.

But the Marvel Cinematic Universe, as it came to be known, is an anomaly.

You'd think after 120 years of making movies, someone would have figured out the magic formula for what worked. But nobody has.

Robert Downey Jr. didn't seem to know either.

*How come?*

William Goldman was as successful a screenwriter as you are likely to find. He won Academy Awards for the screenplays to *Butch Cassidy and the Sundance Kid* in 1969 and *All the President's Men* in 1976. He wrote *Marathon Man* and *The Princess Bride* and adapted film versions of both.

He published a hysterically funny account of how Hollywood really works, *Adventures in the Screen Trade*, in which he famously insisted that the single most important fact of the entire film industry was, "NOBODY KNOWS ANYTHING" (his emphasis) about how to make a hit movie or if it will be a hit. There's a long list in the early part of the book about famous movies that all the Hollywood studios passed on. When he got to the part that every studio in town turned down *Raiders of the Lost Ark*, one of the most successful movies of all time, he noted there was one exception:

> But did you know that *Raiders of the Lost Ark* was offered to every single studio in town—and they all turned it down? All except Paramount. Why did Paramount say yes? Because nobody knows anything. And why did all the other studios say no? Because nobody knows anything. And why did Universal, the mightiest studio of all, pass on *Star Wars*, a decision that just may cost them, when all the sequels and spin-offs and toy money and book money and video-game money are totaled, over a billion dollars? Because nobody, nobody—not now, not ever—knows the least goddam thing about what is or isn't going to work at the box office.[3]

Goldman was speaking about the movies, but he was inadvertently speaking a much wider truth: nobody knows how to predict the future.

How could that be? Goldman was an expert in his field, but he knew that there were far too many variables to accurately predict if a movie was going to be successful.

This turns out to be a universal problem. It doesn't matter whether you are predicting the future of stocks, what will be a hit at the movies, or forecasting just about anything else in the future.

Why is the future so hard to figure out?

The good news is, we have an increasingly good understanding of why it is so hard to forecast, and there are efforts underway to improve the quality of that forecasting. This is the focus of the next chapter.

## CHAPTER 17

# Why Is Everyone So Bad at Predicting the Future?

=====

Why did nobody notice it?

—*Queen Elizabeth II, on the Great Recession of 2007–2009*[1]

QUEEN Elizabeth II wasn't the only one who noticed that the Great Recession was predicted by almost nobody.

You can forgive stock forecasters and active stock pickers for not getting things right, but it's a little tougher when the people who the Federal Reserve rely on for forecasts can't get it right either.

Simon Potter, the Executive Vice President of the New York Federal Reserve, gave a speech in February 2019 with the title, "Models Only Get You So Far."[2] Potter began by outlining the Fed's then-current survey of market participants on the odds of a U.S. recession at that time and in coming years.

The Fed had been conducting this survey for many years. But Potter took note of the results from a prior Fed survey on the same question, taken in mid-2007. This was the start of the Great Recession; the U.S. was already in a recession. And yet, Potter notes that less than 50 percent of the respondents felt that the United States was in a recession at that time or that it would be in one in six months.

Economists the Fed rely on for their forecasts couldn't even tell we were in a recession, when we were already in a recession.

Potter attempted to be diplomatic by calling this a "cautionary tale," but the evidence is damning: even the people the Fed rely on for forecasts are not very good.

## No one can figure out the future

The Federal Reserve, of course, are not the only ones who have had to eat humble pie on their failure to forecast the Great Recession.

Almost no one can figure the future out.

Why? At first glance, there seems to be a grand conspiracy afoot. It's easy to believe that our future is governed by dark forces that control the world and that everything is unfolding according to some grand conspiracy controlled by the *Illuminati*, whoever they are.

The likely explanation is far simpler: the world is ridiculously complex.

There are so many variables in forecasting that making predictions about the future beyond the very short term is almost impossible. Add in the many biases that humans—including forecasters—exhibit in their forecasting, which throws off the validity of their observations, and it's a wonder anyone even bothers trying.

But people do try.

## Debunking the experts

Given how long soothsayers have been around, and how bad their predictions are, you'd think scientific studies of forecasting and the experts who do the forecasting would be a very old business, but it isn't. It's been studied for around 70 years.

Back in 1954, Paul Meehl, a professor of psychology at the University of Minnesota, wrote a seminal book with a very dull-sounding title: *Clinical Versus Statistical Prediction: A Theoretical Analysis and a Review of the Evidence*.[3] Meehl reviewed 20 studies in which clinical predictions (based on direct observation) were pitted against mechanical predictions (based on rules, not observations) and concluded that rules-based mechanical predictions were more reliable.

This was controversial at the time, but it was one of the earliest studies to highlight that experts exhibited numerous biases and weren't so great at predicting outcomes.

From there, the evidence kept mounting.

In a 2005 book, *Expert Political Judgment*, University of Pennsylvania professor Philip Tetlock studied the predictions of almost 300 experts in many different fields, including politics, economics, and the social sciences. It included academics, economists, and journalists.

The results? More than 30 years earlier, Princeton economics professor Burton Malkiel had asserted that "a blindfolded monkey throwing darts at the newspaper's financial pages could select a portfolio that would do just as well as one carefully selected by the experts."[4] Tetlock expanded on that assertion by claiming that the average expert was not any better than their stock-picking brethren: "When we pit experts against minimalist performance benchmarks—dilettantes, dart-throwing chimps and assorted extrapolation algorithms—we find few signs that expertise translates into greater ability to make either 'well-calibrated' or 'discriminating' forecasts."[5]

Most importantly, Tetlock noted that expertise itself—greater knowledge of the subject matter—did not necessarily translate into greater insight into the future: "In this age of academic hyperspecialization, there is no reason for supposing that contributors to top journals—distinguished political scientists, area study specialists, economists, and so on—are any better than journalists or attentive readers of *The New York Times* in 'reading' emerging situations."*⁶

Tetlock did not say all experts were fools, or that forecasting was useless.

Quite the contrary, he noted that some were indeed more accurate than others—not because of expertise, but rather because of the way they thought. Those that were more open-minded and synthesized many different ideas and viewpoints (Tetlock called them "foxes" in reference to a famous 1953 essay by Isaiah Berlin, "The Hedgehog and the Fox") were better forecasters than those who viewed the world through the lens of a single idea or ideology ("hedgehogs").

What all the experts tended to be good at was telling stories. "The one undeniable talent that talking heads have is their skill at telling a compelling story with conviction, and that is enough," Tetlock noted in his next book, *Superforecasting: The Art and Science of Prediction.*⁷

A compelling narrative delivered with conviction is persuasive and leads people to trust the person delivering the narrative: "[P]eople trust more confident financial advisers over those who are less confident even when their track records are identical. And people equate confidence and competence, which makes the forecaster who says something has a middling probability of happening less worthy of respect."⁸

## The forecasting tournament

*Superforecasting* came out of a forecasting tournament sponsored by the Intelligence Advanced Research Projects Activity (IARPA), a U.S.

---

* Louis Menand, in a review of Tetlock's book for *The New Yorker*, concluded that "the best lesson of Tetlock's book may be the one that he seems most reluctant to draw: Think for yourself."

government organization that conducts research for the intelligence community. They, too, were trying to improve the accuracy of forecasting, in this case intelligence forecasting, particularly in the aftermath of the failure to find weapons of mass destruction in Iraq.

By Tetlock's account, the United States had 20,000 intelligence analysts assessing everything from the most obscure occurrences to major events like the likelihood of an Israeli sneak attack on Iranian nuclear facilities, or the departure of Greece from the eurozone.

How good were all these analysts? How accurate were their predictions? Incredibly, no one knew. "[L]ittle can be said with any confidence about how good it is, or even whether it's as good as a multibillion-dollar operation with twenty thousand people should be," Tetlock said.[9]

So IARPA sponsored a tournament in which five teams competed to generate accurate forecasts on a series of scenarios. Tetlock and his research (and life) partner Barbara Mellers created the Good Judgment Project, which was one of the teams that competed. Over the next four years, from 2011 to 2015, Tetlock signed up 20,000 "intellectually curious" laypeople to see if anyone could accurately predict the future.

Over those four years, IARPA posed almost 500 questions on world affairs to the five teams. They were required to submit forecasts at 9 AM Eastern Time every day. Most forecasts involved time frames from one month out to less than one year. In all, there were over one million individual forecasts.

The result? The Good Judgment Project beat the official control group by 60 percent in the first year, and by 78 percent in the second year. They also beat the competing teams to such an extent that IARPA dropped the other teams after two years.

Tetlock came to two conclusions: 1) foresight is real. Some people do have an ability to make much more accurate forecasts than others; and 2) that foresight comes about not because of who they are, their level of expertise, or what they thought, but *how* they thought: "It is the product of particular ways of thinking, of gathering information, of updating beliefs. These habits of thought can be learned and cultivated by any intelligent, thoughtful, determined person."[10]

## *Why is the future so hard to figure out?*

Even Tetlock's superforecasters had problems: the farther out they looked, the harder it was to figure things out.

"It was easiest to beat chance on the shortest-range questions that only required looking one year out, and accuracy fell off the further out experts tried to forecast—approaching the dart-throwing-chimpanzee level three to five years out," Tetlock wrote. "That was an important finding. It tells us something about the limits of expertise in a complex world—and the limits on what it might be possible for even superforecasters to achieve."[11]

It doesn't seem to matter much what the subject is: the weather, the economy, death rates, stock prices, the GDP of the United States, or anything else. Predicting the future is very difficult.

The first problem is that predictions are riddled with bias and noise that limit the quality of those predictions.

In his 2021 book, *Noise*, Daniel Kahneman and his colleagues, Oliver Sibony and Cass R. Sunstein, demonstrate how bias and noise (which they define as "variability in judgments that should be identical") conspire to derail the judgments of even the most well-intentioned individuals.[12]

Like Paul Meehl decades before, Kahneman noted that many studies had demonstrated rules-based methods—where the same rule or rules are applied in all cases—were superior to human judgments, because rules helped combat biases and noise.

One 2000 metastudy looked at 136 cases of applying human judgment against rules-based judgments across a wide variety of endeavors, from medical diagnosis to the success of business startups, career satisfaction, job success, occupational choices, and business failures. The conclusion: "Superiority for mechanical prediction techniques was consistent, regardless of the judgment task, type of judges, judges' amount of experience, or the types of data being combined."[13]

This has implications for stock picking as well. If you are following a rules-based system for picking stocks, you might have a rule that says I will only buy the 100 largest stocks in the U.S. by market capitalization. You might also add a second rule, which says you will rebalance the portfolio every three months—that is, every three months you will add whatever new stock has advanced into the top 100 and remove whatever stocks have fallen out of the top 100.

A very large part of U.S. investing, including most of the Exchange Traded Fund (ETF) market, now uses these types of rules-based methodology.

Given the advantages of following rules-based systems, why don't experts use them more often?

One obvious explanation is the fear that machines will put them out of work.

Indeed, Kahneman notes a 1996 study that cites "fear of technological unemployment" as one major reason why professionals resist following rules-based systems.[14]

Another reason: a lot of people don't trust computers and algorithms and prefer to trust their gut. In doing that, they display the most common of biases, overconfidence—in this case, overconfidence in their own judgment.*[15]

---

* There are other reasons to consider using rules-based methods over human intuition. Kahneman notes that the growth of sophisticated artificial intelligence data mining techniques may make rules-based methods even more valid: "[t]he data is sometimes rich enough for sophisticated AI techniques to detect valid patterns and go well beyond the predictive power of a simple model."

# *Is the future knowable?*

There's a second problem with predicting the future. Many aspects of the future are unknowable. It's unknowable for two reasons: because we don't have complete information, and because events occur that are unpredictable and can affect outcomes.

Think about trying to predict where the price of a stock will be one year from now. Every company has millions of different variables, each of which can affect the outcome.

While there is more and more data being collected all the time, we can never know every piece of detail about a company or the economic data that may impact it.

Think about all the things that can go wrong in making an economic prediction, say the GDP of the United States one year from now. Or the price of a stock.

Some factors may be predictable, but many are not. On the macro level, the economy may face new shocks or surprises, such as inflation, a rise in interest rates, a war that disrupts critical supplies, or a cyberattack. The company may face a new competitor. It may be bought out or engage in an unforeseen merger. The visionary CEO may fall ill and suddenly retire.

And that's not even considering a Black Swan event like Covid, which rendered all forecasts useless.

Making predictions about how human beings are going to perform in the future is just as difficult as making predictions about stock prices.

You would think that predicting the future of human performance has got to be easier, especially if we are just talking about one person.

It's not. Kahneman points out it's just as hard trying to figure out how an individual human being is going to perform.

We can never know all the personal details about a person and how those details may impact their professional career.

And predicting what will happen to someone in the future is just as difficult as predicting what will happen to companies. Some encounter mentors who believe in them and guide them in their careers. Some encounter demoralizing failures. Most encounter events in their personal life that affect job performance.

All this conspires against understanding the future: "Both intractable uncertainty (what cannot possibly be known) and imperfect information (what could be known but isn't) make perfect prediction impossible," Kahneman says.[16]

This should make prognosticators—of political races, of the stock market, of the future in general—very humble: "None of these events and circumstances can be predicted today—not by you, not by anyone else, and not by the best predictive model in the world," Kahneman writes.[17]

## *Why bother?*

Knowing this, a rational person might wonder why it's worth bothering at all.

The answer is, it's critical for anyone seeking advice to understand the problems with making predictions and interpretations. This is important when making decisions on investing, but understanding biases and noise is also critical for understanding judicial rulings, an X-ray diagnosis, giving odds on a political race, or anything else.

Tetlock has demonstrated we can improve our decision-making abilities. His Good Judgment Project (GJP) has become a mini-industry. There is now a GJP 2.0, part of a new IARPA program called FOCUS that is seeking to tackle even bigger issues, focusing on "forecasting on questions that ask how history would have unfolded if some key factor or event had been different. What if Hitler had been born a girl? Would World War II ever have happened?"[18] This is known as "counterfactual forecasting"—examining statements about what would have happened if different circumstances had occurred.

It's not just a historical what-if exercise: the goal is to "develop evidence-based guidelines that any organization can use to improve its 'lessons-learned' processes."

The battle with noise and bias, and the unknowability of much of the future, boils down to a battle for credibility.

Despite the imperfect nature of humans and the unknowability of the future, we are not helpless.

Still, knowing that bias, noise, and the unknowability of the future conspire against us should make all of us humbler.

If that does not impress you, let me tell you about some people who got to see the future, and still got it wrong.

# CHAPTER 18

# *The Gang That Couldn't Trade Straight*

═══

I'M going to tell you a story about a group of people who had access to the future, and they still couldn't figure out the stock market. I call them The Gang That Couldn't Trade Straight.

One of the most important determinants of future stock prices is corporate earnings reports. These reports not only contain the performance of the prior quarter, but they also often provide commentary on current and future activity. These reports can and do move stock prices.

Here's a thought experiment. Suppose I gave you access to those earnings reports, as well as other corporate announcements, several days before anyone else. You could tell if the company met or exceeded expectations for earnings or revenues. You could see if they were optimistic or pessimistic about current and future business.

That would be a gold mine, right? Based on that information, you could buy more of the stock if you thought the price was going to go up, or short it if you thought it was going down.

This actually happened. And it turns out, it's not that easy interpreting the future.

# Five years of seeing the future
## ahead of everyone else

From 2011 to 2015, a group of sophisticated hackers (mainly from Russia and Ukraine) illegally obtained early access to corporate earnings press releases. They got these announcements by hacking into the servers of three commercial newswire services that were storing the announcements prior to public dissemination.

This was not a small-scale operation: the hackers gained unlimited access to over 150,000 unique press releases, largely earnings reports, but also including patent results, clinical trial updates, and acquisition announcements.

It was a veritable gold mine. And they had access for five years!

The hackers turned around and sold the information to an international group of financial professionals. They made a sweet deal: the hackers would get 50 percent of the profits generated from trading on the stolen information in exchange for continued access to the newswire servers, according to Chloe Xie, a researcher from the Graduate School of Business at Stanford University.

Xie examined 1,029 trades that were done with this information over this five-year period. Xie also examined thousands of the actual press releases the companies disseminated.[1]

The investors who traded on the information before the releases were made public appeared to be pretty smart. They deliberately looked for announcements they thought would contain surprising news that would move the respective stocks. They were selective: they stuck with more liquid stocks to avoid detection and chose to trade only 9.25 percent of the illegal obtained earnings announcements.

You'd think these guys would clean up, right? That they would blow away an average investor, right?

They didn't. After studying more than 1,000 of the trades made, Xie concluded: "Despite this informational advantage, the informed traders performed poorly."

Huh? How is this possible? These guys had access to information any trader would kill for.

To be sure, the traders made money. It was estimated they had returns of roughly $100 million over the five-year period.

That sounds amazing, but that is not the question. The issue is: armed with the stolen information, could the traders accurately identify the earnings announcements that would produce the largest returns after the announcements were made public?

Xie concluded they could not.

The problem, as Xie explains it, is that the traders assumed 1) that the information in the earnings announcements predicted how stock prices would move in the near future, and 2) that they could successfully separate those releases that had information that would move prices from those that didn't.

It didn't, and they couldn't. Xie concluded that because earnings and other corporate announcements were inherently "noisy," it was difficult to determine whether the information would cause the stocks to go up or down.

Xie found that the "signal quality" (in this case, whether the information in the releases would move the stocks) of these corporate releases is very low: "This low signal quality implies that individuals cannot infer stock market responses from the information in earnings announcements."

What does all this mean? Xie concluded that:

The informed traders had 'perfect foresight' from stolen earnings announcement press releases, but they were only able to enjoy mixed success in predicting next-day stock returns. Their poor performance implies that capital market participants have difficulty mapping earnings information to stock price reactions.[2]

*You can't predict how stocks will move based on earnings announcements?*

Yep. Humans just aren't very good at figuring that out: "[E]arnings announcements are complex, and investors differ in their ability to process the plethora of hard and soft information."

## Are markets efficient?

Nicholas Colas, who runs DataTrek, a terrific quant-driven financial analytics firm, read Xie's paper and offered two conclusions: 1) "Markets are pretty efficient even in edge cases (those where sophisticated investors thought their informational advantage would yield an outsized profit)," and 2) "Corporate communications outside the earnings release, such as the typical management-led conference call, can be more important than the reported financial results."[3]

That's for sure. Today, traders and analysts are more likely to pay attention to what is said on the conference call than in the earnings press release, because there is more nuance in these conference calls where management is responding to analyst questions.

What does all this mean? For the past several chapters, I've spoken about how difficult it is to forecast the future in almost any endeavor, and the farther out we go the more difficult it gets. Forecasting the future is difficult, and now we see it is so difficult that even with advance information that should be helpful, it still can't be done.

Forecasting the future is not only difficult—it can be painful when people you are close to rely on you to do that.

What should you do when your family calls and asks you for financial advice? I'll describe a particularly difficult moment with my father at the height of the Great Financial Crisis in the next chapter.

# CHAPTER 19

# *On Giving Financial Advice to Your Family*

=====

When a man comes to me for advice, I find out the kind of advice he wants, and I give it to him.

—*Josh Billings*

F OR nearly 30 years, I have adhered to a rule: *do not provide anything other than broad investment advice to your friends or family.*

I did not make this rule because of a lack of desire or a lack of opinions.

My reasoning was grounded in simple logic: if I offered investment advice and I was right, they would want more. If I was wrong, they'd be pissed off, even if they didn't say it.

I have supplied broad investment advice. I've helped my nieces and nephew set up Roth IRAs and talked about the value of long-term investing. When my sister asked for help with investing, I offered a financial advisor whom I respected. She is still with him, more than a decade later.

On the rare occasions anyone asks, I have described the type of investments I own (almost all index funds, which I describe in Chapter 20), but I don't tell anyone what to own and avoid any discussion where I am forced to opine on any particular stock or investment.

I made one exception.

## *What I told my father*

My father called me in the spring of 2008. The S&P was about 15 percent off the historic high it had hit in October of the year before. So far, this was a garden-variety correction, but there was already concern.

My father had moved to Palm Beach Gardens in 1996, to an idyllic gated golf course community. He designed and built his own house, a single-story home with a guesthouse and a pool. His days were spent on the golf course and playing cards with his friends, many of whom, like himself, were transplanted New Yorkers.

It was a crowd with a significant amount of money in the markets. Naturally, CNBC was on in the clubhouse and my father was regularly asked what his son, "the stock market expert," had to say about the markets.

Whenever I went to visit, my father proudly paraded me around the dining room to introduce me to his friends. I avoided talking about the markets.

"Robert, I need your advice," he said on this particular day, and before I could say anything he added, "I don't want to hear any of your 'I don't provide investment advice' crap. I need your advice and I expect you will provide it."

Oh boy. This is one of those "you don't say no" conversations.

"OK."

"I'm only going to ask two questions. First, is Bank of America in danger of going under?"

This was a puzzling question. I didn't know much about my father's portfolio, but he had never told me he had a significant position in Bank of America.

It didn't matter. Almost certainly, it had been a topic at the clubhouse.

It was a good question, because the banks were the leading edge of what was about to become known as The Great Financial Crisis. After years of rapid growth, the housing boom had topped out. Homeownership rates peaked at 69 percent in 2004 and were now dropping rapidly. Mortgage delinquencies had been rising through 2007, a source of concern since one-third of mortgage loans in 2006 were no- or low-documentation loans. That meant there was room for a lot more delinquencies.[1]

Which meant losses, especially for banks that held the mortgages. Because of those concerns, banks were in the middle of a serious correction of their own. While the S&P had only topped out a few months prior, banks had been in a downturn for nearly a year and a half. Many—like Bank of America—were already 30 percent off their 2006 highs by the time my father called me.

In January 2008, Bank of America bought subprime mortgage lender Countrywide Financial for $4 billion in stock. The rationale—B of A was eager to expand its mortgage lending business—would prove to be the wrong move at the wrong time. The subprime mortgage crisis was already rippling through the financial system. A month before, in December 2007, the Federal Reserve announced the creation of a Term Auction Facility designed to supply credit to banks with subprime mortgages.[2]

Other banks and investment houses that had significant mortgage exposure were reeling. The biggest blow came on March 17, 2008, when Bear Stearns, with $46 billion in mortgage assets and facing imminent bankruptcy, was sold to JPMorgan Chase. The Federal Reserve had stepped in, guaranteeing the trading obligations of the firm. The initial price was $2 a share, later adjusted to $10 a share. The week before, it had traded at $60.[3]

This was the context of the question my father was asking. It was a minefield. I had no idea where this was going to end, but the markets were already in a panic.

"I don't think Bank of America will go under," I said, talking very slowly. "There may be a chance they could get acquired, but that's very unlikely because they're so big. They are likely an acquirer of assets, if they can get the Fed's help."

Based on the Fed's action with Bear Stearns, this was a reasonable answer to the question.

"Thank you," my father said. The logical follow-up question would have been what was going to happen to the stock price.

Thank God he didn't ask me, because I had no idea.

"My second question is, I need to get more income from my investments. I want something simple. What do you recommend?"

This was an even bigger minefield than the Bank of America question. My father at that time was 78 years old, hardly a great age to move into riskier high-yield investments.

That's what I told him. I said if he was truly concerned with the markets in the next year or so, at his age the right thing to do would be to take some money out and go to bonds or cash.

That was the correct, "traditional" advice to give in a situation like that. It wasn't good enough for my father.

"Let me ask you a different question," he said. "You must have some kind of bond funds. What do you own that gives you the highest yield?"

Ugh. I had to hand it to my father: this was precisely the right question to ask. *You're so damn smart they put your face on TV, so what do you own, and why?*

Now I'm starting to sweat, because my father is intimating that any investment I own would be good enough for him.

I was in too deep to back out. I told him I owned the Vanguard High Yield Corporate Fund. These funds bought bonds from companies that had a much higher chance of defaulting, so they paid a higher yield than investment-grade bonds. Vanguard's fund had rock-bottom fees and a reputation as the most conservative of the high-yield funds, buying bonds with the highest possible rating that were still rated as junk.

I felt like fainting. I wasn't advising my father to do anything, but just describing this fund at that time seemed like a terrible idea. The high-yield market was in complete turmoil in the middle of 2008. Yields were going through the roof—they had passed 10 percent and were still going higher—because default risk had gone through the roof and prices were plunging.

I explained that to him. I told him prices were going down, and I had no idea where it would end. I told him during recessions, high-yield corporate bond funds act a lot like stocks, not bonds. They can drop fast.

I also told him that I was 26 years younger than him, and it would be much easier for me to weather a once-in-a-generation drop in prices than it would for him.

But he seemed unperturbed. He said he would be holding the investment for some time, so he wasn't concerned with the price. Those yields north of 10 percent were what intrigued him.

"That sounds like what I'm looking for," he said. "Thank you."

And he hung up.

## My father's investment

On September 15, Lehman Brothers declared bankruptcy after the Federal Reserve declined to guarantee its loans, as it had done for Bear Stearns. Other disasters followed: the Federal Reserve soon took over American International Group.

I was at least right on one front: Bank of America was indeed an acquirer. On September 21, it bought Merrill Lynch in an all-stock deal. There was, briefly, discussion that Bank of America might buy Lehman itself, but that never came to fruition.[4]

The world might have been different had they done so. Lehman's bankruptcy stunned everyone. Investors had assumed the Fed would backstop something as big as Lehman, as they had done with Bear Stearns. When they declined to do so, the S&P 500 dropped 4.7 percent that day, its worst day since September 17, 2001, when it dropped 4.9 percent.

As for Bank of America, my father never brought it up again. It would drop 90 percent from its high to the bottom in early 2009 before beginning a long, slow recovery. It did indeed survive, but its investment in Countrywide became what many called the worst financial services deal in history.[5]

As for the Vanguard High Yield Corporate Fund, my father did put money in some time after we talked. He was right: it did prove to be a good long-term investment. He still owned it on the day he passed away, in August 2021. He told me many times he was happy with the yield, which slowly diminished as the spread between high-yield and investment-grade corporate bond yields shrank in the 2010s.

What's the takeaway from this story? I was put in a very difficult position. My father was asking me for financial advice at a moment when it was almost impossible to give it. And he wasn't taking no for an answer.

Looking back, I believe I answered his questions but stuck to my position of not telling him what to do.

Over the years, I've become a little more comfortable talking to friends and even family about investing. I still don't offer specific advice, but, like Josh Billings, I'm pretty good at figuring out what kind of advice people want. I'm able to describe the parameters of their options without making specific recommendations. If they are confused, I have referred some to financial planners.

The most difficult issue is giving yourself investment advice.

And if you think being Stocks Correspondent for CNBC for 25 years makes you any wiser, let me disabuse you of that notion.

In the next chapter, I'm going to describe my personal investment journey. I'm going to show you what I own, and why. I'm also going to tell you about some things I used to own, and why I don't own them anymore.

It is, to paraphrase Shakespeare, a tale told by an idiot, full of sound and fury.

Unlike Shakespeare, however, this tale does not signify nothing.

## CHAPTER 20

# *Trading Hits and Misses: What I Learned Investing My Own Portfolio*

═══

W HEN I think of some of the stupid investing decisions I've made, it's amazing I'm not living in a homeless shelter.

I would like to tell you that, as a Jack Bogle disciple, when I started investing in 1993 I immediately diversified by putting money into an S&P 500 fund, an international fund, and a bond fund and left it that forever.

The evidence suggests otherwise.

## *Why doesn't anyone ever ask what I own?*

When people who are interested in the stock market meet me for the first time, the first question they usually ask is, "What do you think is happening in the markets?"

They usually mean short term, in the next six months.

The discussion usually devolves into exchanging opinions on what is interesting to buy or sell, or whether the market can be "trusted."

Almost no one ever asks me what I would consider to be the single most important question: "You've been around a long time. What do you own?"

I'm not the first person who works on Wall Street who has noticed this odd phenomenon. My friend Josh Brown, co-founder and CEO of Ritholtz Wealth Management, noted that he has been appearing on financial television for nearly 10 years, "And in all that time, not one person has ever asked me about what I do with my own money. Not one."[1]

I'm going to show you what I own. But first, let me show you how stupid I have been.

## *My father tries to turn me into an investor, and fails*

When I was 14, as a Christmas present my father gave me two shares in a company called Kawecki Berylco Industries. Kawecki Berylco made beryllium, which was used in spacecraft and satellites because it was a lightweight metal and could also be applied as a heat shield.

Neil Armstong and Buzz Aldrin had landed on the moon a year before. I was enamored with the space program and seriously thinking of majoring in physics.

It was a thoughtful way to get a 14-year-old interested in the stock market. He chose a subject that interested me—space exploration—and found a company that had a hand in that business.

"Robert, I want you to know that I invest in the stock market, and I hope you will too," my father told me. He had made his money as a real estate developer building apartment houses in Philadelphia and Bucks County, but he was always a dabbler in the markets.

I ignored the advice. I wasn't interested in the markets, I was interested in my three passions: physics, journalism, and the 1960s.

Norman Mailer had just published *Of a Fire on the Moon*, an exploration of the space program, which I devoured. Tom Wolfe had written *The Electric Kool-Aid Acid Test*, about Ken Kesey and the LSD experiments in San Francisco, a couple of years before. The following year, Hunter S. Thompson would publish *Fear and Loathing in Las Vegas*, first in two parts in *Rolling Stone* magazine, then as a book.

I knew what I wanted. I wanted to be like those guys, writing about all the crazy stuff going on.

I was too young to be a part of the 1960s, but I was an avid music fan. In 1965 my mother bought me my first phonograph player, and my first record: "Puff, the Magic Dragon" by Peter, Paul and Mary. In the next several years, I bought 45s (singles) by the Beatles, the Rolling Stones, the Doors, the Righteous Brothers, the Zombies, the Box Tops, Neil Diamond and even Frank Sinatra (I played the grooves off "That's Life"). In 1969, I bought my first albums: Procol Harum's first album, and the first Bee Gees album, both of which had been released a couple of years before.

Physics, journalism, and music. I sure as hell didn't want to be a stock market investor.

Besides, it was an odd time for my father to encourage an interest in stocks. After roaring through the first half of the 1960s, the stock market had sputtered in the last five years. By the end of 1970, the Dow was hovering around 838, about where it was in 1964.

I wanted no part of it.

My father was undeterred. He was Horatio Alger incarnate. He didn't know if the market was going to be up or down, but he believed it reflected the future of the country. He believed in that future and in the greatness of the United States.

And why shouldn't he? He was a poor Italian kid from Arthur Avenue in the Bronx, whose father could not speak English, who went to night school at NYU and escaped to the suburbs of Bucks County, Pennsylvania in the late 1950s via a job at American Airlines, and who had gotten into the real estate development business, first by selling swimming pools, then by building apartment buildings.

By the time he gave me those two shares of Kawecki Berylco he was living in a beautiful home in New Hope, Pennsylvania surrounded by farmland. Paul Simon lived down the street. My dad would go on to make—and lose—a lot of money in the next 15 years, but on that December morning the future seemed bright.

Because he believed the country was growing and the stock market reflected that growth, he seemed unworried about whether the market would be up or down that year. He simply believed it would be up over time.

He wanted me to start investing.

I ignored him.

## Investing Mistake #1: waiting too long to start saving

It was a mistake my entire generation made: for the next decade and beyond, we didn't do much investing or saving. I travelled extensively, all over the world. I hitchhiked through Europe and the Middle East. I went to hundreds of concerts. After working for my father in the 1970s, I considered—and rejected—going deeper into the real estate development business with him, though we co-taught a course on Real Estate Development at the Wharton School at the University of Pennsylvania in the 1980s.

I struggled as a writer, worked for a law firm, and published articles in various periodicals. I wrote a newsletter on affordable housing that did reasonably well.

In 1989, my father and I published *Investing in Land: How to be a Successful Developer*, based on the curriculum we taught at Wharton, which was published by John Wiley.

CNBC went on air in April, the month the book came out. One of the first interviews my father did to promote the book was with Bill Griffeth, then an anchor for our rival, FNN.

CNBC hired me as Real Estate Correspondent in 1990. My father loved to give me a hard time about my refusal to make a career in the real estate business: "You wanted to be a journalist," he used to say. "I told you to go into real estate. You ended up being a real estate journalist. I didn't do so bad by you!"

When I got hired by CNBC, I hadn't given a thought about the stock market since my father tried to interest me nearly 20 years before.

On the surface, ignoring the market looked like a smart move. After a rally into 1972, where the Dow briefly closed over 1,000, the market tanked on the oil crisis in 1974. The rest of the 1970s was a long, protracted battle with high inflation, high unemployment, and low growth. The market didn't bottom until July 1982, with the Dow still hovering around 800.

The rest of the 1980s were better: Federal Reserve Chair Paul Volcker finally broke the back of inflation, though it took a painful recession to do so. The Dow rose 228 percent that decade and had only two down years: 1981 and 1984.[2]

But thinking low returns meant investing wasn't worth it was the wrong way to look at it, and my willful ignorance cost me dearly. I understood the concept of compounding interest and the law of large numbers, but the concepts only seemed real for some distant retirement that I could scarcely imagine.

The inability to imagine myself living in the future, a much older version of myself, was a serious error. Twenty years of no saving and no investing cost me later in life when I realized my investing goals were never going to be met unless I took more risk.

It's a problem facing my entire generation, and one reason there is a serious retirement issue.

I spent the rest of the 1970s and the 1980s ignoring the stock market, even though my father would bring up the subject often.

## NO TO MERGERS!

My hostility extended even to my measly investment in Kawecki Berylco stock that my father had gifted to me in a vain attempt to spark interest in the markets.

On May 31, 1978, Cabot Corporation acquired Kawecki Berylco Industries for $29 per share. On June 18, 1979, I received a letter from Jerry L. Allen, then the Treasurer of the company, asking me to tender my two shares.

"The records show that shares registered in your name are still outstanding," Mr. Allen said. "Since no interest or dividends can be paid on the KBI shares, we urge you to submit your stock to the Distributing Agent, the First National Bank of Boston, in order to receive the $29 per share."

I not only refused to tender my shares, I wrote a letter expressing my outrage at the merger.

I had no idea what I was talking about. I had no solid grounds to object to the merger, I was merely expressing my disapproval of the whole process and the stock market in general.

I still have the stock certificate.

## THE START OF MY INVESTING CAREER

I arrived at CNBC in September 1990, right in the middle of the Gulf War. I was 34 years old and working at a financial network, but even then, I didn't begin investing for another three years.

It was yet another stupid mistake.

When I finally did start investing, I made one rational decision, and yet another stupid decision.

From the outset, those of us in the News Division were restricted in what we could own. We could not own individual stocks or bonds, but we could own mutual funds and Exchange Traded Funds (ETFs).

The one exception to the ban on buying individual stocks or bonds was our company stock. We could own General Electric, which owned NBC at the time.

I began investing in the GE US Equity Fund, a broad, actively managed fund.

That was Smart Investing Decision #1: diversifying.

I also began investing heavily in General Electric stock.

This was good news and bad news. It was good news because the ban on owning other individual stocks prevented me from believing that I could pick stocks over professionals, who were themselves poor stock pickers. Jack Bogle, the founder of Vanguard, who came to have an enormous influence on the way I look at investing, always said, "Forget the needle, buy the haystack," meaning risk could be greatly reduced by avoiding individual stocks and buying the broader market.

The bad news was it didn't prevent me from drinking the Kool-Aid on my own company.

## Investing Mistake #2: putting too much money into one basket, in this case my company's stock

There is a simple rule: do not put much money into the company you work for. It should not be a dominant part of your investment portfolio. The risk is too high.

How much should you own? There is no law, but most investment advice follows the "10 percent guideline": don't invest more than 10 percent of your overall portfolio in the company you work for, and most suggest no more than five percent.

The broader rule is, do not fall in love with an investment.

I was aware of this. Hell, I was more than aware, I wrote a book about it: the book my father and I had written and published in 1989 (*Investing in Land*) specifically warned budding real estate investors about the dangers of falling in love with real estate and overpaying or putting too much money into a single investment:

*Every developer has found a property they have fallen in love with and are willing to throw economic sense to the winds to obtain. Don't do it! Set your upper limits and stick to them; if you cannot get a deal with those figures, walk away.*[3]

I wrote that! And when it came time to act on the principle, I ignored it.

Getting over-invested in anything was not considered a sound business practice, a principle my father reminded me of repeatedly. If you let emotion get involved, your judgment is clouded.

I opened my 401(k) and immediately began investing a third of my savings into GE stock. Why? Even then, as the Real Estate Correspondent, I was aware of the risk of lack of diversification. But I didn't care. I worked for General Electric.

And I worked for Jack Welch, the CEO of General Electric.

## THE JACK WELCH MYTHOS

If you weren't there, it would be hard to understand the influence that GE and Jack Welch had on corporate America and the investment community in the 1990s. Welch was a corporate God. He was 46 when he became the youngest CEO in General Electric's history in 1981.

Welch declared that every GE business must be No. 1 or No. 2 in its industry. He sold old businesses, bought new ones, and re-arranged GE's portfolio. He wiped out entire layers of bureaucracy. He sought input from workers with an ongoing series of "town meetings" between managers and employees. He ranked managers into three groups and insisted the bottom 10 percent had to move up or get fired, helping him earn one of his two nicknames, "Neutron Jack."

Investors preferred the other nickname. *Fortune* magazine dubbed him "Manager of the Century" in 1999.

Most importantly for all of us at NBC, Jack had an interest in television. He had engineered the purchase of RCA, which owned NBC, in 1985. There was some obvious overlap (both companies had an aerospace division, both made TV sets), but it was clear Welch's biggest desire was to own the NBC Television Network. The deal, valued at $6.28 billion, was at that time the largest non-oil merger in U.S. corporate history.[4]

Fortunately, there were visionaries at NBC who recognized the disruptive nature of cable television, then in its infancy.

I bought into the whole story, and why shouldn't I have? These visionaries were about to change my life.

## THE BIRTH OF CNBC

Bob Wright, then-president and CEO of NBC Broadcasting, and Tom Rogers, the first president of NBC Cable, were instrumental in diversifying NBC into the cable business. In early 1989, just before CNBC went on air, they made a deal with Charles Dolan, the founder of Cablevision, whereby NBC invested in many of Dolan's cable properties, including Bravo, American Movie Classics, and the History Channel.

Their first big joint venture was CNBC, which Welch enthusiastically endorsed: "I loved the idea from the start," he wrote in *Jack: Straight From the Gut*. "I thought there was an opportunity for a business channel, and unlike entertainment and sports, business programming wouldn't involve any rights fees."[5]

Welch may have liked the idea, but it was still a ballsy move on Wright's part. At the time, no one was making money in cable, not even CNN. Even worse: the NBC affiliate stations viewed cable as a threat to their business models and actively fought against the creation of CNBC or any cable network.

An even bigger problem was getting a cable operator to carry the station. Wright got the cooperation of John Malone, who ran Tele-Communications Inc. (TCI), the nation's largest cable operator. Malone wanted help with his struggling Tempo Television channel and agreed to carry CNBC if Wright would take Tempo off his hands.

Wright agreed, and with a leased satellite transponder provided by Malone, CNBC launched on April 17, 1989, in 10 million homes. Half of them came from Tempo.[6]

And when crunch time came, Welch, Wright and Rogers pulled it off again.

Two years in, CNBC was still losing money. We had only 18 million subscribers in 1991. Our competitor, Financial News Network (FNN), had filed for bankruptcy. Wright and Rogers convinced a skeptical Jack Welch to make a bid for the assets. GE paid $154.3 million for FNN on May 21, 1991. It was $60 million more than Jack Welch intended to spend, according to Wright.[7]

It would turn out to be one of the great media investments of all time. The acquisition doubled our subscriber base to 40 million households and secured the future of the station. In the mid-1990s, we launched CNBC Asia and CNBC Europe.

Wright, Rogers and David Zaslav (who had hired me in 1990) pulled off another coup in 1996 when they created MSNBC out of America's Talking, a network that was being run at the time by Roger Ailes, who was also running CNBC. Wright and the team convinced a skeptical Bill

Gates, the CEO of Microsoft, about the value of creating a melding of television and the internet. Gates wanted to create an internet news giant using NBC's resources. NBC was looking to find a partner to build out an internet presence. It was a far-reaching agreement, ahead of its time, the value of which would only become apparent years later.

"MSNBC became ground zero for breaking the corporate mold and playing by new rules in the new cable and Internet arenas," Tom Rogers wrote.[8]

By 1997, Wright, Rogers, and Zaslav had created a cable powerhouse. NBC owned CNBC, MSNBC, and seven regional sports networks, all valued at about $2.5 billion.[9]

Welch and the NBC team loved us, and we loved them back.

## OVERCONFIDENCE AND
## THE ILLUSION OF GENIUS

And that was a problem: my overconfidence in the GE team led me to believe that there was little risk in staying long—very long—in my company's stock.

Initially, there was good reason to be overconfident.

After years of underperformance, Welch had turned GE into a colossus.

Forget the internet companies. They were fleas; toddlers on the horizon. Most of them didn't exist in 1993. That's when GE began to pull away from the S&P 500, and up until early 2000 far outperformed the broader market. By late 1999, it was the second most valuable company in the world after Microsoft, with a market capitalization of $400 billion.[10] It would go on, briefly, to become the most valuable company in the world.

Initially, I looked like an investment genius.

By the end of 1998, almost 50 percent of my 401(k) was in GE stock.

And still I kept buying, into 2000. It didn't top out until August of that year.

It had risen about 600 percent in the six or so years I had been buying, and split its stock three times, in 1994, 1997, and 2000.

Then it all went to hell.

## Investing Mistake #3: refusing to rebalance a portfolio

In the late summer of 2000, GE began a long, slow descent.

On October 19, 2000, Welch came on the floor of the NYSE with Azim Premji, the CEO of Wipro, an Indian firm that was listing that day. Premji had turned Wipro from a vegetable products company into a manufacturing and technology colossus in India. The two had become friends following a 1989 joint venture to manufacture diagnostic and imaging products.

After the close, I did a brief interview with Premji and then turned to Jack. My colleague David Faber had just reported that United Technologies was in negotiations to buy Honeywell.

I asked Jack what he thought about the potential mega-deal.

"It's an interesting idea," he said, but he didn't look so calm. He looked stunned. He later admitted he "damn near fell on the floor" when I broke the news to him.[11]

"What are you going to do about it?" I asked.

Welch quickly cut off the interview and said he had to make a phone call. It was a Thursday night.

The next morning, at 10:30 AM, Welch called Honeywell's headquarters in Morristown, New Jersey, and was able to get Mike Bonsignore, Honeywell's CEO, on the phone, five minutes before he was going to close the deal with United Technologies. Welch convinced him to hold off with the promise that a counteroffer was coming.

By Saturday, they had a deal.[12]

None of us knew it, but GE stock had just topped out.

By then, Welch had already put off his retirement several times. It was delayed again so that he could finish the deal, in what would have been the capstone of his career.

It ended in failure in June 2001, when European regulators blocked the merger.

Jack's hand-picked successor, Jeff Immelt, took over the reins of GE a few days before the September 11, 2001 attacks.

By August 2002, GE was half the price it was two years earlier.

Other than disposing of a small options grant I received in 1997, I did not sell.

## Investing Mistake #4: refusing to acknowledge a loss and move on

By then, I was aware of the basic principles of behavioral finance, one of which was "loss aversion"—that the fear of a loss is greater than the expectation of a gain.

And yet, it wasn't the fear of the loss that prevented me from acting as much as a misplaced loyalty to my company. I was a loyal employee, and I believed in GE, even after Jeff Immelt took over from Jack.

It was a stupid sentiment that clouded my judgment, and I knew it. This is classic cognitive dissonance. I held two conflicting beliefs at once: that I should not own too much of my own company's stock, and that I should stay loyal to General Electric.

The loyalty won out. I did nothing.

# *Learning to ignore the daily fluctuations of the market*

Fortunately, by then I had begun absorbing other lessons I had learned from Bogle, Malkiel, Siegel, and Shiller that partially offset my willful stupidity with the GE investment.

The lessons were somewhat counterintuitive to what I was doing.

As a journalist covering the stock market, I was obsessed with the daily machinations of the market, everything from earnings to economic data to global events.

As an investor, I struggled mightily to ignore most of it.

The main principles that came to dominate my investing philosophy were:

- Diversify, both broadly and within asset classes.
- Stay in low-cost index funds and avoid high-cost actively managed funds (low-cost actively managed funds which had a strong track record were OK).
- Stay fully invested to the limits of your risk tolerance.
- Do not engage in market timing.

Looking back, I was successful in diversifying, staying in low-cost funds, and staying fully invested.

Market timing, not so much.

# *My investment history*

After speaking on the phone with Jack Bogle, the head of Vanguard (see Chapter 10), I opened a Vanguard account for my wife in 1997. Her first investment, Vanguard Real Estate Index Fund, was a passively managed fund of the biggest real estate companies. She was a real estate agent, and I had been Real Estate Correspondent. Investing in what you know had been popularized by Peter Lynch a decade before.

This was not a sound investment strategy for the long term, but we had at least started our indexing voyage. She also put money into Vanguard Explorer, a highly regarded actively managed fund.

In the next few years, we began diversifying into still more low-cost funds, mostly index funds like Vanguard Mid-Cap Index and Vanguard Small Cap Value.

I was still not a complete convert on passive investing. By then, Bogle and others had made me aware that precious few funds beat their benchmarks, but there were a few.

We put money into Vanguard Health Care Fund, an actively managed fund run by Ed Owens, who had an amazing ability to pick and rotate between pharmaceuticals, biotech, services, and medical devices. In a 28-year career running Health Care, from 1984 to 2012, Owens was able to pull off a 16 percent annual return. It was one of the greatest runs in stock market history, beating the S&P 500 by almost six percentage points a year.[13]

We kept that fund for many years, only selling after several years of disappointing performances following Owens' departure. My wife switched to Vanguard Health Care Index Fund, a passively managed fund with an ultra-low (0.1%) expense ratio.

We also bought several bond funds, including Vanguard High Yield and Vanguard Intermediate-Term Investment Grade, both well-known corporate bond funds.

The Great Financial Crisis of 2008–2009 rocked many investors to their core. It was the ultimate test of mental discipline: after a dismal start to the new century (the S&P declined in 2000, 2001, and 2002), the markets had been up for five straight years, finally beating the 2000 high in October 2007.

The next two years saw investors dump stocks and real estate on a level not seen in decades. By then, I had weathered a lot of investing storms: the Gulf War in 1990, the Russian debt default in 1998, the dot-com bust in 2000, and the World Trade Center attacks and the accompanying recession.

In mid-2008, I took some money out of my stock funds and made a down payment on an investment condominium, the first real estate investment we had made outside of our home.

It was a good move selling the stock funds, but not a great move buying real estate, which came to a crashing halt about that time.

The S&P 500 declined more than 50 percent from the peak in 2007 to the bottom in March 2009. A year later, in April 2010, it was up almost 80 percent.

## *The Great Financial Crisis: changed assumptions*

The Great Financial Crisis affected the way I look at investments. I was still a believer in Bogle's main precept, the market portfolio is the most sensible decision.[14] That is, the best long-term decision is to own the broad market.

However, having witnessed the Great Financial Crisis first-hand and the response of the Federal Reserve, I made several assumptions in the years after the Financial Crisis and adjusted my portfolio. I assumed that:

- Rates were going to stay low for a very long time, and that this would favor stocks over bonds.
- The Fed was going to continue to pump huge amounts of money into the economy, some of which would find its way into the stock market, leading to asset price inflation.

- The "Fed put" (the belief the Federal Reserve was going to backstop large parts of the economy, thus providing a floor to the economy and the markets, allowing investors to take more risk) was very real.

Broad index funds remained the core investment, but based on these assumptions, I "tilted" the portfolio a bit.

**Stocks have preference over bonds.** Because I was so late to the investing game, I decided a long time ago to take more risk by tilting heavily toward stocks over bonds, which continues even into my 60s. The dismal yields bonds provided (the yield on the 10-year Treasury had dropped below two percent by the end of 2011) made the decision easier. But it was more than just the necessity to take risk: even by 2010, the old 60-40 stock/bond split or the "bonds should be the same percentage of your portfolio as your age" rule (which Bogle had championed earlier on) did not seem to make much sense when many people in my age group were going to live close to 90 years old.

The stock/bond/cash ratio has varied in the 2010s, but has usually been 75/20/5, with sometimes a slightly higher portion in cash.

**Large stocks have preference over small stocks.** I have always had money in small and midcap index funds, but my largest exposure was to big cap funds. Another investing belief is that small-cap stocks outperform large-cap stocks over long periods of time. I found this was partially true, but that small-cap stocks had significantly more risk associated with them, including interest rate risk and economic risk. Jack Bogle himself came to this conclusion in a 2002 speech and noted that small caps and large caps had essentially identical returns from 1945 to 2002, hardly worth the higher risk.[15] Finally the S&P 500—a proxy for the mid- and large-cap market—is now 80 percent of the entire stock market and should do fine in matching the overall market returns.

**Growth has preference over value.** This was the toughest decision to make. The academic research suggested that value outperforms growth over long periods. But my bet was that the post-Great Financial Crisis period was not by any means normal. With growth scarce, the Fed backstopping the economy, and interest rates at record low levels, my bet was that investors would bid up growth stocks.

Through much of the 2010s, I owned growth funds like Vanguard International Growth and Vanguard Growth.

In taking this risk, I revealed an additional bias: a preference for technological disruption, which is usually represented in growth stocks.

I'm not the only one with this bias.

"Disruption always wins," Merrill Lynch's Equity Strategist, Haim Israel, wrote in a 2021 note to clients, noting that only 1.5% of public companies have generated 100 percent of the net global market wealth in the past 30 years. "Only a handful of disruptors ('superstar firms') really influence long-term financial markets growth. Furthermore, accelerating innovation places incumbents at greater risk of displacement. In 1958, the average company lasted 61 years on the S&P 500; by 2016, this was 24 years and is forecast to be just 12 years by 2027."[16]

The question, of course, is how to pick those winners (you don't: you stay with broad funds) and how much you're willing to bid up the prices for growth, which can get crazy overvalued. Investors in particular bid up growth stocks after Covid emerged in 2020.

This emphasis on "tilting" the portfolio away from strict indexing may seem odd from someone who touts himself as a Jack Bogle disciple, but I would beg to differ.

First, the tilt toward growth was not a full-on conversion. Most of the portfolio remained in broad index funds.

Second, Jack Bogle himself was not tone deaf to the demand to "scratch the itch." Vanguard always had actively managed funds. Following the creation of the Windsor Funds in the 1960s, which had a value tilt, Bogle launched the PRIMECAP fund in 1984, and later the Capital Opportunity Fund. Both were actively managed but with a growth tilt.*17

The secret, as with all of Vanguard's funds, active and indexed, was to keep costs low.

## The Fed again forces a change in my portfolio

In late 2021, I made some modest changes in my portfolio. It became obvious the Fed was going to raise rates in 2022 and that the decades-long decline in yields was likely at an end.

Was the flood of liquidity the Fed unleashed since 2009 a factor in the market? It sure seems that way: the S&P 500 climbed an average of roughly 15 percent a year between 2009 and 2021, well above the historic norm of 8–10 percent. That outsized gain is not all attributable to the Fed's intervention (other countries like Japan and the United Kingdom also had aggressive central bank intervention and their markets did not perform nearly as well), but it is reasonable to assume that the Fed was a factor in the market's decade-long outperformance.

If it is reasonable to assume the Fed adding liquidity was a factor in the market's rise, it would be reasonable to assume that the Fed withdrawing liquidity might be a factor in producing sub-par (below 10 percent) gains in the next few years.

In bonds, I wanted less volatility, so I sold my long-standing position in Vanguard High Yield, and even my position in Intermediate-Term

---

* You can read how Jack created these funds, with the help of very capable managers, in his intellectual autobiography, *Stay the Course: The Story of Vanguard and the Index Revolution.*

Investment Grade, and put the money into a relatively new fund, Vanguard Core-Plus Fund, which was an actively managed fund that had a small percentage in high yield. In addition to less volatility than High Yield, Core-Plus offered more diversification.

Why stay in an actively managed bond fund? I reasoned that there would be far more volatility in the bond world in the coming years, and this was one of the rare instances where I felt active management might have a chance to outperform.

For stocks, despite my growth bias, I put more money into Vanguard Small Cap Value Index and Mid-Cap Index, on the theory that the Fed raising rates would provide some headwind to high-valuation tech stocks. I switched from Vanguard International Growth to Vanguard Total International, reasoning that I wanted less exposure to global growth in general and to emerging markets and China.

I also held on to Vanguard Growth and Vanguard Health Care Index.

The largest single holding (about 30 percent of my portfolio) is in the S&P 500. I also keep a small allocation in cash.

I did not change the stock allocation, which has remained in the 75 percent range. I've seen no reason to change my belief that I will live to about 90, which gives me another 25 years in the market. I will gradually reduce that percentage in the coming years.

## MY PORTFOLIO, JANUARY 2022

Equities: S&P 500 index fund, Vanguard Mid-Cap Index (VIMAX), Vanguard Small Cap Value Index (VSIAX), Vanguard Total International Index (VTIAX), Vanguard Health Care Index Fund (VHCIX), Vanguard Growth ETF (VUG), two miscellaneous equity funds.

Bonds: Vanguard Core-Plus Bond Fund (VCPAX).

The "miscellaneous equity funds" has been a mix of two or three equity funds that rotate every few years and which I use to satisfy my itch for "trend picking," which Bogle explicitly warned about. I've put money into—and out of—buyback funds, aggressive growth funds, small cap growth, and others, and what I've noticed is it works for a few years, and then it usually doesn't.

Will this work over the long run? In the 11 years since 2010, this small tilt toward large caps and growth proved to be a good performer, and now I have pushed the portfolio back toward broad index funds, but who knows in the long run. Mean reversion is a powerful force, and it's possible—as has been the case for a good part of 2021—that small caps and value will come roaring back.

## Grading my investment acumen

What grade would I give myself for adherence to my investment principles in the past 30 years?

I'd give it a B, at best.

Let's look down the list of my principles, which I enumerated earlier in the chapter.

*Diversify, both broadly and within asset classes*: in the early years, I made a major mistake with the GE investment. After that, much better. Broad mix of domestic and international funds, and bond funds.

*Stay in low-cost index funds and avoid high-cost actively managed funds*: good grade on that. Even when I owned actively managed funds, they were almost always low cost.

*Stay fully invested to the limits of your risk tolerance*: pretty good here. Because I started investing late in life, I had to take more risk.

*Do not engage in market timing*: here, it gets tricky. I "stayed the course" (to use Jack Bogle's famous phrase) pretty well from the 1990s to the mid-2000s. I made some changes during the height of the Great Financial Crisis and then adopted a pro-growth tilt in the early 2010s that served me well, then shifted more to straight indexing as the Fed signaled it would be raising rates at the end of 2021.

That's market timing. I only did it in a major way a few times in 30 years, but it is market timing.

I've made peace with the fact that I haven't always strictly adhered to my investment precepts. The urge to "scratch the itch" and act is very powerful, and I am not immune to those urges.

Bogle famously said, "Don't do something, stand there!" I've done well just standing there for 30 years, but every once in a while, I had to dance.

# *My thoughts on 30 years of investing*

## FIGURE OUT HOW MUCH TIME YOU WANT TO SPEND UNDERSTANDING THIS STUFF

I'm a classic self-directed investor, so I'm comfortable doing this without a financial advisor.

Most people are not, and that's why I think a reasonably priced financial advisor is a worthwhile investment. As you can see, being very well informed and self-directed didn't prevent me from making mistakes.

Regardless, before you do anything you should be able to answer the most basic questions about your goals, your risk tolerance, and how long you're going to live.

Here's my answers:

**How much risk do I want to take?**
Because I didn't start saving until my mid-30s, I have taken on more risk. Moderate to high.

**How comfortable would I be if the stock market dropped 20 percent in a year?**

This has already happened several times to me, including a 50 percent drop during the Great Financial Crisis. I took some money out during the height of that crisis, but for the most part I have swallowed hard and rode everything out.

**How long do I think I'm going to live?**

I'm 65 as of this writing, expecting to live to 90, which is (hopefully) conservative.

**How comfortable am I with owning stocks versus bonds?**

Very comfortable, and because I expect to live another 25 years I plan to have 70 percent plus of my portfolio in stocks for the foreseeable future and then begin reducing that allocation.

**How much can you save?**

It started out small and increased as my income increased. I'm close to 15 percent.

**What kind of returns am I expecting?**

I go by historic averages. Long term the S&P 500 has returned slightly over 10 percent a year, including dividends. In the last decade, the overall market has returned closer to 15 percent a year, so I am expecting some mean reversion in the coming years and likely sub-10 percent returns, and likely a down year or two.

**What are my future financial needs?**

Between my pension, Social Security, and personal savings, I could stop working in a few years and live comfortably. But I likely will not. I plan to keep working into my 70s, but also plan to start drawing down on my retirement account at a roughly four percent rate at the same time.

## WHETHER YOU CHOOSE ACTIVE OR INDEXED, ALWAYS GO WITH LOW COST

I showed you in Chapter 10 that Bogle had long ago determined that high costs destroy returns. Even great fund managers who might outperform their benchmarks for a few years can underperform on a total return basis because their high fees eat into the returns.

The funds I own are all very low-cost, with almost all charging 10 basis points or less per year (one basis point is one-hundredth of one percent, so 100 basis points is one percent—10 basis points is $10 per year for every $10,000 invested). The exception is Core-Plus Bond Fund, which is actively managed and charges 20 basis points, at the very low end for actively managed bond funds in general.

## PAY LESS ATTENTION TO THE NUMBERS AND MORE ATTENTION TO HOW YOUR BRAIN CHEMISTRY CAUSES YOU TO MAKE STUPID DECISIONS

Once you have a broadly diversified portfolio, are comfortable with your risk level, and you have a clear investment horizon, almost invariably the best course of action is to do nothing.

You will really have to work at this. You will hear about investments you think you should be in. You will watch periods where the market dips down—it may last for several years. You will want to panic and sell.

Almost invariably, if you are truly comfortable with your risk level and your investment time horizon, you should resist that urge to do something.

If you do have that urge—and who doesn't think they are an investment genius—than do what I do. Take 5–10 percent and try investing it actively. Odds are, you would have been better off leaving it in an indexed fund.

## DON'T OVERANALYZE

I look at my investments twice a year. Any changes I make are almost entirely to rebalance, though there were years (2008, the early 2010s, and 2021) when I made more substantive changes.

## MINIMIZE TAXES

It's amazing how many people spend hours trying to find the lowest cost fund but don't pay much attention to taxes. It's a big mistake. Indexed funds are more tax-efficient than actively managed funds. ETFs are more tax-efficient than mutual funds. There's a general rule that you should keep bond funds in tax-deferred accounts and stock funds in taxable accounts, but I keep most of my investments in 401(k) accounts.

## DON'T GET TOO COMPLICATED

When I look at my portfolio, I can practically hear Jack Bogle laughing at me. "You say you're a Jack Bogle disciple, so why do you have so many investments? If you're that big on growth, you can do what you're doing with three or four funds instead of nine or 10, and get the same performance, likely paying less fees!"

He's right. I could pare the funds down and likely get the same amount of exposure for the same (or lower) risk levels.

What I called "tilting" Jack called "slice and dice," the very human tendency of trying to add to your portfolio asset classes you believe are likely to outperform. He cautioned against it, but said if you had to scratch that itch he recommended keeping 55 percent in a total market portfolio, and taking the other 45 percent and dividing it up equally between three other funds or sectors you think will outperform.[18]

With that said, I'm comfortable with the number of holdings I have. It's big enough for me to get my head around it and still feel that I have broad exposure.

I have seen individuals that have dozens and dozens of holdings. They seem to believe that many holdings demonstrate they are deeper and more profound investors, or that it spreads out risk. None of that is necessarily true.

## *Bogle practiced what he preached*

Many years ago, in the mid-2000s, I called Jack Bogle on the phone and played a game of "you show me yours, I'll show you mine" with him. I came right out and asked him what he owned. He declined to answer directly, perhaps because he had a son who had a hedge fund that he had put some money into. But he clearly implied, in our telephone conversation, that for his retirement (tax-deferred) account most of his investment money was in Vanguard's Total Stock Market and Total Bond Market funds.

A few years later, at a 2010 investment conference, Bogle said that he had 81 percent of his personal assets, including his retirement plan, in bonds and 19 percent in stocks. He was then 81 years old, so he was an adherent to his belief that an investor should put his age into bonds.

For his retirement portfolio, Bogle confirmed that he indeed had most of his assets in Total Bond Market, but also added he had one-third of the bond portfolio in Vanguard's Short-Term Investment Grade Bond Fund. His personal (taxable) portfolio also included Vanguard Intermediate-Term Tax-Exempt bond fund and Vanguard Limited-Term Tax-Exempt bond fund.[19]

I couldn't beat that kind of concentrated portfolio, and I certainly split with Bogle on his opinion on bond exposure.

## Consider getting even simpler

It's possible to get a lot simpler. To this day, if someone asks me for the simplest, broadest fund portfolio they could own, I point them to the Bogleheads.

The Bogleheads are a group of Jack Bogle disciples that began meeting informally in 1998 to discuss Jack's investment principles. It was started by Taylor Larimore, a Miami resident, and was initially known as the "Vanguard Diehards," but the name was changed to Bogleheads by 2007.

In *The Boglehead's Guide to the Three-Fund Portfolio: How a Simple Portfolio of Three Total Market Index Funds Outperforms Most Investors with Less Risk*, Larimore recommends a simple three-fund portfolio:

1. Vanguard Total Stock Market Index Fund
2. Vanguard Total Bond Market Index Fund
3. Vanguard Total International Stock Index Fund

The exact allocation would be based on the investor's goal, time frame, risk tolerance and personal financial situation.[20]

All self-directed investors must make these kinds of decisions. The Bogleheads' main message is: keep it as simple as possible. I highly recommend their website, www.bogleheads.org, which contains a wealth of investment advice.

I like to tell people that if you're good as an investor, you can write down what you own on an index card. Whenever I do this, describing in general the kind of indexed ETFs and mutual funds I own, the listener usually says, "That's it? You're the Senior Stocks Correspondent for CNBC and this is the stuff you own?"

And then they stare at me. They're waiting for me to tell them what I really own, the inside stuff, the obscure stuff that would show them I was one of the Illuminati.

They're always disappointed. Other than a little real estate and a vintage collection of 1960s rock posters (hey, everyone should have a hobby), that's it.

## *Goodbye to GE*

The dot-com bust, 9/11, a bust in the energy and insurance businesses, the near blowup of GE Capital during the Great Financial Crisis, and the unwillingness of investors to pay a premium for complicated conglomerates like GE, all combined to make the 2000s a disastrous decade for the company. GE would eventually sell off many of its most prized units, including appliances, plastics, light bulbs, locomotives, and eventually, in 2011, even NBC itself.

By then, it was NBC Universal. In 2004, Bob Wright pulled off one of the great media deals of the century, acquiring 80 percent of Vivendi's film and television subsidiary, Vivendi Universal Entertainment. The newly christened NBCUniversal, or NBCU, now owned Universal Pictures, Universal Parks & Resorts, and valuable cable assets like USA Network.

But Wright had left by 2007, to be replaced by Jeff Zucker.

In 2009, desperate for cash and still reeling from losses in reinsurance, mortgage-backed securities, and power generation, GE agreed to sell a 51 percent stake in NBCU to Comcast in a deal that valued NBCU at $30 billion.[21] Two years after the deal closed in 2011, GE sold the remaining 49 percent.

It was a bitter pill for Wright, who believed that GE, in its desperation to shed assets, had sold NBCUniversal dirt cheap, contending that it was worth closer to $45 billion than $30.[22]

He had reason to be bitter. Wright's foresight in getting into cable with CNBC, MSNBC, and then the Vivendi deal, was what made Comcast bite. Even Steve Burke, who was president of Comcast Cable and became CEO of NBCUniversal in 2009, made it clear it was Wright's foresight that made the deal possible: "The NBC we bought had 100 percent of its earnings come from the cable channels, which is remarkable considering that CNBC had only been around 25 years and MSNBC half that time."[23]

It didn't matter. By then, we were nothing but a ledger note to GE. We were a far better fit under Comcast, which had pipes to send out the channels but very little content. That's what we provided.

GE had gone from a high of $600 billion in market capitalization, to a low of $70 billion. Wright, who witnessed the debacle first-hand, called it "the greatest loss of market capital in business history."[24]

## *"I couldn't take it anymore"*

Meanwhile, I had my own capital loss to deal with.

With GE plunging at the start of the Great Financial Crisis, I sold my entire position in mid-2008. I never calculated exactly how much I had invested from 1993 to 2000, but I am sure it was sold at a loss.

In 2010, I saw Jack Welch at a party. I was a bit nervous to tell him what I had done, but I had to say something.

"Jack, I hope you won't be mad, but I sold all my GE stock. I couldn't take it anymore."

He looked at me, smiled, and patted me on the shoulder. "It's OK, Bob, I understand. And if anyone asks, you tell them, I never sold."

I had no idea if that was true or not, but half of me wanted to believe it, and the other half wanted to believe that, unlike me, Jack Welch was the kind of man who knew exactly when to cut his losses.

## *Older but no wiser*

If you think these experiences turned me into an investing wise man, you'd be wrong.

I still make mistakes, but they're usually not intellectual mistakes. They're emotional mistakes. That's why I pay so much more attention to behavioral finance than I did 20 years ago: it shows the stupid things we are doing and offers a reason why.

What studying behavioral finance has taught me is, I know I can't entirely trust myself.

For example, "Don't overpay for an investment" is a cliché, but it's true. I'm going to tell you about how I violated that very simple precept just a short while ago.

It involves a Black Sabbath poster.

# CHAPTER 21

# *Black Sabbath and Why I Am Still Not Rational*

═══

I F you think knowing something about behavioral economics prevents you from doing stupid things, let me tell you about the Black Sabbath poster I bought.

I have a hobby: I collect 1960s rock posters.

I know, it's a little strange, but it's fun. It's about the golden age of rock: Jimi Hendrix, the Doors, Cream, Grateful Dead, Jefferson Airplane.

The style—usually referred to as "psychedelia"—had a tremendous impact on the visual arts of the 1960s, and continues to have an impact today. The artists who created this style—Wes Wilson, Rick Griffin, Stanley Mouse, Alton Kelley, Lee Conklin, Randy Tuten, David Singer, Victor Moscoso, and Bonnie MacLean, in my opinion, are the Toulouse-Lautrecs of their day.

Most of these posters were given out at concerts at the Fillmore in San Francisco or a few other venues, then were quickly hung on walls, torn up, and thrown away. There's not a lot of copies of the early posters from the dawn of psychedelia (1966–1968), and a small community of collectors that trade these posters has grown up in the last 50 years.

During the pandemic, I displayed a few of the posters I had framed on my wall behind me when I was broadcasting.

They were an instant hit. My coolness factor on social media went through the roof. Room Rater—a Twitter group that rated the rooms of reporters that were broadcasting from their homes and apartments—gave me a 9 out of 10, then upped it to 10 out of 10.

Who knew there were so many Deadheads and old hippies watching CNBC?

## Who's the idiot here?

One day I was monitoring an online auction of rock posters. A 1975 Black Sabbath poster came up for sale. I was not a Black Sabbath fan in the 1970s. The music was too turgid for my taste. I was into Led Zeppelin and the Who. I never even went to a Black Sabbath concert.

But this was a cool poster, with Ozzy Osbourne waving his hands in the air.

The opening bid was $200. On a lark, I bid $400. I figured that $400–$500 was a fair price and the auction would quickly be over.

Immediately, someone counterbid $500.

Hm. I don't really want this poster, but I'm intrigued. Who wants it?

I bid $600. Immediately, there's a counterbid for $700.

Hm. I bid again. Another counterbid.

In two minutes, we're at $1,000.

Now I'm getting annoyed. Who the hell wants this poster so badly? It's not like Black Sabbath has an intense cult of collectors, like Zeppelin or the Velvet Underground.

At least I didn't think so.

I bid again. Another counterbid, immediately.

Two minutes later, we are at $2,000.

Now I'm yelling at my computer. I don't want this goddamn poster. I *hate* Black Sabbath.

A minute or so later, we are at $2,500, then $3,000.

Now I don't care what the hell the price is. I want to find out who this person is, get a meeting, roll up the poster and force it down his or her throat.

I want to make them *eat* this goddamn poster.

A few minutes later, I won the poster, at $3,499, plus a 10 percent buyer's fee.

The next day, I did something I almost never do. I called the person who ran the auction, a very respected dealer who specialized in rock posters.

It's not common to ask who the competing bidders are at auctions, but the auction was over and I had to know. Who was this person? Was I bidding against Ozzy Osbourne himself?

Who the hell was willing to spend $3,500 for a goddamn Black Sabbath poster? Who is this idiot, I demanded to know?

The dealer said, "I can tell you who the idiot was, Bob. It was you. You're the idiot who bought it."

And he was right.

Collectors will tell you that to be a successful long-term collector of anything, you must be disciplined. You must know what you are willing to pay for something, and not go over that price. You cannot be carried away by the emotion of an auction. You must be willing to walk away.

I have walked away from most auctions a loser, because I wasn't willing to pay more than I thought a poster was worth.

What did I think that poster was worth? $400–$500.

How did I know that? I had several decades of experience bidding on rock posters, and based on what I had seen I thought that was a reasonable price.

But it was all a guess, as it is with all collectibles. With stocks, at least you have the appearance of trying to figure out what the "intrinsic value" of the stock might be, based on what kind of dividend it pays, and the present value of a future stream of cash flow that might turn into earnings.

This is known as "fundamental analysis" and it is the basis for most long-term stock investing.

But there's none of that when it comes to posters, or any other kind of collectible.

A rock poster doesn't do anything. It doesn't pay a dividend, or provide a future cash flow you can try to discount into the present.

It just sits there.

Same story with gold, and with Bitcoin as well.

What's this poster worth? It's worth whatever anyone is willing to pay for it at that moment.

It doesn't have an intrinsic value, but it does have a price.

And when you have two bidders who suddenly, for whatever reason, decide they are price-insensitive, watch out.

The price can get stupid fast. Which is exactly what happened.

I bid $400 and ended up with a $3,500 poster of Ozzy Osbourne staring me in the face.

With that damn Black Sabbath poster, I violated all the rules. I lost it. Something snapped.

## *Why did I lose it?*

I consulted Dr. Brad Klontz, a Certified Financial Planner, psychologist and a member of the CNBC Financial Wellness Council. He's an expert in financial psychology, behavioral finance, and financial planning, and he's author of several books, including *Money Mammoth: Harness the Power of Financial Psychology to Evolve Your Money Mindset, Avoid Extinction, and Crush Your Financial Goals.*

Brad showed me several ways my thinking had been skewed:

- *Competition:* Cooperation is more common in relationships and competition is more common with unrelated individuals. Competition increases when supply is low and demand is high. It's possible that the anonymity of my competitor made me more competitive.
- *The psychology of scarcity:* When we believe that we lack something we become less rational and are more prone to engaging in self-defeating behaviors to try to get it.
- *The Endowment Effect:* We have a tendency to overvalue what we already possess. The degree to which I fantasized about already having that poster on my wall would have increased the price I was willing to pay for it.
- *Social Facilitation:* Being in the presence of others changes our behavior. Sometimes this improves our performance and at other times it can compromise our commitment to stick to our plans, including engaging in more risky behaviors than we would have done if we were alone.[1]

There are other explanations, including one offered indirectly by the dean of behavioral economists, Daniel Kahneman. In *Your Money and Your Brain: How the New Science of Neuroeconomics Can Help Make You Rich*, Jason Zweig quotes Kahneman as saying, "Financial decision-making is not necessarily about making money. It's also about intangible motives like avoiding regret or achieving pride."[2]

Those were certainly factors lurking in the back of my mind. I didn't want to miss out on acquiring a rare poster (I had never seen it before), and I probably wanted the bragging rights to owning it.

All these explanations are feasible, but I still remember being annoyed that anyone was willing to pay so much for the damn poster. It was irrational!

Maybe not entirely. The competing bidder, I was told, was a Los Angeles poster dealer who frequently sold to the Hollywood crowd and wealthy Angelinos.

Figures. Who else would be dumb enough to pay $3,500 for a Black Sabbath poster? Some stupid actor with too much money and a weird fixation on Black Sabbath. Idiot.

I framed it, which cost me another $500. I had to drastically curtail my spending for a few months just to pay it off. It hangs on my living room wall—a reminder of my own stupidity and biases.

It is a pretty cool poster, though.

## What's it worth?

I try to avoid "what's it worth?" questions when it comes to investments outside the stock market.

What's gold worth? What's Bitcoin worth? It's worth whatever anyone is willing to pay for it at that moment.

When I was a kid in the 1960s, I collected comic books. Most 1940s comic books, in 1966, were selling for $10–$50.

Between 1990 and 2010, a large group of new collectors came into the marketplace, many of whom had never owned comic books and had no emotional attachment to them. They were just interested in owning collectibles as alternative investments.

Prices went up. In 2010, the first Superman comic book, *Action #1*, sold for $1 million. It was the first comic book to ever sell for $1 million.

That was a famous comic book even in the 1960s, but I remember thinking, "Man, $1 million is crazy money for a comic book. I'd like to meet the idiot who spent $1 million for a comic book."

In 2021, a high-quality copy of *Action #1* sold for $3.25 million.

I wanted to meet that idiot, too.

I have no doubt there were people watching that rock poster auction where I bought that Black Sabbath poster who were wondering, "Man, I'd like to meet the idiot who spent $3,500 for a Black Sabbath poster."

I may not have much faith in my ability to control my auction impulses, but I do have a few core beliefs about the stock market, which I will share with you in the next chapter.

## CHAPTER 22

# *What I Believe about the Stock Market*

===

I T'S often been said that the stock market is a casino.

I never understood this. In a casino, you walk in, place a bet, and hope to win. Over time, it is well established that the odds are in favor of the casino, regardless of whether you are playing slots, blackjack, or craps.

In the long run, almost all players in a casino will lose.

That's not how the stock market works.

The stock market is the *opposite* of a casino: over long periods of time, the broad stock market outperforms most other investments.

In this chapter, I share the reason why I hold this view and a series of my other beliefs about investing.

# Belief #1: Over long periods of time, stocks outperform bonds and cash

This is the most important idea to grasp, but it is only true over long periods of time, and I mean decades.

Since 1928, the S&P 500 has gone up, year-over-year, 72 percent of the time. That includes dividends, which are an important part of the total return. That is an impressive achievement.

**S&P 500 year-over-year returns (since 1928, including dividends)[1]**

| Up | 72% |
|------|-----|
| Down | 28% |

During that 94-year period, the S&P has averaged a yearly return of 11.7 percent, again including dividends (not adjusted for inflation).

The gains and losses have not been evenly distributed: there have been far more years with big advances than big declines. The S&P has advanced 10 percent or more in a year 57 percent of the time, and declined 10 percent or more only 12 percent of the time:

**S&P 500 (percentage advance each year)**

| 20%+ advance | 36% |
|-----------------|-----|
| 10%–20% advance | 21% |
| 0%–10% advance | 15% |
| 0%–10% decline | 15% |
| 10%+ decline | 12% |

This beats bonds and cash by a wide margin.

**Stocks beat bonds ($1 return, 1926–2019)**

| Inflation | $14 |
|---|---|
| Long-term government bonds | $175 |
| U.S. Large-cap stocks | $9,237 |
| U.S. Small-cap stocks | $25,617 |

Source: Dimensional funds.

Now for the bad news.

Pessimists on the markets like to trot out all sorts of reasons why you should stay away from investing. Many of the basic facts are true, but they shouldn't scare anyone away.

Let's look at some of them.

## OBJECTION #1: THE STOCK MARKET CAN UNDERPERFORM FOR LONG PERIODS

It's true.

One often-cited example is returns after the stock market peaked in September 1929. It took 14 years (until 1943) to get back to even (including dividends) on the S&P 500 and 25 years (until 1954) using only prices (excluding dividends).

There are other long periods where stocks had flat or negative multi-year returns: during the high-inflation period in the mid-1970s when the S&P was essentially flat (on a price basis) between 1973 and 1980; and in the 2000s following the dot-com bust from mid-2000 to mid-2007.

## OBJECTION #2: INFLATION AND HIGH INTEREST RATES CAN KILL MARKET RETURNS

Also true, but with caveats.

The 1970s, a period of high inflation and high rates, was one of the worst times to be a stocks investor. There were many years during this period when government Treasuries, or even gold, were a better investment.[2] Fortunately, inflation and interest rates have—for the most part—trended lower for the past 30 years, and that has mostly benefitted stocks.

However, because stocks represent claims on future earnings, and because companies can and do raise prices to adjust for inflation, stocks can be an excellent hedge against inflation, as long as inflation occurs in moderation.

## OBJECTION #3: STOCKS ARE RISKY

True again.

Stocks are riskier to own than other investments, and that's why they offer a higher expected return.

Wes Crill is Senior Researcher at Dimensional Fund Advisors, a highly regarded investment firm that specializes in low-cost index funds and includes Nobel Memorial Prize in Economic Sciences winner Eugene Fama on its Board of Directors. He says that compared to bonds, there is a higher probability of large losses owning stocks because "you are not promised cashflows on a particular schedule, and you are further down the pecking order in the event that the company in which you've invested goes bankrupt. It would not make sense for an investor to hold equity securities for the same rate of return as fixed income."[3]

Ben Carlson is with Ritholtz Wealth Management and writes one of my favorite investment blogs, *A Wealth of Common Sense*. He put it best: "It's likely true that the reason returns have been so high over the long-run for U.S. stocks is *because* of the fact that there is so much risk involved at times."[4]

An investor *should* be compensated with higher returns over long periods for holding riskier investments.

## OBJECTION #4: STOCK PRICES
## MOVE AROUND A LOT

They do.

Price declines of 5–10 percent happen all the time. Between 1946 and 2019, there have been 84 instances where the S&P has dropped 5–10 percent, according to Guggenheim.[5]

That's a lot. That's more than once a year.

Fortunately, the market usually bounces back fast from these modest declines. The average time it takes to recover from those losses is one month.

Far deeper declines have happened, but they occur less frequently.

**Declines in the S&P 500 (since 1946)**

| Decline % | # of declines | Average time to recover (months) |
|-----------|---------------|----------------------------------|
| 5–10      | 84            | 1                                |
| 10–20     | 29            | 4                                |
| 20–40     | 9             | 14                               |
| 40+       | 3             | 58                               |

Source: Guggenheim.

Declines of 10–20 percent have happened 29 times (about once every 2.5 years since 1946), 20–40 percent nine times (about once every 8.5 years) and 40 percent or more three times (every 25 years).

Two key takeaways: first, most pullbacks above 20 percent have been associated with recessions (there have been 12 since 1946).

Second, for long-term investors, it tells you that even relatively severe pullbacks of 20–40 percent don't last very long—only 14 months. Your average long-term investor can easily weather that storm.

The rare instances of severe pullbacks—40 percent or more—do represent a problem for investors near retirement age, or those who might need the money immediately. That's because the average recovery period—58 months—is nearly five years.

That kind of decline and the long recovery is one reason retirees need to be especially mindful of the potential of those (very rare) types of market declines.

But don't let that scare you. Oft-used phrases like "The S&P 500 declined 50 percent from the market top in 2007 to the bottom in 2009" are true but not very relevant to the average investor.

Think about it: how many people do you know who invested all of their money at a market top, and pulled it all out at the market bottom? Yes, I know people who panicked at bottoms, but not one of them invested all their money at the very top. Most people engage in some form of dollar-cost averaging where they invest money over many years.

That means that when stocks pull back, they are almost certainly pulling back from a higher price than you paid for them.

Why are the returns so lumpy? Why does the market gyrate so much? Because the free enterprise system goes through periods of boom and bust, and because humans are, well, just kind of crazy sometimes.

Jack Bogle, in a famous 2002 speech, put it this way:

Part of the reason is that the course of our economy is not smooth. We have prosperity and recession, even boom and bust. Those are simply the economics of enterprise, and while they may be tamer than in the past, they are not tamed. But there is more: The emotions of investors, whose greed leads them to value stocks too dearly at one moment and whose fear leads them to value stocks too cheaply at another. It is this combination of economics and emotions that shapes stock market returns.[6]

What does it all mean? It means you should be optimistic about investing. My old friend Dan Wiener, who has run the Independent Adviser for Vanguard Investors newsletter for decades and manages a considerable amount of money as Chairman of Adviser Investment Management, put it best:

> Cutting through all the numbers, your baseline expectations in any given year should be for gains; if I just say I expect the stock market to go up next year, I'll be right about eight out of 10 times. Additionally, you should expect stocks to beat bonds, which in turn should outpace cash. In other words, the burden of proof should always be on the pessimists calling for bear markets and crashes. Yes, they'll be right from time to time, but most of the time, and importantly over time, it is the optimists who triumph.[7]

## Belief #2: Market timing doesn't work

In theory, putting money into the market when prices are down, then selling when they are higher, then buying when they are low again, in an infinite loop, is the perfect way to own stocks.

The problem is, no one has consistently been able to identify market tops and bottoms, and the cost of not being in the market on the most important days is devastating to a long-term portfolio.

There are many studies that indicate what happens to portfolios when they are not invested on days when the markets move up (or down) significantly. It does not matter who does the studies, they all come to the same conclusion: *don't bother with market timing.*[8]

Here's an example from Dimensional Fund Advisors.

**Hypothetical growth of $1,000 invested in the S&P 500 in 1970 (through August 2019)**

| Total return | $138,908 |
|---|---|
| Minus the best performing day | $124,491 |
| Minus the best 5 days | $90,171 |
| Minus the best 15 days | $52,246 |
| Minus the best 25 days | $32,763 |

Source: Dimensional Funds.[9]

These are amazing statistics. Missing just one day—the best day—in the last 50 years means you are making more than $14,000 less. That is 10 percent less money—*for not being in the market on one day.*

Miss the best 15 days, and you have 35 percent less money.

Why is it so difficult to time the market? Because to time the market, you have to get two variables right, not one. You need to know when to buy, and when to sell. The need to get two variables right introduces much more complexity.

Another Nobel Memorial Prize in Economics laureate, Robert Merton, put it this way:

> Timing markets is the dream of everybody. Suppose I could verify that I'm a .700 hitter in calling market turns. That's pretty good; you'd hire me right away. But to be a good market timer, you've got to do it twice. What if the chances of me getting it right were independent each time? They're not. But if they were, that's 0.7 times 0.7. That's less than 50–50. So, market timing is horribly difficult to do.[10]

Because no one knows when these best days occur, it's best not to gamble. "While favorable timing is theoretically possible, there isn't much evidence that it can be done reliably, even by professional investors," Dimensional Funds advises its clients.

## Belief #3: Some investing styles do seem to do better than the overall market over long periods, but don't kill yourself trying to figure it out

This is one of the Holy Grails of stock investing: if you can't time the market, can you at least outperform by investing in certain sectors or styles? What if you just owned stocks that kept increasing profits every year? Or companies that increased their dividends every year? Or just owned Utilities? Or just bought stocks that saw price increases greater than the market, a style known as momentum investing?

There are literally hundreds of different ways to invest in the market. Do any of them work in the long term?

The smartest people I know have spent decades trying to figure this out.

Back in the 1950s, the Capital Asset Pricing Model (CAPM) was developed to try to figure this out. It concluded that the most important factor in determining which stocks outperformed was the amount of risk associated with owning each stock.

Some stocks are just riskier to own than others. Most investors would agree that a stock that can fluctuate 100 percent in price over a one-year period is more volatile and riskier to own than a stock that fluctuates only 10 percent a year.

Because of this, investors want to be more highly compensated for taking a bet on riskier stocks.

The issue is, how does an analyst determine an expected return, and how much more should the investor be compensated for owning riskier stocks?

The CAPM was developed to quantify those risks.

Analysts have developed all sorts of fancy metrics to measure risk. The simplest is beta—which is a measure of how a stock's price moves in comparison to the market as a whole. There are many benchmarks, but typically stocks in the S&P 500 are compared to the movement in the S&P 500 as a whole.

The S&P 500 has a beta of 1.0, so if XYZ stock has a beta of, say, 1.1, on a day when the S&P 500 went up one percent, XYZ stock would be expected to rise 1.1%.

There are wide variations in the betas of stocks in the S&P 500. Johnson & Johnson, for example, which is considered a "low-beta" (i.e., low-volatility) stock, has a five-year beta of 0.69, while Tesla, which is considered a "high-beta" stock, has a five-year beta of 1.69. This tells the analyst that Tesla is going to be more than twice as volatile on any given day than Johnson & Johnson.

How is this useful to investors? It implies that adding Tesla to a portfolio might increase the risk to the portfolio, but it might also increase the return. In fact, because Tesla is more volatile than most other stocks, rational investors are expecting higher returns to compensate for the risk.

In 1992, Eugene Fama and Kenneth French published an influential paper that studied return on companies listed on the NYSE, the AmEx and Nasdaq from 1963 to 1990. They concluded that in addition to beta, there was evidence that over long periods value stocks (stocks that trade below their fundamental values) outperformed growth stocks (stocks whose earnings are growing faster than the market), and that small-cap stocks outperformed large-cap stocks.[11]

So should investors load up on value stocks and small-cap stocks, and could they double-down by overweighting their portfolios with small-cap value funds?

A 2021 research paper that reviewed hundreds of investing styles concluded that only a small number show promise of outperforming.[12] Larry Swedroe, the Chief Research Officer for Buckingham Strategic Wealth and the author of many books on investing, reviewed the paper and concluded: "For investors, the important takeaway is that despite the proliferation in the literature of a zoo of hundreds of factors, there are only a small number needed to explain the vast majority of differences in returns of diversified portfolios."[13]

Those few include styles that track:

- *Profit growth*: this is the bedrock of all investing. Companies are ultimately judged on whether they are profitable or not, and also by how profitable they are against other companies.
- *Momentum*: stocks that are moving up tend to keep moving up, and vice versa.
- *Quality*: companies with stable and growing earnings, high profit margins (how much of sales have turned into profits), and low debt.
- *Value*: companies that are trading below the value of the company, known as intrinsic value.
- *Low volatility*: stocks that don't go up or down as much as the market does on a regular basis.

You can knock yourself out buying and selling all sorts of investing styles (I told you about my tilt toward growth in my own portfolio in Chapter 20), but Swedroe and others suggest it's mostly a waste of time in the long run: "Once you have gained exposure to the factors we recommend, there is not a great deal of potential to add much, if any, benefit through exposure to additional factors."

## *Belief #4: The average investor is getting a better deal buying and selling stock than they ever did in the past*

Don't pay much attention to press accounts that high-speed traders are ripping off poor, disadvantaged retail traders. It's true that trading has moved into an almost entirely electronic sphere, and that high-speed electronic market makers have almost completely displaced human broker transactions. But there is little if any evidence that the average investor is being ripped off.

Trading costs are a significant part of the calculus of buying and selling stocks. They fall into two buckets: the price to buy and sell stocks, and commission costs. The good news is that thanks to changes in the law and advances in technology, those costs have declined dramatically in the past 50 years, and the average retail investor has been the beneficiary.

There are two reasons:

First, *prices to buy and sell stocks from brokers have dramatically improved.*

Investors are getting much better prices than they did in decades past.

The simplest way to see this is to look at the bid-ask spread, which is the difference between the bid (the highest price a buyer is willing to pay) and the ask (the lowest price a seller is willing to accept). The spread is the cost of the transaction. The broker gets to keep the difference.

If XYZ stock were bid at $100.00, and the ask was at $100.04, a broker would make money by buying XYZ at $100.00 and selling it at $100.04, thus pocketing 4 cents per share. This can also be stated in percentage terms, as a percentage of the lowest ask (selling) price. In this case 4 cents per share / $100.04 = 0.04 percent.

The wider the bid-ask spread, the more money the broker is making, which means costs to investors are higher.

A 2002 paper by Charles Jones of Columbia University clearly shows that the bid-ask spread in dollar terms between Dow Jones stocks has been declining since the 1960s.[14]

**Bid-ask spreads on Dow Jones stocks (all DJ stocks 1900–1928, DJIA stocks 1929-present)**

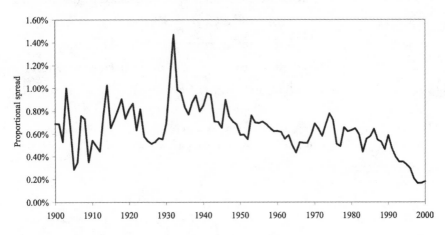

Source: Charles Jones.

Why did the bid-ask spread decline? In 1997, the tick size—the minimum price variation for quoting stocks—was reduced from one-eighth of a dollar (12.5 cents) to one-sixteenth (6.25 cents), and in 2001 again reduced to one cent. Also, reforms on the Nasdaq in 1997 allowed more competition from market makers, further reducing the bid-ask spread.[15]

Second, *commissions have almost disappeared.*

It's hard to believe, but all the way into the mid-1970s fixed commissions were charged on trading. And it wasn't just x-dollars per trade; it was typically a percentage of the dollar volume, usually at least one percent plus a fixed dollar charge.

Here's an example. In mid-1973, IBM's share price was roughly $20. Buying 100 shares would have cost $2,000. The commission was $12 plus 1.3 percent of the amount traded, so the cost of the transaction was $38 ($20,000 x 1.3% = $26 + $12 = $38).[16]

The commission was almost two percent! And this is only for 100 shares—the dollar cost of the commissions went higher depending on how much was traded.

No wonder the stock brokerage business was so lucrative.

On May 1, 1975, fixed commissions were abolished. This allowed for the rise of discount brokers like Charles Schwab. For the first time, commissions were set by competition rather than a fixed commission.

That competition proved to be a good deal for the average investor. By 2000, commission costs had come down dramatically.[17]

**Average commissions on round-lot transactions in NYSE stocks (based on fixed schedule pre-1968 and member commission revenue thereafter)**

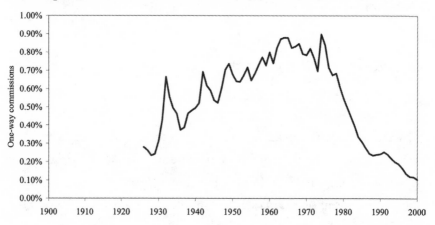

Source: Charles Jones.

Commissions continued to decline after 2000. By 2017 or so, most online brokerages were charging around $7.99 per trade, regardless of share volume, and by 2019 most had abolished commissions altogether.

In recent years, a lively debate has been underway about payment for order flow (PFOF), the practice whereby a broker receives compensation in exchange for routing its clients' trades to a market maker.

Proponents argue that PFOF has enabled many brokers to eliminate or drastically reduce commissions. Opponents argue that there is a hidden cost to this trading: by pushing retail trading mostly onto these market makers that execute the orders mostly internally, it's not clear if investors are getting the best prices because they are not exposed to the entire market. Opponents also argue that there is a potential for conflict of interest, since the broker may be more interested in routing orders to those who are willing to pay the highest amount for the orders.

This debate has not been resolved, but it should not detract from the fact that we are still dealing with a very low cost to investors because everyone is still required to provide best execution: the best possible price at that time.

I'm following the PFOF debate very closely, but regardless, the average investor is still getting a better deal than they ever have before.

## *Belief #5: The average investor is better off owning a diversified portfolio of index funds than picking stocks or paying higher fees for actively managed funds*

The active vs. passive debate is the Great Divide in the investing world; you're usually on one side or the other.

I have many friends who are active traders or who cater to the active trading community. Some invest their own money. Some are employed as strategists by large firms to advise clients on where to put their money, most of it geared toward strategies that last for a few months. Others run their own small firms and manage money for clients.

These friends of mine are very dedicated and very much believe that they are adding value for their clients.

I don't doubt their sincerity, but more than 20 years ago I concluded that—with a few exceptions—the average investor should stick with index funds and index-based ETFs.

I described my own personal investing journey in Chapter 20. You shouldn't be surprised that I am a Jack Bogle disciple and most of my investments (with a few exceptions) are in those index-based funds.

I think most people would benefit from sticking to that philosophy—and many (I am tempted to say most) investment professionals who have studied this dispassionately would agree.

Larry Swedroe has studied stock market returns for decades. In a 2021 paper, "Most Stocks Are Duds (Yes, You Read That Right)," Swedroe reviewed several studies of market returns over many decades and concluded, "Most common stocks do not outperform Treasury bills over their lifetimes."

How is that possible? The major indexes like the Dow and the S&P do indeed outperform Treasuries over many decades. The gains from the indexes, Swedroe says, "was attributable to outsize gains generated by a relatively few high-performing stocks."

Of course, almost no one can identify those stocks in advance!

Swedroe concluded that strategies that involve actively trading individual stocks are far riskier than owning broad swaths of the market: "Such results help explain why active strategies, which tend to be poorly diversified, most often lead to underperformance."[18]

David F. Swensen was the Chief Investment Officer for Yale University. After an initial foray into index investing, Swensen and his team switched to active investing and from 1985 to 2015 amassed an extraordinary record: a return of 12.9 percent per year, far exceeding the 8.8 percent return of a passive portfolio of 60 percent U.S. equities and 40 percent U.S. bonds.[19]

If that isn't an advertisement for active management, I don't know what is.

And yet, Swensen recommended that individual investors forget about active management.

Why? Swensen had 30 professionals scouring the world for investments, something that is not available to the average investor. Writing the introduction to the seventh edition of Charles D. Ellis' investment classic, *Winning the Loser's Game*, Swensen surveyed his extraordinary career and offered this advice: "Without having substantial financial resources and a high-quality dedicated staff, it is nearly impossible to succeed in the cutthroat world of active management... I concluded that individuals should avoid active management entirely."[20]

Yikes. Why was Swensen so unhappy that he recommended that the average investor should not put money into active management? Because his overall experience with the investment industry and particularly mutual fund managers was not a pleasant one: "The crux of the problem is that mutual fund managers generally fail to discharge their fiduciary responsibility to investors," he said. He accused fund managers of "succumbing to the siren song of bloated funds that generated bloated profits."

He said mutual funds were too big, held too many positions, traded too much (which generated additional tax bills for investors) and, worst of all, charged too much: "Overwhelmingly, mutual fund managers collect excessive fees and spend their days in the rate of return hall of shame."[21]

Double yikes! And yet, Swensen's experience has been verified empirically time and again. Most fund managers do indeed underperform their benchmarks and spend their days in the "rate return hall of shame," as I discussed in Chapters 15–17.

Charles Ellis himself said it best: "The cruel irony is that so many active managers are so skillful, hardworking, and capable that they collectively dominate the market. So few, if any, can beat the expert consensus *and*, disconcertingly, investors cannot tell which ones will."[22]

---

In this chapter, I've laid out a few things I believe about investing.

In the next chapter, I'm going to sum up what watching the markets for 32 years has taught me about how to approach life in general.

I know that sounds ambitious. But I'll reveal to you the half-dozen principles I try to adhere to, why I am a lot less cocky than I was 30 years ago, why I am a fox and not a hedgehog (and what that means), and why, when I am in doubt, I ask myself: what would Captain Kirk do?

# CHAPTER 23

# *Bob 2.0: On Being a Fox and Other Things I've Learned*

═══

I like to think I'm a Captain Kirk kind of guy.

I grew up watching the original *Star Trek* series, which ran for only three seasons, from 1966 to 1969. After *The Twilight Zone* and *The Outer Limits*, it was, and still is, my favorite TV show.

By 1966, when I was 10 years old, *The Twilight Zone* and *The Outer Limits* were gone, but it was still a great year to be a 10-year-old, and particularly a 10-year-old science fiction fan.

On TV, there was *Voyage to the Bottom of the Sea,* with Richard Basehart piloting a super-submarine of the distant future (the 1970s!). There was *Lost in Space,* a somewhat silly Robinson Crusoe story about a family marooned in a hostile universe. There was *The Time Tunnel,* about several men trapped in time that keep moving from one great historical event to the next.

In the movies, there was *Fantastic Voyage,* about a scientist who had figured out how to miniaturize atoms, who then survives an assassination attempt while trying to come to the West. His colleagues must build a ship to go inside his body to destroy a blood clot. It had a book by Isaac

Asimov (which he adapted from the screenplay), and Raquel Welch as the star.

What else could a 10-year-old boy ask for?

## Why Star Trek mattered

*Star Trek* debuted on September 8, 1966. It was, on the surface, about the effort "to explore strange new worlds, to seek out new life and new civilizations, to boldly go where no man has gone before," as the famous opening voiceover goes.

As with all great shows and stories, it was really about something else.

It was about trust and family. It boiled down to a conflict between three guys and how they resolved those conflicts.

Dr. Spock (Leonard Nimoy) was cold and logical, though the Vulcan salute he made popular ("Live long and prosper"), seemed like profoundly human advice, at least to a 10-year-old.

Dr. McCoy (DeForest Kelley) was temperamental and hot-headed, the opposite of Spock.

Captain Kirk (William Shatner) was right in the middle. He could think critically, but he also had strong emotions that helped guide his actions, though he tried hard not to let those emotions become too dominant.

Kirk was the synthesis of Spock and McCoy.

In a now-famous 1953 essay, *The Hedgehog and the Fox*, Isaiah Berlin referenced a fragment from the Greek poet Archilochus ("A fox knows many things, but a hedgehog knows one big thing") and used it as a springboard to divide thinkers into two categories: hedgehogs who view the world through a single big idea, and foxes who do not have a single overarching idea but synthesize many different ideas.[1]

I told you about the work of Philip Tetlock in Chapter 17. His book,

*Expert Political Judgment,* drew heavily upon Berlin's insight and noted that forecasters who displayed fox-like tendencies were generally more accurate than forecasters who had hedgehog-like tendencies.

Captain Kirk was a fox. He took in the opinions of many different people, synthesized them, and came up with a judgment. He had opinions, but he wasn't particularly ideological. He was flexible. When new information came in, he weighed the new facts. He didn't try to make the new facts fit into any mental framework he had constructed.

I'm a fox too. I try to be open-minded and willing to change if facts present themselves that should cause me to change.

Of course, I have opinions, and I've shared some of my beliefs about investing in this book. But I strive mightily to avoid appearing rigid or ideological. I avoid going around stomping my feet and insisting I am right and the rest of you are a bunch of fools.

That can be a tough position to maintain in the internet age, when everyone is supposed to have a strident opinion on everything.

## The traits of good forecasters

As we saw in Chapter 17, in his 2015 book, *Superforecasting: The Art and Science of Prediction,* Philip Tetlock surveyed the characteristics of the small group of people who were "superforecasters," those who were far more successful at predicting future events than a control group or even so-called "expert" forecasters.

What made them successful as superforecasters? It wasn't what they thought, it was how they thought. They had a way of looking at the world that enabled deeper insights than those who didn't share those characteristics.

In sketching a composite of successful superforecasters, Tetlock noted that they were:

- *Pragmatic:* they were not wedded to any idea or plan.
- *Dragonfly-eyed:* like the compound eye of the dragonfly, they saw many different points of view and synthesized them into their own.
- *Humble:* they recognized the world was "infinitely complex" and were comfortable with the inability to understand or predict the future.[2]

Humbleness has been a difficult trait to cultivate, particularly after I had been around for a long time and began to believe that I knew a lot more than anyone else and that this allowed me special insight.

But knowledge is not understanding, and it doesn't necessarily convey prescience. I know as much as any human being could reasonably be said to know about the stock market, and yet as time goes on, I have become more humble, not less humble, about what I know and my ability to see into the future.

This doesn't mean that I'm paralyzed, or I think all my experience amounts to a lot of nothing. Tetlock discusses the talents of leaders, particularly confidence and decisiveness, and how to balance that with humbleness:

The humility required for good judgment is not self-doubt—the sense that you are untalented, unintelligent, or unworthy. It is intellectual humility. It is a recognition that reality is profoundly complex, that seeing things clearly is a constant struggle, when it can be done at all, and that human judgment must therefore be riddled with mistakes. This is true for fools and geniuses alike. So it's quite possible to think highly of yourself and be intellectually humble. In fact, this combination can be wonderfully fruitful. Intellectual humility compels the careful reflection necessary for good judgment; confidence in one's abilities inspires determined action.[3]

# *When someone throws the glass at you, duck and carry on*

Trying to be open-minded, curious and a bit playful is not easy when dealing with hedgehogs or people who have a close-minded view of the world.

Even a simple outlook on life can get you into conflict.

I'm going to stick my neck out and make a grand pronouncement:

*There are four kinds of people in the world: those who believe the glass is half full, those who believe it is half empty, those who believe the glass doesn't exist, and those who will pick up the glass and throw it at you.*

I'm a glass-half-full guy. I look for reasons to be optimistic about the future, rather than pessimistic. I look for reasons to like people, rather than dislike them. I look for reasons to get along with people, rather than not get along. I look for reasons to support people, rather than reasons to tear them down.

This seems like a sensible way to go through life. Yet I'm amazed by the number of people that think I am naïve and don't understand the way the world really works.

The glass-half-empty people are the kind who get up every morning thinking, "Life sucks and it's not going to get any better." The people who look for reasons to dislike people, who look for reasons to sow discord and distrust.

I used to think the world was divided into these two groups, with the belief that there were more people like me than like the others.

But in my 30 years covering the financial world, and watching a lot of people, I've realized there are more glass-half-empty people than I'd care to believe exist, and that there are other groups I never realized existed.

There are people, if you scratch them hard enough, who will tell you the glass doesn't exist. They're nihilists who believe it's all a crock.

There are people so angry they don't care if the glass is half full or half empty. They just want to throw the glass at you.

That kind of thinking—the glass half empty, the glass doesn't exist, and the throw-the-glass-at-you mentality—are examples of thinking that is closed. Those people tend not to be good forecasters.

I have strived to acquire what Tetlock calls a "growth mindset": a belief that it is possible to improve myself through continual learning and introspection.

It means the next time someone throws a glass at me, literally or figuratively, I just duck and carry on.

Being a fox means more than just allowing a lot of diverse viewpoints to occupy your brain. It means you must be curious about the world and keep learning, continually.

Here are some of the precepts I try hard to integrate into my life.

## *Six precepts to live by*

### KEEP UPDATING YOUR KNOWLEDGE

In surveying the characteristics of people who were good forecasters, Tetlock found that not all characteristics were equal. There was one that mattered above all others: "The strongest predictor of rising into the ranks of superforecasters is perpetual beta, the degree to which one is committed to belief updating and self-improvement. It is roughly three times as powerful a predictor as its closest rival, intelligence."[4]

Superforecasters, in other words, were constantly updating their information and willing to change what they thought when the information changed in a convincing way. Those that didn't update, or weren't willing to change, were not as good.

I keep a list of all the things that interest me, not just from the business world but hobbies like music and posters. I use Google Alerts to track people and ideas that I care about.

That sounds a bit mechanistic, but the point is I'm always looking to add to my understanding of the world.

It's Bob 2.0 and beyond.

## LIMIT THE SIZE OF CONTACTS
## BUT KEEP UP THE QUALITY

Some years ago I stumbled on my 1999 contact list. It was a list of the people I talked to that year. There were about 500 people on the list.

I was astonished that I had talked to that many people on a regular basis. I'm sure I believed that talking to as many people as possible increased my chances of being a better reporter.

Today, I talk to less than half that amount on a regular basis. I discovered that, for example, I didn't need to talk to six analysts about Apple. I needed to know two analysts whose opinion I trusted, who knew what they were doing and could give me an honest opinion.

Of course, if I was just a reporter on Apple, I would be talking to a much wider group. But I'm not. I'm Senior Markets Correspondent, so becoming more discerning in who I speak with has enabled me to spend less time weeding out people that are a waste of time. That means that I ignore some people who are very famous, and some who keep pestering me but whom I've decided can't help me improve my understanding of markets.

I also spend more time with lesser-known people who I find have surprisingly good insights.

## UNDERSTAND YOUR BIASES

Start with the idea that you are not going to eliminate all your biases, but that becoming aware of them will help control them.

One of the biggest mistakes I made as a journalist was largely ignoring the conclusions of behavioral economists, which were being widely disseminated by the time I got to the NYSE in 1997. There's a difference between being intellectually aware of an idea and integrating it into your thinking and belief system.

I was aware, but I stubbornly resisted integrating behavioral finance into my belief system. I don't know why, but it's likely because I like to believe I am a rational person and invest in a rational manner and that others do as well. The findings of behavioralists, that many investors do indeed behave in an irrational manner and are subject to numerous biases that warp their thinking, was deeply upsetting to my worldview.

I was, to adopt the behavioralists' terminology, in a state of *cognitive dissonance*. I was experiencing two contradictory ideas in my head at once and was profoundly uncomfortable.

When I started paying closer attention to the behavioralists, I was able to more clearly think about my own biases (overconfidence first among them) and got much better at explaining market trends as examples of biases and group behavior.

## AVOID GROUPTHINK

James Surowiecki's bestselling book, *The Wisdom of Crowds,* popularized the idea that decisions made in groups are often better than decisions made by any individual member of the group.[5]

But there's a downside to the wisdom of crowds: groupthink. People, including investors, crave a coherent narrative. They crave the need to belong to a group. The need to conform can result in irrational decision-making.

Reporting leaves you vulnerable to groupthink. The stock market is a particularly good example of groupthink, where large numbers of people will collectively convince themselves that companies with no hope of future profits are worth exorbitant sums of money (2000 and the dot-com bust), that Bitcoin will somehow change the world of fiat currencies forever (it won't), or that certain meme stocks like GameStop are worth hundreds of times more than their underlying fundamentals suggest (they aren't).

There are more subtle, less flamboyant, examples of groupthink. The stock market is a massive experiment in groupthink every day. The market operates under a series of narratives that guide the trend. Is the direction of earnings up or down? Is the economy expanding or contracting? Is the Federal Reserve raising or lowering interest rates? Is the money supply expanding or contracting? The answer to these, and other questions, will determine whether the majority are bullish, or bearish.

Those narratives can and do change, and in an age when information is disseminated in sub-second intervals, those narratives can change overnight.

Constantly questioning those narratives is a daily exercise. It doesn't just involve updating information. You must be willing to turn the narratives upside down and evaluate the likelihood that the trend will indeed soon move in the other direction.

That does not mean that nothing matters and everything is relative. The laws of financial gravity have not changed. Most investments, for example, do indeed mean-revert over time. It is not "different this time."

But it does mean being a lot more comfortable with uncertainty.

## SUPPORT INNOVATION

It's hard to believe, but online banking is less than 20 years old. The most ubiquitous financial innovation in modern times—the bank teller machine—has been around less than 50 years.

Financial innovation has been a constant throughout the entire 400-year history of capitalism, from the creation of joint stock companies, to futures, options and other derivatives markets, to warrants and a dizzying array of bond instruments, as well as new investment products like Exchange Traded Funds (ETFs).[6]

We need more of it. Innovation creates new wealth, improves efficiencies of markets, and helps manage risk. Yes, it can sometimes lead to more volatility, as we have seen with certain volatility products in the ETF space. But those risks can be managed.

Supporting innovation doesn't mean throwing your weight behind every hair-brained idea, trend, or investment concept that gets thrown at you. You can believe in innovation and still understand that many of the paths to innovation are going to be dead ends.

Yale economist Robert Shiller has been one of the most eloquent advocates for the continuing expansion of financial innovation. In his 2013 Nobel Prize lecture Shiller looked back on a lifetime of advocacy and stated:

> We want such innovations, if not exactly the ones I and others have been advocating to date, because their predecessor innovations, the financial institutions we already have today, have brought such prosperity, despite the occasional big disruptions caused by bubbles and financial crises. There is no economic system other than financial capitalism that has brought the level of prosperity that we see in much of the world today, and there is every reason to believe that further expansion of this system will yield even more prosperity.[7]

Shiller has been particularly active in promoting ways to improve the real estate market, particularly for single-family homes, which he describes as "woefully inefficient." He has discussed the creation of a home futures market, which might allow homeowners to hedge their investments using products like home equity insurance.[8]

One of the key precepts of financial innovation is that technology stimulates innovation.[9] Today we have one of the great innovations of all time—the internet—to accelerate innovation. Modern financial innovation—what we call today "FinTech"—only became possible with the internet. We can invest, get a mortgage, transfer money—all online.

Financial products we use every day today were considered outliers when they were created—on the internet. PayPal, now one of the world's most dominant payment platforms, was only created in 1998.

Amazon was started in 1994. eBay, one of the most dominant e-commerce sites, was only invented in 1995.

Two innovations of the last 15 years seem especially promising:

## 1. Blockchain

Will Bitcoin replace the world's fiat currencies?

I seriously doubt it, but the blockchain concept—a list of records that are linked together using cryptography, listed on a publicly distributed ledger that can be seen by anyone—has tremendous financial potential.

At its simplest, decentralized finance—which is the blockchain applied to financial issues—can help answer the age-old question, how do I know I own anything?

Entire industries exist to answer this question. How do I know I bought a piece of real estate? There are title insurance companies that will confirm it. How do I know I bought 100 shares of IBM? There are clearance companies that will guarantee the seller delivers, or they will cover the transaction. How do I know I sent $1,000 to my friend in London? There are big banks that will act as intermediaries and make sure it gets in your friend's account.

All of these intermediaries charge significant fees. Decentralized finance platforms hold out the potential it could be done quicker, more efficiently, and cheaper.

## 2. Crowdfunding

Rewards-based crowdfunding—funding a project or venture by getting a large number of people to contribute a small amount of money—has been around for a while, but the growth of online platforms like Kickstarter, which offer rewards or experiences to investors who back creative projects, or GoFundMe, which allows people to raise money for almost anything from birthday celebrations to helping pay for operations, or even Patreon, which allows content creators to run a subscription service, has greatly expanded the ability to support creative activities.

There's another kind of crowdfunding—equity crowdfunding. The JOBS Act, signed into law by President Obama in 2012, allowed online fundraising for small investors. It was a tricky process—the SEC had to balance the need for financial innovation with the need to protect investors from fraud. Funding is conducted either through a registered broker or a new type of entity called a "funding portal."[10]

The final rule, Regulation Crowdfunding, went into effect in 2016 and permitted individuals to invest in securities-based crowdfunding transactions subject to certain investment limits.[11]

Unfortunately equity crowdfunding has had a mixed history, but not because it's a bad idea. It's had a mixed history because of the high regulatory standards and because a lot of companies aren't ready to go public or are not investible.[12]

## DON'T FIGHT CHANGE

I was miserable after the dot-com bust and 9/11. The world had changed, and I only learned to be less miserable when I stopped fighting the changes and learned to, if not embrace them, at least understand them.

One change I learned to embrace was the move from human-centered, floor-based trading to electronic trading.

In 1999, the Securities Traders Association of New York (STANY) held their annual holiday party at the Marriott Marquis in Times Square. The stock trading community was at the very top of its game. Four thousand people showed up. Kool and the Gang played.

STANY still exists, and still provides top-notch educational services and conferences to its members, but the trading community has shrunk to a fraction of what it once was.

The floor of the New York Stock Exchange is also a very different place than when I first came in the summer of 1997. There were 4,000 people on the floor then that did over 80 percent of the trading in all NYSE-listed stocks. Today there are a few hundred that trade less than 20 percent of the volume.

Watching the transition over a 15-year period from roughly 1995 to 2000 was painful, but it was for the good.

The volume of trading has dramatically increased, and most professionals would agree electronic trading has made the markets more efficient.

More importantly, the NYSE is now owned by Intercontinental Exchange (ICE), which owns not only the NYSE but also futures and options exchanges for financial products and commodities, equity options exchanges, as well as clearinghouses. In 2018 it formed a new company, Bakkt, to manage digital assets. In 2020, ICE bought Ellie Mae, a software company that processes 35 percent of U.S. mortgage applications.

The bottom line: the NYSE today is part of a much larger organization that has helped make it stronger.

Since the early 2000s, I've dramatically widened the community of people I talk to. I talk less to people on the floor and less to the sell-side in general, and more to hedge funds, strategists, the ETF community, and a smattering of people on social media.

But there is still information on the floor, still bell ringings with CEOs, and still, post-Covid, after-trading drinks with strategists, analysts, and hangers-on.

The world has changed, the trading world has changed, and I've had to change too.

# The Financial District
## has changed

Downtown New York has changed dramatically as well. The Covid pandemic affected the Financial District, as it did everywhere.

But the World Trade Center site is almost completely rebuilt. Prior to Covid, more than a quarter-million people a day commuted through Santiago Calatrava's magnificent transit hub. Eataly, that homage to all things Italian, is going strong. The Ronald O. Perelman Performing Arts Center (PAC) is scheduled to open in 2023.

The most startling change is not the rebuilt Trade Center: it's that Downtown has become a 24/7 environment. Prior to 9/11, there were very few people who lived Downtown. The area around the NYSE and Trade Center was practically a ghost town after 6 PM.

Not anymore. Sixty-four thousand people live Downtown now, many of them millennials who have filled up the buildings that formerly housed Wall Street firms. Thousands of new apartments have been constructed.

The Covid pandemic hurt the tourist business Downtown, but they too are starting to come back. About 14 million came in 2019, 60 percent of which were international visitors, so many that on most days there are more tourists than locals on the street. [13]

Mostly, they come to see the 9/11 Memorial. When it was first completed, I was baffled. It's two holes in the ground with waterfalls on all four sides. I kept walking around them, trying to understand what they were trying to say. How is this a memorial?

I finally came around to exactly what they had done. It draws the mind inward. It's peaceful. The visitors are respectful but not unduly somber. The names of those who died are engraved around the two Memorials. There is commercial development around the site, but it is not intrusive. The tone feels right.

And what about my friend Bill Meehan from Cantor Fitzgerald, who I told you about in Chapter 7, who died in the North Tower on September 11, 2001, along with 657 other Cantor Fitzgerald employees? He's still there. He lives on in my memory and the memory of all others who knew and loved him.

If you're by the Memorial, stop by to pay your respects. William J. Meehan, Jr., Panel N-27, North Memorial Pool.


## *When in doubt, consult Captain Kirk*

As for me, whenever I feel the need to relearn something I've forgotten but don't want to work too hard, I'll turn on an old *Star Trek* episode, and there they are—Kirk, Spock, McCoy, Uhuru, Chekov, Sulu, and Scottie.

In one of my favorite episodes, "The Enemy Within," which aired in the first season, Kirk is involved in a transporter accident that splits him into two different people. One Kirk is wild, impulsive, and so lustful and aggressive that he sexually assaults a female crew member. The other is compassionate but so docile he can't make a decision.

Dr. Spock, of course, sees the mishap as an opportunity to observe human nature.

"We have here an unusual opportunity to appraise the human mind, or to examine in Earth terms the rules of good and evil in a man," he tells the docile Kirk and a skeptical McCoy. "His negative side, which you call hostility, lust, violence, and his positive side, which Earth people express as compassion, love, tenderness."

Spock then addresses the docile Kirk's greatest fear: that he is losing his ability to be a leader.

"What is it that makes one man an exceptional leader?" Spock asks. "We see here indications that it is his negative side which makes him strong, that his evil side, if you will, properly controlled and disciplined, is vital to his strength. Your negative side, removed from you, the power of command begins to elude you."

The trio eventually figures out a way to get the two Kirks together in the transponder and merge them back into one person.

"I've seen a part of myself that no man should ever see," Kirk tells Spock at the conclusion.

It's a great lesson in how to balance impulsiveness against endless deliberation, and how to show leadership without being overbearing.

And so it went, 80 episodes over the course of three years. After a brief hour (I can only take one at a time) I will turn off the TV, happy to have learned another life lesson, but mostly happy because for that short hour I am 10 years old again, with my crew cut, my red-striped t-shirt, my baggy jeans, and my Converse sneakers, sitting cross-legged on the basement floor of our home in Bucks County, Pennsylvania with our Zenith black-and-white TV and a TV dinner (preferably fish sticks), waiting for Captain Kirk, at some critical juncture, to launch into a pseudo-Shakespearean monologue about the perils of being in command, or why aliens are people too.

Live long and prosper.

# PART FOUR

# *Encounters on the NYSE Floor, and Elsewhere*

=

## CHAPTER 24

# *A Head-Scratcher with Fidel Castro*

═══

S OMETIMES things work out, and sometimes it all goes to hell. It was the latter for my one and only meeting with Fidel Castro.

It was January 2008. Pope John Paul II was set to arrive for a five-day visit of Cuba, the first time a Pope had visited the island. It was, in theory, a big deal.

Everyone, of course, wanted something. The Pope wanted to strengthen the church against competing faiths, including African-based Santeria faiths. Castro wanted a platform to rail against the American embargo.

And the Cuban government desperately wanted the dollars that reporters like us were bringing, an estimated $25 million windfall.

An army of 3,000 reporters descended on Havana. We checked into the Habana Libre, the former Havana Hilton that was Fidel Castro's headquarters after the capture of Havana in 1959. Everyone was there: Dan Rather, Ted Koppel, Peter Jennings, Tom Brokaw. Even Martha Stewart came.[1]

I went to the government office in charge of dealing with the foreign media, presented my credentials, and asked for an interview with Fidel Castro.

The woman looked at me and frowned, as if to say, *sure you and 2,000 other gringos.* She took down my information and said they would be in touch.

And that, I assumed, would be the end of it.

The Pope's arrival was more than a week away, so my producer, Stephanie Krikorian, my cameraman, Angel Ortiz, and I set about discovering the island.

There was a lot to discover.

It was a strange time for Castro and Cuba. The Cuban economy had been kept afloat by trade with the Soviet Union, so when the Russian government collapsed in the early 90s, it was a disaster for Castro.

As corrupt as the 1950s government that preceded Castro had been, his own regime had proven inept at producing even staples.

They couldn't even harvest sugar, which was the heart of the Cuban economy. Production hit a 50-year low three years before thanks to a massive, inefficient bureaucracy. Some of the harvest was still cut by hand. We went to sugar fields and saw turbines that dated to the early 1900s.

In the past the Cubans had sold sugar at inflated prices to the Soviet Union in exchange for oil, but with the collapse of the Soviet Union that changed. At the time, 85 percent of Cuba's oil was imported. The Cubans desperately needed to become more self-sufficient but were struggling. They were trying to bring in Western companies to drill for oil, with limited success.

They had one modest success, with tourism. It had become the number one source of hard currency.

We went to Varadero, about 60 miles east of Havana, a tourist city filled with Canadian, European and Latin American tourists staying in hotels financed via joint ventures with the Cubans and Western countries, mostly Canadian and European. But no Americans.

With the country in ruins, Castro was forced to open the economy. He allowed small family-owned businesses to operate, and actively sought foreign investment.

I interviewed a fellow named Roglia Conde Acosta, a barber. When Castro allowed small businesses to open, he started a seafood restaurant above his home, which prospered.

But 10 months before I interviewed him, the authorities shut him down.

"They closed me down because in this country it is not permitted to sell seafood, be it fish, shrimp, lobster, to the Cuban population," he told me.

Seafood, he said, was a high-profit item and Castro wanted the higher-profit restaurants to be controlled by the government.

The Cuban government was competing against its own people for money.

And not the local money: the competition was for dollars. Castro had allowed Cubans to legally possess dollars since 1993, and it quickly became the second currency on the island. Some stores we visited accepted only dollars, especially those that had the latest Western goods.

How did the Cubans get dollars? About half the population had access, either through money sent by relatives living in the United States, or through running small businesses like restaurants, or by contact with foreigners.

That made us very popular, wherever we went.

It also created a dual-class citizenship. Those that had dollars sent to them by relatives suddenly had access to expensive consumer goods. I visited a store where a pair of Nikes were $90. The average Cuban worker made about $10 a month.

If you didn't have access to those dollars, you were screwed.

Which was strange, considering there was a 37-year-old U.S. embargo that was supposed to prevent any U.S. product from being sold there.

Except there was no embargo. We went to a grocery story that had baby food, camera film, sneakers, and soft drinks, all from the U.S.A. Young Cubans were walking around with Nike t-shirts and New York Yankees baseball caps.

Most of it had been coming through Mexico, where wholesalers were buying from American subsidiaries and then re-selling to Cubans.

The hunt for dollars was particularly acute when we did interviews for Cuba's most famous export: cigars. We spent a day at the largest Cuban cigar factory. They were Cuba's sixth biggest dollar earner (after tourism, family remittances, sugar, nickel, and fish), but as with almost everything we saw, the whole production was labor-intensive and low-tech, from moistening the tobacco leaves, to hanging them on racks, sorting by color and texture, to the actual rolling of the cigars, accompanied by a professional reader who read the newspaper, or a novel, to the workers (one roller told me he preferred listening to Mexican soap operas).

A box of Cohibas (Castro's favorite brand) sold at the factory for nearly $300, a princely sum considering the workers at the factory were making roughly $10 a month.

For all its poverty and 1950s American cars, Havana was a vibrant city. We went to the Tropicana nightclub (the real one) and saw a show. It looked like 1955, with the dancers dressed in sequined bikinis.

I drank daiquiris at El Floridita at the same bar Hemingway sat at, and mojitos at La Bodeguita del Medio, where they were (supposedly) invented.

And then, a day or so after our arrival, the phone rang in my hotel room.

It was 2:30 AM.

A voice was on the other line, sounding very distant.

"El Jefe will see you."

What? El Jefe?

"El Jefe. El Jefe will see you!" she repeated, more insistently.

El Jefe. The Chief. Castro.

She told me to assemble my crew and meet at the airport at 5:30 AM. Three hours from now. We were to be flown to Santiago de Cuba, where Castro would vote and speak at a hospital.

We arrived at the airport on time and were surprised that there were only two other foreign journalists there. We were told that other Cuban journalists would join us in Santiago.

We flew to Santiago de Cuba and were driven to a local hospital where Castro, we were told, would vote in elections and give a speech.

We waited several hours in the blazing sun. Several hundred people had assembled, many of them barefoot.

On the surface, it seemed like a strange place to fly a few foreign journalists to witness a speech by Castro. He was scheduled to be with the Pope in a massive square in front of tens of thousands of people in a few days.

But Santiago de Cuba was more than just a town. It was the birthplace of the Castro mythos and the Cuban revolution.

On July 26, 1953, Castro and a small group of supporters attacked a military garrison, the Moncada Barracks, outside Santiago. The attack failed. Castro was subsequently arrested, tried and sentenced to 15 years in prison. While in prison, he formed the "26th of July Movement" and started a school for prisoners.

He was released in May 1955. Three and a half years later, on January 2, 1959, he entered Santiago de Cuba, two days after dictator Fulgencio Batista had fled the country. Castro was now in control of the country. He reached Havana on January 9, and took up residence at the Havana Hilton, the now-renamed Habana Libre where we were staying.

I was eager to meet this man. Castro had a reputation for being one of the great orators of the world, and one of the most long-winded. He famously spoke for four and a half hours at the UN General Assembly in 1960, said to be the longest speech ever given by a Head of State at the General Assembly.[2]

I had asked a few of the reporters at the hotel about Castro's health. The word was that, at 71, he was not in great condition, but formal details about Castro's health were impossible to come by. The government simply did not talk about it.

After almost two hours, a caravan of jeeps drove up. Castro pulled up in one of them, right in front of me.

It was an odd moment. I stared at him. I was grinning, and with good reason: the man looked *exactly* like Fidel Castro. The olive-green cap. Military fatigues. The beard. Everything.

It was Fidel as the eternal revolutionary.

It was like meeting Elvis.

He walked over to the porch, turned to the cheering crowd, and began speaking. He did not have notes.

An hour and a half later, he was still talking.

My Spanish is limited to tourist menus, but I could tell this was not a man that was in imminent danger of collapse. He gesticulated, his voice rose and fell, and the audience applauded at all the right moments. I only knew we were reaching the end when his voice began to rise steadily and he said, "*Socialismo o muerte!*" and "*Viva la Revolution!*"

He walked into the building, and we were told he voted in the local election. Our handler then came over and said he would see us.

We were brought into a large room. The two other foreign journalists were on my left. We were surrounded by a group of what we were told were Cuban journalists.

Castro spoke perfect English but would not speak it to foreign journalists, so I had an interpreter ask about what he expected when he met the Pope.

He gave a fairly innocuous answer. I asked a brief follow-up, then reached up to scratch my head.

That's when the room moved.

Or, rather, I was moved. In seconds, I was in the back of the room. Both of my arms were pinned against the wall by two men who had been behind me.

The Cuban "journalists" were security agents.

Another man had grabbed my microphone and was dismantling it in the presence of yet another man, who was carefully examining the dismantled parts.

I looked to my left, and I could see they had my cameraman Angel against the wall as well and had taken his camera from him.

While I was pinned to the wall, watching these men dismember my microphone, I figured out what likely had happened. I had reached up to scratch my head briefly, holding the microphone in the same hand. The security people around me must have believed that I was raising my hand with the intention of striking Castro with the microphone.

This, of course, was completely absurd, but only if you didn't know anything about the history of the man I had just been snatched away from.

They say you're not paranoid if they really are out to get you, and in the case of Fidel Castro, they really were out to get him.

He had good reason to be paranoid, even in the heartland of the revolution. There had been numerous—dozens, perhaps hundreds—of attempts to assassinate him over the years.

Hundreds? Fabian Escalante, the former head of Cuban counterintelligence, published a book in 2006, *Executive Action: 634 Ways to Kill Fidel Castro*, where he reviewed more than 600 plots to kill Castro.[3] Many were confirmed years later by columnist Jack Andersen and the 1975 Church Commission headed by Senator Frank Church, which detailed early plans by the CIA, in conjunction with the Mafia, to assassinate Castro using poison pills.[4] There were attempts at cyanide poisoning in restaurants. Poison capsules in chocolate milkshakes. Cyanide-laced bullets.

That's just for starters. Some of the other attempts strain the imagination.

There were explosive devices of all kinds. Under a speaker's platform. Under bridges. In storm drains. There were exploding mollusks (Castro was an avid scuba diver).

And cigars: exploding cigars. Cigars containing poison. LSD-impregnated cigars.

If someone wasn't trying to kill him, they were trying to make his life miserable. There were thallium salts that would cause his beard to fall out. There was a custom-made diving suit impregnated with bacteria.

My favorite: according to Escalante, Elio Hernandez Alfonso, a "counterrevolutionary" who worked in a steel mill, hatched a plot to make El Jefe fall into a large vat of melted iron when he passed by.

The attempt failed. No word on what happened to Elio, other than that he was arrested.[5]

There were numerous other attempts, including a plot involving a revolver placed inside a TV camera. There were toxic fountain pens.[6]

Yikes.

If a toxic fountain pen seemed plausible, why not a microphone that concealed a hidden dagger? Or something inside a TV camera?

That's what I was thinking while I was pinned against the wall, watching these guys dismantle my microphone. After a few minutes, they reassembled it. One of them handed it back to me, said "Thank you," and walked away.

And that was it. The interview was over.

After that, everything else was anticlimactic. We shot additional interviews and stand-ups for the stories we had done on the Cuban economy and left before the Pope arrived.

The Pope did give Castro a bit of what he wanted: a criticism of the embargo.

"May Cuba, with all its magnificent potential, open itself up to the world, and may the world open itself up to Cuba," he said as he arrived.[7]

Castro, predictably, denounced the embargo as "genocide" and told John Paul "We choose a thousand deaths rather than abdicate our convictions."

But by the time the Pope arrived, much of the world's media had diverted its attention. The entire meeting was eclipsed by the Clinton-Lewinsky scandal, in which President Clinton declared, "I did not have sexual relations with that woman, Miss Lewinsky" in a White House news conference at the same time the Pope was in Havana.

In the end, very little changed. The Catholic Church was a modest winner: Castro did eventually declare Cuba to be a secular state, which at least implied the government was not actively hostile to religion and allowed for greater religious expression.[8]

But the Pope's plea for Cuba to "open itself up to the world" never happened. The hopes for more democracy following the Pope's visit never happened, either. Other Popes came: Pope Benedict XVI in 2012 and Pope Francis in 2015, with little effect.

"The capital of hope awakened by John Paul II has drained away after almost two decades of no real improvements in the country's socioeconomic and political situation, and in the spiral of poverty that stifles much of the population," Havana-based writer Miriam Celaya wrote in *The Atlantic* magazine on the eve of Pope Francis' visit in 2015.[9]

Castro, however, continued on. He relinquished his presidential duties in 2006 to his brother Raul after surgery for intestinal bleeding, but continued his involvement in government affairs. There were reports, never confirmed by the government, that he suffered from diverticulitis.

Fidel Castro died on November 25, 2016 at the age of 90. He was cremated the following day and his ashes were transported the 560 miles from Havana back to Santiago de Cuba, the birthplace of the revolution, reversing the route he had taken after taking control of the country in 1959.

His ashes were interred at the Santa Ifigenia Cemetery in Santiago de Cuba, not far from where I saw him give that speech.

By all accounts, he died of natural causes. He had outlived all those assassination attempts, many of which were so comical it made you scratch your head.

Scratching your head, it turned out, could easily have implicated you in one of those plots.

## CHAPTER 25

# *Barry Manilow: On Perseverance and the Art of the Comeback*

===

W HO knew Barry Manilow could teach me anything about the right way to look at my career?

In May 2017, he came on the NYSE floor just after he played the Nassau Veterans Memorial Coliseum in Uniondale, New York to a sold-out crowd of roughly 15,000. Manilow hadn't had a significant hit in years, but here he was selling out a 15,000-seat arena.

I was not a Barry Manilow fan, but the sellout at the Coliseum amazed me. How did he pull it off?

Starting with "Mandy" in 1974, Manilow had been a massive hit machine, a string that continued into the early 1980s. But while he continued to put out albums and made occasional appearances on the Adult Contemporary charts after that, he hadn't appeared on the Billboard Hot 100 in nearly 30 years.[1]

He finished a brief on-air interview with two of my colleagues—Kelly Evans and Bill Griffeth—and after he had walked off the set, I approached him.

If you want to get famous people who are interviewed often to say

336

something revealing, you have to find out what animates them. Manilow had a new album he was promoting, *This is My Town*, which had primarily been the subject of the interview with Kelly and Bill.

That wasn't what interested me, and I doubted it was what interested Manilow. My experience talking to movie stars and performers taught me that while it was important for them economically to talk about their new product, it was rarely what truly interested them.

Two subjects always sparked an emotional response: the "correct" way to look at their legacy, and the reason behind their longevity.

After introducing myself, I said, "I just have two questions for you. First, did you really write the State Farm jingle and sell it for just $500?"

It was well-known that Manilow had written the jingle ("Like a good neighbor, State Farm is there"), along with many other jingles in the 1970s ("I'm stuck on a Band-Aid, and a Band-Aid's stuck on me"), before he hit it big. Still, I wanted to ask a simple, friendly question before getting to the issue I wanted to bring up.

He said he did, and he never regretted it: "Five hundred dollars was a lot of money back then!" he told me, and that being a jingle writer was the best music college he could have gone to.

Then I got to the longevity question. He had just sold out Nassau Coliseum. He had put out many albums in the last few decades, but hadn't had a significant hit in years. Why did people keep showing up for his shows?

That's when Barry Manilow surprised me. I expected him to talk about his loyal (mostly female) fan base, which was the obvious answer. Instead, he talked about his career, how after his first string of big hits (26 Top 100 hits between 1974 and 1983), he continued to churn out albums and continued performing, even after the hits stopped coming.

"I'm one of the lucky guys, the well hasn't run dry yet, I always have ideas," he had said during the on-air interview.

He was surprisingly reflective about the arc of his career—the early hits, the lull after the hits stopped coming, and his status as a musical legend, despite the endless critical derision he had received. Even his biographer, Patricia Butler, referred to Manilow as "our national punchline" and "everyone's favorite celebrity fall-guy."[2]

It's clear the criticism bothered him, but he kept plugging along, and scored several comebacks, even after the hits stopped coming in the early 1980s.

His 2002 compilation, *Ultimate Manilow*, reached No. 3 and went double-platinum. His theme-based albums, *The Greatest Songs of the Fifties*, *The Greatest Songs of the Sixties*, and *The Greatest Songs of the Seventies*, had hit No. 1, No. 2, and No. 4, respectively, on the U.S. album charts in 2006 and 2007. Those albums produced a couple of minor Adult Contemporary hits, "Unchained Melody" and "Love is a Many-Splendored Thing."

That view of the arc of his career fit the mold of many successful people I had known: an initial period of apprenticeship, followed by success, followed by a middle period where, while most are not stuck, their careers are simply cruising along. Many switch jobs or careers at this point. Manilow had stopped producing pop hits but had stayed close to musical idioms he was most comfortable with—Broadway show tunes, jazz, and the Great American Songbook.

He had stayed with what made him passionate, made it through the challenging middle part of his career, and had stuck with it long enough to emerge on the other side as a legend.

What Manilow was saying to me was that there was a reward for sticking to something long term, even if it's not always apparent along the way. "If you take away something from tonight's show, it would be don't be afraid to do what you love to do," he told an audience in Milwaukee during the Live 2002! tour.[3]

He also advised against going with fads. In a 1991 interview with *The New York Times*, Manilow described his years as a hitmaker:

It was like being in golden handcuffs… It's only recently I've figured out how to have my cake and eat it—by being honest about my own musical desires and not just being led around by what I think the audience wants to hear.[4]

I could have used that advice earlier in my career. It would have saved me the many hours of soul-searching I had to engage in to come to the same conclusion Manilow had come to.

I had begun as the Real Estate Correspondent in 1990. I had worked at it for six years and was moderately successful, but my career moved to a higher profile when I switched to On-Air Stocks Correspondent in 1997 and went to the NYSE.

CNBC had started getting significant ratings only about 1995. But the ratings were not going up because I was the Real Estate Correspondent— they were going up because the stock market was beginning to rise due to the internet boom, which took off in August 1995 when Netscape went public.

The time after I became On-Air Stocks Editor in 1997 was a wild, three-year period where all of us on-air at CNBC went from relative unknowns to practically household names. But the dot-com bust in 2000, the 9/11 disaster the following year, and the brief recession that followed changed the public's opinion toward investing. Suddenly, we weren't the hottest thing on television anymore.

Many of my colleagues took advantage of the change to switch jobs. After a lot of soul-searching, I decided to stay. I stayed because I loved CNBC, I loved being a journalist live on television, I loved the stock market, I loved the NYSE, and I loved meeting the famous people who rang the bell every day.

I made that decision back in 2002. Sticking with it despite the disappointment was the difficult middle part of my career. Like Barry Manilow, I simply decided to stay with what I loved to do.

In deciding to stay on as the On-Air Stocks Editor, I became known as "inch wide, mile deep." I accumulated a vast trove of personal experience about a small part of the world—the stock market. In making that decision, I eventually became well-known for my expertise in that area.

Most successful people I have met ringing the NYSE bell have done just that. If you love what you're doing, stick out the difficult middle part, because there is a lot of satisfaction in becoming well-known for a specific skill.

Art Cashin, the dean of floor traders at the NYSE, has spent nearly 60 years on the floor. Every day, after stopping in at the bar at the NYSE (or at Bobby Van's steakhouse across the street) for a couple of tumblers of Dewar's, he went home and studied stock charts. The next day he produced "Cashin's Comments," one of the most widely read commentaries on the markets.

For many years, I interviewed him every day at 11:30, and often he told me what I needed to look for in my own commentaries.

"You've got to work your craft," he said time and again, usually after I failed to notice a connection between two events where the link was obvious to him but not apparent to me. "Pay attention!"

Art realized very early that the world is paying for particular skill sets and that experience was the way to hone those skill sets. Tech entrepreneur Josh Linkner, who writes a blog on leadership and creativity, said, "Being the worldwide expert in one area will simply outpunch those who diffuse their energy, passion, and expertise into many. To scale your business and career, focus your aperture and become jaw-droppingly great at just one thing."[5]

There's a problem with becoming an expert: it takes a long time, and many do not have the patience or the motivation. Some love their work but get burnt out.

That's happened to me several times: in 1993 after working nonstop for three years at the startup that was CNBC, in 2001 after the dot-com bust and the 9/11 disaster, and in 2009 in the aftermath of the Financial Crisis. Each time, I thought of quitting, and each time I looked at my circumstances and decided to keep going.

If your job bores the hell out of you and you truly can't take it anymore, I'm not going to convince you to stay, even if you are well-paid for your expertise (if you're not well paid, that's a different problem).

I am saying that most people don't honestly think through their circumstances. Most people overestimate how bored they are and underestimate the impact of lower pay and the time and effort it will take to become a sufficiently well-paid expert in another field, whether it's computer programming, running a pizza shop, or playing the soprano saxophone in a jazz band.

And there are plenty of ways to overcome the "I'm not motivated anymore" story. In my case, I realized I could handle burnout by evolving and growing in other parts of my life.

After my first burnout in 1993, I took more vacation and went home earlier in the day.

After 9/11, I learned to meditate and went much deeper into a hobby (photography) that I had only dabbled in during the 1990s. After the Financial Crisis, my wife Suzanne and I began to travel extensively. I went deeper into yet another hobby I dabbled in for many years: collecting 1960s rock posters.

As a journalist, something else happens when you stick around for a long time: your knowledge deepens.

You end up knowing as much as many of your sources.

Few of us could be described as legends for simply surviving, but those few minutes chatting with Barry Manilow left a profound impression on me. The hits, when the hits stop coming, and the importance of sticking with what you love to do.

He still loved what he was doing. He was still performing: "It's the only place" anyone makes money anymore, he said.

And he was at peace with the course of his career. When Bill Boggs, in an interview done a year later, asked him what the best period of his life was, Barry Manilow said, "Right now."[6]

That's the right attitude. To have a career where you feel the best part is "right now."

Who knew Barry Manilow was such a sage?

## CHAPTER 26

# Mike Wallace and the First Commandment of Broadcast Journalism

━━━

P ISANI'S First Law of Broadcast Journalism is: Thou Shalt Make Air. If you don't make air, nothing else matters.

And—when faced with the prospect of not making air—you'd be surprised what you'd be willing to do.

Like the day Mike Wallace saved my butt.

It was 1992. It was a glorious time to be a reporter at CNBC.

CNBC had been founded only three years earlier, in 1989, by Tom Rogers and NBC Broadcasting CEO Bob Wright, partly to compete against Ted Turner's CNN.

I had been hired in the summer of 1990 as Real Estate Correspondent and was put in charge of my own show, *The Real Estate Report*, which I co-anchored with Ted David and Wayne Shannon.

By 1992, we had merged with our main rival, Financial News Network, and while we were not the hottest thing on television—that would come a few years later—we were young, scrappy, and—working out of Fort

Lee, New Jersey—far, far, less expensive to run than our NBC parent that occupied 30 Rock in Manhattan.

In the beginning, we were the Consumer News and Business Channel (CNBC), and while we were immediately associated with the stock crawl at the bottom of the screen, we were still working out exactly what we wanted to be.

During the day, we had begun coalescing around a single idea: the stock market, or "the horse race," as we liked to call it. We soon dropped the old name, Consumer News and Business Channel, and were simply CNBC. Consumer news was generally out; stocks and business were in. From then on, it would be about who and what was winning and losing in the business world, but particularly in the stock market.

At night, it was different. We had general news and entertainment shows, hosted by stalwarts like Morton Downey Jr., Dick Cavett and John McLaughlin, along with shows like *Steals & Deals*, our investigative consumer finance show hosted by Janice Lieberman, and *Real Story*, a *Today* show-styled amalgam of general news and entertainment.

As Real Estate Correspondent, during the day I covered new home sales, home prices, mortgage rates, real estate taxes.

But at night, it was a different story. If you were a reporter that was a bit curious about the world, you only had to propose a story that started with, "The business of (fill in the blank)" and you had a good shot at getting the story on the air.

And that's what I did—I put all my interests on the air. The business of jazz. Historic hotels. Historic diners. Almost anything could be turned into a business story.

I expanded the Real Estate beat as well. I covered insurance nightmares. Hurricanes. The safety record of elevators—and the hazards of escalators.

I turned stories around the history of my favorite buildings (the Empire State Building, the Waldorf Astoria), and always tried to cover them in a different way than the competition. For the 60th anniversary of the Empire State Building in 1991, every TV reporter in New York went to the Observation Post on the 102nd floor to file their story. Not me. I went to the lowest part of the Empire State Building—the sub-basement seven stories below the street and stood by the original stream that had run on the land when it was first developed in the 1830s and was still there—still being pumped out of the building.

## The Russian Tea Room

When the chance came to do a story around one of my favorite restaurants—the Russian Tea Room—I jumped at the chance.

By then, the Tea Room was already more than 60 years old, having been founded by members of the Russian Imperial Ballet in the late 1920s. By the 1930s, thanks to its location next to Carnegie Hall, it had become a haven for artists and celebrities, and later a favorite spot to shoot movies, including *Tootsie*.

By the early 1990s, it was a long way from its heyday in the 1950s and 1960s, but it was still a formidable presence among the older celebrity crowd. They pulled in a huge mix of New Yorkers and tourists and had the numbers to prove it: 3,000 pounds of caviar served each year (the most of any restaurant in America), and 6,000 bottles of vodka poured each year, also the most for any restaurant.

And that was what I was looking for: a chance to hang out in the fabled red banquettes for a couple days, interview a few celebrities, throw in some history and some old stills, and put it on the air.

I spent a day tailing Faith Stewart-Gordon, who had run the Tea Room for more than 30 years. She showed me the nooks and crannies, told some funny stories, but I quickly got down to business: I needed some of her celebrity friends to talk.

No problem, she said. Liz Smith was having a birthday party upstairs the next day. I was welcome to attend, and chat with anyone who was willing to chat with me.

That was more than I could have possibly hoped for. Liz Smith, in 1992, was the most successful gossip columnist in America. Hell, she was one of the most successful journalists in America, period. She had just moved from *The Daily News* to *Newsday*, but she had made the jump with no loss of influence. She was a staple of New York nightlife. Everyone who mattered would be at her party.

I arrived the next day, went up the stairs, and tried to walk into the room where the party was being held. A very large bouncer stood in my way, his arms crossed.

"Hi, Bob Pisani from CNBC," I said cheerfully. "I'm here for Liz Smith's party."

"You can't come in." He stared down at me, malevolently.

"I'm sorry, but Ms. Stewart-Gordon said I could come. I'm sure Ms. Smith knows I am coming."

"She knows, and she told me to tell you that you can't come in."

That was a smack in the face that I should have anticipated: Liz Smith, queen of gossip columnists, didn't want me gossiping with her guests. The guard was there to make sure I didn't bother anyone.

I was screwed.

This was supposed to be fun and easy, and it was neither. It was supposed to be a few quick interviews, cut it in the morning, air it that night.

The First Law of Broadcast Journalism flashed in front of my eyes: Thou Shalt Make Air.

Panic. I did the only thing I could possibly do: I excused myself, walked down the hallway with my cameraman, set the camera up in front of the ladies room, and waited with a stick mike in my hand.

Fifteen minutes into my vigil, Barbara Walters came sauntering out of the party, and walked straight towards me. Barbara Walters! Surely she had wonderful stories about the place. I was saved.

"Ms. Walters, I'm Bob Pisani from CNBC. We're doing a story on the anniversary of the Russian Tea Room, and I was wondering if you could…"

That was as far as I got.

"Move the camera away from the door, NOW!"

She glared at me malevolently. Was this Barbara Walters, the famous TV journalist?

I could have just sandbagged her. I had permission to be on the property. I could have just rolled the camera and stuck a mike in her face, recorded the minor tirade, and used it in the piece.

But no, I had to ask. A nice guy, I was about to finish last, something Barbara Walters would certainly not have allowed had she been doing the story.

I moved the camera.

Five minutes later, Kathleen Turner came through the door! Kathleen Turner! She looked smashing in a black leather jacket and miniskirt.

She was also visibly swaying.

"Ms. Turner, Bob Pisani from CNBC. We're doing a story on the 50th anniversary of the Russian Tea Room. Care to share any anecdotes about coming here?"

She stared at me, lowered her head, and smiled. "I don't know too much about the place, and I really don't think I should say anything at all, don't you agree?"

Again it went through my head: I have permission to be on the property. Roll the goddamn tape.

"Of course, I understand Ms. Turner." I stepped aside and she brushed past me.

Idiot. Nice guy. And what you have is: nothing.

And then Norman Mailer came through the door.

Now, with a few exceptions, I don't give a damn about TV personalities or movie stars; it's not my scene. But this was Norman Mailer, my childhood hero, the guy I most wanted to be, as a kid growing up dreaming of being a writer.

In the late sixties and early seventies, Mailer seemed to be everywhere. His books—*The Armies of the Night*, about the 1967 march on the Pentagon, *Miami and the Seize of Chicago*, about the 1968 Republic and Democratic National Conventions, and *Of A Fire On The Moon*, about the space program, were bestsellers and made a profound impact on me. They made me want to be a writer.

And Mailer was the writer I wanted to be. He wrote all the big books, he got into all the brawls with all the right people, and he was in the middle of all the big issues of his day.

He had all the fun, and as a 13-year old in Bucks County, Pennsylvania in 1969, that's what I wanted to do.

I had met him briefly at a lecture he gave at Berkeley in 1975. By then, he could write about anything he wanted: Marilyn Monroe, the Ali-Foreman fight, even the virtues of graffiti. He was combative and witty, everything I wanted to be.

He was also a jerk toward women, which even in the 1970s was not cool and I knew it, but he personified so many of the qualities I wanted to possess that I ignored that very serious flaw.

Don't meet your heroes or you'll be disappointed? Bullshit, I remember thinking.

He had seen better days; he was nearly 70 when I saw him outside that men's room. He waddled back and forth as he walked. He looked like he was in pain.

But he was still Norman Mailer.

"Mr. Mailer, Bob Pisani from CNBC. I know you used to come here in the fifties, I'm doing a piece on the 50th anniversary. Care to tell us a few stories about hanging out here?"

He stopped in front of the camera. This was it—I was going to get some juicy story about him getting shitfaced here, writing pieces that went into *Advertisements for Myself*, sitting in the banquettes and getting into fights with all the right people. I signaled to my cameraman to get ready to start rolling.

"To tell you the truth, kid, I never liked this place or the people in it, and I didn't come very often. Now if you don't move that goddamn camera I'm going to pee right on the fucking door!"

Kid? Pee on the fucking door? This was Norman Mailer, the Mailer I loved.

But it wasn't the Mailer I needed. I moved the camera. Again.

And so it went, all night. No one would talk to me. I was screwed.

The party was winding down. The guests went down another set of stairs and out the front door, so they didn't have to go past me in the back.

The Prime Commandment loomed large. I was on air the next day, and aside from a brief interview with the actor Jack Palance and one or two others, I had very little to hang a story on.

I needed a name.

I needed more firepower. I walked up to the guard, who was standing with his arms crossed.

"Listen, everyone's leaving," I said, leaning into him and lowering my voice, like I was sharing a secret. "At least let me into the room and ask if someone wants to come out and do an interview."

"Sorry, can't do it." He still had his arms crossed. He was enjoying himself, sticking it to me.

I looked past him, into the room, watching helplessly as the guests left.

Then I saw him: Mike Wallace, getting up, putting on his Humphrey Bogart trench coat.

I jumped up and down, waving over the guard. "Mr. Wallace, Mr. Wallace! Got a minute?" The guard stared malevolently at me, put his hand on my chest. He looked like he was going to punch me in the stomach.

Wallace came to the door. "Mr. Wallace, Bob Pisani from CNBC! I'm doing a piece for air tomorrow on the 50th anniversary of this place, and I really need a few good stories from people who used to hang out here. I know you did—can you help me?"

He smiled. "Sure, happy to help."

And for the next 10 minutes Mike Wallace stood outside the door and told me stories about the Russian Tea Room in the 1950s and 1960s.

"For those of us who are of a certain age, certain spots mean New York—the center of Manhattan. This is one of them."

"There's only one objection I have to the Tea Room. It used to be—it used to be easier to pay the bill."

It was all I needed. The next morning the Executive Producer of *The Real Story* called.

"You got what you need for that piece on the Russian Tea Room?"

"Yep. Got Mike Wallace, Jack Palance, Jerry Ohrbach, Stiller and Meara, Margaret Whiting."

"Good. Cut it now. You're on tonight."

I never met Mike Wallace again, but every time I saw him on the air I smiled and remembered. And every time someone stops me in the street and wants to ask my opinion about the stock market because they watch me every day on CNBC and I don't feel like talking, I think of Mike Wallace and what he did for me.

And that tenaciousness—that willingness to stand in front of the ladies room with a stick mike and a cameraman and block the door, and shout over large bouncers—would serve me well in the coming years.

## CHAPTER 27

# *Aretha Franklin: People Will Open Up to You if You Find What Animates Them*

═══

T HE trick to getting someone to open up to you is to find the subject that animates them the most. That may or may not be the subject that most interests the people watching or reading.

Aretha Franklin came to the NYSE on December 4, 2008, for the annual Christmas party and to debut her first Christmas album.

I had a subject that I believed would get her talking.

By then, we were all desperate for some holiday cheer. It had been a disastrous year.

Lehman Brothers had gone under less than three months before. The S&P 500 was 45 percent below its recent high in October 2007, only 14 months earlier, and, though we didn't know it, would not bottom for another three months.

Everyone was hopeful that Aretha Franklin, and the NYSE Christmas party that came with it, would be a welcome distraction.

It came at a transitional moment for Aretha. A few months before, she had left her label of the past 28 years, Arista. The album she was promoting, *This Christmas, Aretha* was released by DMI, and was sold exclusively through Borders bookstore, an unusual arrangement for that time.

It was a tough time for the recording industry. Total physical album sales were down a shocking 14 percent from 2007, and though digital sales increased it was not enough to make up for losses in physical sales.[1] Old alliances were falling apart, and Aretha smartly experimented with new arrangements, not just musically but also in business.

To emphasize those new arrangements, she brought along Tena Clark, the CEO of DMI, the producer of the album, and Rob Gruen, the executive vice president of merchandising for Borders. She asked that they be included in the interview.

I had no problem with that. The bigger problem was Aretha.

I was, first and foremost, nervous. When you are on the floor of the NYSE every day, you meet a lot of famous people. But most don't have a personal connection. It's different when you meet someone who was a large part of your life growing up.

Aretha fits into that category. Growing up in the Philadelphia area in the 1960s, her records were a fixture on WFIL and WIBG, two of the radio stations I listened to.

But that was a long time ago. By 2008, the most prominent artists of the 1960s—the Rolling Stones, James Brown, Ray Charles, Bob Dylan, and Aretha Franklin—had long since stopped being "pop stars" and had graduated into a much more exalted status—that of cultural icon. Those that had passed away—John Lennon, Marvin Gaye, Sam Cooke, Jimi Hendrix—were spoken of reverentially. Those that were still alive—like Aretha—were treated with the greatest of deference.

That deference was only getting bigger. That summer, *Rolling Stone* magazine named her the #1 singer of all time, ahead of Ray Charles, Elvis Presley, and Sam Cooke.

"Aretha is a gift from God," Mary J. Blige wrote in *Rolling Stone*.[2]

Still, deference only went so far.

She was known to be difficult and prickly in interviews. She had good reason to be: she had lived a long life (she was 66 that year), full of highs and lows, but despite the success of her recording career (17 top-ten pop singles, 18 Grammy Awards, 75 million records sold), much of the ink spilt on her had been devoted to salacious tidbits of her personal life, particularly on her relationships with her ex-husbands, her jealousies of other female artists, or her struggles with alcohol.

I had no interest in asking about her personal struggles. I had a different agenda.

In 2004, a biopic of Ray Charles, *Ray*, had been released. It was a critical and commercial success. Jamie Foxx garnered rave reviews as Ray Charles and won the Academy Award for Best Actor and the Golden Globe, BAFTA, Screen Actors Guild, and Critics' Choice. It was only the second time an actor had won all five major lead actor awards for the same performance. *Ray* was also a commercial success, grossing $124.7 million worldwide.[3]

Ray Charles never saw the picture (he died a few months before the premiere), but it introduced a whole new generation to Ray Charles. As entertaining as the film was, it served a great educational purpose: it showed why he was so famous. Charles was more than just a great voice: he had helped to create the genre now known as soul by crossing secular lyrics with gospel music. This idea was controversial and even blasphemous among the black community that bought Charles' early music.

It was first and foremost an *educational* film about how Ray Charles helped invent soul music.

That's what I wanted to get at with Aretha Franklin. What was her role in all this, and how strongly did she feel about the need to educate a whole new generation about her contributions?

After chatting about her Christmas album, I got right to the heart of what interested me: what new projects was she working on?

"Well I'm looking for someone to work with on my autobiography," she told me. "We had something in the works about two years ago and then we went through a lot of different producers, a lot of problems here and there, it is back on the front burner now, so I'm hoping to see a rewrite, something that went into rewrite. We're waiting for a first draft now. If that doesn't happen, I'd like a lot of backup!"[4]

How about a movie about her life?

"I would love that. That is what we're working on," she told me.

"I think people need to know," I said. "Look what happened to that Ray Charles biopic how important that was to educate people about how soul and gospel music influenced American culture. And I just think a whole generation of young people learned about Ray Charles as a result of that movie and then you can learn more about you and your contributions. I mean, particularly the younger people they need to understand your contributions."

"Thank you so much," she said. "Yes, he was one of the greatest artists of all time."

I was hoping for a little more on the biopic, but I didn't get it.

When the interview ended, I told her I hoped she would do something with a biopic because that is how people educate themselves today. Video is the critical medium, not books.

She said she understood that and was very eager to get a project going. She loved *Ray* and understood why it was important. She talked very animatedly about what she wanted to do, and a biopic was a big priority.

I was disappointed that I couldn't get this excitement out of her on the interview but I wasn't surprised: after what she had been through with the press a certain reserve in front of a TV camera was probably the right attitude to adopt.

I also realized there wasn't a lot for her to tell. The biopic was just in a discussion stage.

After the interview was over, her manager came up to me.

"I don't know what you just said to her, but she normally does not spend any time chatting with reporters after an interview. Whatever you said got her interested."

That made me feel good. I was right: I had gotten to the core of what was animating her. She was indeed thinking about her legacy, and a biopic was a part of that.

The Christmas party, unfortunately, was not as festive as we had hoped. Aretha Franklin did show up to light the tree, but it was raining by then. She performed briefly and left.

Aretha Franklin died 10 years later, in 2018, of pancreatic cancer, at the age of 76.

That biopic she talked with me about? It took much longer than even Aretha likely anticipated. A big-screen production, *RESPECT*, starring Jennifer Hudson, was finally completed in 2021, 13 years after we had spoken. A separate biopic, *Genius: Aretha*, debuted on the National Geographic channel in 2021 and was denounced by her family, who said they had not been consulted, though National Geographic said they had permission to make the film from Franklin's estate.[5]

What's it all mean? Why did it take 13 years to get a biopic done when she had been so enthusiastic about the idea when I spoke to her?

I don't know, but it likely means that even the most talented people, with many smart people around them, sometimes face impossible odds. What endures is the music.

# CHAPTER 28

## *Joey Ramone: "I Got Mutual Funds!"*

═══

T HE variety of people who watch CNBC has always amazed me. You'd think most people watching a financial channel would be older types with staid attitudes, but that's not what I've experienced.

One of CNBC's biggest fans came from the least likely source: punk rock.

On one particular night in 1992, when I was Real Estate Correspondent, I had a story on CNBC's show *Real Story*. I walked into the tiny makeup room in CNBC headquarters in Fort Lee, New Jersey.

Joey Ramone was sitting there, waiting to go on.

Most of the time when you meet famous people, you say hello, but most of them don't have a lot of personal connection.

This was different. This was Joey Ramone, co-founder of the Ramones, the greatest punk rock band of all time. I had first seen the Ramones in March 1978 at the Tower Theater in Philadelphia (a very young Joan Jett, with the Runaways, opened the show).

I was very excited to meet him and told him I went to all the shows back in the day.

He looked at me, smiled, and said, "Yeah, yeah, I know who you are. You're Bob Pisani, you're the Real Estate Correspondent. I know who you are, because I watch CNBC now. See, I've got mutual funds."

My first thought was, "Oh man, Joey Ramone knows who I am, how cool is that!"

My second thought was, "Joey Ramone owns mutual funds? Oh no! Not cool!"

But it was cool. Very cool. He was very excited to talk about his investments. He loved CNBC, which amazed me.

I went to see Joey and the band later that year, 1992, at the Roseland Ballroom. I always thought he might make a good spokesperson for investors: Joey Ramone, hawking mutual funds.

It never happened.

Joey Ramone died in 2001 after a long battle with lymphoma, a month before his 50th birthday. A year later, in 2002, a posthumous solo album, *Don't Worry About Me*, was released. Joey was a CNBC fan to the end. That album contained a song about my colleague, Maria Bartiromo.

What's happening on Wall St.
What's happening at the Stock Exchange
I want to know
What's happening on Squawk Box
What's happening with my stocks
I want to know…
I watch you on the TV every single day[1]

In June 2021, I attended a Ramones Recollection Dinner at Bar Primi in the Bowery with Joe Dente, a friend from the NYSE floor. In attendance were the Ramones old tour manager, Monte A. Melnick, along with Lenny Kaye, Patti Smith's guitar player and a noted rock historian.*

It was just a block from the old CBGB club where the Ramones had broken out in 1976, along with Blondie, Television, and so many others. It was by then a very different neighborhood.

"Let's not romanticize that time too much," Lenny Kaye said during the dinner, noting that they had to step over bums and junkies to get to the club.

It was hard not to notice the difference, 45 years after the Ramones had become famous. Gone were the bums and junkies, and the abandoned buildings. CBGB had turned into a John Varvatos store. The old flophouses and single room occupancy hotels that defined the Bowery were long gone. The hip Bowery Hotel up the street charged $400 a night.

Nobody may have been in a mood to romanticize the past, but everyone in attendance was certainly nostalgic. And why shouldn't they be? A plaque—"Joey Ramone Place"—hung on a lamppost outside Bar Primi, which had itself morphed into an upscale Italian joint that served pricey Barolo wine.

Melnick, who was hawking his book, *On the Road With the Ramones*, told stories about life on tour with the band, including their favorite foods (pizza—they liked Domino's because it was consistent—and tacos) and their favorite restaurants (Cracker Barrel, because the band discovered they could get free meals if they autographed photos).

During the Q&A, I told Melnick about meeting Joey in 1992 and his interest in CNBC and investing.

Melnick confirmed that Joey was a regular CNBC viewer, even on the road. The problem, Melnick said, was that Joey had obsessive-compulsive

---

* Kaye's 1973 anthology of 1960s garage rock bands, *Nuggets,* spawned several albums and helped spur many of us to seek out obscure bands from the mid to late 1960s. I bought *Nuggets* in a record store in Horsham, Pennsylvania in 1973 and it changed my life.

disorder (OCD), and the ticker tape that ran at the bottom of the screen drove him crazy—he couldn't watch the screen because the ticker distracted him.

To solve the problem, Joey stuck a piece of paper or whatever was handy across the bottom of the screen to block out the ticker.

It's a great image: Joey Ramone in a hotel room, Domino's Pizza boxes scattered about, taping paper across the bottom of the TV screen while trying to get the latest stock news.

## A gift from Joey Ramone

On my 40th birthday in February 1996, my wife Suzanne and I went to see the Ramones at Hammerjacks in Baltimore for their final tour, Adios Amigos! We were only able to get one ticket, and the show was sold out when we got there. We stood in line waiting to get in, hoping a miracle would happen.

As the doors opened, a guy walked up to me and said, "You looking for a ticket?" I said, "Yeah, you got any?" and he handed me a ticket.

I was dumbstruck. I said, "Gee thanks man, how much do I owe you?" and he said, "Nothing. Next time it's your turn to do someone a favor." And he walked away.

For the past 25 years, whenever I go to a concert and I have an extra ticket, I look around for someone looking as forlorn as I looked 25 years ago, and I walk up and say, "You looking for a ticket?" and if the answer is yes, I give it to them, and when they ask, "What do I owe you?" I say, "Nothing. It's a gift from Joey Ramone."

# *Appendices*

# APPENDIX 1

# *ETFs and the Origin of Indexing*

===

## *Buffett wins the bet*

No one can pinpoint the exact date when it became clear that investing in index funds had won out over investing in active management (particularly high-cost active management), but Warren Buffett declaring it to be so is certainly a pivotal moment.

Buffett had entered into a bet with Protégé Partners, a New York City money management firm that runs funds of hedge funds, that an index fund could beat an active manager.

The bet was this: over a 10-year period commencing January 1, 2008, and ending December 31, 2017, the S&P 500 would outperform a portfolio of five hedge funds of funds, when performance was measured on a basis net of fees, costs, and expenses.[1]

Buffett, who chose the Vanguard Index Fund as a proxy for the S&P 500, won by a landslide. The five fund of funds had an average return of only 36.3% net of fees over that ten-year period, while the S&P index fund had a return of 125.8%.[2]

In his 2017 letter to shareholders, Buffett took note of the high fees of hedge fund managers and offered what he called a simple equation: "If Group A (active investors) and Group B (do-nothing investors) comprise the total investing universe, and B is destined to achieve average results before costs, so, too, must A. Whichever group has the lower costs will win."[3]

His advice to investors: "When trillions of dollars are managed by Wall Streeters charging high fees, it will usually be the managers who reap outsized profits, not the clients. Both large and small investors should stick with low-cost index funds."[4]

Buffett was saying something that had been known to savvy investors and traders for almost a century, but which had taken a long time to seep into the average investor's consciousness.

## How I got on the indexing bandwagon

By the time I arrived at CNBC in 1990, the myth that active investors outperformed the markets was beginning to evaporate and attitudes about index investing were changing fast.

CNBC was changing fast as well.

I had been hired as the Real Estate Correspondent in 1990. During the day, we covered the financial world, mostly the stock market. At night, I covered real estate investing stories for our consumer show, *Steals and Deals*.

It was all great fun, but I was already thinking of moving away from real estate and toward the stock market. About this time, I started hanging out with one of our anchors, Ron Insana, because he already had the experience covering the markets that I wanted.

Insana was one of the most knowledgeable stock reporters I knew. He had been with our competitor, Financial News Network (FNN), since

1984. CNBC acquired FNN and it ceased operations on May 21, 1991, after a bidding war with Dow Jones/Westinghouse that cost NBC $154.3 million but sealed our place as a viable business channel.

It all happened thanks to the visionary thinking of NBC's leaders, Bob Wright and Tom Rogers, who had convinced a skeptical Jack Welch, CEO of our parent General Electric, to make the additional investment to get us into more homes.

It worked. Overnight, our subscribers doubled, from 18 million to 40 million. Most important of all, we were now carried in New York City. National advertisers could no longer ignore us. It was the great turning point.[5]

Insana and his fellow anchor, Bill Griffeth, had been with FNN from the beginning. Standing in the newsroom in Fort Lee, I watched Ron and Bill sign off together on FNN's last night. They immediately flew from California to New Jersey to join us.

## The KBW Bank Index

One day in 1992, Insana told me that a new index had just started, the KBW Bank Index. Keefe Bruyette Woods (KBW) started in 1962 as a boutique brokerage firm specializing in bank stocks. They created an index that tracked 24 of the largest bank stocks that went back to 1961. The index was unlisted, but it was useful to track the movement of bank stocks, and especially useful for KBW's clients.

On March 6, 1992, the firm listed the KBW Bank Index (BKX) on the Philadelphia Stock Exchange, with values going back to October 21, 1991. That meant derivatives (options) could be created off the product.[6]

That casual conversation piqued my interest. KBW's clients were obviously interested in trying to figure out where bank stocks were going, and KBW found a way to do that. Indexes were not new, but finding a way to make them investible was very difficult.

That started me thinking: why isn't it investible? How could it be made investible?

It turned out, an entire industry was just being born trying to answer those questions—one that would turn the investing world upside down.

## Unmasking the Wall Street game

Considering how long the stock market has been around, it took an awfully long time for researchers to figure out that much of the advice Wall Street was giving was bad advice.

Legendary Wall Street trader Jesse Livermore, speaking through journalist Edwin Lefevre, came to the same conclusion Buffett had come to way back in 1922: "I have said many times and cannot say it too often that the experience of years as a stock operator has convinced me that no man can consistently and continuously beat the stock market though he may make money in individual stocks on certain occasions."[7]

That was 100 years ago.

But getting hard evidence was not easy in the days before computers.

In 1932, Alfred Cowles III, whose grandfather had founded the *Chicago Tribune*, conducted an exhaustive survey of 16 financial services that had made 7,500 stock recommendations between January 1, 1928, to July 1, 1932; 20 fire insurance companies that had picked stocks from 1928 through 1931; and 24 financial publications that that made market forecasts from January 1, 1928, to June 1, 1932.

The results were terrible.

On the track record of the financial services, Cowles concluded that "Statistical tests of the best individual records failed to demonstrate that they exhibited skill, and indicated that they more probably were results of chance."

On the track record of the fire insurance companies: "The best of these records... fails to exhibit definitely the existence of any skill in investment."

On the track record of the financial publications: "the most successful records are little, if any, better than what might be expected to result from pure chance."[8]

A follow-up study Cowles conducted in 1944 also failed to show that stock pickers had any predictive ability.[9]

Cowles' achievement was notable because of the difficulty he faced in a pre-computer age. Just compiling the data was an immense task.

While the Dow Jones Industrial Average had been around since 1896, investors did not have a comprehensive stock market database. Absent a database, there was no way a truly comprehensive study of the markets could be conducted.

## Mutual funds take off

And that was a problem, because the bull market of the early 1950s (the S&P 500 was up six out of seven years from 1950–1956) caused a surge of interest in a then relatively new investment vehicle: mutual funds.

Open-ended mutual funds with redeemable shares had been around since the 1920s. The Securities Act of 1933, created in the wake of the 1929 stock market crash, required that all investments sold to the public, including mutual funds, be registered with the government. The following year, the Securities Exchange Act of 1934 created the Securities and Exchange Commission (SEC) as the primary regulator of securities, including mutual funds. The Investment Company Act of 1940 required even more disclosure about each investment company.

Interest in mutual funds were slow to develop, but the 1950s bull market was the initial impetus for the expansion of the mutual fund business. By the end of 1951, the total number of mutual funds surpassed 100, and the number of shareholder accounts exceeded one million for the first time. By 1954, net purchases of mutual fund shares exceeded that of corporate stock.[10]

It was the perfect moment for the American investor, and fortunately there was some brilliant work being done on investing at the time.

# Wall Street enters the computer age

In 1959, Louis Engel, then vice president of Merrill Lynch, Pierce, Fenner & Smith, funded a study done by Professor James H. Lori at the University of Chicago. Engel was interested in knowing what the investment performance in the stock market relative to other types of investments had been.

Engel had an obvious motivation: if stocks did outperform other investments, it would be a valuable marketing tool to an investment firm like Merrill Lynch.

But no one seemed to know the answer to the question.

This led to the creation of the Center for Research in Security Prices (CRSP) in 1960. Lori set about gathering the first comprehensive database of the prices, dividends, and rates of return of all NYSE stocks since 1926. When the initial database was completed in 1964, it was estimated to contain between two and three million pieces of information.[11]

Lori's database enabled an accurate calculation of how much return an investor was getting from the stock market. From 1926 to 1960, the rate of return on NYSE listed stocks (with reinvestment of dividends), was nine percent per year.[12]

Lori did not directly answer Engel's initial question about how stocks performed against other investments, but that nine percent figure was high enough for Lori and his co-author Lawrence Fisher to proclaim: "These rates are substantially higher than for alternative investment media for which data are available."[13]

That was good news for Engel, who promptly made the results public and pushed the investing public to put more money into stocks.

## The evidence mounts: Wall Street can't pick stocks

Engel may have liked the absolute returns stocks were generating, but he certainly did not want to hear that this mountain of data was beginning to generate some disturbing implications for Wall Street.

By the mid-1960s, the evidence was mounting that most investors (and investment professionals) were, as Cowle had suspected, terrible stock pickers, and that the cost of fees and commissions substantially ate into any profits that were made.

Even mutual funds were coming under fire. In a 1968 paper, Michael C. Jensen at the University of Rochester College of Business evaluated the performance of 115 mutual funds from 1955 to 1964. His conclusion:

> The evidence on mutual fund performance discussed above indicates not only that these 115 mutual funds were *on average* not able to predict security prices well enough to outperform a buy-the-market-and-hold policy, but also that there is very little evidence that any *individual* fund was able to do significantly better than that which we expected from mere random chance.[14]

This was a serious problem. It was one thing to say that the public were terrible stock pickers. To a certain extent, this played into Wall Street's hands. Don't know how to pick stocks? Let a professional pick them for you through a mutual fund.

And yet, there was now growing academic evidence that even mutual funds weren't able to generate excess returns, once fees and commissions had been deducted.

At the same time, there was even more evidence that investors were better off avoiding stock picking altogether.

## *Diversification: the only free lunch there is?*

In 1952, Harry Markowitz was a Research Associate at the Rand Corporation. As a student at the University of Chicago, he had worked at the Cowles Foundation for Research in Economics, a think tank Alfred Cowles had established 20 years before. In 1952, he published a dissertation called *Portfolio Selection* in which he mathematically demonstrated that diversifying across a large number of stocks reduced risks for investors.[15]

It didn't sound like much, but the implications were revolutionary. *Financial Times* Global Finance Correspondent Robin Wigglesworth summarized Markowitz's thesis in his book on the history of indexing, *Trillions: How a Band of Wall Street Renegades Invented the Index Fund and Changed Finance Forever*:

Markowitz suggested that all investors should really care about was how the entire portfolio acted, rather than obsess about each individual security it contained. As long as a stock moved somewhat independently of the others, whatever its other virtues, the overall risk of the portfolio— or at least its volatility—would be reduced. Diversification, such as can be achieved through a broad, passive portfolio of the entire stock market, is the only "free lunch" available to investors, Markowitz argued.[16]

Markowitz's thesis became the foundation for what is now called Modern Portfolio Theory (MPT) and would win him the Nobel Memorial Prize in Economic Sciences in 1990.

The idea that an investor could reduce risk through diversification was now in the air.

Another important impetus to indexing came in the mid-1960s, when Eugene Fama and others developed the Efficient Market Hypothesis, which I discussed in Chapter 14. It held that asset prices reflect all available information, and because prices reflect all available information about the future payout of dividends and earnings, there is no good or bad time to enter the market.

These two concepts—Modern Portfolio Theory and the Efficient Market Hypothesis—combined to produce a powerful conclusion:

The best way to reduce risk through diversification is to own the entire market.

The issue was, how could that be accomplished?

## *The birth of indexing*

In the early 1960s, Ransom Cook, the chairman of Wells Fargo, attended an IBM conference in which a Smith Barney analyst, John McQuown, talked about using computers to pick stocks. McQuown had a degree in mechanical engineering from Northwestern University, and was keenly interested in statistical analysis of the stock market and how an index fund might be set up.[17]

Cook was so intrigued he offered McQuown a job immediately. For the next decade, McQuown was a director of the Management Sciences Group at Wells Fargo, a think tank that reported directly to Cook. He eventually became the founder of Wells Fargo Investment Advisors, the bank's investment advisory subsidiary.

The first index portfolio was begun in 1971 and funded by an unlikely source: the Samsonite luggage company's $6 million pension fund. It was indexed to the 1,500 stocks on the NYSE, but the difficulty in managing the constant updating of 1,500 stocks caused Wells Fargo to soon set up a separate fund, this one indexed to the S&P 500, and to fold the Samsonite fund into it.[18]

An index fund was now in existence, but it attracted very little attention.

In Chapter 10, I told you about Jack Bogle's somewhat lonely quest to develop a fund tied to the S&P 500. Jack was aware of the efforts at Wells Fargo, and in 1976 launched his own fund, the First Index Investment Trust.

But getting investors to sign on to a fund that merely mimicked the S&P 500 was no easy task; fund managers openly ridiculed the idea, claiming that investors should be trying to beat the market, not merely perform in-line with the market.

There was an additional problem: these funds could not be traded during the day.

Smart people began asking the next logical question: is there another way to buy, sell and own an index fund?

## The birth of the ETF business

The October 1987 stock market crash helped create the impetus for the next big development: the birth of Exchange-Traded Funds (ETFs). The SEC issued a long report analyzing the crash four months later and suggested that had investors had a market-based instrument like the S&P 500 that could be traded intraday, it might have mitigated the impact.

What they were describing was what became known as an Exchange-Traded Fund, which could wrap the 500 stocks of the S&P 500 into a single security and that could trade intraday, just like a stock.

Nate Most and Steven Bloom were listening. Most was head of product development at the American Stock Exchange, and Bloom was his right-hand man.

The Amex, as it was known, was in serious trouble.

Long home to younger companies, it was losing the competition for those companies to its upstart rival, the Nasdaq, which had developed strong ties to the technology community. It was also losing market share to other competitors who were paying participants to trade on their platforms, a process that came to be known as "payment for order flow."

To make up for the lost trading, Amex had begun aggressively moving into options trading and was looking to develop new business.

Princeton University economist Burton Malkiel was a governor at the Amex and chaired the new products committee. When Most brought up the ETF concept, Malkiel enthusiastically endorsed the idea.

And with good reason. Malkiel's 1973 book, *A Random Walk Down Wall Street*, had helped popularize the idea that stocks exhibit a "random walk" pattern, that it was not possible to consistently outperform the stock market, and that investors were better off in broadly diversified index funds.

In the 20 years since its publication, it had become an investment classic.

"I was a strong proponent of indexing, and I thought this [ETFs] was a great idea," Malkiel told me. "I suggested to Nate that he speak with Jack Bogle at Vanguard, but Jack hated ETFs and thought they would only be used by speculators. He refused to consider it. Nate then went to State Street, and they were very enthusiastic."[19]

After several false starts and battles with the SEC and the Commodities Futures Trading Commission (CFTC), Most and Bloom joined forces with State Street Global Advisors to launch the Standard & Poor's Depositary Receipt (symbol SPY), the first U.S.-based ETF, on January 29, 1993.*[20]

Like the Vanguard 500 Index Fund, the SPDR, as it came to be known, tracked the S&P 500. But the ETF structure had several advantages over a mutual fund:

- It was structured as a Unit Investment Trust (UIT), which unlike a mutual fund did not need an asset manager or a board of directors, which kept costs lower.
- It could be traded intraday, just like a stock.
- It had no minimum purchase requirement.
- The annual fees were lower than most comparable mutual funds.
- It was more tax efficient than a mutual fund. When mutual funds sell shares, it usually generates capital gains that become taxable for shareholders. An ETF may have to sell shares to meet investor redemptions, but these sales are made to a market maker (known as an "authorized participant") and do not create a taxable event.

## *No love for ETFs from Wall Street*

Malkiel had no problem convincing the Amex floor traders that there was potential in the new product.

"While the floor traders were not always enthusiastic about new

---

* The Toronto Stock Exchange had already launched a similar product that tracked the Toronto Stock Exchange 35 Index in 1990.

products, they were about this one, because they could create derivative products and if you had a long position, this was a way to hedge that position with the futures market."

Despite the advantages, the SPDR did not initially take off. Like Jack Bogle's Vanguard 500 Index Fund, much of Wall Street was not in love with the product.

"There was tremendous resistance to change," Bob Tull, who was developing new products for Morgan Stanley at the time and was a key figure in the development of ETFs, told me.[21]

Mutual funds and broker-dealers quickly realized there was little money in the product.

"There was a small asset management fee, but the Street hated it because there was no annual shareholder servicing fee," Tull told me. "The only thing they could charge was a commission. There was also no minimum amount, so they could have got a $5,000 ticket or a $50 ticket."

It was retail investors, who began buying through discount brokers, that helped the product break out, thanks to a strong marketing push from the Amex.

"The Amex was manning the 800-line, answering questions from investors or broker-dealers. They had people answering the phone, visiting offices of regional broker-dealers. They went into anyone's office who called and asked, 'Would you come in and talk to my staff about the SPDR?'"

The SPDR was quickly followed by the MidCap SPDR (now the SPDR S&P Midcap 400 ETF) in 1995.

In 1996, Tull, while still at Morgan Stanley, helped launched a series of 17 products, World Equity Benchmark shares (WEBS), that tracked indexes tied to different countries.

"Now any retail investor could get international exposure, where it was almost impossible to do that prior to the ETFs," Tull told me.

These new products differed in one important way from the SPDR products: they were structured as an open-end fund, rather than a Unit Investment Trust (UIT). This offered several advantages: dividends could be reinvested, shares could be lent out, and open-end funds had an asset manager that wasn't required to own each company in the index in exact proportion to the weighting in the S&P 500.[22]

## The right product at the right time

While it started off slowly, the ETF business came along at the exact right moment.

Its growth was aided by a confluence of two events: 1) the growing awareness that indexing was a superior way of owning the market over stock picking; and 2) the explosion of the internet and dot-com phenomenon, which helped the S&P 500 rocket up an average of 28 percent a year between 1995 and 1999.

In 1997, there were just 19 ETFs in existence (17 of which were international products, the WEBS). By the end of 2000, there were 80. The dot-com bust slowed down the entire financial industry, but within a few years the number of funds began to increase again.

## The gold ETF makes commodity investing viable

The year 2004 was an important year for the ETF business. The market was coming out of its 2000 dot-com funk, and the ETF business was growing again.

It was a year one of the world's most recognizable investments—gold—was available to buy as an ETF.

Investors who wanted to own gold had limited choices up until then. They could own gold bars or gold coins, but storage was not an easy matter. They could own gold futures, but that involved another layer of complexity. They could own gold mining stocks, but there was an imperfect relationship between gold and gold stocks.

When the StreetTracks Gold Shares (now called SPDR Gold Shares, symbol GLD) went public on November 18, 2004, it represented a quantum leap in making gold more widely available. The gold was held in vaults by a custodian. It tracked gold prices well, though as with all ETFs there was a fee (currently 0.4%). It could be bought and sold in a brokerage account, and even traded intraday.

A few days before it began trading at the NYSE, I called the World Gold Council and spoke with George Milling Stanley, who was Managing Director. The Council, through a subsidiary, was the sponsor of the ETF.

This was a big deal for gold investors and for the ETF business, I told George. I wanted him to come on the floor of the NYSE the day it started trading and explain how it works.

He turned me down.

I was flabbergasted. I assumed they would be eager to talk about the new product.

He told me the Council was concerned that the SEC might view them promoting the ETF as a violation of securities laws.

I had encountered this problem before. It all boiled down to what their lawyers were telling them. Some ETF providers never brought the issue up. Others had more conservative legal advisors and didn't want to get involved until after their securities started trading.

George, and World Gold Council, were in the latter camp.

I was determined to push through with something theatrical.

I got George to agree to a deal.

After some back and forth, the World Gold Council agreed to lend me several gold bars to show on the floor. It came complete with two armed guards.

The day the ETF went public, I stood in front of the camera, picked up one of the gold bars, held it over my head, and said:

This is gold. This is a gold bullion bar here. It's 25 pounds, it's worth about $180,000, and I've got three of them here along with a lot smaller amounts of gold, as well as these two burly guards I've been married to for the last half hour—thank you, guys. Why am I talking about gold today? Because finally a gold ETF is available—today, for the first time thanks to the World Gold Council and State Street, you are able to buy gold just like it's a stock![23]

It was a fortuitous moment to launch a gold ETF.

Gold had been outperforming the S&P 500 since the dot-com bust in mid-2000. For the next several years, with the exception of a pause in 2008, gold went almost straight up.

# The ETF business takes off

The GLD was the first commodity-based ETF in the U.S., but others quickly followed.

The GLD was benefitting from the upward trend in gold, but the entire ETF industry benefitted from increasing awareness that active management was not, for the most part, producing market-beating returns.

Jack Bogle was slowly winning the argument.

From almost nothing in 1996, ETF assets under management in the U.S. went up almost 400 percent between 2000 and 2005.

Staying in low-cost, well-diversified funds with low turnover and tax advantages (ETFs) gained even more adherents after the Great Financial Crisis in 2008–2009, which convinced more investors that trying to beat the markets was futile, and that high-cost funds ate away at any market-beating returns most funds could claim to make.

## The Bank Index flourishes as an ETF

That's what happened to the KBW Bank Index, that index that Ron Insana introduced me to 30 years ago.

By 2005, KBW had licensed the index to State Street, and it could be bought as an ETF.

Assets under management skyrocketed in 2010 as many investors bought into ETFs and indexing in the wake of the Great Financial Crisis.

In 2015 Nasdaq was brought in and it's now called the KBW Nasdaq Bank Index, and since 2011 it has been licensed to Invesco as the Invesco KBW Bank ETF (symbol KBWB).

State Street has renamed its bank ETF the SPDR S&P Bank ETF (symbol KBE) and now uses the S&P Banks Select Industry Index, which competes with the KBW Bank Index.

## ETFs: poised to take over from mutual funds

After pausing during the Great Financial Crisis, ETF assets under management took off and have been more than doubling every five years.

**U.S. ETF assets under management**

| | |
|---|---|
| 1996 | $2.4 billion |
| 2000 | $65.5 billion |
| 2005 | $300.8 billion |
| 2010 | $991.9 billion |
| 2015 | $2.1 trillion |
| 2020 | $5.5 trillion |

Source: Investment Company Institute.[24]

The Covid pandemic pushed even more money into ETFs, the vast majority into index-based products like those tied to the S&P 500.

By the end of 2021, over $7 trillion was in U.S.-based ETFs. The mutual fund industry still had significantly more assets (about $23 trillion), but that gap is closing fast.

From a measly 80 ETFs in 2000, there are now over 2,200 ETFs operating in the U.S.

Mutual funds, by contrast, have seen their numbers decline in the past 20 years, even as the dollar value has risen due to the rise in the stock market.[25]

"ETFs are still the largest growing asset wrapper in the world," Bob Tull, who has built ETFs in 18 countries, told me. "It is the one product regulators trust because of its transparency. People know what they are getting the day they buy it."[26]

# APPENDIX 2

# *Understanding Bubbles*

≡

I can calculate the motion of heavenly bodies, but not the madness of people.

—*Sir Isaac Newton, commenting on the South Sea Bubble of 1720*[1]

I'VE seen a lot of bubbles in my 30-plus years at CNBC. I'm constantly asked if tech stocks, or real estate, or Bitcoin, are in a bubble.*

There are two problems: most people don't know how to frame the question right (there are very few real "bubbles"), and second, if something is in a real bubble, it's usually impossible to tell when it will burst.

Asset classes—stocks, bonds, gold, commodities, currencies, real estate—are always going up and down, but every few years, something blows up and gets everyone hot and bothered.

A bubble is a rapid rise in prices over a short period that, in retrospect, is not supported by fundamentals, followed by a subsequent rapid decline. The word "fundamentals" can be a bit tricky to define,

---

* The study of the history of market bubbles is a sub-genre of investing: see Chancellor, Kindleberger, Mackay, and Reinhart.

since some investments (gold, Bitcoin, collectibles in general) don't have "intrinsic" value—that is, they don't throw off a dividend or the potential for a steady stream of cash flow, as stocks or bonds do. These kinds of investments are worth whatever the forces of supply and demand dictate.

Here's just a few crazy bubbles that have happened in recent decades:

- *Gold: 1976–1980.* During the high-inflation period of the mid-1970s, gold went from $100 an ounce in 1976 to over $800 in January 1980. By 1982 it was back in the $300 range and did not begin rising again for another 20 years, in 2002. The 2000s were again a golden era for the precious metal: it went from $300 in early 2002 to $1,900 in mid-2011.

- *The Japanese real estate/stock market bubble: 1985–1989.* Fueled by a strong yen and a Tokyo real estate boom that greatly inflated net corporate assets, the country's leading stock barometer, the Nikkei-225, increased 224 percent between January 1985 and December 1989, when it hit a historic high. After the Bank of Japan began raising rates, the Nikkei was down over 40 percent. It has never returned to its December 1989 highs.

- *The U.S. tech bubble: 1991–2000.* The Nasdaq 100, the largest 100 non-financial stocks in the Nasdaq, went from roughly 100 at the start of 1991 to 4,800 in March 2000, an astonishing gain of 2,300 percent in 10 years, far outperforming the S&P 500's approximately 300 percent gain in the same period.

- *The Asian Financial Crisis: 1997.* High interest rates and dramatic growth in exports resulted in a stock market boom in Asian emerging market countries including Thailand, the Philippines, and Malaysia. When the U.S. dollar strengthened, governments were forced to devalue their currencies. Much of the foreign investment left. From mid-1996 to mid-1998, the Thai stock market dropped more than 80 percent.

- *The U.S. housing bubble: 2002–2007.* The average sale price of a new home went from $228,700 in 2002 to $313,600 in 2007, a gain of almost 40 percent.[2] Between 2007 and 2009, average house prices in the largest metropolitan areas dropped by one-third.[3]
- *The China equity/commodity bubble: 2006–2007.* Chinese equities, as measured by the CSI-300, went up over 400 percent in two years from 2006 to the end of 2007, corresponding with a spike in global commodities like copper. By October 2008, less than one year later, the CSI-300 had dropped 70 percent.
- *Bitcoin: 2016–2017.* The cryptocurrency went from $400 in early 2016 to a peak of $19,000 in December 2017. One year later, it was back to $2,700. Then it went from $10,000 in late 2020 to $60,000 in April 2021, then down to $30,000 four months later, then back to over $60,000 in late 2021.
- *FAANG stocks.* Tech stocks are another group that burst and have had a resurgence, though much of it is confined to a narrow group. My colleague Jim Cramer coined the word "FAANG" in 2013, referring to a group of five companies (Facebook, Apple, Amazon, Netflix, and Google) that were dominant in their industries. Microsoft was also later included in this group. These stocks were up 600–800 percent between 2014 and mid-2021.

Some of these bubbles burst and never came back (Japanese stocks), while some burst and have had resurgences (gold in the 2000s, tech stocks in the mid-2010s, U.S. home prices in the mid-2010s, Bitcoin in mid-2020). Others argue that FAANG stocks were never in a bubble since their stock price rises were accompanied by enormous profit growth.

Why do bubbles happen? Why do bubbles form and then burst? Why do people buy things when they know, or should know, the value isn't there? William Bernstein, the author of many excellent books on investing and the history of capitalism, put it this way: The anatomy of bubbles "consists of the 'four ps': promoters, public, politicians, and press."*[4]

In other words, you need a vehicle that is investible, someone to promote it, someone to buy it, and some medium to spread the information.

That last factor is crucial. It's no coincidence that the birth of the stock market as an investment and newspapers as a means of spreading information both happened at roughly the same time, in the 1600s.

Of course, not every investment becomes a bubble; most do not. Bernstein reviewed the work of economist Hyman Minsky, who studied bubbles carefully and concluded that most also needed two other conditions: low interest rates, which made it easy to borrow money cheaply, and an exciting new technology.[5]

And that's when we see the first bubbles, beginning with the famous Dutch tulip mania craze, where a pound of tulips bulbs in 1637 sold for about four years of income for a master carpenter. The whole craze collapsed later that year, though there is considerable debate in modern times about the extent of the "mania."†[6]

Most early bubbles do indeed revolve around new technologies: turnpike construction in England (1600s), U.S. canals (1820s), railroads (1830s), the telegraph (1830s), undersea cables (1860s), the telephone (1870s), and radio (1920s), which was the internet of its time.[7] All had significant run-ups in stock prices, and all collapsed at some point.

There are other theories about why bubbles form. However, they boil down to one point: it's essentially a matter of psychology, with a bit of economics thrown in. Assets move up and down all the time, but to get a true "bubble," there needs to be a combination of several factors present:

---

* Bernstein is an excellent interpreter of complex economic and investing subjects.
† The whole conception that tulip mania was an example of a modern financial bubble has been challenged in the last decades, arguing it was not nearly as dramatic as depicted in Charles MacKay's famous account.

- *Easy money*, where interest rates are low or the supply of money is plentiful, so it's easy to borrow money cheaply (the U.S. housing bubble, the China stock market).
- *A new disruptive technology* that creates intense demand and speculation (the internet in the 1990s, Bitcoin).
- *New financial innovations*, such as the many new mortgage products that emerged during the U.S. housing bubble in the mid-2000s.
- *A supply/demand imbalance*, where demand exceeds supply or supply is limited (China equities and commodity inflation in the mid-2000s).
- *A need to hedge* against some other part of a portfolio (gold in the 2000s, bitcoin).

The most important thing to understand about bubbles is that *they are primarily a psychological phenomenon.*

Paul S. L. Yip, an economics professor at Nanyan Technological University in Singapore, identified three "stages" that all bubbles go through:

1. *Seeding stage.* This is the initial price rise where an asset moves above a prior trough for a few months or quarters.
2. *Development stage.* The rise in prices attracts the attention of other investors, creating an expectation of a further rise in prices. Crowd behavior now begins to take over, which leads to vicious upward cycles.
3. *Herding stage.* This final stage drags in other participants who have not yet participated, in a frenzy of FOMO (fear of missing out)—mainly from fund managers who are fearful of underperforming should they not be in the asset class that is outperforming.

At some point, however, 100 percent of all the investors who want in, will be in. At that point, the same psychological factors that drove the investment up, will drive it down. That's the top, Yip says:

At this time, even a very mild negative shock can cause a fall in the asset price, which will in turn trigger herding behavior in the downward direction and causing a reversal of the above vicious cycles, spirals, financial leveraging, and changes in economic behaviors and expectation until the asset price plunges to a level well below the normal equilibrium level.[8]

These psychological factors are extremely powerful. For example, during China's stock market bubble of 2006–2007, Yip notes that tens of millions of people—including businesspeople, employees, homemakers, retirees and students—suddenly became investors for the first time in a frenzy of speculation.

William Quinn, in his book *Boom and Bust: A Global History of Financial Bubbles*, also noted the role new technologies play in promoting bubbles, but added that they needed three elements to thrive:

1. *Marketability:* there must be an asset that can be easily bought and sold. Bubbles are often preceded by an increase in marketability. The dot-com bubble, for example, was associated with the growth of internet trading. A particularly egregious example was the mass issuance of mortgage-backed securities during the run-up to the Great Financial Crisis of 2007–2009, "which turned previously illiquid mortgage debt into an asset that could be bought, sold and speculated in," Quinn writes.[9]

2. *Money and credit:* investors need money to invest, so periods with low interest rates and abundant credit are often associated with bubbles. Low rates make it cheap to borrow money, and also force investors to look for anything with higher yields.

3. *Speculative investors:* there are always speculators (short-term investors) in the market, but during bubbles large numbers of speculators, many of them novices, come in. The earliest investors make quick profits,

which drags in even more investors. These new, typically novice, investors usually end up buying high and selling low.

Why aren't bubbles easy to spot and predict? Why do prices shoot up and often stay up for some time? Quinn notes that while new technologies are often touted as the start of a "new era," the economic impact is very hard to gauge: "This means there is limited information with which to value the shares accurately." The financial press is also complicit, since coverage of the rising prices helps drag in additional investors.

Not surprisingly, behavioral economists have had a field day studying asset bubbles, and also not surprisingly they emphasize investor psychology as a leading reason why bubbles grow, well, into bubbles.

Yale economist Robert Shiller, who has studied bubbles extensively, noted in his Nobel Prize lecture that investors themselves are part of the reason bubbles form, due to a "house money effect" that can help make bubbles grow even bigger: "an analogy to gamblers at casinos who, after they have won some money, become very risk tolerant with that money because they frame it as somebody else's money that they can afford to lose."[10]

The key point I have learned about watching bubbles of any type: they are largely driven by psychology and you will drive yourself mad trying to figure out a "fundamental" value of the investment while it is in a bubble, or even when the bubble will end.

## APPENDIX 3

# *58 Maxims on Life, Television, and the Stock Market*

===

T HE maxim (a short statement of a general truth, principle, or rule for behavior, according to the *Cambridge Dictionary*) seems out of fashion today. I don't know why.

Perhaps it's because they can seem cynical or contrived, which can put them out of touch with the raw honesty ("authenticity," a word I detest) so valued today.

One thing's for sure: whenever I ask someone to summarize their career or what they have learned, the response is usually phrased as a maxim.

Whether they are lawyers, doctors, rock stars, or stock pickers, the successful ones also realize that what they have experienced was like a metaphor for life.

*I think that way as well.*

Here are some of my observations.

# On television

1. Thou shalt make air.

   *Woody Allen once said that 80 percent of success was just showing up. It's amazing how many people never show up.*

2. Your name is not Tolstoy.

   *The art is in the brevity.*

3. At any moment, 10 percent of the viewers think you're a genius, 10 percent think you're a moron, and the rest are indifferent or undecided.

4. Talk, make sense, employed. Don't talk, don't make sense, unemployed.

5. Always push for more time on air, and higher up in the rundown.

   *Never assume anyone recognizes your talent or cares if you live or die. Sell yourself and explain why on earth anyone should pay attention to you.*

6. In television, you can be forgiven for almost any atrocity except lousy ratings.

7. There are only four words a News Director needs to know: Yes, No, and Hell No.

8. The viewers must always believe that you know something more than they do.

9. When every day is a crisis, no day is a crisis.

10. Ignore the vast audience you mistakenly think are watching: speak to a single person who has an intense interest in what you are saying. Answer their questions.

11. We are not actors, but there are elements of acting in everything we do.

# On Style

12. Content always trumps presentation, but make sure your tie is straight.

13. Don't get nervous, but always remain in a state of mild agitation.

14. Authenticity is always preferable.

15. Authenticity is always preferable, but if you're an authentic asshole, work on a convincing alternative persona.

16. Authenticity is always preferable, but it's just as much a construct as phoniness.

17. Don't be controversial for the sake of being controversial, but strive to be the one who drives the conversation.

## On competition and success

18. In debate, a more knowledgeable opponent can be defeated by an adversary who is better prepared and can control the conversation.

19. It's not always about megalomania, but that's a good place to start.

20. An intense, all-consuming motivation to succeed can sometimes trump talent. For many, intense motivation *is* the talent.

21. Your greatest competition is always inside your head, not outside.

## On journalism

22. Everyone agrees that journalism operates under a set of Grand Principals, but no one can agree on what they are.

23. You're only as good as your last hit.
*The old guys on the floor were right: they used to say, "It's a long race, but the runners have a short memory."*

24. There are only two kinds of people in the world: those who have the information you need to get through your next hit, and those who don't.

25. You know you're in trouble when your best sources call and ask YOU what's going on.

26. There is no necessary relationship between the number of people you talk to and how well informed you are.

27. The most valuable sources are those who both know what they are talking about and who can provide an honest opinion. They are not necessarily the same.
28. The risk of being early on a story is minimal, but the risk of being late is that the story may not be worth reporting at all.
29. Your sources are not your friends.
30. Do not become what you are reporting.

## On interviewing

31. Avoid interviewing anyone wearing sunglasses.
32. An interview should sound to the interviewee like a conversation, not an interrogation.
33. The follow-up to an insufficient answer should be silence, not another question. Wait for your subject to fill the dead space.
34. Most issues are shades of gray, not black and white. Think carefully before you demand to know "the truth" from anyone.

## On traders and the stock market

35. Everyone talks their book. Be cognizant of the motives of the people you are talking to.
36. Don't yell at the stock market. You're not the lone genius that recognizes the coming catastrophe.
37. When stock traders talk about what's affecting trading and the subject is outside the stock market, pay very close attention, because it means they are afraid of something they don't understand.
38. When drinking with traders, stay one drink behind, and shut up.

## On where you fit in

39. If you knew what your "friends" really thought about you, you'd have a hard time getting out of bed every morning.

40. The joy lies in the process of creation, not in the reception.
    *You'll be amazed how many people can't stand you. Much of the time, it is not about you.*

41. Bullshit the world if you must, but never bullshit yourself.
    *Stand naked in front of a mirror every morning. Look at yourself. Not pretty, is it? Note: don't do this in a public restroom.*

42. When someone screws you and justifies it by saying, "It's nothing personal," it's personal.

43. Very few things matter in the long run, and even less that you can control.
    *Focus on the intersection between the things that matter and the things that you can control.*

## On social media

44. There's always someone who knows one fact more than you do on the most obscure subject imaginable, and they are eager to let you know it.

45. Aggrievement is a poor branding strategy. Find something else to stand for.

## On goals

46. Making friends is important, but not making enemies is a superior strategy.

47. Learn to live in the future.

48. Take notes: they are memos you send to yourself in the future.

49. There are only two kinds of people in the world: those who have product, and those who don't.

50. Be perceived as a problem solver, not a problem maker.

51. Surround yourself with people smarter than you are.

52. It is not different this time: you may not believe in gravity, but gravity very much believes in you.

53. Invest more time in relationships and less in stocks.

54. A friend is someone who will return your phone call after you've stopped being who you used to be.

55. Stop the theft of your attention: you cannot buy more time, but it can be stolen from you.

## On taking risks

56. Very few people ever get hit by a bus, but if it happens to you, you will have a very different perspective when you cross the street again.

## On speaking your mind

57. Honesty is the best policy, but it rarely behooves you to tell everyone exactly what you're thinking.

58. Say nothing, and mean it. You don't need to have an opinion on everything.

# Acknowledgments

═══

I T'S a fortunate person who can say, "For 30 years, I have been with a wonderful company."

It's rare indeed to be able to say, "For 30 years, I have been with *two* wonderful companies."

I can make that claim.

I joined CNBC in 1990, a little after its first year in existence. I watched it grow from a tiny cable operation with no ratings situated in a backwater of New Jersey to a network that became an important part of NBC and General Electric, and later for Comcast as well.

I first came to the New York Stock Exchange in 1995 and was there on a full-time basis by 1997. By then it was already 205 years old, one of the great institutions of America, and one of the most recognizable brand names in the world.

Television news is a chaotic world, full of uncertainty because, try as you might, no one can really know what is going to happen on any given day. It's full of hard-working writers, producers, reporters and anchors who strive mightily to decipher what is going on.

Managing a group like this is no easy task. TV can be a cutthroat business, but CNBC, in my experience, has always been a congenial place to work in a turbulent business.

My deepest thanks to the visionary men and women who founded CNBC, but particularly Bob Wright and Tom Rogers, and the two men who took a chance on me in the summer of 1990: Bob Davis and David Zaslav.

My thanks to CNBC's Chairman, Mark Hoffman, my boss and friend for many years, who made many of the initial investments in the NYSE floor that made it possible for us to become the dominant news force on Wall Street.

A special thanks to my producers through the years: Anna Levine (1998–2001), Bianna Golodryga (2001–2003), Robert Hum (2003–2010), Kristin Scholer (2010–2013), Jill Harding (2013–2016), and Kirsten Chang (2016–present), all of whom worked with me in a small room and were unfailingly cheerful despite my long silences and general weirdness.

Thanks to the Assignment Desk and the many people in the News Division who help decide what goes on our air every day: Dan Colarusso, Senior Vice President of News, Jason Gewirtz, Ellen Egeth, Brad Quick, Tom Rotunno, Peter Schacknow, Alex Crippen, Jim Forkin, Katie Slaman, Leslie Yevak and Ryan Ruggiero, and especially Lacy O'Toole, Managing Editor, who has the unenviable job of keeping track of what everyone is doing, where they are, where they are supposed to be and making sure all the troops are marching in the same direction.

CNBC has a morning and afternoon call, where reporters pitch stories to the Assignment Desk and the producers and Executive Producers, including Matt Quayle, Todd Bonin, Chip Aiken, Marc Gilbert, Maria Boden, Lisa Villalobos, Kevin Flynn, Sandy Cannold, and Regina Gilgan, as well as Matt Cuddy, Washington Bureau News Director, John Melloy, who runs the all-important market coverage for CNBC.com, Mary Duffy, in charge of Talent Development, Jay Yarrow, the head of CNBC Digital, and Nick Dunn, Executive Editor of CNBC Events.

I listen very carefully to these calls because there are no finer reporters covering their beats: Julia Boorstin, Contessa Brewer, Dominic Chu, Jeff Cox, Bertha Coombs, Patti Domm, Sharon Epperson, Frank Holland, Robert Frank, Eamon Javers, Phil LeBeau, Ylan Mui, Steve Liesman, Seema Mody, Diana Olick, Kristina Partsinevelos, Leslie Picker, Courtney Reagan, Kate Rogers, Kate Rooney, Rick Santelli, Mike Santolli, Rahel Solomon, Hugh Son, Kayla Tausche, and Meg Tirrell.

I'm proud to say I have worked with every single anchor in the history of CNBC, including our current roster: Morgan Brennan, Jim Cramer, Sara Eisen, David Faber, Jon Fortt, Kelly Evans, Wilfred Frost, Joe Kernen, Melissa Lee, Becky Quick, Carl Quintanilla, Tyler Mathisen, Andrew Ross Sorkin, Shepard Smith, Brian Sullivan, and Scott Wapner.

Given the many things that can go wrong with technology, it's amazing how well everything works (most of the time).

The CNBC crew on the floor of the NYSE, particularly Brad Rubin and Gillian Austin, have held down the fort for many years and are responsible for making sure guests get in on time and all the technology is functioning for a smooth broadcast.

I am grateful to the NYSE's archivist, Peter Asch, for his help in uncovering obscure facts about the history of that wonderful institution and for locating old photographs, to the NYSE's Josh King and Farrell Kramer for their help arranging interviews and meeting with NYSE staff, and to Judy Shaw for her eternal cheerfulness and her many years of work shuffling visitors around the floor.

My deepest thanks to the members of the NYSE, particularly those on the floor in my earliest days who provided commentary and allowed me to watch them work, but particularly Bob Fagenson, Mike LaBranche, James Rutledge, Jimmy Maguire, Bob Hardy, Bob Seijas, Chris Quick, Lou Pastina, Larry Leibowitz, and Joe Mecane.

Bob Zito, former Executive VP for the NYSE, and former NYSE CEO Richard Grasso, brought television to the NYSE floor in 1995, transformed the NYSE opening and closing bells from staid affairs to media events, and help turn the NYSE into one of the most recognizable brand names in the world.

Art Cashin, Director of Floor Operations for UBS, has been a friend and mentor since I came to the NYSE in 1997. He has been a steady hand through all the changes in trading and has been a constant source of inspiration.

I am indebted to the following friends who read parts of the manuscript and offered many helpful comments and suggestions:

- Burton Malkiel, author of the investment classic, *A Random Walk Down Wall Street*, for reviewing the chapter on indexing and ETFs;
- Bob Tull, who while at Morgan Stanley and other firms was instrumental in the creation of Exchange Traded Funds (ETFs) in the 1980s and 1990s, also read sections on indexing and the creation of ETFs;
- Robert A. Schwartz, Marvin M. Speiser Professor of Finance and University Distinguished Professor in the Zicklin School of Business, Baruch College, City University of New York, for reading parts of the manuscript related to market history;
- Larry Leibowitz, formerly Chief Operating Officer for NYSE Euronext, who also read parts of the manuscript related to market history.

Any errors or omissions are of course my own.

While hundreds of people have shaped my reporting over the years, I am particularly indebted to a very small group whom I first encountered in the 1990s and whose writings and personal contact have had a profound influence on the way I view the markets: Jack Bogle, founder of Vanguard and author of *Common Sense on Mutual Funds*; Jeremy Siegel, Russell E. Palmer Professor of Finance at the Wharton School of the University of Pennsylvania and author of *Stocks for the Long Run*; investment consultant Charles D. Ellis, author of *Winning the Loser's Game*; Burton Malkiel,

Chemical Bank Chairman's Professor of Economics, Senior Economist at Princeton University and author of *A Random Walk Down Wall Street*; and Robert Shiller, Sterling Professor of Economics at Yale University, 2013 Nobel Economics Laureate, and author of *Irrational Exuberance*.

One of the great joys of being a financial reporter for the past 30 years has been watching the explosive growth of the Exchange Traded Funds (ETF) business, a low-cost, tax-efficient method of owning stocks that has revolutionized investing and helped spur the growth of indexing, a fancy word that means simply owning the broad market. Many people have contributed to this revolution, but I have had the good fortune of having three friends whose expertise I have been able to draw upon for many years: Dave Nadig and Tom Lydon from ETF Trends, and Matt Hougan, Chief Investment Officer of Bitwise Asset Management.

Suzanne Petruzel, my wife and best friend for 40 years, read the entire manuscript as it was being written and offered many helpful comments. Most importantly, she put up with my long absences over the two years this book was written.

My attorney, Paul Julian, has been a friend and counselor for 20 years and provided much appreciated advice and guidance.

My editor at Harriman House, Craig Pearce, has been an excellent collaborator and made many helpful suggestions to improve the final form of the book.

Thanks to three friends: Joe and Cathy Zicherman, who have helped expand my horizons through travel, music, and wine and brought me into their wonderful family, and to Chris Botti, trumpeter and band leader extraordinaire, with whom I have shared many fine nights talking about music, the stock market, and politics.

Finally, a special thanks to those who helped build CNBC dayside in the very early days and who stayed for decades: Alex Crippen, Tom Anthony, Scott Cohn, Bill Griffeth, Ron Insana, Sue Herera, Angel Perez, Brigid Scire, Chris Maurer, Peter Schacknow, Jim Forkin, Matt Quayle, Rob

Contino, John Schoen, Mario Schettino, Fritz Mott, Pat Bucci, Victor Calderin, Jerry Frasier, Mike Vaughan, and Rich Fisherman.

Thanks to the many others who contributed so much to dayside and primetime in the early days and moved on to other careers: Jaime Avery, Maria Bartiromo, Art Benger, John Bollinger, Gail Buckner, Stacey Cahn, Ed Caldwell, Allan Chernoff, Dan Clark, Conway Cliff, Jerry Cobb, Ted David, Ken & Daria Dolan, Brian Donlon, Jim Donovan, Lynn Doyle, Bruce Francis, Andy Friendly, Alison Gibbs, Karen Gibbs, Doreen Herbert, Lynn Keller, Mabel Jong, Kim Kennedy, Judy Kuriansky, Jeff Leshay, Lidj Lewis, Janice Lieberman, Leslie Linton, Susan Lisovicz, Mike Mammana, Kevin McCullough, John McLaughlin, John Metaxas, Juliette Meeus, Larry Moscow, Darby Mullaney Dunn; John Murphy, Mark Neschis, Monica Orbe, Diane Petzke, Glen Rochkind, Bobbi Rebell, Marc Rosenweig, Glenn Ruppel, Sasha Salama, Michael Salort, Bahman Samiian, Ed Scanlon, Dawn Schefler, Dean Shepherd, Alec Sirken, Cathy Stevens, Kristen Strand, Felicia Taylor, Jon Teall, Alison Tepper, Elizabeth Tilson Ailes, Karen Toulon, Michele Treacy, Billy Toth, Mary VanHorn, Donald Van de Mark, Caroline Vanderlip, and Chuck Woodruff.

And special thanks to Mark Haines, who left us way too soon. The plaque is still by the stairs at the NYSE, old buddy.

One last thanks—and this really is the last thanks: good night, Wayne Shannon. Thanks for the laughs. I still have your dictionary. Come by and pick it up some time.

## THE PRESIDENTS OF CNBC

Mark Hoffman, 2005–present (Chairman, 2015–present)
Pamela Thomas-Graham, 2001–2005
Bill Bolster, 1996–2001
Roger Ailes, 1993–1996

Al Barber, 1990–1993
Mike Eskridge, 1989–1990

## CNBC EXECUTIVE VICE PRESIDENTS, NEWS

Dan Colarusso, 2019–present
Nik Deogun, 2011–2018
Jeremy Pink, 2009–2011
Jonathan Wald, 2006–2009
David Friend, 2002–2006
Bruno Cohen, 1997–2002
Jack Riley, 1993–1997
Peter Sturtevant, 1989–1993

## CEOS OF THE NEW YORK STOCK EXCHANGE

Richard Grasso, 1995–2003
John Thain, 2004–2007
Duncan Niederauer, 2007–2014
Thomas Farley, 2014–2018 (President)
Stacey Cunningham, 2018–2021 (President)
Lynn Martin, 2022–present (President)

# *Bibliography*

===

## *The books that influenced me the most*

I don't make any pretense to having read every investment book ever written. But a small number of books (and people) I came in contact with in the 1990s exerted a profound effect on me and continue to do so.

Bogle, John C., *Common Sense on Mutual Funds* (John Wiley, 10th Anniversary Edition, 2009). Originally published in 1999 by John Wiley & Sons. Meeting Jack Bogle in the mid-1990s changed my life. While CNBC were making "TV stars" out of investors like Bill Miller at Legg Mason, Bogle convinced me that: 1) for most investors low-cost index funds were the way to go, 2) the outperformance of the small (very small) group of active managers who did outperform was negated by the high fees they charged, and 3) once you got the mix of assets right for your risk tolerance, the key was to stick with the plan and not freak out when markets dropped. More than anyone—including Warren Buffett—Bogle changed how I look at investing.

Ellis, Charles D., *Winning the Loser's Game: Timeless Strategies for Successful Investing* (McGraw Hill Education, 8th edition, 2021). First published as *Investment Policy: How to Win the Loser's Game* by Dow-Jones Iriwn in 1985. This book distilled much of the wisdom that Malkiel, Bogle, Siegel and Shiller had separately published on beating the markets, the efficient market hypothesis, market timing, and asset allocation.

Malkiel, Burton., *A Random Walk Down Wall Street* (W. W. Norton & Company, 12th edition, 2020). First published in 1973 by W. W. Norton. By the time I met Burton Malkiel this book had already been in print for more than 25 years. It has grown enormously in the last 47 years (the 12th edition that came out in 2020 is 500 small-type pages) but more than any other book it popularized the idea that you can't beat the market. Malkiel was a close friend of Jack Bogle and spent 28 years on the board of Vanguard.

Shiller, Robert, *Irrational Exuberance* (Princeton University Press, 3rd edition, 2015). First published in 2000 by Princeton University Press. The book was named after Alan Greenspan's now-famous comment about how stock market valuations can get absurd. Shiller was prescient: this explanation of how markets can be dominated by irrational thinking and herd behavior (what came to be known as "behavioral economics") was published in March 2000, the exact height of the dot-com stock market bubble. It addresses the causes of asset bubbles and how to mitigate risk, much of it built around Shiller's study of behavioral economics. Subsequent editions have covered the housing crisis (2005) and the bond market (2015).

Siegel, Jeremy J., *Stocks for the Long Run: The Definitive Guide to Financial Market Returns & Long-Term Investment Strategies* (McGraw-Hill Education, 5th edition, 2014). Originally published in 1994 by Richard D. Irwin, Inc. Siegel examined stock and bond returns going back 200 years and concluded that on average stocks produced inflation-adjusted returns of 6.5%–7% a year, far outperforming bonds. This was a pivotal study that helped convince many that a simple "buy and hold" strategy was the best long-term investment.

Wurman, Richard Saul, Kenneth M. Morris and Alan M. Siegel, *The Wall Street Journal Guide to Understanding Money and Markets* (Access Press, 1989). I read many books preparing to transition from Real Estate Correspondent to On-Air Stocks Editor in 1997, but this was far and away my favorite and likely the shortest. Wurman was trained as an architect but became a legend in a series of books that could be described as "information design," books that combine graphics and texts that explain complicated subjects in an interesting and easy-to-digest manner. He designed a series of city "walking guides" beginning with Access L.A. in 1980 that revolutionized city travel books. In 1989, he published this book, which spawned numerous imitators. He also founded the now-legendary TED conferences, beginning in 1984. The book's core style has continued, in slightly different form, as *The Guide to Money & Investing*, by Virginia B. Morris and Kenneth M. Morris, published by Lightbulb Press.

## *History of indexing and ETFs*

Bogle, John C, *Stay the Course: The Story of Vanguard and the Index Revolution* (John Wiley, 2019). Bogle's intellectual autobiography.

Carrel, Lawrence, *ETFs for the Long Run: What They Are, How They Work, and Simple Strategies for Successful Long-Term Investing* (John C. Wiley, 2008).

Ellis, Charles, with James R. Vertin, *The Index Revolution: Why Investors Should Join it Now* (John Wiley, 2016). Foreword by Burton Malkiel.

Hebner, Mark T., *Index Funds: The 12-Step Recovery Program for Active Investors* (IFA Publishing, 2018). An outstanding distillation of the history of indexing and the early pioneers of stock market research.

Lehman, Ralph, *The Elusive Trade: How Exchange Traded Funds Conquered Wall Street* (Brown Books, 2019).

Wigglesworth, Robin, *Trillions: How a Band of Wall Street Renegades*

*Invented the Index Fund and Changed Finance Forever* (Penguin Publishing Group, 2021). An outstanding overview of the men and women who revolutionized investing by creating the first index funds and ETFs from the *Financial Times* global finance correspondent.

# Investing/trading

Bernstein, William, *The Four Pillars of Investing: Lessons for Building a Winning Portfolio* (McGraw-Hill Education, 1st edition, 2010).

Bogle, John C., *Bogle on Mutual Funds: New Perspectives for the Intelligent Investor* (Richard D. Irwin, 1994).

Bogle, John C., *The Little Book of Common Sense Investing: The Only Way to Guarantee Your Fair Share of Stock Market Returns* (John Wiley, 2007, 10th Anniversary Edition updated and revised 2017).

Brown, Joshua, and Brian Portnoy, editors, *How I Invest My Money: Finance Experts Reveal How They Save, Spend, and Invest* (Harriman House, 2020). Financial advisor Josh Brown experienced the same bizarre behavior I saw: everyone always asked him about the market, but no one ever asked him what he owned. It's the most important question! So he and Portnoy edited a book asking contributors to describe how they navigate their own investments.

Buffett, Warren, and Lawrence Cunningham, *The Essays of Warren Buffett: Lessons for Corporate America* (Carolina Academic Press, 5th edition, revised 2019). A collection of letters Buffett wrote to shareholders over several decades. The best distillation of his investment philosophy.

Edelman, Ric, *The Truth About Your Future: The Money Guide You Need Now, Later, and Much Later* (Simon & Schuster, 2017).

Ellis, Charles, with James R. Vertin, *Classics: An Investor's Anthology* (Irwin, 1989).

Ellis, Charles, with James R. Vertin, *Classics II: Another Investor's Anthology* (Irwin, 1991).

Ellis, Charles, with James R. Vertin, *The Investor's Anthology: Original Ideas From the Industry's Greatest Minds* (John Wiley & Sons, 1997).

Graham, Benjamin, and David L. Dodd, *Security Analysis* (Mc-Graw Hill, 6th edition, 2008). First published in 1934 and still the most important book on fundamental analysis of stocks.

Graham, Benjamin, *The Intelligent Investor: The Definitive Book on Value Investing* (Harper-Collins Business, Revised Edition, 2009). First published 1949.

Greenberg, Alan. C., *Memos from the Chairman* (Workman Publishing Company, 1996).

Kaufman, Peter D., *Poor Charlie's Almanac: the Wit and Wisdom of Charlie Munger* (2005). Munger popularized the idea of "mental models", explanations of how things work. The book is long and often repetitive, but worth the slog.

Larimore, Taylor, and John C. Bogle, *The Bogleheads' Guide to the Three-Fund Portfolio: How a Simple Portfolio of Three Total Market Index Funds Outperforms Most Investors With Less Risk* (John Wiley, 2018).

Lowenstein, Roger, *When Genius Failed: The Rise and Fall of Long-Term Capital Management* (Random House, 1989).

Malkiel, Burton G., and Charles D. Ellis, *The Elements of Investing: Easy Lessons for Every Investor* (John Wiley & Sons, 10th Anniversary Edition, 2021).

Murphy, John C. *Technical Analysis of the Financial Markets: A Comprehensive Guide to Trading Methods and Applications* (New York Institute of Finance, 1999). Murphy was the Technical Analyst at CNBC during its very early days.

O'Neil, William J., *How to Make Money in Stocks* (McGraw-Hill Education, 4th edition, revised 2009). Despite evidence that actively trading stocks regularly is a losing game, many investors ask me how it could be done systematically. Bill O'Neill, the founder of Investors Business Daily, certainly has a method. His CANSLIM system focuses on growth stocks and employs both technical and fundamental analysis. It has a dedicated following.

O'Shaugnessy, James P., *What Works on Wall Street* (McGraw-Hill Education, 4th edition, 2011). Jim O'Shaugnessy was a guest on CNBC for many years. His book looks at several investment strategies, most of them based off fundamental analysis. He disagrees with Bogle and others by claiming that investment opportunities still persist, even after becoming widely known.

Patterson, Scott, *Dark Pools: High-Speed Traders, A.I. Bandits, and the Threat to the Global Financial System* (Crown Publishing Group, 2012).

Schwager, Jack D., *Market Wizards: Interviews with Top Traders* (John Wiley & Sons, 2012). First published in 1989, this book helped make stars out of traders like Paul Tudor Jones, William O'Neill, Jim Rogers, and Michael Steinhardt, and spawned a whole series of spin-offs.

Schwager, Jack D., *The Little Book of Market Wizards: Lessons from the Great Traders* (John Wiley & Sons, 2014).

Swedroe, Larry, *Reducing the Risk of Black Swans: Using the Science of Investing to Capture Returns With Less Volatility* (BAM Alliance Press, 2018).

Swedroe, Larry, and Andrew L. Berkin, *The Incredible Shrinking Alpha: How to be a Successful Investor Without Picking Winners* (Harriman House, 2020).

Swedroe, Larry, *Wise Investing Made Simple: Larry Swedroe's Tales to Enrich Your Future (Focused Investor)* (Charter Financial Publishing Network, 2007).

Zuckerman, Gregory, *The Man Who Solved the Market: How Jim Simons Launched the Quant Revolution* (Portfolio/Penguin, 2019).

# *Behavioral economics*

Cialdini, Robert, *Influence: The Psychology of Persuasion* (Harper Business, 2021). First published in 1984. This book explores how our minds can be easily influenced—and how to prevent it. It's therefore no surprise that an investor like Charlie Munger, who popularized the idea of mental models, loves the book.

Kahneman, Daniel, and Olivier Sibony and Cass R. Sunstein, *Noise: A Flaw in Human Judgment* (Hachette Book Group, 2021).

Kahneman, Daniel, *Thinking, Fast and Slow* (Farrar, Straus and Giroux, 2011).

LeBon, Gustave, *The Crowd: A Study of the Popular Mind* (Unwin Hyman Limited, 1977). Originally published 1895. Excerpts reprinted in Charles D. Ellis and James R. Vertin (eds.), *The Investors Anthology: Original Ideas From the Industry's Greatest Minds* (John C. Wiley & Sons, 1997), pp. 9–10.

Lewis, Michael, *The Undoing Project: A Friendship That Changed Our Minds* (W. W. Norton, 2017). A moving account of the friendship between Daniel Kahneman and Amos Tversky.

Surowiecki, James, *The Wisdom of Crowds: Why the Many are Smarter than the Few* (Doubleday, 2004).

Tetlock, Philip E., and Gardner, Dan, *Superforecasting: The Art and Science of Prediction* (Crown, 2015).

Tetlock, Philip E., *Expert Political Judgment: How Good Is It? How Can We Know?* (Princeton University Press, 2009).

Thaler, Richard, *Misbehaving: The Making of Behavioral Economics* (W. W. Norton, 2016).

Thaler, Richard H., and Cass R. Sunstein, *Nudge: The Final Edition: Improving Decisions About Money, Health, and the Environment* (Yale University Press, 2021). First published 2008.

Zweig, Jason, *Your Money and Your Brain: How the New Science of*

*Neuroeconomics Can Help Make You Rich* (Simon & Schuster, 2007).

# Economic history

Bernanke, Ben, *Essays on the Great Depression*. Princeton University Press (January 10, 2009).

Bernstein, Peter, *Against the Gods: The Remarkable Story of Risk* (John Wiley & Sons, 1998).

Bernstein, William J., *The Birth of Plenty: How the Prosperity of the Modern World Was Created* (McGraw-Hill Education, 2010).

Chancellor, Edwin, *Devil Take the Hindmost: A History of Financial Speculation* (Plume, Reissue Edition, June 1, 2000).

Cowing, Cedric B., *Populists, Plungers, and Progressives: A Social History of Stock and Commodity Speculation, 1890–1936* (Princeton University Press, 1965).

Fox, Justin, *The Myth of the Rational Market: A History of Risk, Reward and Delusion on Wall Street* (HarperCollins e-books, Reprint Edition, June 2, 2009).

Galbraith, John Kenneth, *The Great Crash 1929* (Houghton Mifflin, 1955). There's a lot of books written about the 1929 crash, but this 1955 classic is the most famous because it's the most accessible and the best written.

Karabel, Zachary, *The Leading Indicators: A Short History of the Numbers That Rule Our World* (Simon & Schuster, New York, 2014).

Lowenstein, Roger, *When Genius Failed: The Rise and Fall of Long-Term Capital Management* (Random House, 1989).

Sobel, Robert, *Panic on Wall Street: A History of America's Financial Disasters* (Beard Books, Washington, DC, 1999, reprint of 1968 edition).

Weatherall, James Owen, *The Physics of Wall Street: A Brief History of Predicting the Unpredictable* (Houghton Mifflin, New York, 2014).

# History of ideas

Berlin, Isaiah, *The Hedgehog and the Fox: An Essay on Tolstoy's View of History* (Princeton University Press, 2nd edition, 2013).

Diamond, Jared, *Guns, Germs, and Steel* (W. W. Norton & Company; Revised edition, 2005).

Harari, Yuval Noah, *Sapiens: A Brief History of Humankind* (Harper Perennial, 2018).

Harari, Yuval Noah, *Homo Deus: A Brief History of Tomorrow* (Harper Perennial, 2018).

Harari, Yuval Noah, *21 Lessons For the 21st Century* (Random House Publishing Group, Reprint Edition, 2019).

Taleb, Nassim Nicholas, *The Black Swan: The Impact of the Highly Improbable* (Random House, 2007).

# Investing classics

Bachelier, Louis, *Theory of Speculation* (Princeton University Press, December 12, 2011), Mark Davis & Alison Etheridge, tr.

De la Vega, Joseph, "Confusion de Confusiones," in Martin S. Fridon (ed.), *Extraordinary Popular Delusions and the Madness of Crowds* (John Wiley & Sons, New York, 1995). If you think there is anything new under the sun, read this account of investing on the Amsterdam Stock Exchange and specifically trading in the stock of the Dutch East India Company, first published in 1688.

Keynes, John Maynard, *The General Theory of Employment, Interest and Money* (Harcourt, Brace & World, 1st edition, 2016). First published by Macmillan in 1936.

Lefevre, Edwin, and Markman, Jon D., *Reminiscences of a Stock Operator: With New Commentary and Insights on the Life and Times of Jesse*

*Livermore* (John Wiley & Sons, 2012). Published in 1922 but still relevant for its insight into investor psychology.

Schwed Jr., Fred, *Where Are the Customers' Yachts?: or A Good Hard Look at Wall Street* (John Wiley, 1st edition, 2006). Originally published in 1940 by Simon & Schuster. This is one of the wisest and funniest books ever written about Wall Street.

## Bubbles and manias

Bernstein, William, *The Delusion of Crowds: Why People Go Mad In Groups* (Atlantic Monthly Press, 2021).

Chancellor, Edward, *Devil Take the Hindmost: A History of Financial Speculation* (Plume, Reissue Edition, 2000).

Kindleberger, Charles P. and Robert Z. Aliber, *Manias, Panics, and Crashes: A History of Financial Crises* (Palgrave Macmillan, 7th edition, 2015). This book has a large and dedicated following.

Mackay, Charles, and De La Vega, Joseph, *Extraordinary Popular Delusions and the Madness of Crowds & Confusion de Confusiones* (Wiley Investment Classics, 1996).

Reinhart, Carmen C., and Kenneth C. Rogoff, *This Time Is Different: Eight Centuries of Financial Folly* (Princeton University Press, Reprint Edition, 2011).

Sobel, Robert, *Panic on Wall Street: A History of America's Financial Disasters* (Beard Books, Washington, DC, 1999, reprint of 1968 edition).

## Wall Street history

Cowing, Cedric B., *Populists, Plungers, and Progressives: A Social History of Stock and Commodity Speculation, 1890–1936* (Princeton University Press, 1965).

Emery, Henry Crosby, "Speculation on the Stock and Produce Exchange of the United States" (New York, 1896).

Geisst, Charles R., *Wall Street: A History* (Oxford University Press, Updated Edition, 2012), Kindle Locations 790–795.

Hochfelder, David, "Where the Common People Could Speculate: the ticker, bucket shops, and the origins of popular participation in financial markets, 1880–1920," *Journal of American History* 93 (September 2006).

Leinweber, David, *Nerds on Wall Street: Math, Machines and Wired Markets* (John Wiley, Hoboken, NJ, 2009).

Nairn, Alasdair, *Engines That Move Markets: Technology Investing from Railroads to the Internet and Beyond* (John Wiley & Sons, New York, 2002).

Seligman, Joel, *The Transformation of Wall Street: A History of the Securities and Exchange Commission and Modern Corporate Finance* (Aspen Publishers, 3rd edition, 2003).

Smith, B. Mark, *A History of the Global Stock Market: From Ancient Rome to Silicon Valley* (University of Chicago Press, 2003).

Sobel, Robert, *Inside Wall Street* (W. W. Norton & Company, New York, 1977).

Sobel, Robert, *The Big Board: A History of the New York Stock Market* (Beard Books, 2000).

Weatherall, James Owen, *The Physics of Wall Street: A Brief History of Predicting the Unpredictable* (Houghton Mifflin, New York, 2014).

## *My favorite investing blogs*

The Rekenthaler Report. Rekenthaler is Vice President of Research for Morningstar. Consistent fact-based research on investing, particularly the virtues of index investing.

www.morningstar.com/collections/7/rekenthaler-report

The Reformed Broker. Josh Brown is a financial advisor at Ritholtz Wealth Management and a regular on CNBC. Funny and refreshingly irreverent. thereformedbroker.com

A Wealth of Common Sense. Ben Carlson manages portfolios for individuals and institutions at Ritholtz Wealth Management. His blog focuses on wealth management, investments, financial markets and investor psychology. awealthofcommonsense.com

DataTrek. Jessica Rabe and Nicholas Colas are probably the most data intensive researchers on Wall Street today. They are particularly strong on describing the effects of disruptive technologies on the economy and markets. datatrekresearch.com/category/blog

# *Notes*

===

## *Chapter 1*

1 Zito, Bob, "How Television Got to the NYSE Trading Floor," zitopartners.
com (June 18, 2020).

## *Chapter 2*

1 "Securities and Exchange Commission, Ten of Nation's Top Investment
Firms Settle Enforcement Actions Involving Conflict of Interest," sec.gov/
news/press/2003-54.htm (April 28, 2003).
2 Personal communication from John Butters, FactSet (July 20, 2021).

## *Chapter 3*

1 About the NYSE bell: www.nyse.com/bell/history.
2 Personal communication from Peter Asch, NYSE Archivist (August 4, 2021).
3 Demos, Telis, "Alibaba IPO Biggest in History as Bankers Exercise 'Green
Shoe' Option," *The Wall Street Journal* (September 21, 2014).
4 Tangel, Andrew, and Walter Hamilton, "Stakes are high on Facebook's first
day of trading," *Los Angeles Times* (May 17, 2012).
5 Personal communication, Matt Kennedy, Renaissance Capital (August 9,
2021).

6 Kharpal, Arjun, "Ant Group to raise $34.5 billion, valuing it at over $313 billion, in biggest IPO of all time," CNBC.com (October 26, 2020).

7 Go, Brenda, "Alibaba's Jack Ma makes first public appearance in three months," Reuters (January 19, 2021).

8 Nagarajan, Shalin, "Jack Ma's wealth tumbles by $12 billion in 2 months as China seeks to shrink the billionaire's financial empire," Markets Insider (December 30, 2020).

9 Richard Grasso, personal communication (July 21, 2021); and David Shields, personal communication (August 20, 2021).

10 "An Old New-Yorker Gone: The Sudden Death of Anthony J. Bleecker," *The New York Times* (January 18, 1884).

# Chapter 4

1 Lewis, Michael, *The Undoing Project: A Friendship That Changed Our Minds* (W. W. Norton, 2016), p. 250.

2 Interview with Art Cashin, Bobby Van's Steakhouse (December 16, 2019).

3 Ibid.

4 Ibid.

5 Ibid.

6 Ibid.

7 Zak, Paul J., "Why Inspiring Stories Make Us React: The Neuroscience of Narrative," *Cerebrum* (January–February 2015).

8 Ibid.

9 Interview with Art Cashin (December 20, 2018).

10 Heath, Thomas, "Arthur Cashin, wise to the ways of Wall Street," *The Washington Post* (September 19, 2019).

11 Interview with Art Cashin, Bobby Van's Steakhouse (December 16, 2019).

12 Unrecorded interview with Art Cashin, Bobby Van's Steakhouse (January 14, 2020).

# Chapter 5

1 Securities and Exchange Commission, "Trading Analysis of October 27 and 28, 1997," sec.gov (September 1998).

2  nyse.com.

3  Jarzemsky, Matt, and Michael Driscoll, "New Circuit Breakers Would Have Halted 'Flash Crash'," *The Wall Street Journal* (June 1, 2012).

4  Securities and Exchange Commission, "Trading Analysis of October 27 and 28, 1997," sec.gov (September 1998).

5  "List of largest daily changes in the Dow Jones Industrial Average," wikipedia.org.

## *Chapter 6*

1  "Issues in Labor Statistics," U.S. Department of Labor, Bureau of Labor Statistics, Summary 99-4 (March 1999).

2  Duggan, Wayne, "This Day In Market History: The Netscape IPO," Yahoo Finance (August 9, 2018).

3  "Crank It Up," *Wired* (January 2000).

4  Fishman, Charles, "The Revolution Will Be Televised (on CNBC)," *Fast Company* (May 31, 2000).

5  Ibid.

6  Serwer, Andy, and Angela Key, "I Want My CNBC," *Fortune* (May 24, 1999).

7  Ibid.

8  "About the NYSE Bell," nyse.com

9  Mulligan, Thomas S., "Ringing at NYSE Has Become Belle of the Ball," *Los Angeles Times* (December 26, 2003).

10  Nelson, Valerie. J., "Walter Cronkite dies at 92; longtime CBS anchorman," *Los Angeles Times* (July 18, 2009).

11  Cronkite, Walter, *A Reporter's Life* (Ballantine Books, 1997), p. 353.

12  Boyer, Peter J., "Cronkite Idea for Special Is Rejected by CBS," *The New York Times* (June 8, 1988).

13  Mansfield, Stephanie, "Walter Cronkite, Loving It the Way it Was," *The Washington Post* (July 29, 1986).

14  "The Partnership Program: Be Part Of It," NYSE television ad (2003), YouTube.com.

15  Whitefoot, John, "Market Crash: What Caused the Dotcom Bubble to Burst in 2000?" Lombardi Letter (March 23, 2017).

16 "Merrill buys market maker," CNNMoney (June 6, 2000).

17 McGeehan, Patrick, "Goldman Sachs to Acquire Top Firm on Trading Floors," *The New York Times* (September 12, 2000).

18 "LaBranche & Co. Inc. History," Funding Universe.

# Chapter 7

1 McCullough, Brian, "A revealing look at the dot-com bubble of 2000 — and how it shapes our lives today," Ted.com (December 4, 2018).

2 "Nasdaq tumbles on Japan," CNNMoney (March 13, 2000).

3 Willoughby, Jack, "Burning Up," *Barron's* (March 20, 2000).

4 "MicroStrategy Plummets," CNNMoney (March 20, 2000).

5 "Nasdaq sinks 350 points," CNNMoney (April 3, 2000).

6 "Bleak Friday on Wall Street," CNNMoney (April 14, 2000).

7 "Here's Why The Dot Com Bubble Began And Why It Popped," Business Insider (December 15, 2010).

8 Amadeo, Kimberly, "Fed Funds Rate History: Its Highs, Lows, and Charts," The Balance (November 9, 2021).

9 Haig, Matt, *Brand Failures: The Truth About the 100 Biggest Branding Mistakes of All Time* (Kogan Page Limited, 2003), pp. 170–174.

10 "Amazon.com Announces Investment in Pets.com," amazon.com (March 29, 1999).

11 Planes, Alex, "The IPO That Inflated the Dot-Com Bubble," The Motley Fool (August 9, 2013). See also Kelly, Haywood, "What's $10 Billion to AOL?" Morningstar (April 5, 1999).

12 Kawamoto, Dawn, "TheGlobe.com's IPO one for the books," CNET News (November 13, 1998).

13 Shim, Richard, "TheGlobe.com to cut staff, fold sites," CNET News (August 3, 2001).

14 Shiller, Robert J., *Irrational Exuberance* (Princeton University Press, 1st edition, 2000), p. 71.

15 Hoye, Bob, "Net Destinies," *Barron's* (June 28, 1999).

16 Shiller, *Irrational Exuberance* (2000), p. 95.

17 Ibid.

18 Id., p. 112.

19  Shiller, Robert J., *Irrational Exuberance* (Princeton University Press, revised and expanded 3rd edition, 2015).

20  Id., p. 114.

21  Mills, D. Quinn, "Who's to Blame for the Bubble?" *Harvard Business Review* (May 2001).

22  Greenspan, Alan, "The Challenge of Central Banking in a Democratic Society," Remarks at the Annual Dinner and Francis Boyer Lecture of The American Enterprise Institute for Public Policy Research, Washington, D.C. (December 5, 1996).

## *Chapter 8*

1  Lefevre, Edwin, and Markman, Jon D., *Reminiscences of a Stock Operator: With New Commentary and Insights on the Life and Times of Jesse Livermore* (John Wiley & Sons, 2012), p. 464.

2  Schwager, Jack D., *Market Wizards: Interviews with Top Traders* (John Wiley & Sons, 2012), p. 214.

3  Stewart, James B., *Den of Thieves* (Simon & Schuster, 2012), p. 95.

4  Id., p. 423.

5  Id., pp 421, 427.

6  Id., p. 528.

7  Johnson, Edward C. II., "Contrary Opinion in Stock Market Techniques," reprinted in Charles D. Ellis and James R. Vertin (eds.) *The Investors Anthology: Original Ideas From the Industry's Greatest Minds* (John C. Wiley & Sons, 1997), p. 98.

8  Id., p. 99.

9  Buzzy Geduld, personal communication (November 9, 2021).

10  Bartlett. Sarah, "Where the Ace is King," *The New York Times* (June 11, 1989).

11  Greenberg, Alan. C., *Memos from the Chairman* (Workman Publishing Company, 1996).

12  Id., p. 32, 33, 40.

13  Id., p. 17.

14  Id., p. 21.

15  Id., p. 66.

16  Id., p. 19.

17  Id., p. 109.

18  Id., p. 16.

19  Id., p. 122.

20  Joe Zicherman, personal communication (August 21, 2021).

21  LeBon, Gustave, *The Crowd: A Study of the Popular Mind* (Unwin Hyman Limited, 1977, originally published 1895). Excerpts reprinted in Charles D. Ellis and James R. Vertin (eds.), *The Investors Anthology: Original Ideas From the Industry's Greatest Minds* (John C. Wiley & Sons, 1997), pp. 9–10.

22  "Merrill buys market maker," CNN Money (June 6, 2000).

23  Intindola, Brendan, "Rich and famous mourn Wall Street's John Mulheren," *Forbes* (December 19, 2003).

24  "Viagra Falls," *People Magazine* (June 29, 1998).

## *Chapter 9*

1  Steve Swanson, personal communication (April 5, 2021).

2  "The Institution of Experience: Self-Regulatory Organizations in the Securities Industry, 1792–2010," Securities and Exchange Commission Historical Society.

3  Nelson, Brian, "NASDAQ Stock Market History," PocketSense (July 27, 2017).

4  "The Institution of Experience: Self-Regulatory Organizations in the Securities Industry, 1792–2010," Securities and Exchange Commission Historical Society.

5  "Stock Exchanges," Library of Congress.

6  "They are not just faster than the slowest market-maker, they are faster than the average market-maker." Harris, Jeffrey H., and Paul H. Schultz, "The trading profits of SOES bandits," *Journal of Financial Economics* 50 (1998), 39–62.

7  Berryhill, Michael, "Watch Out, Stock Market, Here Comes the SOES Bandits," *Houston Press* (June 13, 1996).

8  Christie, William G., and Paul H. Schultz, "Why Do Nasdaq Market Makers Avoid Odd- Eighth Quotes?" *Journal of Finance* 49 (December 1994), 1813–40. Also see Christie and Schultz, "Did Nasdaq Market Makers

Implicitly Collude?" *Journal of Economic Perspectives* 9:3 (Summer 1995), pp. 199–208.

9  "Report Pursuant to Section 21(a) of the Securities Exchange Act of 1934 Regarding the NASD and the NASDAQ Market," sec.gov (August 1996).

10  Lindsey R., Byrne J. A., and Schwartz R. A., "The SEC's Order Handling Rules of 1997 and Beyond: Perspective and Outcomes of the Landmark Regulation," in Schwartz R., Byrne J., Stempel E. (eds), Rapidly Changing Securities Markets, Zicklin School of Business Financial Markets Series (2017).

11  "Securities and Exchange Commission, Regulation of Exchanges and Alternative Trading Systems," sec.gov (2000).

12  A brief history of Datek can be found at "Datek Online Holdings Corp." on company-histories.com. For more, see Patterson, Scott, *Dark Pools: High-Speed Traders, A.I. Bandits, and the Threat to the Global Financial System* (Crown Publishing Group. 2012).

13  Barboza, David, "Golden Boy?; He's Dazzled Wall Street, but the Ghosts Of His Company May Haunt His Future," *The New York Times* (May 10, 1998).

14  SEC vs. SHELDON MASCHLER, JEFFREY A. CITRON, MICHAEL MCCARTY, ERIK MASCHLER, HEARTLAND SECURITIES CORPORATION, AARON ELBOGEN, MOISHE ZELCER, RAFT INVESTMENTS, INC., JES MANAGEMENT CORPORATION. sec.gov. January 2003, Section 37.

15  "The Island ECN, Inc. History," Funding Universe.

16  "Securities and Exchange Commission, Regulation of Exchanges and Alternative Trading Systems," sec.gov (2000).

17  Ibid.

18  Coffee, Jr., John C., "Competition Among Securities Markets: A Path Dependent Perspective," Columbia Law School, The Center for Law and Economic Studies, Working Paper No. 192 (March 25, 2002).

19  For a brief chronology of trading and technology, see web.archive.org/web/20100515175903/http://www.nyse.com/about/history/timeline_chronology_index.html.

20  "Electronic Communication Networks and After-Hours Trading," SEC Division of Market Regulation, sec.gov (June 2000).

21  Lindsey, R., J. A. Byrne, and R. A. Schwartz, "The SEC's Order Handling

Rules of 1997 and Beyond: Perspective and Outcomes of the Landmark Regulation," in Schwartz, R., J. A. Byrne, and E. Stempel (eds.), *Rapidly Changing Securities Markets*, Zicklin School of Business Financial Markets Series (Springer), p. 7.

22 Robert Schwartz, personal communication (September 27, 2021).

23 Angel, James J., Lawrence E. Harris, and Charles E. Spratt, "Equity Trading in the 21st Century," *Quarterly Journal of Finance (QJF)* 1:1, World Scientific Publishing Co. Pte. Ltd. (2011), pp. 1–53.

24 "Securities and Exchange Commission, Order Approving Proposed Rule Change To Rescind Exchange Rule 390," sec.gov (May 5, 2000).

25 Nelson, "NASDAQ."

26 "Vintage Nasdaq Commercial: The Stock Market for the Next 100 Years," YouTube.

27 Zubulake, Paul, and Sang Lee, *The High-Frequency Game Changer: How Automated Trading Strategies Have Revolutionized the Markets* (John Wiley & Sons, 2011), p. 345.

28 Lindsey, Byrne, and Schwartz, "The SEC's Order Handling Rules of 1997 and Beyond," p. 8. See also Massa, Annie, "NYSE Takes Over 131-Year-Old Exchange Once Tied to Bernie Madoff," Bloomberg (December 14, 2016).

29 "Securities and Exchange Commission, Decimals Implementation Plan for the Equities and Options Markets," sec.gov (July 24, 2000).

30 For a history of automated trading and dark pools, see: Zubulake, *The High-Frequency Game Change*; and Patterson, *Dark Pools*.

31 Joyce, Erin, "Instinet Acquires Island ECN," Internet News (June 10, 2002).

32 Langton, James, "Nasdaq completes acquisition of INET," Investment Executive (December 8, 2005).

33 "SEC Charges Former Day-Trading Principals with Securities Fraud; Others Charged with Fraud or Violating Recordkeeping and Reporting Rules," sec.gov (January 14, 2003).

34 Sorkin, Andrew Ross, "Ameritrade In Deal to Buy Online Rival Datek," *The New York Times* (April 8, 2002).

35 Craig, Susanne, "Ameritrade Agrees to Buy Datek In $1.29 Billion Stock Agreement," *The Wall Street Journal* (April 8, 2002).

36 Stempel, Jonathan, "Citigroup Buys Automated Trading Desk," Reuters (July 2, 2007).

37  Popper, Nathaniel, "High-Speed Trading Executives Shut Firm," *The New York Times* (October 16, 2012). Also Steve D. Swanson profile at College of Charleston.

38  Miller, Stephen, "Father of Day-Trading Sought To Be Investors' Advocate," *The Wall Street Journal* (August 2, 2008).

## *Chapter 10*

1  Bogle, John C., *Common Sense on Mutual Funds* (John C. Wiley & Sons, 10th Anniversary Edition, 2009), p. 120.

2  Bogle, Jack, "The First Index Mutual Fund," in Neuberger, Albert S., *Indexing for Maximum Investment Results* (Routledge. 2014), p. 44.

3  Bogle, "The First Index Mutual Fund," p. 47.

4  Bogle, *Common Sense on Mutual Funds* (2009), p. 151.

5  Bogle, "The First Index Mutual Fund," pp. 44–47.

6  Malkiel, Burton G., *A Random Walk Down Wall Street* (W. W. Norton, 1973), p. 226.

7  Ellis, Charles, "The Loser's Game," *The Financial Analysts Journal* 31:4 (July/ August 1975), pp. 19–26.

8  Samuelson, Paul, "Challenge to Judgment," *Journal of Portfolio Management* (Fall 1974).

9  Bogle, John C., "How the Index Fund Was Born," *The Wall Street Journal* (September 3, 2011).

10  Bogle, *Common Sense on Mutual Funds* (2009), p. 155.

11  Bogle, "The First Index Mutual Fund," p. 56.

12  Id., p. 63.

13  Id., p. 38.

14  Bogle. John C., *Common Sense on Mutual Funds* (John C. Wiley & Sons, 1999), p. 1.

15  CNBC interview (May 6, 1999).

16  Bogle, *Common Sense on Mutual Funds* (1999), p. 79.

17  Bogle, *Common Sense on Mutual Funds* (2009), pp. 78–79.

18  Siegel, Jeremy, *Stocks for the Long Run* (Richard D. Irwin, Inc., 1994), p. 11, 15.

19  Siegel, Jeremy, *Stocks for the Long Run* (McGraw Hill Education, 5th edition, 2014), pp. 5–6, 81.

20 Id., p 82.

21 Id., p. 96.

22 Bogle, *Common Sense on Mutual Funds* (2009), p. 78.

23 Id., pp. 15–16.

24 Id., p. 14.

25 Siegel, *Stocks for the Long Run* (1994), pp. 10–12; and Siegel, *Stocks for the Long Run* (2014), pp. 82–84, p. 375.

26 Bogle, *Common Sense on Mutual Funds* (2009), p. 51.

27 Id., pp. 53–4.

28 Bogle, *Common Sense on Mutual Funds* (2009), p. 214.

29 Id., p. 212

30 Id., p. 169.

31 Id., p. 343.

32 Id., p. 99.

33 Id., p. 421.

34 Id., p. 28.

35 Id., p. 41.

36 Id., p. 34.

37 Id., pp. 36–7.

38 Id., p. 125.

39 Id., p. 307.

40 See Chapter 10, "On Reversion to the Mean," in id., p. 305–28.

41 Id., p. 131.

42 Id., p. 115.

43 Id., p. 139.

44 Id., p. 41.

45 Burns, Scott, "A Visit With John Bogle," *The Seattle Times* (March 13, 2010).

46 Bogle, *Common Sense on Mutual Funds* (2009), back cover.

47 Yager, Fred, "Here Are 15 Business Books that could actually Help Make You Rich," Consumer Affairs (December 18, 2020).

48 Bogle, *Common Sense on Mutual Funds* (2009), pp. 185–7.

49 "Fast facts about Vanguard," vanguard.com.

50 Butler, Dave, "5 Vanguard Funds That Can Help You Retire a Millionaire," The Motley Fool (March 12, 2021).

## *Chapter 12*

1 Pottker, Jan, *Janet and Jackie: the Story of a Mother and Her Daughter, Jacqueline Kennedy Onassis* (St. Martin's Press, 2014), p. 50.

2 Id., p. 65.

3 Klein, Edward, *All Too Human: The Love Story of Jack and Jackie Kennedy* (Pocket Books, 1997), p. 155.

4 Andersen, Christopher, *These Few Precious Days: The Final Year of Jack with Jackie* (Gallery Books, 2013), p 90.

5 Bouvier, Kathleen, *Black Jack Bouvier: the Life and Times of Jackie O's Father* (Pinnacle Books, 1979), p. 243.

6 See Securities and Exchange Commission Historical Society. "The Institution of Experience: Self-Regulatory Organizations in the Securities Industry, 1792–2010."

7 Fleckner, Andreas M., "Stock Exchanges at the Crossroads: Competitive Challenges," Harvard Law School, p 18.

8 Id., p. 19.

9 "Settlement Reached With Five Specialist Firms for Violating Federal Securities Laws and NYSE Regulations; Firms Will Pay More Than $240 Million in Penalties and Disgorgement," sec.gov (March 30, 2004).

10 Fleckner, "Stock Exchanges at the Crossroads," p. 19.

11 "NYSE Stock Surges in First Day of Trading," NBC News (March 8, 2006); and "Investor FAQs," Nasdaq.com.

12 "Final rules and amendments to joint industry plans," sec.gov (June 9, 2005).

13 Personal communication from Larry Leibowitz (November 18, 2021).

14 Pisani, Bob, "Plundered by Harpies: An Early History of High-Speed Trading," *Museum of American Finance Magazine* (Fall 2014).

15 Conerly, Bill, "High Frequency Trading Explained Simply," *Forbes* (April 14, 2014).

16 Bondi, Bradley J., "Memo To Michael Lewis: The Excesses Of High-Speed Trading Are A Direct Result Of SEC Micromanagement," *Forbes* (April 29, 2014).

17 Lewis, Michael, *Flash Boys: A Wall Street Revolt* (W. W. Norton, 2014).

18 Bartash, Jeffrey, "U.S. markets 'not rigged,' SEC boss says," MarketWatch (April 29, 2014).

19  NYSE Annual Report 2006, p. 11.

20  "NYSE Euronext merger with Deutsche Boerse blocked by EU," BBC News (February 1, 2012).

21  "The Institution of Experience: Self-Regulatory Organizations in the Securities Industry, 1792–2010," Securities and Exchange Commission Historical Society.

22  "The NYSE Market Model," nyse.com.

23  NYSE Aims to Maximize Market Quality and Competitiveness With Newly Approved Enhancements of Trading Model (October 24, 2008).

## *Chapter 13*

1  "The Great Recession," federalreservehistory.org (November 22, 2013).

2  Siegel, *Stocks for the Long Run* (2014), p. 25.

3  Id., p. 25–8.

4  Id., p. 24.

5  Id., pp. 26–7.

6  Id., p. 31.

7  CNBC report (September 29, 2008).

8  Bernanke, Ben, *Essays on the Great Depression* (Princeton University Press, 2000).

9  "The Great Depression," federalreservehistory.org (November 22, 2013).

10  Bernanke, Ben, "Remarks at Conference to Honor Milton Friedman On the Occasion of His 90th Birthday," (November 8, 2002).

11  Siegel, *Stocks for the Long Run* (2014), p. 210.

12  "The Great Recession," federalreservehistory.org (November 22, 2013).

13  Mutual Funds; Mutual Fund Shares; Liability, Transactions. FRED. fred.stlouisfed.org/series/MFMFSLQ027S.

14  Kahneman, Daniel, and Amos Tversky, "Prospect Theory: An Analysis of Decision under Risk," *Econometrica* 47:2 (1979), pp. 263–91.

15  Tversky, Amos, and Daniel Kahneman, "Advances in Prospect Theory: Cumulative Representation of Uncertainty," *Journal of Risk and Uncertainty* 5:4 (1992), p. 311.

16  A good summary is provided by the Chartered Financial Analyst Institute website. "The Behavioral Biases of Individuals."

17  Kahneman, Daniel, *Thinking, Fast and Slow* (Farrar, Straus and Giroux, 2011), p. 86.

18  Tetlock, Philip E., and Gardner, Dan, *Superforecasting: The Art and Science of Prediction* (Crown, 2015), p. 232.

19  Zweig, Jason, *Your Money and Your Brain: How the New Science of Neuroeconomics Can Help Make You Rich* (Simon & Schuster, 2007).

20  The Sveriges Riksbank Prize in Economic Sciences in Memory of Alfred Nobel 2002.

21  Appelbaum, Binyamin, "Nobel in Economics is Awarded to Richard Thaler," *The New York Times* (October 9, 2017).

22  Shiller, Robert J., "Speculative Asset Prices," Prize Lecture, nobelprize.org (December 8, 2013).

23  Guszcza, Jim, "The importance of Misbehaving: A conversation with Richard Thaler," Deloitte Review Issue 18 (January 25, 2016).

# Chapter 14

1  Fama, Eugene F., "The Behavior of Stock-Market Prices," *The Journal of Business* 38:1 (1965), pp. 34–105.

2  For a history of Efficient Market Hypothesis, see Sewell, Richard, "History of the Efficient Market Hypothesis," UCL Department of Computer Science (January 20, 2011).

3  Siegel, *Stocks for the Long Run* (2014), p. 323.

4  Shiller, Robert J., "Do Stock Prices Move Too Much to Be Justified by Subsequent Changes in Dividends?" *The American Economic Review* 71:3 (1981), pp. 421–36.

5  Id., p. 434.

6  Shiller, Robert J., "Speculative Asset Prices," Prize Lecture (December 8, 2013).

7  Id., p. 460.

8  Id., p. 460.

9  Id., p. 485.

10  Siegel, *Stocks for the Long Run* (2014), p. 316.

11  Buffett, Warren, and Lawrence Cunningham, *The Essays of Warren Buffett: Lessons for Corporate America* (Carolina Academic Press, 5th edition, revised 2019), p. 177.

12  Tetlock and Gardner, *Superforecasting*, p. 205.

## *Chapter 15*

1  www.brainyquote.com/quotes/mike_tyson_369869

2  "How Mike Tyson KO'd adversity," CNBC interview (November 13, 2013).

3  Keynes, John Maynard, *The General Theory of Employment, Interest and Money* (London: Macmillan, 1936), p. 150.

4  Ibid.

5  Id., p. 157.

6  Id., p. 151.

7  S&P Dow Jones Indices, SPIVA U.S. Scorecard, mid-year 2021.

8  S&P Dow Jones Indices, SPIVA U.S. Scorecard.

9  S&P Dow Jones Indices, Fleeing Alpha: The Challenge of Consistent Outperformance, p. 2.

10 Barber, Brad M., and Xing Huang, Terrance Odean, and Christopher Schwarz, "Attention Induced Trading and Returns: Evidence from Robinhood Users," ssrn.com (November 24, 2020).

11 Chague, Fernando and De-Losso, Rodrigo and Giovannetti, Bruno, "Day Trading for a Living?" ssrn.com (June 11, 2020).

12 Barber, Brad M., Yi-Tsung Lee, Yu-Jane Liu, Terrance Odean, "The Cross-Section of Speculator Skill Evidence from Day Trading," (May 2011).

13 Barber, Brad M., Yi-Tsung Lee, Yu-Jane Liu, Terrance Odean, "The Cross-Section of Speculator Skill: Evidence from Day Trading," *Journal of Financial Markets* (March 2014).

14 Barber, Brad M., and Terrance Odean, "Trading Is Hazardous to Your Wealth: The Common Stock Investment Performance of Individual Investors," *The Journal of Finance* (April 2000).

15 Swedroe, Larry, *Wise Investing Made Simple: Larry Swedroe's Tales to Enrich Your Future*, Focused Investor, Charter Financial Publishing Network (2007), p. 113.

16 Barber, Brad M. and Reuven Lehavy, Brett Trueman, "Ratings Changes, Ratings Levels, and the Predictive Value of Analysts' Recommendations," ssrn.com (December 24, 2007).

17 Stotz, Andrew and Lu, Wei, "Financial Analysts Were Only Wrong by 25%," (November 24, 2015).

18  Kubik, Jeffrey D., and Harrison G. Hong, "Analyzing the analysts: Career concerns and biased earnings forecasts," *Journal of Finance* 58:1 (2003), pp. 313–51.

19  Hope, Ole-Kristian, and Tony Kang, "The association between macroeconomic uncertainty and analysts' forecast accuracy," *Journal of International Accounting Research* 4:1 (2005), pp. 23–38.

20  Wolinsky, Jacob, "This Study Proves Hedge Fund Performance Has Worsened In Recent Years," *Forbes* (June 30, 2021).

21  Lahiri, Kajal, and J. George Wang, "Evaluating Probability Forecasts for GDP Declines Using Alternative Methodologies," *International Journal of Forecasting* 29:1 (2013), pp. 175–90.

22  Chang, Andrew C., and Tyler J. Hanson, "The Accuracy of Forecasts Prepared for the Federal Open Market Committee," Finance and Economics Discussion Series 2015-062. Washington: Board of Governors of the Federal Reserve System (2015).

23  Paul, Pascal, "Does the Fed Know More about the Economy?" FRBSF Economic Letter (April 8, 2019).

24  Guisinger, Amy Y., Michael T. Owyang, and Hannah G. Shell, "Economic Forecasting: Comparing the Fed with the Private Sector," Federal Reserve Bank of Saint Louis (2019).

25  "Mike Tyson: 'I was totally out of my league'," CNBC interview (December 7, 2015).

26  "Mike Tyson returns to ring, draws in exhibition with Jones," CNBC interview (November 29, 2020).

## *Chapter 16*

1  Bean, Travis, "All 24 Marvel Cinematic Universe Films Ranked At The Box Office—Including 'Black Widow'," *Forbes* (April 24, 2020).

2  "'Iron Man' Meets 'Market Man'," CNBC.com (April 30, 2013).

3  Goldman, William, *Adventures in the Screen Trade: A Personal View of Hollywood and Screen Writing* (Grand Central Publishing, 1983), p. 40.

# Chapter 17

1   Pierce, Andrew, "The Queen asks why no one saw the credit crunch coming," *The Telegraph* (November 8, 2008).

2   Potter, Simon, "Models Only Get You So Far," Federal Reserve Bank of New York (February 22, 2019).

3   Meehl, Paul, *Clinical Versus Statistical Prediction: A Theoretical Analysis and a Review of the Evidence* (Echo Point Books & Media, 2013).

4   Malkiel, *A Random Walk* (1973), p. 16.

5   Tetlock, Philip, *Expert Political Judgment: How Good Is It? How Can We Know?* (Princeton University Press, 1st edition, 2005; revised edition 2017), p. 20.

6   Id., p. 233; and Menand, Louis, "Everybody's An Expert," *The New Yorker* (November 27, 2005).

7   Tetlock and Gardner, *Superforecasting*, p. 5.

8   Id., p. 138.

9   Id., p. 17.

10  Id., p. 18

11  Id., p. 5.

12  Kahneman, Daniel, Oliver Sibony, and Cass R. Sunstein, *Noise* (Little, Brown and Company, 2021).

13  Grove, William M., David H. Zald, Boyd S. Lebow, Beth E. Snitz, and Chad Nelson, "Clinical Versus Mechanical Prediction: A Meta-Analysis," *Psychological Assessment* 12:1 (2000).

14  Kahneman, Sibony, and Sunstein, *Noise*, p. 134.

15  Id., p. 133.

16  Id., p. 140.

17  Id., p. 139.

18  Good Judgment Project 2.0: Learn to think like a Superforecaster, www.gjp2.org. For more on FOCUS, see www.iarpa.gov/index.php/research-programs/focus.

# Chapter 18

1   Xie, Chloe L., "The Signal Quality of Earnings Announcements: Evidence from an Informed Trading Cartel," (November 1, 2019).

2   Id., p. 7.

3   DataTrek client note (December 4, 2019).

## Chapter 19

1   Lerner, Michael, "10 years later: How the housing market has changed since the crash," *The Washington Post* (October 4, 2018).

2   Press Release of the Board of Governors of the Federal Reserve System (December 12, 2007).

3   Falkenstein, Eric, "The Bear Stearns Books Still Don't Answer The Interesting Questions," Business Insider (May 18, 2009).

4   Isidore, Chris, "Bank of America to buy Merrill," CNN Money (September 21, 2008).

5   Zarroli, Jim, "Looking Back On Bank Of America's Countrywide Debacle," NPR (January 11, 2013).

## Chapter 20

1   Brown, Joshua and Brian Portnoy, *How I Invest My Money: Finance Experts Reveal How They Save, Spend, and Invest* (Harriman House, 2020), p. 1.

2   en.wikipedia.org/wiki/Dow_Jones_Industrial_Average

3   Pisani, Ralph R. and Robert L. Pisani, *Investing in Land: How to be a Successful Developer* (John Wiley & Sons, 1989), p. 62.

4   "General Electric Co., in the largest non-oil merger in history," UPI (December 11, 1985).

5   Welch, Jack and John A. Byrne, *Jack: Straight from the Gut* (Warner Business Books, 2001), p. 287.

6   Wright, Bob and Diane Mermigas, *The Wright Stuff: From NBC to Autism Speaks* (Rosetta Books, 2016), p. 104.

7   Id., p. 107.

8   Id., p. 197.

9   Id., p. 112.

10  Geoffrey Colvin, Geoffrey, "The Ultimate Manager In a time of hidebound, formulaic thinking, General Electric's Jack Welch gave power to the worker and the shareholder," *Fortune* (November 22, 1999).

11 Welch and Byrne, *Jack*, p. 387.

12 Id., p. 390.

13 Huang, Nellis S., "Vanguard Health Care Fund Gets a New Boss," *Kiplinger's* (November 6, 2012).

14 Bogle, Jack, "The Telltale Chart," Keynote Speech by John C. Bogle Founder and Former CEO, The Vanguard Group Before the Morningstar Investment Forum (June 26, 2002).

15 Ibid.

16 Israel, Haim, "To the Moon(shots)! – Future Tech Primer," B of A Securities (September 14, 2021).

17 Bogle, Jack, *Stay the Course: The Story of Vanguard and the Index Revolution* (John Wiley, 2019), pp. 165–203.

18 Bogle, "The Telltale Chart."

19 Powell, Robert, "Bogle's in bonds, but should you be?" MarketWatch (May 20, 2010).

20 Larimore, Taylor, *The Boglehead's Guide to the Three-Fund Portfolio: How a Simple Portfolio of Three Total Market Index Funds Outperforms Most Investors with Less Risk* (John Wiley & Sons, 2018).

21 Wilkerson, David B. and Steve Goldstein, "Comcast scores controlling stake in NBC Universal," Marketwatch (December 3, 2009).

22 Wright, *The Wright Stuff*, p. 204.

23 Id., p. 205.

24 Id., p. 211.

## *Chapter 21*

1 Brad Klontz, personal communication (May 25, 2021).

2 Zweig, *Your Money and Your Brain*, p. 10.

## *Chapter 22*

1 "Historical Returns on Stocks, Bonds and Bills: 1928–2020," NYU Stern (January 2021).

2 Carlson, Ben, "9 Uncomfortable Facts About the Stock Market," A Wealth of Common Sense (January 24, 2021).

3  Wes Crill, personal communication (February 24, 2021).

4  Carlson, "9 Uncomfortable Facts."

5  "Putting Pullbacks In Perspective," Guggenheim Investments.

6  Bogle, John C., "The Telltale Heart: Keynote Speech by John C. Bogle Founder and Former CEO," The Vanguard Group Before the Morningstar Investment Forum Chicago, IL (June 26, 2002).

7  Independent Adviser for Vanguard Investors (January 2021), p. 3.

8  See e.g., Nadig, Dave, "The Folly of Market Timing," (February 19, 2019); and "Opposite Thinking for Investors," Calamos Investments (December 6, 2017).

9  "What Happens When You Fail at Market Timing," Dimensional Fund Advisors.

10  "Timing Isn't Everything," Dimensional Fund Advisors.

11  Fama, Eugene, and Kenneth French, "The Cross-Section of Expected Stock Returns," *Journal of Finance* (1992).

12  Jensen, Theis Ingersley, Bryan T. Kelly and Lasse Heje Pedersen, "Is There a Replication Crisis in Finance?" ssrn.com (March 5, 2021).

13  Swedroe, Larry, "Is There a Replication Crisis in Finance?" (March 23, 2001). See also, Asness, Cliff, "The Replication Crisis That Wasn't," AQR (March 24, 2021).

14  Charts from Jones, Charles, "A Century of Stock Market Liquidity and Trading Costs."

15  Sapp, Travis R. A., and Xuemin (Sterling) Yan, "The Nasdaq-Amex Merger, Nasdaq Reforms, and the Liquidity of Small Firms," *The Journal of Financial Research* (Summer 2003), p. 226.

16  For a list of NYSE trading commissions through 1975, see Jones, Charles, "A Century of Stock Market Liquidity and Trading Costs."

17  Chart from Jones, Charles, "A Century of Stock Market Liquidity and Trading Costs."

18  Swedroe, Larry, "Most Stocks Are Duds (Yes, You Read That Right)," The Evidence-Based Investor (September 3, 2021).

19  Ellis, Charles, *Winning the Loser's Game: Timeless Strategies for Successful Investing* (McGraw Hill Education, 7th edition, 2017), p. xi.

20  Id., p. xii.

21  Id., p. x.

22  Id., p. 261.

# Chapter 23

1 Berlin, Isaiah, *The Hedgehog and the Fox: An Essay on Tolstoy's View of History* (Princeton University Press, 2nd edition, 2013).

2 Tetlock and Gardner, *Superforecasting*, p. 190.

3 Id., p. 228.

4 Id., p. 190.

5 Surowiecki, James, *The Wisdom of Crowds: Why the Many are Smarter than the Few* (Doubleday, 2004).

6 For a useful discussion on the history of financial innovation, see Peter Tufano, "Financial Innovation," Harvard Business School (June 16, 2002).

7 Shiller, Robert J., "Speculative Asset Prices," Prize Lecture (December 8, 2013).

8 "Speculative Asset Prices," Robert J. Shiller, Prize Lecture (December 8, 2013), p. 490.

9 For a brief history of how the telegraph, telephone and undersea cable changed trading in the 1800s, see Pisani, "Plundered by Harpies."

10 SEC Adopts Rules to Permit Crowdfunding. Securities and Exchange Commission (October 30, 2015).

11 Jumpstart Our Business Startups Act: Frequently Asked Questions About Crowdfunding Intermediaries, Securities and Exchange Commission (May 7, 2012).

12 Nead, Nate, "Why Equity Crowdfunding Has Failed to Live Up to the Hype and Expectations (and What To Do About It)" investmentbank.com.

13 "Lower Manhattan Real Estate Year In Review 2020," Downtown Alliance (February 22, 2021).

# Chapter 24

1 Rohter, Larry, "With Pope Due, the Cubans Wrest Dollars From Heaven," *The New York Times* (January 21, 1998).

2 Dag Hammarskjold Library.

3 Escalante, Fabian, *Executive Action: 634 Ways to Kill Fidel Castro* (Ocean Press, 2006).

4 Kessler, G., "Trying to Kill Fidel Castro," *The Washington Post* (June 27, 2007).

5 Escalante, *Executive Action*, pp. 202–231.

6 Campbell, Duncan, "Close but no cigar: how America failed to kill Fidel Castro," *Guardian* (November 26, 2016).

7 Simpson, Victor L., "AP WAS THERE: Pope John Paul II arrives in Cuba," *San Diego Union Tribune* (September 18, 2015).

8 "Pope to Visit Cuba, Mexico," Voice of America (December 8, 2011).

9 Celaya, Miriam, "What Happens the Day After Pope Francis Leaves Cuba?" *The Atlantic* (September 19, 2015).

## *Chapter 25*

1 en.wikipedia.org/wiki/Barry_Manilow_discography

2 Butler, Patricia, *Barry Manilow: The Biography* (Omnibus Press, 2002), p. 226.

3 Id., p. 235.

4 Holden, Stephen, "Barry Manilow: Yes, He Still Writes the Songs," *The New York Times* (October 13, 1991).

5 Linkner, Josh, "Inch-Wide, Mile-Deep," joshlinkner.com (July 8, 2018).

6 Bill Boggs interviews Barry Manilow, YouTube.com (November 19, 2018).

## *Chapter 27*

1 Sisario, Ben, "Music Sales Fell in 2008, but Climbed on the Web," *The New York Times* (January 1, 2009).

2 "100 Greatest Singers of All Time," *Rolling Stone* (2008).

3 en.wikipedia.org/wiki/Ray_(film)

4 "Aretha Franklin at NYSE on Christmas album and possible biopic," cnbc.com (2008).

5 "Aretha Franklin's Family Rejects Genius Biopic," msn.com (March 22, 2021).

## *Chapter 28*

1  "Maria Bartiromo," from the album, *Don't Worry About Me*. Lyrics by Jeffrey Ross Hyman. Lyrics © BMG Rights Management, Warner Chappell Music, Inc.

## *Appendix 1*

1  Loomis, Carol, "Buffett's Big Bet," *Fortune* (June 2008).

2  Kabil, Ahmed, "How Warren Buffett Won His Multi-Million Dollar Long Bet," Medium (February 17, 2018). A more detailed discussion can be found in *Buffett, Warren and Lawrence Cunningham, The Essays of Warren Buffett: Lessons for Corporate America* (Carolina Academic Press, 5th edition, revised 2019), pp. 180 ff.

3  Buffett, Warren, Berkshire Hathaway Letter to Shareholders 2016, p. 24.

4  Ibid.

5  "Purchase Of FNN Boosts NBC's Cable-Market Share," *Seattle Times* (May 26, 1991).

6  Personal communication from Melissa Roberts, KBW, January 26, 2021.

7  Lefevre, Edwin and Markman, Jon D., *Reminiscences of a Stock Operator: With New Commentary and Insights on the Life and Times of Jesse Livermore* (John Wiley & Sons, 2012), p. 485.

8  Cowles, Alfred, "Can Stock Market Forecasters Forecast?" A paper read before a joint meeting of the Econometric Society and the American Statistical Association, Cincinnati, Ohio (December 31, 1932).

9  Cowles, Alfred, "Stock Market Forecasting," *Econometrica* (July–Oct. 1944), pp. 206–214.

10  Investment Company Institute, 2021 Factbook, p. 305.

11  History: CRSP Timeline. www.crsp.org/about-crsp/history

12  Fisher, L. and J. H. Lorie, "Rates of Return on Investments in Common Stocks," *The Journal of Business* 37:1 (January 1964), pp. 1–21.

13  Id., p. 9.

14  Jensen, Michael C., "The Performance of Mutual Funds in the Period 1945–1964," *Journal of Finance* (May 1968).

15  Markowitz, Harry, "Portfolio Selection," *The Journal of Finance* 7:1 (March 1952), pp. 77–9.

16 Wigglesworth, Robin, *Trillions: How a Band of Wall Street Renegades Invented the Index Fund and Changed Finance Forever* (Penguin Publishing Group, 2021), p. 40.

17 A fuller account of McQuown's pivotal role in the creation of ETFs can be found in Lehman, Ralph, *The Elusive Trade: How Exchange Traded Funds Conquered Wall Street* (Brown Books, 2019), pp. 9 ff; and Wigglesworth, Robin, *Trillions: How a Band of Wall Street Renegades Invented the Index Fund and Changed Finance Forever* (Penguin Publishing Group, 2021), pp. 55 ff.

18 Wigglesworth, Robin, "Passive attack: the story of a Wall Street revolution," *Financial Times* (December 20, 2018).

19 Burton Malkiel, personal communication (January 5, 2022).

20 See Carrel, Lawrence, *ETFs for the Long Run: What They Are, How They Work, and Simple Strategies for Successful Long-Term Investing* (John C. Wiley, 2008), p. 23.

21 Bob Tull, personal communication (January 4, 2022).

22 Ibid.

23 Pisani, Bob, "Top gold ETF turns 15. Here's what SPDR's chief gold strategist sees ahead," (November 15, 2019).

24 Investment Company Institute, 2021 Factbook, p. 220.

25 Investment Company Institute, 2021 Factbook, p. 214.

26 Bob Tull personal communication, id.

## *Appendix 2*

1 Quoted in Chancellor, Edward, *Devil Take the Hindmost: A History of Financial Speculation* (Plume; Reissue Edition, June 1, 2000).

2 Paulin, Geoffrey, "Housing and expenditures: before, during, and after the bubble," U.S. Bureau of Labor Statistics (June 2018).

3 Pfeffer, Fabian T., Sheldon Dangier, and Robert F. Schoeni, "Wealth Levels, Wealth Inequality, and the Great Recession," Russell Sage Foundation (June 2014).

4 Bernstein, William, *The Delusion of Crowds: Why People Go Mad In Groups* (Atlantic Monthly Press, 2021), p. 168.

5 Id., p. 168.

6 Kuper, Simon, "Petal power," *Financial Times* (May 12, 2007); and Goldgar,

Ann, *Tulipmania: Money, Honor, and Knowledge in the Dutch Golden Age* (University of Chicago Press, 2008).

7  Hoye, Bob, "'Net Destinies," *Barron's* (June 28, 1999).

8  Yip, Paul S. L., "Some Important Characteristics of Asset Bubbles and Financial Crises," *Modern Economy* 9:7 (July 2018), pp. 1137–1168.

9  Quinn, William and John D. Turner, *Boom and Bust: A Global History of Financial Bubbles* (Cambridge University Press, 2020). A summary is at "A New History of Financial Bubbles," *Financial History* (Spring 2021), p. 10–13.

10 Shiller, Robert J., "Speculative Asset Prices," Prize Lecture (December 8, 2013). p. 485.

# Index

437